Contemporary International Relations:
A Guide to Theory

Contemporary International Relations: A Guide to Theory

Edited by
A.J.R. Groom and Margot Light

PINTER
PUBLISHERS
LONDON, NEW YORK

Distributed exclusively in the United States and Canada by St. Martin's Press

Pinter Publishers Ltd.
25 Floral Street, London WC2E 9DS, United Kingdom

First published in 1994

Distributed exclusively in the USA and Canada by St. Martin's Press, Inc., Room 400, 175 Fifth Avenue, New York, NY 10010, USA

British Library Cataloguing in Publication Data

A CIP catalogue record for this book is available from the British Library

ISBN 1 85567 078 X (hb)
ISBN 1 85567 128 X (pb)

Library of Congress Cataloging-in-Publication Data

Contemporary international relations : a guide to theory / edited by
    A.J.R. Groom and Margot Light
        p.   cm.
    Includes bibliographical references and indexes.
    ISBN 1–85567–078–X. – ISBN 1–85567–128–X (pbk.)
    1. International relations.   I. Groom, A.J.R.   II Light, Margot.
JX1391.C662   1994
327.1'01–dc20   94–15115
                                                                        CIP

Typeset by Mayhew Typesetting, Rhayader, Powys
Printed and bound in Great Britain by Biddles Ltd., Guildford and King's Lynn

Contents

Preface

This volume is the third in a series by British or British-based scholars on the conceptual state of the field of International Relations (IR). The first volume, published by Frances Pinter in 1978, was edited by A.J.R. Groom and C.R. Mitchell under the title *International Relations Theory: A Bibliography*. Its successor, again published by Frances Pinter, but this time edited by Margot Light and A.J.R. Groom, was published in 1985 as *International Relations: A Handbook of Current Theory*. The present volume seeks to repeat the exercise. Many of the contributors to the previous volumes have written new chapters for this book, other authors are contributing for the first time. While the present volume represents our view of the present state of the field, together the three volumes chart our vision of the changes in IR. The aim has not been to provide a textbook, but rather to provide a *vade mecum* to be used in conjunction with such a text.

Having set out to present a selective survey of the field as it is presently conceived, we asked contributors to present overviews of their topics, mentioning some classics in the field but focusing primarily on new trends and pointing to probable growth points. Contributors were asked to concentrate on the literature published after 1985, since reference can be made to the previous volumes for earlier works. In general, we have sought to emphasize conceptual rather than empirical work, and, while expecting our contributors to reflect general interests in the field of IR, we have encouraged them to stress their own particular views. In short, while each chapter represents a general guide to a particular topic, it is not intended to be encyclopedic but rather to provide guidance from an acknowledged expert in that aspect of the field. Where contributors have quoted 'telling phrases' from the literature, we have cited the general source but not necessarily the page number.

Although we, as editors, are responsible for the choice of subjects, we consulted a number of colleagues. The change in the contents of the three volumes we have produced in itself conveys how the field has developed. In 1978 we had chapters on methodology, research techniques, systems approaches, international stratification, power, influence and authority, conflict and war, strategy, order and change, integration theory, foreign policy analysis, psychological aspects, anthropological aspects and ways of analysing world society. By 1985 the important elements of the subject seemed to have changed somewhat. At that point, although methodology, power, influence and authority, conflict, war and conflict management, strategy, foreign policy analysis, anthropological aspects and psychological aspects still seemed important, we included chapters on the inter-paradigm debate, normative approaches, world society and human needs, development and dependency, structuralism and neorealism, integration and disintegration and textbooks. For the present volume it has again been necessary to add new subjects.

The debate on critical theory and postmodernism clearly requires a chapter of its own. In some respects it is linked to a growing awareness of feminist approaches to IR. Gender issues, ethnic politics and more traditional concepts of nationalism reflect the new emphasis in IR on identity studies. Interesting work is now being done in the field of political geography, often with a structuralist aspect, and this subject, an old tradition in the study of IR, has returned to the mainstream. In some respects we see here examples of theory catching up with, and reflecting, the enormous changes that have taken place in the international system in the last decade.

Our previous volumes were, if not parochial, then certainly Anglo-Saxon-centric. They surveyed the literature published in English in Britain and North America. They paid some attention to the literature from other countries published in English, but they did not venture beyond the medium of English. In this volume we have recognized our parochialism and have made an effort to bring to readers' attention significant contributions to the literature in other languages. To do this we required the help of many colleagues abroad and we would like to thank them for their cooperation. We hope these first efforts will stimulate responses that will enable us to improve our coverage in the future.

One aspect of the field, in particular, has gone through an interesting metamorphosis in the three volumes. In the first volume, there was a chapter on integration theory. In the second we linked integration with theories of disintegration. In the 1990s we have had to conceive the subject in a different manner. On the one hand integration is concerned with patterns of global politics and governance; on the other, disintegration has given nationalism a renewed salience. Another subject that has gone through a significant metamorphosis is that of strategy, as Ken Booth's contribution demonstrates. It may seem perverse that we have included a chapter on Marxist theories of IR. However, political changes do not necessarily reflect intellectual validity, and, as Hazel Smith indicates, the contribution of Marxist analysis to IR theory is multiform. Moreover, Marxist analyses contribute to the study of large-scale historical change – a subject that now is of growing interest and importance to IR scholars, as Richard Little demonstrates.

But what aspects of IR have we omitted from our survey? In 1978 systems approaches to IR were still current, but we no longer felt justified in including them in 1985, since little new had been written on that subject and the promises had not been fulfilled. In 1985 the literature on structuralism was in full flow and the *Handbook* reflected this. In 1994, however, structuralists have made their point, or rather we are all, to some extent, structuralists now and structuralist analyses can be found in many of the chapters of this volume. The decline of realism and, indeed, neorealism is also a feature of the three volumes. We no longer felt it necessary to have a separate chapter on the subject in this volume, although realism and neorealism, like structuralist approaches, appear in many chapters that follow. Indeed, the inter-paradigm debate can no longer be subsumed easily in a tripartite superstructure. There are debates and there are cutting edges – in conflict studies, in the notion of global governance, in identity studies, in critical theory and in political geography – but we can discern no new dominant paradigm. We hope, too, to have our eyes opened by the literature beyond the English language.

We owe thanks to many people and not least to our contributors. We have learned a great deal from them, and we appreciate their responses to our pressures. We must also thank Fran Pinter for her constant encouragement of our endeavour. Our gratitude and appreciation are due to Rick Fawn, Helena Sjursen and Vassiliki Koutrakou who acted as our research assistants and contributed much of great usefulness to this volume. We have been blessed with excellent and unstinting secretarial support from Marilyn Spice and her colleagues at the University of Kent and Martina Langer at the LSE. This has indeed been a team enterprise, but ultimately the responsibility rests with us.

A.J.R. Groom
Margot Light
Canterbury and London
January 1994

Contributors

Peter Bennett studied physics and philosophy of science and became interested in the study of decision making in conflicts as a researcher at Sussex University. He maintains an interest in analysing international conflict while working within a management science perspective stressing the use of models to improve decision making. He is currently Reader in the Management Science Department at Strathclyde University. His publications include *Analysing Conflict and its Resolution*, editor (1987), 'Modelling Complex Conflicts: Formalism or Expertise?', *Review of International Studies*, vol. 17, 1991, no. 4, pp. 349–64.

Ken Booth holds a Personal Chair in the Department of International Politics, University of Wales, Aberystwyth. He has been Scholar-in-Residence at the US Naval War College, Senior Research Fellow at the Center for Foreign Policy Studies, Dalhousie University (Canada) and Visiting MacArthur Professor in the Faculty of Social and Political Sciences, Cambridge University. He has lectured to academic and military audiences in many countries. Among his books are *Strategy and Ethnocentrism*, *Law, Force and Diplomacy at Sea* and *New Thinking about Strategy and International Security*.

Chris Brown is senior lecturer in Politics and International Relations at the University of Kent at Canterbury. His publications include *International Relations Theory: New Normative Approaches* (1992), *Political Restructuring in Europe: Ethical Perspectives*, editor (1993) and numerous articles on international relations theory and international political economy.

John Burton was an Australian delegate to the United Nations Charter Conference in 1945 and was appointed Permanent Head of the Australian Foreign Office in 1947. From 1963 to 1978 he taught international relations at University College London where he founded the Centre for the Analysis of Conflict. After 1978 he was associated with the University of Kent, the University of Maryland Center for Development and Conflict Resolution and the George Mason Center for Conflict Analysis and Resolution. In 1989 he was a Distinguished Jennings Randolph Fellow at the United States Institute of Peace. His many books include *International Relations: A General Theory* (1965), *Conflict and Communication* (1969), *World Society* (1972) and a four-volume series on Conflict.

Stephen Chan is Director of the University of Kent London Centre of International Relations and Honorary Professor of the University of Zambia. He has held visiting appointments at Oxford, Wellington, Geneva and Natal and was a member of the Commonwealth Secretariat for six years, stationed in both London and southern Africa. He has published eight books on international relations, including *Kaunda and Southern Africa: Image and Reality in Foreign Policy* (1991) and one hundred papers.

A.J.R. Groom is Professor of International Relations at the University of Kent. A past chairman of the British International Studies Association, he is founder and chairman of the European Standing Group for International Relations of ECPR and Director of the Centre for Conflict Analysis. His principal publications include some 17 monographs and books and over one hundred articles. Recent publications include *Frameworks for International Cooperation*, edited with Paul Taylor (1990), *International Relations: Then and Now* with William Olson (1991) and *The European Community in Context* (1992).

Fred Halliday is Professor of International Relations at the London School of Economics. His publications include *The Making of the Second Cold War* (1983) and *Rethinking International Relations* (1994). He is currently working on a study of the international dimensions of revolutions.

Richard Higgott is Professor of Government, University of Manchester. Until January 1994 he was Professor of International Relations and Public Policy, Research School of Pacific Studies, Australian National University. His recent publications include *Relocating Middlepowers: Australia and Canada in an Evolving World Order*, co-authored with Andrew F Cooper and Kim Richard Nossal (1993); *Pacific Economic Relations in the 1990s: Cooperation or Conflict?*, co-edited with Richard Leaver and John Ravenhill (1993) *International Relations: Global and Australian Perspectives on an Evolving Discipline*, co-edited with James L. Richardson (1993).

Mark Hoffman is lecturer in International Relations at the London School of Economics. His main publications are in international relations theory, third-party mediation and conflict resolution. He is the editor (with Ian Forbes) of *Political Theory, International Relations and the Ethics of Intervention* (1993). He is currently working on two projects: one on third-party mediation and ethnic conflict, the other on critical international theory.

Margot Light is senior lecturer in International Relations at the London School of Economics. She is the editor, with A.J.R. Groom of *International Relations: A Handbook of Current Theory* (1985), author of *The Soviet Theory of International Relations* (1988) and editor of *Troubled Friendships: Moscow's Third World Ventures* (1993).

Richard Little is Professor of International Politics at the University of Bristol. Before moving to Bristol, he spent over 20 years at Lancaster

University. He also worked for three years at the Open University where he helped to prepare the course on Perspectives in World Politics. For the past four years he has been the editor of the *Review of International Studies*. His publications include *Intervention: External Involvement in Civil Wars* (1975), *Global Problems and World Order*, with R.D. McKinlay (1986) and *The Logic of Anarchy: From Neorealism to Structural Realism* with B. Buzan and C. Jones (1993).

James Mayall has worked at the London School of Economics and Political Science since 1966. He is currently Professor of International Relations and Chairman of the Centre for International Studies. He is the author of *Nationalism and International Society* (1990) and has also published widely on the Third World and international relations theory.

Christopher Mitchell joined the academic exodus from Britain in the 1980s and is Druce French Cumbie Professor of International Conflict Analysis at George Mason University, Virginia and, currently, Director of that university's Institute for Conflict Analysis and Resolution. He continues to work on various aspects of peace processes and has recently published articles on the theory of entrapment, ending asymmetric conflicts and a multi-role model of mediation. His major works are *The Structure of International Conflict* (1981), *Peacemaking and the Consultants' Role* (1981), and (with Keith Webb) *New Approaches to International Mediation* (1988). His forthcoming publications are *Gestures of Conciliation* and *A Handbook on Problem Solving Approaches to Protracted Conflicts*.

Michael Nicholson took both undergraduate and doctoral degrees in economics at the University of Cambridge. He subsequently held faculty positions in various universities in Britain and North America. From 1970–82 he was Director of the Richardson Institute for Conflict and Peace Research, first in London and later at the University of Lancaster. He became Professor of International Relations at the University of Kent and Director of the university's London Centre of International Relations. He is now Professor of International Relations at the University of Sussex. His most recent book is *Rationality and the Analysis of International Conflict* (1992).

Geoffrey Parker is senior lecturer in Political Geography and Geopolitics at the University of Birmingham. He has lectured widely, especially in the United Kingdom, Western Europe and India. He has a particular interest in European political geography and in European and Asiatic geopolitical thought. His principal works include *The Political Geography of Community Europe* (1983), *Western Geopolitical Thought in the Twentieth Century* (1985) and *The Geopolitics of Domination* (1988). He has also contributed to a number of books, journals and reference works including the *Dictionary of Geopolitics* (1994).

Dominic Powell graduated from Indiana University in 1991. He is currently conducting postgraduate research on just war theory at the University of

Kent and is an editor of *Paradigms*, the International Relations journal of the University of Kent.

Hazel Smith is a lecturer in International Relations at the University of Kent's London Centre of International Relations. She studied at the University of Essex and London School of Economics. Her books include *Nicaragua: Self-determination and Survival* (1993) and *The European Community and Central America: the structural limits to EC foreign policy* (1994).

Tarja Väyrynen is a Ph.D. student at the University of Kent at Canterbury. Her doctoral thesis deals with problem-solving conflict resolution from a theoretical point of view. She has done research on the Central European peace process at the University of Tampere in Finland. Her research interests include international conflict analysis, the philosophy of the social sciences and phenomenology.

Introduction: the past as prelude
A.J.R. Groom

International Relations (IR) in practice and as an academic subject is both ancient and modern. While it was one of the last elements of social science to achieve disciplinary status with the establishment of a Chair at the University of Wales at Aberystwyth in 1919, a simple perusal of the classics of political science and political thought points to its ancient status in theory and practice. Where there are large groups that interact within a societal framework, there is IR, as practice and usually as discipline. Even if we reach back to the earliest civilizations with the help of Mann's [23] wonderful study of the bases of social power throughout recorded history, we can see IR in practice and in embryo as a discipline. The interaction of Mann's four bases of social power – economic, ideological, political and military – provide the very stuff of IR in an ancient context as much as they do in the 1990s.

The purpose of this Introduction is to acknowledge the past rather than to reach back into it. In comparison with Mann's sweep of civilizations, Parkinson [28] and Knutsen [16] both provide us with a history of thought and practice reaching back into the roots of our own Western civilization in their surveys of the period from mediæval times to our own. Both works give a healthy sense of context. However, for other writers, the modern period is a half-millennium stretching back to approximately 1500. Wallerstein [37] and Modelski [25] both accept that the world-system that emerged about that time is, at the global level, still recognizably that which pertains today. Although Wallerstein sees it essentially as a world economy without a world empire, and Modelski concentrates on political leadership in a society which, although it has anarchical elements, is still nevertheless a society, their time-scale is the same. Their writings have given rise to a lively debate about whether the contemporary world system of the last half-millennium is rooted in economic or political relationships. Thompson's volume [35] gives an account of this debate. Others take a similarly long time-span in looking at the gradual evolution of geopolitical relationships whereby slow, deep processes lay or destroy the foundations of the stage on which princes and prime ministers strut, seemingly in charge but

1

structurally constrained (Ashley [1], Braudel [2], Choucri and North [4], Mackinder [21], Mahan [22], Scott [31], Harold and Margaret Sprout [32]).

If our time-scale is that of the formal discipline of IR now some 75 years old, then Olson and Groom [27] have sketched the intellectual history of the discipline. Their work is organized around the now conventional triptych of frameworks, namely realism, world society approaches and structural approaches, and they demonstrate how such approaches were evident in 19th-century theory and practice, be it in the concert system (realism), in the growth of international pressure groups, international public unions, international arbitration procedures and peace conferences (world society approaches) or in the structuralist Marxist and geopolitical traditions. In the last years of the 19th century, and the first quarter of the 20th century there was a substantial debate, particularly among intellectuals in central Europe, about the nature of capitalism and in particular its relationship with imperialism. Did imperialism constitute the highest stage of capitalism as an organic part of that phenomenon, as Lenin [18] asserted, or was the association of imperialism with capitalism accidental and not necessary for the flourishing of capitalism as Hobson [13] argued? Similarly, the geopoliticians had room for debate as the sea-based theories of Mahan [22] were challenged by the land-based theories of Mackinder [21]. Would the heartland or the rimland prevail as the time-space ratio changed under the impact of new technology and in particular the building of railways across the continents of the world?

Olson and Groom [27] also pay attention to the development of political thought in the context of the emerging modern state system which received recognition of its full flowering in the Peace of Westphalia in 1648 and the subsequent Treaty. Among the realists were Hobbes [12] and Machiavelli [20]. Callières [5] set out a Treatise on Diplomacy, and Grotius was a towering figure in the development of the new international law. On the other hand, the Duc de Sully [7] and that remarkable man Kant [14], who barely strayed from the confines of Königsberg in his physical presence but whose mind encompassed the world, both sought to create the conditions for a permanent and working peace system.

But the 19th century had many great writers in the unacknowledged field of IR, as Hinsley [11] points out. Gentz [8] became the father of modern diplomacy. De Tocqueville [6] saw clearly the outlines of mid-20th-century international relations, whereas von Clausewitz [36] made us aware that war was the continuation of politics by other means even if statesmen, time and again, refused to learn his lesson other than the hard way. As we have seen, the geopoliticians flourished and the Marxist tradition was born.

The point of crystallization was the First World War, where all these trends and the urgent necessity for a practical solution to the problem of war gave birth to the discipline of IR. The purpose of IR was to examine the causes of war and the conditions of peace in a 'scientific manner'. The new-found discipline was dedicated to improving the lot of humankind through the application of science and scientific method to social problems. That was how progress had been made in the creation of a welfare state and an increasingly liberal form of democracy. That was how famine and disease, two of the great inflictions on humankind, were being conquered (at least in parts of Western Europe and on the Atlantic seaboard of the United States). It was, therefore, surely the way to broach the problem of war and to establish conditions for the peace. Thus IR was founded at a time of unprecedented political engineering at the practical level, with the creation of many new states based in theory, if not in practice, on nations and the creation of the first general international organization with a secretariat, namely the League of Nations. There was briefly in the 1920s a consensus in theory and practice on the precepts of liberal internationalism associated with the name of Woodrow Wilson.

This consensus had its underpinnings in the belief that rationality was shared among free men and women, that the world was at least in part subject to our manipulation and that whenever free peoples met together the harmony of interests would provide a foundation for fructuous relations. In short, the purpose of liberal internationalism was to create at the global level those conditions of shared values and collective security which were deemed to be evident within democratic nation-states. This consensus provides the framework within which the textbooks of IR of the first decade of the new subject were written. Olson and Groom [27] provide appendices in which they list the most prominent textbooks of the years 1916–31, 1932–44 and 1945–62. The literature of that period was adorned by major studies whose significance is both historical and contemporary, such as those of Keynes [15], Richardson [29] and Lasswell [17], since they were important in their time and they still bear reading now.

As the international situation changed, so did the academic discipline. In the last months before the Second World War, Carr [3] wrote his magisterial study of the 20-years' crisis. He argued that harmony of interests could not be assumed, but on the other hand, he was not prepared to embrace a Hobbesian world. His was a prudential realism. Schwarzenberger [30] went further and asserted that power politics was axiomatic, but the most widely read statement of realism was that of Morgenthau [26]. Starting from the premise that the drive to dominate is universal in time and space, Morgenthau elaborated six principles of political realism. For Schwarzenberger and for Morgenthau there could be no peace but merely a truce based upon the overwhelming power of the dominant states of the day. The manipulation of threats and, where necessary, their implementation was the constant feature of the eternal dialogue between status quo and revisionist Powers. At that time, however, the geopolitical tradition was not absent, as the influential works of Strausz-Hupé [34] and Spykman [33] attested. The Anglo-American tradition of liberal internationalism had been subject to brutal and frank questioning by scholars who had been trained in the European continental tradition and whose personal lives had been scarred by the rise of Hitler and Fascism in a Europe in which the liberal democracies were on the defensive and in isolation. When the threat of national socialism and Fascism had been defeated, the Cold War began. The second great consensus was, therefore, on realism.

Not all writing in the post-war period was steeped in the intellectual maelstrom of the Cold War. One of the founding fathers of the subject, Quincy Wright [40], an outstanding international lawyer, also developed a study of war rooted in an empirical base. But Wright, ever a man of ideas, was never a mindless datamonger as his survey of IR proves [41]. Waltz's analysis of the interaction between man, the state and war [38] was a more philosophical study of war, analysing theories of war according to different levels: that of the individual, the internal organization of the state and the nature of the international system. The nature of the international system excited the minds and imagination of two eminent scholars at the London School of Economics and Political Science, Manning [24] and Wight [39]. Wight saw power politics through a Christian lens, whereas Manning sought to seize the essence of the nature of international society. They brought a nuance to the cruder analyses of a Schwarzenberger or a Morgenthau, but their subtleties did not prevent a more radical challenge to the dominance of realism.

The world was changing yet again. In the 1950s there was the dramatic reconciliation of France and Germany after a conflict lasting nearly a century. Nuclear weapons had to be assimilated into the political calculations of politicians and peoples. Colonialism was coming rapidly to an end, opening up a north–south dimension to international politics to expand the dominant east–west dimension. New actors had forced themselves on to the international scene, buffeting states as they did so. The discipline of IR had been founded on the notion that international politics were in essence state-centric and that the dominant mode of relations between states was power politics. Both of these axioms were now under fierce challenge. The second consensus was beginning to crack. The prelude was giving way to the present – a present which can be traced through the predecessors of this volume [9, 19].

Where then do we stand in the mid-1990s? Our world has changed over the last 30 years, and the change has seemed particularly dramatic in the last half-decade. Do we have the necessary concepts to understand it, or are we condemned to broach the questions of the 21st century with the intellectual tools of the 19th? The pages which follow seek to provide a basis on which a judgement can be made. They reflect conceptual thinking in the field of international relations as it exists in the mid-1990s.

Bibliography

1. Ashley, Richard K. *The Political Economy of War and Peace*. London, Pinter, 1980.
2. Braudel, Fernand *The Mediterranean*. New York, Harper & Row, 1972.
3. Carr, E.H. *The Twenty Years Crisis, 1919–1939*. London, Macmillan, 1981.
4. Choucri, Nazli and North, Robert C. *Nations in Conflict*. San Francisco, W.H. Freeman, 1975.
5. de Callières, François *On the Manner of Negotiating with Princes*. Lanham, University Press of America, 1983.

6. de Tocqueville, Alexis *Democracy in America*. New York, Harper & Row, 1966.
7. Duc de Sully *The Grand Design of Henry IV*. Boston, Ginn & Co., 1909.
8. Gentz, Friedrich *Fragments on the Balance of Power*. London, Peltier, 1806.
9. Groom, A.J.R. and Mitchell, C.R. (eds) *International Relations Theory*. London, Pinter and New York, Nichols, 1978.
10. Grotius, Hugo *The Law of War and Peace*. New York, Bobbs-Merrill, 1925.
11. Hinsley, F.H. *Power and the Pursuit of Peace*. London, Cambridge University Press, 1963.
12. Hobbes, Thomas *Leviathan*. Oxford, Oxford University Press, 1952.
13. Hobson, J.A. *Imperialism: A Study*. London, Unwin Hyman, 1988.
14. Kant, Immanuel *Perpetual Peace*. New York, Bobbs-Merrill, 1957.
15. Keynes, J.M. *The Economic Consequences of the Peace*. New York, Harcourt, 1919.
16. Knutsen, Torbjörn L. *A History of International Relations Theory*. Manchester, Manchester University Press, 1992.
17. Lasswell, Harold D. *World Politics and Personal Insecurity*. New York, McGraw-Hill, 1935.
18. Lenin, V.I. *Imperialism: The Highest Stage of Capitalism* in *Collected Works*. London, Lawrence & Wishart, 1964, pp. 185–304.
19. Light, Margot and Groom, A.J.R. (eds) *International Relations: A Handbook of Current Theory*. London, Pinter and Boulder, Lynne Rienner, 1985.
20. Machiavelli, Niccoló *The Prince*. New York, Penguin, 1984.
21. Mackinder, Halford J. *Democratic Ideals and Reality*. London, Constable, 1919.
22. Mahan, Alfred Thayer *The Influence of Sea Power upon History 1660–1783*. London, Methuen, 1965.
23. Mann, Michael *The Sources of Social Power*. Cambridge, Cambridge University Press, 1986.
24. Manning, C.A.W. *The Nature of International Society*. London, Macmillan, 1975.
25. Modelski, George *Long Cycles in World Politics*. London, Macmillan, 1987.
26. Morgenthau, Hans J. *Politics among Nations*. New York, Alfred Knopf, 1985.
27. Olson, William C. and Groom, A.J.R. *International Relations Then and Now*. London, Routledge, 1992.
28. Parkinson, F. *The Philosophy of International Relations*. London, Sage, 1977.
29. Richardson, L.F. *Arms and Insecurity: a mathematical study of the causes and origins of war*. Pittsburgh, Boxwood Press, 1960.
30. Schwarzenberger, Georg *Power Politics: A Study of World Politics*. London, Stevens, 1964.
31. Scott, Andrew M. *The Dynamics of Interdependence*. London, University of North Carolina Press, 1982.
32. Sprout, Harold and Margaret *The Ecological Perspectives in Human Affairs*. Princeton, Princeton University Press, 1965.
33. Spykman, Nicholas J. *America's Strategy in World Politics*. Hamden, Archon Books, 1970.
34. Strausz-Hupé, R. *Geopolitics*. New York, Putnam, 1942.
35. Thompson, William R. (ed.) *Contending Approaches to World System Analysis*. London, Sage, 1983.
36. von Clausewitz, Carl *On War*, translated and edited by Michael Howard and Peter Paret, Princeton, Princeton University Press, 1976.
37. Wallerstein, Immanuel *The Capitalist World Economy*. London, Cambridge University Press, 1979.

38. Waltz, Kenneth N. *Man, the State and War.* New York, Columbia University Press, 1959.
39. Wight, Martin *Power Politics.* Leicester, Leicester University Press, 1978.
40. Wright, Quincy *A Study of War.* Chicago, University of Chicago Press, 1983.
41. Wright, Quincy *The Study of International Relations.* New York, Irvington Publishers, 1980.

Part 1
Philosophical approaches

1 International relations and large-scale historical change*
Richard Little

There has been an important convergence of interest in recent years between students of International Relations (IR) and students of large-scale historical change. On the one hand, the complex series of events which eventually led to the demise of the Soviet Union has made IR scholars much more aware of the processes associated with large-scale historical change [34]. On the other hand, there has been a growing recognition that it is not possible to understand large-scale historical change without taking account of the international system. Large-scale historical change refers to transformational moments in world history: for example, the demise of antiquity, the rise of feudalism and the emergence of modern capitalism. The disintegration of the Soviet Union is sometimes placed into this category of events because it is seen to mark the ultimate triumph of liberal capitalism over all other rival ideologies [68]. Fukuyama [44] has even associated this event with the 'end of history'. Although such an assessment has, unsurprisingly, been subjected to substantial criticism, it has helped to fuel the widespread interest in large-scale historical change [75].

As awareness of this interest has developed, IR specialists have started to explore beyond the boundaries of their own discipline for a better understanding of change in international relations [71, 72, 98]. It has been recognized for some time now that IR has relied on a very static conception of the international system and has lacked the necessary theoretical tools to accommodate processes which precipitate change [22, 58, 112]. At the same time students of large-scale historical change, acknowledging the importance of international relations, have started to mine IR research [47, 80, 81, 82, 83, 109]. When these two areas of literature are viewed from a wider perspective, however, it becomes evident that their mutual concerns reflect three complicating factors.

First, having come to recognize the significance of the global arena, students of large-scale historical change have drawn very extensively on ideas

* The author gratefully acknowledges the financial assistance of the ESRC in the completion of this article.

9

which are associated in IR with the realist perspective. They have identified a link between international competition and the survival of the state, with the consequence that a significant role is ascribed to power, particularly military power, in the processes associated with large-scale historical change [8, 40, 108]. In IR, the same link has long been associated with realist thinkers and, in recent years, the logic which underpins this perspective has been articulated most explicitly by the neorealist school of thought associated with Waltz [121,122]. Yet, paradoxically, in the IR literature, far from being identified with an historical outlook, it has been argued that neorealism draws on an unredeemed form of ahistoricism and, as a consequence, is completely unable to offer a coherent account, never mind an explanation, of either contemporary [67] or historical [31, 96] developments in the international system. Because the link with realism is indirect and probably inadvertent, the deep-seated conflicts within IR between realists and their critics have not been acknowledged by students of large-scale historical change.

Second, despite the growing interest in large-scale historical change, IR has failed to develop a framework which can fully embrace the evolution of world history at a global level. This is because of the tendency to rely on what Walker [114] sees as the rather constrained or delimited history of the international system associated with the realist viewpoint. Waltz and his colleagues have very successfully propagated the view that world history has occurred within an unchanging anarchic international system. This ahistorical perspective has, in fact, made it more difficult to develop a view of world history from a global perspective. Although susceptible to criticism, the so-called 'English school of international relations' [53, 62, 128] associated with Wight, Bull and Watson [18, 19, 123, 127] has been endeavouring to break loose from these neorealist constraints for some time, but with the growing interest in large-scale historical change, their work has been reinforced if not overtaken by theorists working inside and outside of international relations.

Finally, as interest in large-scale historical change has grown, so it has become increasingly important to find answers to a number of difficult methodological and epistemological questions which have always bedeviled the social sciences but which are raised in an acute form when attention is drawn to issues relating to large-scale historical change. At the heart of these questions is the problem associated with the relationship between structure and agency. A review of the literature reveals that the problem surfaces in particular when attempts are made to develop a theory of the state. Many social scientists have, over the last decade, claimed to have rediscovered the state [6, 38], and it is argued that the state has the potentiality to be an autonomous agent. Much effort has been invested in developing a theory which will accommodate the complex and variable role played by the state in world history [13, 101]. Although realists in IR have never doubted the autonomy of the state, IR scholars are beginning to recognize that realists, in fact, operate on the basis of a very undernourished conception of the state and, indeed, lack any explicit theory of the state [60]. The need for such a theory represents a constant refrain which runs through this assessment of the convergence of large-scale historical change and IR.

It is surprising, at first sight, that it has taken so long to identify the common links between IR and large-scale historical change because the antecedents of the contemporary study of IR are so often identified in the work of historians who were interested in questions about large scale-change [33]. In the ancient world, for example, Thucydides explained how a major war brought about the collapse of the Athenian Empire; and at the start of the 16th century Guicciardini, who recovered historical method for the modern historian, struggled to account for the collapse of the city states in Renaissance Italy when they were confronted by the nascent nation states of Europe [48].

Yet despite the centrality of large-scale historical change in these texts, this feature has not been highlighted. Instead, attention in IR has almost invariably been drawn to the importance of contingent or unforeseen events in historical accounts [114, 126]. A sharp distinction has been drawn in IR, as a consequence, between the approaches adopted by historians and social scientists [93]. Historians are seen to rely on narrative accounts which use hermeneutic methods to reveal how one contingent event gives rise to another. Social scientists, by contrast, are seen to provide scientific accounts which draw on the assumption that human behaviour is constrained by social structures. Although there have been attempts by some philosophers of a positivist predisposition [55] to suggest that historical and scientific accounts do in fact rely on the same mode of explanation, this position has not generally been accepted by either historians or social scientists.

When it comes to accounts of large-scale historical change, the division between historian and social scientist largely breaks down. Nevertheless, for the purpose of this review, a distinction is drawn between historical sociologists and world historians (WH). In practice, the division can be difficult to sustain. Nevertheless, it remains a useful starting point to distinguish between the work of analysts who see themselves as sociologists and those who see themselves as historians.

The development of historical sociology (HS)

Contemporary historical sociologists fiercely attack the division between history and social science. Although there have always been historians [27] and sociologists [84] who have questioned the idea of a methodological and substantive division of labour between historians and social scientists, the desire to abolish the division constitutes a defining characteristic of historical sociologists, who insist that any boundary between history and social science looks 'increasingly quaint, contrived and unnecessary' [2: p. x, 46, 104, 107].

The origins of historical sociology have been traced back to the Enlightenment, when for the first time it began to be taken for granted that it was possible to improve the human condition by unmaking and remaking human institutions. During the 18th century there were tentative attempts to compare societies and, in particular, to understand why some societies were more successful than others [45]. Statesmen, of course, have always kept a wary eye on the relative military strength of other countries. But by the 18th century it was becoming clear that the traditional indicators for assessing the international balance of power were increasingly inadequate. As Britain moved to the centre of the world stage, success in the international arena began to be associated with progressive political systems by thinkers such as Montesquieu. By the 19th century, moreover, there was also an awareness that momentous social changes were taking place within societies as the result of industrialization and, in an attempt to understand this process, extensive systematic social analysis began to take place. Underlying this analysis was the desire to discover how Europe had managed to surge ahead of other centres of civilization.

Some of the most important social thinkers of the 19th and early 20th century are seen to represent the first wave of historical sociology [2, 104]. Marx and Weber, for example, both accepted the importance of comparative historical analysis in any attempt to understand large-scale social change. It can be argued, in addition, that they also provided the foundations for contemporary critical theory because they were interested in the existence of hidden social structures which frustrate some human aspirations and make others realizable. The attempt to reveal these structures was a product of the desire to redraw the parameters of society in a way which would permit a greater fulfilment of human aspirations. This desire brought HS into confrontation with 20th-century totalitarian regimes which sought to bring about change on the basis of historical myth rather than an empirical analysis of history. With the defeat of Fascism, however, there was a resurgence of interest in HS. Initially, the mainstream emphasis was on structural functional analysis as exemplified in the work of Parsons [89, 90] and Smelser [90, 103]. But the methods and approaches of HS became more varied with the emergence of major social theorists such as Eisenstadt [36, 37], Lipset [73, 74] and Bendix [9, 10, 11]. The implications of their work for HS have been summarized by Smith [104].

Most of these theorists, like their 19th-century counterparts, treated the state as a closed system. No account was taken of the international arena within which social systems existed. As a result, after the Second World War, a major intellectual gulf existed between IR, which studied relations between states, and sociology, which studied social behaviour within states. But not all early historical sociologists ignored the international dimension. Bendix, for example, argued that treating society as a self-contained unit was an unacceptable historical generalization drawn from the distinctive experience of France and Britain [95]. And in *The Great Transformation*, Polanyi [91, 14] argued that although the formation of the 'self-regulating' market which emerged during the 19th century was intimately connected to the growing power of the state, the survival of independent states depended upon the existence of an international balance of power.

While the work of Bendix and Polanyi had virtually no impact on IR, Wallerstein's incursion into the field of HS [5, 115, 116, 117, 118, 119, 120] in the 1970s did very quickly begin to make a mark [57]. Wallerstein became a focal point of attention in part because unwittingly he posed a major challenge to the state-centric framework so closely associated with realism. Although IR analysts such as Keohane and Nye [66] were questioning the continuing relevance of realism at that time – suggesting that states were losing their autonomy and coherence with the rise of transnational actors – they continued to accept the historical validity of a state-centric model. By contrast, Burton [20, 21] insisted that the state system had always been only one of many overlapping systems. He endeavoured to replace the billiard ball model with the image of the international system as a cobweb. He failed, however, to provide an historical dimension, whereas Wallerstein demonstrated that a state-centric model was inappropriate for understanding the capitalist world system which has evolved and consolidated during the last five hundred years. Wallerstein also locates his discussion in a much broader historical framework. From his perspective, world history can be conceptualized most effectively in terms of co-existing world systems which take the form of either world empires or world economies. In the case of a world empire, the economy and the polity are both centralized so that the political centre of the empire can extract economic resources from the periphery and then use the resources to maintain the stability of the centralized structures which define the empire. A world economy, by contrast, has a polity which is fragmented into independent political units; these are located within an integrated economy, defined by a single division of labour, so that trade represents an essential feature of the relations between the fragmented political units.

Although Wallerstein has shown no interest in using his theoretical framework to develop a world history, he could, in principle, provide such a history revealing how world empires and world economies have repeatedly replaced each other over time. Instead, he has focused his attention on the aftermath of European feudalism – an epoch defined by self-sufficient economic and political units. Wallerstein's analysis presupposes that the feudal era operated in the absence of the kind of overarching or integrating economic or political structure which defines the existence of a world system. It follows that it was only when trade began to take place between these feudal units and an economic division of labour developed, linking all the units, that a world economy evolved and a new world system came into existence. The underlying theoretical question which intrigued Wallerstein was why this world economy, in contrast to earlier examples, failed to transform into a world empire.

Traditionally realists have answered this question by reference to the existence of a balance of power. But although Wallerstein makes provision for competition between the major states in the system – the central feature of any balance of power – he does not see this factor as providing a sufficient explanation for the system's survival because the balance of power failed to prevent previous world economies from being transformed into world empires. Wallerstein's complex explanation for the survival of the capitalist world economy relies on the emergence of strong states at the core of the world economy which were able to exploit the weak states in the periphery. The existence of competing strong states also ensured that capital remained mobile, and the conjunction of these two factors effectively prevented the system from becoming politically centralized. Wallerstein is defining strength here, as realists do, in terms of a capacity to exert power over other states.

Wallerstein's theory has provided the foundations for a growing body of research, and his admirers consider his work to be a major intellectual achievement of the late 20th century [92]. Nevertheless, he has been attacked both for his historical interpretations [52, 63] and his unsound theoretical premises [100, 105]. Yet even his critics have acknowledged the importance of locating large-scale historical change in the context of a complex global arena. When Skocpol [101] carried out her comparative analysis of revolutions, for example, she found it necessary to break away from the idea of the state as a closed system. She identified states as potentially autonomous actors, capable of pursuing strategies which could conflict with the interests of the dominant class within the state. What Skocpol demonstrates is that the revolutions she examined occurred because the ruling elite which controlled the state apparatus found itself caught in a pincer movement, under threat simultaneously from powerful domestic and foreign forces.

The need to locate large-scale historical change in an international setting is also evident in another major research project in HS, produced in the 1970s by Anderson [3, 4]. In contrast to Wallerstein, who sees the capitalist world economy emerging autonomously at a particular point in time and space, Anderson argues that the roots of the present system need to be traced back to antiquity. Indeed he argues that the emergence of modern capitalism was the result of a unique concatenation of antiquity and feudalism. In other words, capitalism is seen as the end product of a set of structural trans-formations which took place along a particular historical pathway. In fact, he traces two distinct yet interconnected pathways for Eastern and Western Europe from the time of antiquity. The pathways are interconnected in part because Anderson recognizes that the European experience occurred within a wider international setting.

In antiquity, Anderson identifies a mode of production based on slavery which resulted in technological stagnation. Economic expansion could only take place, therefore, through geographical conquest and, as a consequence, economic growth was more closely linked to military power than in any other mode of production. Anderson goes on to show how successive empires in antiquity – the Athenian, the Macedonian and the Roman – each managed to overcome structural problems in the preceding empire which had limited its capacity for expansion. The Roman Empire even extended into Western Europe, with the end result that a complex synthesis took place between two modes of production, the slave mode imposed by the Romans and the communal or primitive mode of production introduced by the barbarians who migrated into Western Europe.

Central to the resulting feudal mode of production which emerged after the disintegration of the Roman Empire was the 'parcellization of sovereignty' such that the functions of the state were disaggregated and allocated on a vertical basis down through the social system. But for

Anderson, a pure form of feudalism only developed in Western Europe. Although feudalism did emerge in Eastern Europe, where the slave mode of production was never imposed by the Romans, it occurred later and developed along a different pathway. Travelling down the Western pathway, Anderson is able to identify the emergence of structural conflict in the feudal mode of production between the serfs and the nobility. To preserve their position in society, the nobility agreed to the establishment of the absolutist state within which they continued to occupy a privileged position. The formation of these absolutist states, however, posed a threat to the East where the ruling elites were forced to create an alternative and distinctive form of the absolutist state – reflecting their own unique historical pathway.

Critics of Anderson argue that although he sustains his Marxist credentials by establishing a central role for class conflict in his analysis, in fact, he gives a much more important role to military power and inter-state competition. The former plays a vital part in the development of empires, and the latter is a crucial factor in the formulation of the absolutist states [43, 97]. Anderson's orientation corresponds to the general direction being taken by historical sociologists who now accept the crucial role played by war and international competition in the development of the modern state. These historical sociologists have paid considerable attention to the processes whereby the centralization and consolidation of the modern state in Europe have evolved in an international context [8, 40, 47, 81]. But this initial line of research is now being extended and re-evaluated in a number of ways. First, Tilly [109] has attacked the assumption that there is a uniform process which has given rise to the modern nation state. He has drawn attention to the variation in the kinds of state that have existed simultaneously in Europe over the past millennium, although he concludes, in line with Waltz, that in the long haul the need to fight wars eventually eliminated the variation.

Second, Mann [80] has endeavoured to place the formation of the modern state in a much wider historical context. He explores the world historical process whereby people and space have been integrated into 'dominant configurations'. The process is defined by social power, which emerged in the first place in Mesopotamia, around 5000 BC, when individuals became tied to a particular location as the result of sedentary patterns of agriculture; at this juncture, volatile 'social networks' rigidified and were transformed into 'social cages'. From then on, power became a defining feature of all social systems. Mann identifies four sources of social power (economic, ideological, political and military) and then traces how they have developed and inter-related with each other, thereby generating a history of power. On the basis of this history, Mann is able to identify two main types of 'dominant configuration' – empires of domination and multi-power-actor civilizations – and then to explain why one or the other has prevailed in the evolving world historical context.

Mann's overarching framework is very similar to the one adopted by Wallerstein, but unlike Wallerstein, he endeavours to use his framework to provide the basis for a world history. Mann [83] also decries Wallerstein's attempt to give economic factors priority over the other major sources of power, although he has noted the irony that in his later work [119] Wallerstein comes to rely on the political-military factors that historical sociologists like Skocpol, Tilly and Mann have taken so seriously. Mann himself, however, has come under fire for establishing what is seen as an artificial distinction between political and military power [26].

Although Wallerstein has failed to use his framework to develop a world history, other world systems theorists have now started to undertake this exercise. Abu-Lughod [1], for example, has argued that Wallerstein has failed to recognize that the modern world economy was not established in 1500. Its origins need to be traced back to the 13th century when trade began to take place across the Eurasian land mass. This vast trading system eventually collapsed, only to be re-established by the West Europeans after 1500. Western Eurocentric thinking, according to Abu-Lughod, has discouraged Wallerstein from recognizing that the rise of the West was facilitated by the prior existence of a world economy. Frank and Gills [42, 49] have pushed this argument further and insisted that it is possible to trace the emergence of a world system even further back in time.

The work of World Historians

Historical sociologists are not, of course, the only analysts to adopt a macro-historical perspective. Earlier in the century, the attempts by Toynbee and Spengler to develop a macro-historical approach, for example, were given very serious attention. But their work has been out of fashion in recent decades although there is a resurgence of interest at this moment [16, 39]. At the same time, the work of more recent world historians like McNeill and Bozeman [15, 76, 77] has been given a much more sympathetic hearing. World historians are anxious to move away from the Eurocentric character of much contemporary history, and McNeill has endeavoured to establish a framework which places the history of Europe in a global setting. He suggests that world history can be examined in the context of four centres of civilization originating in Greece, India, China and the Middle East. Although these civilizations were quite distinct, there was a degree of direct and indirect contact. As a consequence, any development within one of these centres of civilization giving it a military or economic advantage would be borrowed and adapted by the others. Although there were times when the civilizations intruded on each other, friction between them was minimized because they did not completely occupy the Eurasian landmass. Territory occupied by nomadic peoples separated the civilizations and served to insulate one from another. In this way, the four civilizations coexisted in a rough equilibrium for two millennia between 500 BC and 1500 AD.

The new breed of world historians are, like the historical sociologists, as well as economic historians [61], interested in why the civilization centred on Europe eventually came to overwhelm the others. It is argued that it is not possible to account for this development simply by exploring the evolution of the modern European state system because for the preceding 2,000 years the various civilizations had managed to preserve some kind of equilibrium. As a consequence, Lewis [70] focuses on developments in all the competing civilizations during the Middle Ages. He examines, in particular, how the various civilizations had to adapt as a consequence of nomadic assaults and Christian crusades, and he shows how these adaptations left Western Europe as the overall gainer. Lewis makes it very clear that the successive nomadic empires in Eurasia played a vital role in world history. This theme has been further explored in Barfield's study of the complex relationship between the Chinese civilization and the neighbouring nomadic empires over a 2,000-year period [7].

There are other important themes emerging in the literature currently being generated by world historians. For example, there is growing interest in the development of merchant empires arising from long-distance trade, and world historians are trying to account for the ultimate domination of the Europeans in this area over well-organized and well-financed rivals from other civilizations [109, 110]. McNeill [78, 79], on the other hand, has explored the impact of disease and military technology on world history.

Large-scale historical change and international relations

Although the study of IR often traces its roots back to historians like Thucydides, Guicciardini and Heeren, most contemporary literature in the field has focused resolutely on the present. This tendency has been reinforced by the strong ahistorical predisposition within the discipline noted above which is most apparent in the approach of the neorealists. Waltz, however, has been remarkably unperturbed by the charge of ahistoricism levelled at him by critics such as Ruggie [96] and Cox [31]. In answer to the accusation that he is unable to account even for the momentous shift from the feudal state system to the modern state system, he [121, 122] argues that although there were massive changes in the nature of the units during this shift, the anarchic structure of the system remained the same throughout this period. As far as Waltz is concerned, therefore, world history is characterized by an enduring anarchic system and his theory of the balance of power is designed to explain why this system has never broken down. In essence his theory reveals that the reproduction of the system is an unintended structural consequence of the rational attempts by states to survive.

Once this framework is accepted, it removes the need to ask historical questions about the evolving structure of either states or the international system, and it also becomes perfectly legitimate to draw analogies between Soviet–American relations during the Cold War and the links between Athens and Sparta in antiquity [41]. By the same token, Gilpin [50], drawing on this ahistorical assumption, is able to explore the role of hegemonic powers through the ages. The legitimacy of this assumption, however, has been challenged empirically by Rosenberg [94], who demonstrates that the state systems in ancient Greece and Renaissance Italy are simply not directly comparable.

But the most direct challenge to Waltz has come from the 'long cycle' theorists who assert that it is not possible to characterize the evolution of the world system in terms of a shifting balance of power. Instead, it is necessary to view the history of the modern world system in terms of cycles of war and peace which are then related to the rise and fall of hegemonic powers. Goldstein [51], who has undertaken an extensive review of this literature, identifies three schools of thought in IR which work within this framework. First, there is the leadership cycle school which is most closely associated with the work of Modelski [85, 86]. He argues that the survival of the international system is not an unintended structural consequence of the anarchic system but the result of actions orchestrated by successive leading actors or hegemons in the international political system. Second, a power transition school is tied primarily to the work of Organski [88] who defines the international system in hierarchical rather than anarchic terms. War is related to differential economic growth which makes it possible for challenges to take place to the existing hierarchy. Finally, there is a world-systems school which has drawn Wallerstein's work directly into the field of IR and has endeavoured to establish a link between the interstate system and the world economy [28]. Although these approaches challenge Waltz's theory of international politics, they do not attempt to explore the structure of the international system prior to 1500. Despite the introduction of the idea of cycles, there is a strong presumption that these cycles occur within the structure of an essentially unchanging international system. As a consequence, none of this emerging literature is able to describe or analyse the nature of international relations in the preceding feudal period.

At a more theoretical level, Wendt [124] has argued that Waltz's ahistoricism means that both the state and the international system constitute unexplained or primitive concepts. From this perspective, Waltz ostensibly lacks any theory of either the state or the international system which can account for their genesis or evolution. Waltz acknowledges that he lacks any theory of the state, but a more detailed investigation carried out elsewhere [23] reveals that there is an incipient theory of the state lodged within his theory of the international balance of power. Waltz argues that in order to survive, states have to engage constantly in an internal restructuring process, emulating changes in other states which enhance their power potential. This process constitutes the internal dimension of Waltz's balance of power theory, and the embryonic theory predicts that states will be remarkably similar at any point in time but that their common structures will vary across time. The theory, therefore, ties in very closely with the early work of historical sociologists which examined the emergence of the modern state. This research shows how rapidly feudal states were transformed into absolutist states.

Waltz's theory of the state seems to run foul of Tilly's more recent work [109] which focuses on the structural variations between units in the international system. It is important to recognize, however, that the external dimension of Waltz's balance of power theory, dealing with alliances, could, relatively easily, accommodate Tilly's identification of structural differentiation in the international system. It is worth noting that historical sociologists are now recognizing the significance of alliances for any theory of the state [130]. Kennedy's [64] popular account of the rise and fall of great powers has been attacked on this point [82] and so too has the work of Wallerstein and Anderson [131]. Despite criticism of this kind, Waltz, however, is unlikely to be impressed with these attempts to modify his thesis. Balance of power tactics, from his perspective, can delay but not prevent the elimination of structural differentiation.

But there is obviously a problem with this line of argument. It is true that the contemporary international political system can be defined in terms of the interactions among sovereign states, but this is a very recent phenomenon. Although Waltz provides a powerful logic which can account for this development, his theory does not give any purchase on the origins and evolution of the contemporary international system. His model is both Eurocentric and ahistorical. The growing interest in large-scale historical change is slowly beginning to highlight these features and reveal how much the framework has concealed. His parsimonious approach to theory-building has helped to clarify just how extensively IR theorizing has taken place on the basis of ahistorical assumptions. Slowly but surely, however, his stringent assumptions are being relaxed. Although he probably deplores this development, there is no doubt that it is a necessary procedure in order to establish a more historically sensitive discipline.

The English School has been endeavouring for some time to modify the more extreme ahistorical assumptions of neorealism, drawing a sharp distinction, for example, between an international system and an international society and seeing one evolve from the other [19, 123]. This distinction has been attacked [14, 59], but the critics have failed to provide a more effective alternative. An attempt is now being made from a structural realist perspective to establish a framework which will make it possible to examine world history from a global and international perspective [23, 24, 25]. This structural realist framework starts from the assumption, first, that it is necessary to acknowledge the existence of structural differentiation among the units within the international system. Second, it assumes that the units and the international system are mutually constituted, so that as the structure of the units change, so too does the nature of the international system. It follows that an international system made up of feudal states is very different in character from an international system made up of modern sovereign states. Finally, structural realists argue that it is necessary to explore the international system from separate economic, political and cultural perspectives. Once this distinction is made, it becomes possible to examine, for example, whether an international economic system existed prior to an international political system.

In addition to this attempt to fashion a more historically sensitive approach to international relations, IR scholars [31, 32, 71, 72, 129] are also endeavouring to demonstrate how realism in IR and the Marxist strand of HS can be woven together to produce a more effective critical theory of world politics. At the heart of these endeavours is the recognition that structural transformation of the state is insufficient to bring about human emancipation. Individuals exist within a world system and change must take place at this level before true emancipation can be achieved.

A methodological footnote

One of the central methodological concerns in HS is often seen to be the problem associated with linking structure to agency [2, 26, 46]. There is a desire among many contemporary historical sociologists to move away from the idea that history is structurally determined, and they can only do this by making room for human agency. It is accepted that human beings are constrained by established social structures, but it is denied that these structures are established or changed simply on the basis of abstract historical laws. History involves human intervention. This position establishes the link, so clearly identified by Smith and Linklater [72, 104], between HS and critical theory.

Not all historical sociologists accept this link with critical theory. Skocpol's analysis of revolutions, for example, has been attacked for failing to take sufficient account of human agency [106]. Nor is there any agreement within HS or among sociologists about how to deal with the problem of structure and agency, although it has been subjected to extensive discussion [26, 69]. The attempt by Giddens [46] to solve the problem on the basis of structuration (very similar to Abrams' [2] concept of structuring) has been widely admired, but it has also been extensively criticized [17, 29, 30]. At the heart of Giddens's solution is the assumption that structures and agents are mutually constituted. Structures, from this perspective, represent unintended consequences of the rational actions of human agents. Critics argue that on the basis of this solution structure collapses into agency, but whether or not Giddens' solution is accepted, the debate has helped to focus attention on questions about how structures get reproduced or, alternatively, transformed. The issue has always been salient in HS, but it is now seen to be of central importance within IR.

The problem of structure and agency was raised explicitly in IR by Wendt [124] in a critique of Waltz and Wallerstein. Although his assessment of Waltz has occasioned debate [56, 125], the implications of the problem for an understanding of IR are now in full swing [23, 35, 87]. It has even been suggested that far from being an unreformed structuralist, as is popularly supposed, Waltz's methodology is compatible with the concept of structuration [23]. Certainly his argument that the anarchic structure of the international system is an unintended consequence of actions taken by agents of the state resonates with Giddens's argument that structure and agents are mutually constituted.

The debate about structure and agency, however, is still wide open. Nevertheless, it can be suggested that if the work of historical sociologists and world historians is to be successfully incorporated into IR, then it is essential that the significance of the debate is effectively internalized within the discipline. The first steps in this direction have already been taken, and it is likely that the issue will become one of the central areas of concern in IR.

Bibliography

1. Abu-Lughod, J. *Before European Hegemony: The World System A.D. 1250–1350*. London and New York, Oxford University Press, 1989.
2. Abrams, P. *Historical Sociology*. London, Open Books, 1982 and Ithaca, Cornell University Press, 1983.
3. Anderson, P. *Passages From Antiquity to Feudalism*. London, New Left Books, 1974 and New York, Routledge, Chapman & Hall, 1985.
4. Anderson, P. *Lineages of the Absolutist State*. London, Verso and New York, Routledge, Chapman & Hall, 1974 .
5. Arrighi, G., Hopkins, T.K. and Wallerstein, I. *Antisystemic Movements*. London and New York, Verso, 1989.
6. Banks, M. and Shaw, M. (eds) *State and Society in International Relations*. London, Harvester Wheatsheaf and New York, St. Martin's Press, 1991.
7. Barfield, T.J. *The Perilous Frontier. Nomadic Empires and China 221BC–AD1757*. Oxford and Cambridge MA, Basil Blackwell, 1989.
8. Bean, R. 'War and the Birth of the Nation-State'. *Journal of Economic History*, vol. 33., no. 1, 1973, pp. 203–21.
9. Bendix, R. *Nation-Building and Citizenship. Studies of Our Changing Social Order*. New York, Wiley, 1964; new edition Berkeley, University of California Press, 1977.
10. Bendix, R. *Kings or People. Power and the Mandate to Rule*. Berkeley and London, University of California Press, 1978.
11. Bendix, R. *Force, Fate and Freedom: On Historical Sociology*. Berkeley, University of California Press, 1984.
12. Berridge, G. 'The Political Theory and Institutional History of States Systems'. *British Journal of International Studies*, vol. 6, no. 1, 1980, pp. 82–92.
13. Block, F. 'Marxist Theories of the State in World System Analysis' in B.H. Kaplan (ed.) *Social Change in the Capitalist World Economy*. Beverly Hills, Sage, 1978, pp. 27–37.
14. Block, F. and Somers, M.R. 'Beyond the Economistic Fallacy: The Holistic Social Science of Karl Polanyi' in T. Skocpol (ed.) *Vision and Method in Historical Sociology*. Cambridge and New York, Cambridge University Press, 1984, pp. 47–84.
15. Bozeman, A.B. *Politics and Culture in International History*. Princeton, Princeton University Press, 1960.
16. Brewin, C. 'Research in a Global Context: A Discussion of Toynbee's Legacy'. *Review of International Studies*, vol. 18, no. 2, 1992, pp. 115–30.
17. Bryant, C.G.A. and Jary D. (eds) *Giddens' Theory of Structuration. A Critical Appreciation*. London and New York, Routledge, 1990.
18. Bull, H. *The Anarchical Society: A Study of Order in World Politics*. London, Macmillan, 1977 and New York, Columbia University Press, 1979.
19. Bull, H. and Watson, A. (eds) *The Expansion of International Society*. Oxford, Clarendon Press, 1984 and New York, Oxford University Press, 1985.
20. Burton, J.W. *Systems, States, Diplomacy and Rules*. Cambridge, Cambridge University Press, 1968.
21. Burton, J.W. *World Society*. Cambridge, Cambridge University Press, 1972; new editions Lanham and London, University Press of America, 1987.
22. Buzan, B. and Jones, R.J.B. (eds) *Change and the Study of International Relations: the Evaded Dimension*. London, Pinter and New York, St. Martin's Press, 1981.

23. Buzan, B., Jones, C.A. and Little, R. *The Logic of Anarchy: Neorealism to Structural Realism*. New York, Columbia University Press, 1993.
24. Buzan, B. and Little, R. 'The Idea of International System: Theory Meets History'. *International Journal of Political Science*, forthcoming, 1994.
25. Buzan, B. and Little, R. *An Introduction to the International System: Theory Meets History*. Oxford, Oxford University Press, forthcoming.
26. Callinicos, A. *Making History: Agency, Structure, and Change in Social Theory*. Cambridge, Polity Press, 1987 and Ithaca, Cornell University Press, 1988.
27. Carr, E.H. *What is History?* London, Macmillan, 1986 (second edition) and New York, Random House, 1967.
28. Chase-Dunn, C., 'Interstate System and Capitalist World-Economy: one logic or two?' *International Studies Quarterly*, vol. 25, no. 1, 1981, pp. 19–42.
29. Clark, J., Mogdil, C. and Mogdil, S. (eds) *Anthony Giddens. Consensus and Controversy*. London and New York, The Falmer Press, 1990.
30. Cohen, I.J. *Structuration Theory. Anthony Giddens and the Constitution of Social Life*. London, Macmillan and New York, St. Martin's Press, 1989.
31. Cox, R.W. 'Social Forces, States and World Orders: Beyond International Relations Theory' in R.O. Keohane (ed.) *Neorealism and Its Critics*. New York, Columbia University Press, 1986, pp. 204–54.
32. Cox, R.W. *Production, Power and World Order. Social Forces in the Making of History*. New York, Columbia University Press, 1987.
33. Craig, G.A. 'On the Nature of Diplomatic History: The Relevance of Some Old Books' in P.G. Lauren (ed.) *Diplomacy: Some New Approaches in History, Theory and Policy*. New York, Free Press and London, Collier Macmillan, 1979, pp. 21–42.
34. Deudney, D. and Ikenberry, G.J. 'Soviet Reform and the End of the Cold War: Explaining Large-scale Historical Change'. *Review of International Studies*, vol. 17, no. 3, 1991, pp. 225–50.
35. Dressler, D. 'What's At Stake in the Agent-Structure Debate'. *International Organization*, vol. 43, no. 3, 1989, pp. 441–73.
36. Eisenstadt, S.N. *The Political Systems of Empires*. New York and London, Free Press of Glencoe, 1963, new edition, New Brunswick, Transaction Publishers, 1993.
37. Eisenstadt, S.N. and Rokkan, S. (eds) *Building States and Nations: analysis by region*. Vol. 2. Beverly Hills and London, Sage, 1973.
38. Evans, P., Rueschemeyer, D. and Skocpol, T. (eds) *Bringing the State Back In*. Cambridge, Cambridge University Press, 1985.
39. Farrenkopf, J. 'The Challenge of Spenglerian Pessimism to Ranke and Political Realism'. *Review of International Studies*, vol. 17, no. 3, 1991, pp. 267–84.
40. Finer, S.E. 'State and Nation-Building in Europe: The Role of the Military' in C. Tilly (ed.) *The Formation of National States in Western Europe*. Princeton and London, Princeton University Press, 1975, pp. 84–163.
41. Fleiss, P. *Thucydides and the Politics of Bipolarity*. Baton Rouge, Louisiana State University Press, 1966.
42. Frank, A.G. 'A Theoretical Introduction to 5000 Years of World Systems History'. *Review*, vol. 13, no. 2, 1990, pp. 155–248.
43. Fulbrook, M. and Skocpol, T. 'Destined Pathways: The Historical Sociology of Perry Anderson' in T. Skocpol (ed.) *Vision and Method in Historical Sociology*. Cambridge and New York, Cambridge University Press, 1984, pp. 170–210.
44. Fukuyama, F. *The End of History and the Last Man*. London, Hamish Hamilton, 1992 and New York, Avon Books, 1993.

45. Gellner, E. *Plough, Sword and Book: The Structure of Human History*. London, Collins Harvill, 1988.
46. Giddens, A. *The Constitution of Society. An Outline of the Theory of Structuration*. Cambridge, Polity Press, 1984 and Chicago, University of Chicago Press, 1990.
47. Giddens, A. *The Nation State and Violence*. London, Polity Press and Berkeley, University of California Press, 1985.
48. Gilbert, F. *Machiavelli and Guicciardini. Politics and History in Sixteenth Century Florence*. Princeton, Princeton University Press, 1965; second edition, New York and London, Norton, 1984.
49. Gills, B.K. and Frank, A.G. 'World Systems Cycles, Crises and Hegemonial Shifts, 1700BC to 1700AD'. *Review*, vol. 15, no. 4, 1992, pp. 621–87.
50. Gilpin, R. *War and Change in World Politics*. Cambridge and New York, Cambridge University Press, 1981.
51. Goldstein, J.S. *Long Cycles: Prosperity and War in the Modern Age*. New Haven and London, Yale University Press, 1988.
52. Gourevitch, P. 'The International System and Regime Formation: A Critical Review of Anderson and Wallerstein'. *Comparative Politics*, vol. 10, no. 3, 1978, pp. 419–38.
53. Grader, S. 'The English School of International Relations: Evidence and Evaluation'. *Review of International Studies*, vol. 14, no. 1, 1981, pp. 29–44.
54. Held, D. and Thompson, J. (eds) *Anthony Giddens and His Critics*. Cambridge and New York, Cambridge University Press, 1989.
55. Hempel, C.G. 'The Function of General Laws in History' in P. Gardiner (ed.) *Theories of History*. New York, Free Press, 1959, pp. 344–56.
56. Hollis, M. and Smith, S. 'Beware of Gurus: Structure and Action in International Relations'. *Review of International Studies*, vol. 17, no. 4, 1991, pp. 393–410.
57. Hollist, W.L. and Rosenau, J.N. 'World Systems Debates'. Special Issue of *International Studies Quarterly*, vol. 25, no. 1, 1981, pp. 5–17.
58. Holsti, O.R., Siverson, R.M. and George, A.L. (eds) *Change in the International System*. Boulder, Westview Press and Bowker Publishing Press, 1980.
59. James, A. 'System or Society?'. *Review of International Studies*, vol. 19, no. 3, 1993, pp. 269–88.
60. Jarvis, A. 'Societies, States and Geopolitics: Challenges from Historical Sociology'. *Review of International Studies*, vol. 15, no. 3, 1989, pp. 281–93.
61. Jones, E.L. *The European Miracle. Environments, Economies, and Geopolitics in the History of Europe and Asia*; second edition, Cambridge, Cambridge University Press, 1987.
62. Jones, R.E. 'The English School of International Relations: A Suitable Case for Closure'. *Review of International Studies*, vol. 7, no. 1, 1981, pp. 1–13.
63. Kellenbenz, H. 'The Modern World-System'. *Journal of Modern History*, vol. 48, no. 4, 1976, pp. 685–92.
64. Kennedy, P. *The Rise and Fall of the Great Powers*. London, Fontana, 1989.
65. Keohane, R.O. (ed.) *Neorealism and Its Critics*. New York, Columbia University Press, 1986.
66. Keohane, R.O. and Nye, J.S. (eds) *Transnational Relations and World Politics*. Cambridge MA and London, Harvard University Press, 1971.
67. Kratochwil, F.V. 'The Embarrassment of Changes: Neo-Realism as the Science of Realpolitik Without Politics'. *Review of International Studies*, vol. 19, no. 1, 1993, pp. 63–80.
68. Kumar, K. 'The Revolutions of 1989: Socialism, Capitalism and Democracy'. *Theory and Society*, vol. 21, No. 3, 1992, pp. 309–56.

69. Layder, D. *Structure, Interaction and Social Theory*. London, Routledge and Kegan Paul, 1981.
70. Lewis, A.R. *Nomads and Crusaders. A.D.1000–1368*. Bloomington, Indiana University Press, 1988.
71. Linklater, A. 'Realism, Marxism and Critical International Theory'. *Review of International Studies*, vol. 12, no. 4, 1986, pp. 301–12.
72. Linklater, A. *Beyond Realism and Marxism: Critical Theory and International Relations*. London, Macmillan and New York, St. Martin's Press, 1990.
73. Lipset, S.M. *The First New Nation. The United States in Historical and Comparative Perspective*. London, Heinemann, 1964 and New York, Norton, 1979.
74. Lipset, S.M. *Revolution and Counterrevolution. Change and Persistence in Social Structures*. New York, Basic Books, 1968 and London, Heinemann Educational, 1969; revised edition, New Brunswick and Oxford, Transaction Books, 1988.
75. Little, R. 'International Relations and the Triumph of Capitalism' in K. Booth and S. Smith (eds) *International Political Theory Today*. Cambridge, Polity Press, forthcoming.
76. McNeill, W.H. *The Rise of the West. A History of the Human Community*. Chicago, Chicago University Press, 1963.
77. McNeill, W.H. *A World History*. Oxford, Oxford University Press, 1979 and Chicago, Chicago University Press, 1991.
78. McNeill, W.H. *Plagues and Peoples*. Harmondsworth, Penguin, 1979.
79. McNeill, W.H. *The Pursuit of Power*. Oxford, Blackwell, 1983 and Chicago, University of Chicago Press, 1984.
80. Mann, M. *The Sources of Social Power. Vol. 1: A History of Power from the Beginning to AD 1760*. Cambridge, Cambridge University Press, 1986.
81. Mann, M. *States, War and Capitalism. Studies in Political Sociology*. Oxford, Blackwell, 1988.
82. Mann, M., Giddens, A. and Wallerstein, I. 'Comments on Paul Kennedy's Rise and Fall of the Great Powers'. *British Journal of Sociology*, vol. 40, no. 2, 1989, pp. 328–40.
83. Mann, M. 'Review of Wallerstein's The Modern World-System Vol. 3'. *Contemporary Sociology*, vol. 19, no. 2, 1990, pp. 196–8.
84. Mills, C.W. *The Sociological Imagination*. New York, Oxford University Press, 1967.
85. Modelski, G. *Long Cycles in World Politics*. London, Macmillan, 1987 and Seattle, University of Washington Press, 1986.
86. Modelski, G. and Thompson, W. *Seapower in Global Politics 1494–1994*. London, Macmillan, 1988 and Seattle, University of Washington Press, 1987.
87. Morrow, J.D. 'Social Choice and System Structure in World Politics'. *World Politics*, vol. 41, no. 1, 1988, pp. 75–97.
88. Organski, A.F.K. and Kugler, J. *The War Ledger*. Chicago and London, Chicago, Chicago University Press, 1981.
89. Parsons, T. *Societies: Evolutionary and Comparative Perspectives*. Foundations of Modern Sociology Series. Englewood Cliffs, Prentice Hall, 1966.
90. Parsons, T. and Smelser, N. *Economy and Society. A Study in the Integration of Economic and Social Theory*. International library of sociology and social reconstruction series. London, Routledge & Kegan Paul, 1956.
91. Polanyi, K. *The Great Transformation*; revised edition, Boston, Beacon Press, 1957 [1944].

92. Ragin, C. and Chirot, D. 'The World System of Immanuel Wallerstein: Sociology and Politics as History' in T. Skocpol (ed.) *Vision and Method in Historical Sociology*. Cambridge and New York, Cambridge University Press, 1984, pp. 276–312.
93. Reynolds, C. *Theory and Explanation in International Politics*. London, Martin Robertson, 1973.
94. Rosenberg, J. 'Secret Origins of the State: the Structural Basis of Raison d'état'. *Review of International Studies*, vol. 18, no. 2, 1992, pp. 131–60.
95. Rueschemeyer, D. 'Theoretical Generalization and Historical Particularity in the Comparative Sociology of Reinhard Bendix' in T. Skocpol (ed.) *Vision and Method in Historical Sociology*. Cambridge and New York, Cambridge University Press, 1984, pp. 129–69.
96. Ruggie, J.G. 'Continuity and Transformation in the World Polity: Toward a Neorealist Synthesis' in R.O. Keohane (ed.) *Neorealism and Its Critics*. New York, Columbia University Press, 1986, pp. 131–57.
97. Runciman, W.G. *A Treatise on Social Theory. Volume One: The Methodology of Social Theory*. Cambridge, Cambridge University Press, 1983.
98. Scholte, J.A. 'From Power Politics to Social Change: An Alternative Focus for International Studies'. *Review of International Studies*, vol. 19, no. 1, 1993, pp. 3–22.
99. Shaw, M. (ed.) *War, State and Society*. London, Macmillan, 1984 and New York, St. Martin's Press, 1984.
100. Skocpol, T. 'Wallerstein's World Capitalist System: A Theoretical and Historical Critique'. *American Journal of Sociology*, vol. 82, no. 5, 1977, pp. 1075–90.
101. Skocpol, T. *States and Social Revolutions: a comparative analysis of France, Russia and China*. Cambridge, Cambridge University Press, 1979.
102. Skocpol, T. 'Sociology's Historical Imagination' in T. Skocpol (ed.) *Vision and Method in Historical Sociology*. Cambridge and New York, Cambridge University Press, 1984, pp. 1–21.
103. Smelser, N. *Social Change in the Industrial Revolution*. London, Routledge, 1959.
104. Smith, D. *The Rise of Historical Sociology*. Oxford, Polity Press, 1991 and Philadelphia, Temple University Press, 1992.
105. Stinchcombe, A. 'The Growth of the World System'. *American Journal of Sociology*, vol. 87, no. 6, 1982, pp. 1389–95.
106. Taylor, M. 'Structure, Culture and Action in the Explanation of Social Change'. *Politics and Society*, vol. 17, no. 2, 1989, pp. 115–62.
107. Tilly, C. *As Sociology Meets History*. New York, Academic Press, 1981.
108. Tilly, C. 'War Making and State Making as Organised Crime' in P. Evans, D. Rueschemeyer and T. Skocpol (eds) *Bringing the State Back In*. Cambridge, Cambridge University Press, 1985, pp. 169–91.
109. Tilly, C. *Coercion, Capital and European States AD990–1990*. Oxford, Blackwell and Cambridge, Basil Blackwell, 1992.
110. Tracy, J.D. (ed.) *The Rise of Merchant Empires: long distance trade in the early modern world*. Cambridge and New York, Cambridge University Press, 1990.
111. Tracy, J.D. (ed.) *The Political Economy of Merchant Empires*. Cambridge and New York, Cambridge University Press, 1991.
112. Vincent, R.J. 'Change and International Relations'. *Review of International Studies*, vol. 9, no. 1, 1983, pp. 63–70.
113. Walker, R.B.J. 'Realism, Change and International Political Theory'. *International Studies Quarterly*, vol. 31, no. 1, 1987, pp. 65–86.

114. Walker, R.B.J. 'History and Structure in the Theory of International Relations'. *Millennium*, vol. 18, no. 2, 1989, pp. 163–83.
115. Wallerstein, I. *The Modern World-System I. Capitalist Agriculture and the Origins of the World-Economy in the Sixteenth Century.* New York and London, Academic Press, 1974.
116. Wallerstein, I. *The Capitalist World-Economy.* Cambridge, Cambridge University Press, 1979.
117. Wallerstein, I. *The Modern World-System II. Mercantilism and the Consolidation of the European World-Economy 1600–1750.* New York and London, Academic Press, 1980.
118. Wallerstein, I. *Historical Capitalism.* London, Verso and New York, Routledge, Chapman & Hall, 1983.
119. Wallerstein, I. *The Modern World-System III. The Second Era of Great Expansion of the Capitalist World Economy 1730–1840s.* San Diego, Academic Press, 1989.
120. Wallerstein, I. *Geopolitics and Geoculture. Essays on the Changing World-System.* Cambridge and New York, Cambridge University Press, 1991.
121. Waltz, K.N. *Theory of International Politics.* Reading, MA and London, Addison-Wesley Publishing Co., 1979.
122. Waltz, K.N. 'Reflections on Theory of International Politics: A Response to My Critics' in R.O. Keohane (ed.) *Neorealism and Its Critics.* Columbia, Columbia University Press, 1986, pp. 322–45.
123. Watson, A. *The Evolution of International Society: a comparative historical analysis.* London, Routledge, 1992.
124. Wendt, A.E. 'The Agent-Structure Problem in International Relations Theory'. *International Organization*, vol. 41, no. 3, 1987, pp, 335–70.
125. Wendt, A.E. 'Bridging the Theory/Meta-theory Gap in International Relations'. *Review of International Studies*, vol. 17, no. 4, 1991, pp. 383–92.
126. Wight, M. 'Why Is There No International Relations Theory' in H. Butterfield and M. Wight (eds) *Diplomatic Investigations: essays in the theory of international politics.* London, George Allen and Unwin, 1966, pp. 17–34.
127. Wight, M. *Systems of States.* Leicester, Leicester University Press, 1977.
128. Wilson, P. 'The English School of International Relations: A Reply to Sheila Grader'. *Review of International Studies*, vol. 15, no. 1, 1989, pp. 49–58.
129. Witton, B.J. *Uneven Development and the Logics of International Order Formation.* Ph.D. dissertation, Canberra, Australian National University, 1991.
130. Zolberg, A.R. 'Strategic Interactions and the Formation of Modern States: France and England'. *International Social Science Journal*, vol. 32, no. 4, 1980, pp. 687–716.
131. Zolberg, A.R. 'Origins of the Modern World-System: A Missing Link'. *World Politics*, vol. 33, no. 2, 1981, pp. 253–81.

2 Normative international theory: approaches and issues

Mark Hoffman

Introduction

The late 20th century poses considerable challenges of an intellectual and practical nature which reflect the state of flux which has come to characterize the post-Cold War environment. Within this environment, normative concerns have come to occupy a central place. Questions about the moral standing of states and the nature and extent of our obligations and responsibilities within, between and beyond individual states have taken on a new immediacy.

While these normative questions reconnect the study of IR with concerns which originally animated the discipline, their importance in IR was not always so self-evident. For much of the post-Second World War period, such questions have been located and explored at the margins of IR. It is worth examining briefly why this was so and what has brought about their re-emergence.

The evolution of normative international theory

It is possible to identify four successive phases in the emergence of normative international theory, within each of which the development of theory was conditioned by both theoretical debates and the substantive social, political and economic milieu in which they have taken place. The initial phase coincides with the establishment of IR as an academic discipline. IR was originally constituted as an essentially normative, reformist search for a remedy to the problem of war in an international system populated by sovereign political entities. Rooted in international law, liberal internationalism and employing the 'domestic analogy' [99], this inter-war 'utopianism' proffered the solution of 'peace through law' [100].

The second phase was ushered in by the failure of the League and Carr's pungent critique of 'utopianism' [17]. It came into its own during the Cold War when practical concerns and the intellectual dominance of political realism combined to steer IR away from overt normative orientations. For realists, the anarchic international system constituted a moral vacuum which was not conducive to the pursuit of universalistic, progressivist concerns [54].

As Frost has noted, the realist marginalization of normative theory was subtly and perniciously reinforced by the epistemological and methodological dominance of positivist social science within the study of IR [34]. This recast inherently normative political questions into technical problems with solutions that could be deduced scientifically. It also masked normative assumptions about human nature and the social world and an ontology premised on an unchanging, fixed social order. The consequence of the dominance of positivism has been aptly characterized as a 'bizarre forty year detour' in international theory [96].

During this period, the 'English School' developed an account of 'international society' [14] which had a normative content. The 'classical' approach identified a set of 'settled norms' [34] that inhere in and revolve around the idea and practice of the sovereign state. While starting with the presumption of international anarchy, it quickly identified a 'morality of states'. However, this 'ethic of coexistence' [68] ended up privileging order over justice.

Paradoxically, the 'great methodological debate' between advocates of behavioural and classical realist approaches triggered the third phase of normative international theory. This phase was characterized by a concern with the effect values have on theoretical orientations, especially the questions addressed. These concerns were reinforced by developments in the philosophy of science and the return of 'grand theory' in social and political theory [92], best exemplified by Rawls's work [79]. Second, was the effort by both international and political theorists to extend normative arguments to a wide range of issues in IR – the ethics of the use of force and the ethics of deterrence [18, 26, 40, 50, 78, 110], human rights [23, 28, 44, 61, 88, 108] and distributive justice [3, 7, 26, 31, 75, 82, 88, 91].

The most recent wave of normative theory began in the late 1980s in response to the heightened tensions of the Second Cold War and the unabashed positivism of neorealism. It seeks to link IR with the wide-ranging debates on 'modernity' and 'postmodernism', recasting the study of IR as a form of social and political theory [109]. The resulting 'post-positivist' [56] turn in IR has created the opening for radical forms of theorizing which privilege ontological concerns over epistemological problems and compel IR scholars to recognize its unavoidably normative content and orientation [96].

Traditions of thought in normative international theory

Within the chronological development of normative international theory, a number of traditions of thought can be distinguished which have animated the discussion and debates. Wolfers [118], for example, contrasts the continental and Anglo-Saxon approaches to normative theory. Wight identified his now (in)famous trilogy of realism, rationalism and revolutionism [117].

Donelan [22] extends these categories to five different 'elements' – natural law, realism, fideism, rationalism and historicism – each with its own normative implications. Hoffman [43] identifies utopianism, moral scepticism, the morality of states and cosmopolitanism as the four approaches which have dominated normative international theory. The contributors to Nardin and Mapel's excellent edited collection [70] discuss 12 traditions of thought, highlighting the continuities and discontinuities between contemporary international ethical discourse and its classical roots.

The communitarian–cosmopolitan divide

A central dichotomization underscores this proliferation of traditions: that between particularism and universalism; between our dual identities as members of particularist communities and more extensive, universalist communities. This dichotomization is implicit within Beitz [7] but is most clearly deployed by Linklater [58] in his discussion of our competing identities as 'men' and 'citizens'. Linklater argues that this 'double existence' produces a fragmented moral experience that is specific to the modern state-system and yet offers intimations of a higher form of political life.

More recently these traditions and debates have been brought into sharper focus by characterizing them in terms of 'communitarian' and 'cosmopolitan' approaches. The cosmopolitan–communitarian divide is the central organizing structure of two recent, noteworthy works on normative international theory by Brown [12] and Thompson [103]. For both authors, these two traditions constitute background foundations on which substantive normative theories can be built. Each tradition offers different responses to the question of how we reconcile individual autonomy with political community. This, in turn, allows debates and discussions in IR to connect with parallel debates in social and political theory.

The cosmopolitan tradition has its roots in the Enlightenment, particularly the philosophical and political writings of Kant [21, 52]. It stems from the focus on the reasoning human individual as an autonomous moral agent and affirms the existence of a universal set of self-evident moral truths accessible through human reason. For the cosmopolitan tradition, the ultimate source of moral value is the individual understood as part of a wider species–being. It espouses the ideals of human freedom and argues that the legitimacy of social structures, particularly the state, is instrumental, derivative and contingent on their ability to enable the realization of human autonomy. It refuses to privilege the status of particularist communities and sees such privileging as a hindrance to emancipatory forms of politics.

Communitarians, rejecting the idea of autonomous moral agents, argue that the 'self' is embedded within a concrete set of social relations [86]. Thus, the central source of moral value inheres in particularist communities, and it is only through membership in a political community that the individual finds meaning and gains rights [97]. This shapes our under-standing of who has what legitimate rights claims and against whom those claims can be made – because the individual is constituted by the community, the demands of concrete, socially located ethics override the demands of abstract cosmopolitan morality. For many, Hegel's claim that it is only through the state that individuals can realize freedom epitomizes the communitarian perspective.

Normative issues

It is worth exploring the contrasting cosmopolitan–communitarian positions with regard to some of the most important normative issues facing IR: the autonomy of states, human rights, the ethics of intervention, distributive justice, and environmental degradation.

The autonomy of states

One area in which the cosmopolitan-communitarian divide clearly operates is with regard to the moral standing of states. Do states have a right to autonomy *vis-à-vis* other states and over and above individuals? Or is the moral standing of states derivative and therefore conditional?

For communitarians, the autonomy of states is derived from the nature of the individual as a member of a particular community – in this case the sovereign, territorial state. This 'community' creates and possesses a moral value which is distinct from that assigned to the individual within the community [86, 97, 111, 112]. It is within the community-as-sovereign-state that rights, duties, obligations and, indeed, identity of the individual as citizen are defined and realized. Communitarians reconcile the tensions between sovereignty and rights by arguing that genuine rights can only emerge and be realized within the sovereign state [11, 34, 97]. For communitarians, the tension only arises if one adopts the mistaken view that rights can somehow exist outside of a community. Thus, the only constraints that can be placed on the autonomy of states are those that derive from the community itself; there can be no external imposition of universal standards of behaviour.

In its more extreme variants, this manifests itself as xenophobic nationalism. Most communitarians, however, offer more subtle and complex accounts [12, 34, 68, 112]. While starting with the basic premise regarding the autonomy of states, they accept that not all communities have an equal right to autonomy. Frost [34] argues that the moral autonomy of the state is conditional on the degree to which there is a coincidence between the ethical claims of the state as the basis for the realization of the individual and its actual practices. The failure of most states to satisfy this criteria points to their 'quasi-sovereignty' [49].

For cosmopolitans, however, communitarianism simply provides a rationalization of existing structures of discourse and power. They reject the idea that states have an absolute right to autonomy on both theoretical and empirical grounds. The important question is not the inherent moral qualities of particular political arrangements but whether or not they serve to promote the realization of universal values such as justice and human dignity. They argue that these values entail a prior set of universal rights claims located at the level of the individual and derived from membership of humankind. Universal rights necessarily override state autonomy.

The cosmopolitan-informed arguments of Beitz [7], Shue [88] and O'Neill [72, 73, 74] entail a commitment to the radical transformation of the structure and institutions of world politics so as to create greater scope for human agency and the realization of emancipatory politics. However, cosmopolitanism does not entail a complete rejection of the state. As Hurrell [47] notes, even Kant, the exemplar of cosmopolitanism, adopts a pragmatic approach towards the state, recognizing it as a real-world constraint and calling for its reform along the lines of a 'universal history'.

Human rights

Not surprisingly, differences regarding the moral standing of states extend into claims regarding universal human rights and the balance between them and state sovereignty. There have been several notable efforts at addressing such questions [23, 28, 44, 88, 105]. Vincent noted [106] that rights talk has become the *lingua franca* of international ethics, a part of the everyday language of IR. But the adoption of rights discourse is not unproblematic since there are considerable and important differences in ascertaining the precise nature and justification of rights and the level at which they operate [19, 29, 30, 35, 81]. Thus, rights have been characterized as being negative or positive in nature; rooted in human nature, natural law, individual consciousness and the capacity for reason, or the specificity of particular cultures; and located at the level of the individual, particular communities such as the state or humanity as a whole. Moreover, much of the discourse is a product of Western Enlightenment traditions which has to operate in non-Western contexts. The evolution of these concepts from the ancient to the modern world and their practical implications are discussed in Donnelly [23], Vincent [105, 106] and Shapiro [87].

Cosmopolitans adopt a universalist position with regard to human rights, arguing that human rights are possessed by individuals as autonomous moral agents rather than as members of any particular group. Rights are part of an individual's status as a person and exist independently of any particular culture, ideology or value system. Yet they operate not simply at the level of the individual but for humanity as a whole by virtue of each individual's status as a rational member of a single moral order. This means that claims to human rights are made against all other individuals and not just a select few.

The most noteworthy efforts at articulating a cosmopolitan approach are to be found in Beitz [7] and Shue [88]. Beitz extends Rawls's Kantian-informed 'original position' to the level of the international and reinforces its viability by pointing to the increasing interdependence and globalism within world society. Shue argues that basic human rights to security and subsistence are prior to all other rights claims.

There are obvious problems with the 'universalism' in these claims. First, even if the notion of universal rights is accepted, it is not clear which rights are to be universalized. The predominant orientation is the universality of negative rights such as individual civil and political rights. But there are equally strong assertions regarding the universality of positive, socio-economic rights. Second, and more problematic, is the ethnocentrism of the cosmopolitan's espousal of universal rights. For some, generalizing the values of a particular (Western) culture is little more than a poorly disguised form of cultural and ethical imperialism reflecting a subtle projection of power.

For communitarians, the problem is precisely the presumption that individuals can be abstracted from the community and stripped of their cultural and political heritage. Individuals do not exist as autonomous entities but receive their identity as members of a particular community: to be human is to be a member of a community, to be a citizen of a particular polis. Each polity has the right to develop its own political, social, economic and cultural system; and particularist communities, such as the state, are the repository of rights and the location of obligations [86, 97]. Given the role of the community in the constitution of values and the individual's identity, individuals have moral claims against fellow citizens, but these claims cannot be extended beyond the self-defined limits of the community.

Communitarians reinforce their arguments by pointing to the tremendous political, cultural, ideological and religious differences within the modern international system. These produce competing and irreconcilable African [45, 65], Asian [25, 46] and Islamic [63, 90] conceptions of the 'self', society and rights. This diversity makes apparent that there is no possibility of, nor demand for, a global community or polis. Moreover, communitarians claim that this diversity offers the possibility for tolerance within a diverse world.

The communitarian position has considerable sympathy with the manner in which human rights are dealt with in the international society perspective. The shift from individual to states' rights does not preclude moral criticism of other societies nor discussion of human rights, but the basis on which this takes place is not the universalism of cosmopolitanism but an avowed ethnocentrism, stressing the historical particularity of the idea and practice of human rights and by invoking the standards which a society itself professes to be pursuing. Bull [16], Donnelly [23], Frost [34], Nardin [68] and Walzer [112] exemplify the different efforts to incorporate human rights along such lines. Vincent [105] offers perhaps the most interesting effort at reconciling the autonomy of states and human rights, but in the end his apparent cosmopolitanism is highly conditioned by a communitarian prudentialism which holds back from the necessity of acting on the basis of cosmopolitan injunctions.

The problem with international society's communitarian stance of tolerance is threefold. First, the focus on the state as the embodiment of community points to a problematic tension: if states are the most frequent violators of human rights, can the state be designated as the guarantor of human rights or be allowed to espouse the moral claims of 'community'? Second, its moral criticism loses its forcefulness precisely because it adjures universal standards. In the end, the rights of states will always win out over individuals. Third, and relatedly, it can too readily transform into an ethical relativism [69] which holds that there is no basis for objective value judgements and therefore no basis for criticizing the actions of other societies towards their own members. The danger is that this may too easily slide into a form of quietism in the face of dangerous social forces.

The ethics of intervention

The cosmopolitan and communitarian views on the autonomy of states and human rights have obvious implications for current concern about the ethics of intervention. There is no straightforward correspondence, however, between the communitarian and cosmopolitan approaches and particular attitudes towards intervention. While communitarians usually advocate the norm of non-intervention and cosmopolitans that of humanitarian intervention, for different reasons both approaches are ambivalent about when intervention is appropriate. Useful general discussions of the problem of intervention can be found in Bull [15], Forbes and Hoffman [32], Smith [94], Thomas [101], Walzer [110] and Vincent [107].

In general, communitarians maintain that the norm of non-intervention is the cardinal rule underpinning order in international society. Intervention undermines the very idea of 'communities' as moral arenas [71] and thereby threatens both domestic and international order. Moreover, intervention often results in disastrous consequences and, whether pursued for reasons of national self-interest or cosmopolitan ideals regarding universal human rights, it is rarely effective in promoting its desired goal. [102]. But this is not to say that communitarians would never countenance intervention.

The classic statement of the communitarian position is to be found in J.S. Mill [67]. The core of his argument is that no matter how strong may be the case for intervention, it is not possible to give people freedom; it is something they must gain for themselves as an expression of their community's self-identification. This means that intervention is only justified under certain specified conditions.

Mill's arguments have influenced significantly the effort to establish criteria for intervention. Walzer [110] and Slater and Nardin [93] have reworked them, adding the gross violations of human rights as a criterion for intervention. Mill's arguments also inform the views of the 'English School' [64, 102, 105, 107], but as Wheeler [115] points out, there is considerable tension between the 'pluralist' and 'solidarist' orientations within the 'English School'. And, in advocating Shue's basic human rights as a criterion for intervention, Vincent [105, 107] pushes clearly in the direction of the 'solidarist' orientation.

The problem with the communitarian approach is that it embraces a moral relativism [69] masked as prudentialism which leaves open the prospect that the mistreatment by states of their own population will trigger no external response. In such circumstances it becomes problematic to see the value in espousing the moral claims of community.

Cosmopolitans argue that to prohibit intervention against unjust states places an unjustifiable obstacle in the way of transforming the international system. Thus there is no sacrosanct norm of non-intervention behind which states can hide their internal policies. Indeed, the accounts of the nature of states and international society which form the background assumptions for the norm of non-intervention simply do not stand up to scrutiny [7].

The moral regard we have for others, according to cosmopolitans, is not limited by territorial boundaries or the norm of non-intervention. It thus offers a more permissive set of injunctions regarding intervention, often based on concerns for human rights and social justice [7, 28, 41, 66, 88]. But, while there may be circumstances in which intervention is not only ethically justified but required, this general orientation does not translate into an automatic requirement or right to intervene. As Wicclair's discussion of the implications of Rawls's arguments for the principle of non-intervention makes clear [116], the cosmopolitanist position is nearly as ambiguous as that of the communitarians.

Both approaches to the problem of intervention based on human rights raise the troubling issues of ethnocentrism and cultural imperialism. One response is to argue that there will always be a problem of 'dirty hands' and that justifications for humanitarian intervention will always represent the cultural orientations of those with the power to carry it out [51]. Others, such as Shue [88], have argued that it is possible to identify a non-ideological set of basic human rights in the form of rights to security and subsistence which provide a non-imperial, non-ethnocentric basis for assessing the actions of states towards their own citizens and provide a basis for justifying intervention. Beitz [7] similarly argues that the norm of non-intervention applies only to states whose internal arrangements satisfy criteria commensurate with social justice.

Nevertheless, cosmopolitanism recognizes that there may be prudential reasons which mitigate against intervention in particular circumstances. What differentiates it from communitarianism is that it would not be a prudentialism grounded in state autonomy.

Distributive justice

The tension between the communitarian emphasis on the moral autonomy of states and the cosmopolitan belief in a universal ethic rooted in the community of humankind is equally evident when we turn to the significant economic disparities between the haves and have-nots in the modern international system and the resulting claims for distributive justice.

While justice has been a long-standing concern in social and political philosophy from the Greeks onwards, the focus on distributive justice is relatively recent. It became a central issue in normative theory when Rawls [79] argued convincingly that societal differences needed to be justified. His arguments have become a focal point for debate in political theory [4, 20, 86]. Critiques of Rawls's theory of justice which also address the international context but push in very different directions can be found in Fishkin [31], Sandel [86], Barry [4, 5] and the essays in Luper-Foy [62].

Thompson engages critically with Rawls's arguments in developing her arguments regarding a just world order [103], while authors such as Beitz [7] and Poggee [76] have discussed the extension of Rawls's theory to the international level.

Cosmopolitanism embraces a Kantian account of equality – treating individuals as ends rather than means – as the starting point for thinking about justice. As autonomous moral agents, all human beings have general obligations towards each other entailed by their common humanity which cannot be overridden by the particularist considerations of separate communities. Differences between particular communities are morally irrelevant and do not provide a basis for prioritizing one's fellow citizens over other human beings.

The nature of these obligations is that they should be acted upon by all. Since the fulfilment of such obligations requires access to resources, however, social institutions need to be organized so as to enhance the possibility for realizing such ends. Thus, for cosmopolitans, justice between individuals is intimately connected to the nature and character of social institutions. If they are unjust or unequal, they prohibit the realization of human emancipation. Moreover, if we are to take seriously our obligation as moral agents to assist others to be moral agents, this implies a necessary transformation in individual and structural relations between the haves and have-nots. Thus, basic to any cosmopolitan position is some principle of distributive justice.

This cosmopolitan orientation takes several forms with regard to international distributive justice. One is the radical utilitarianism of Singer [91]. Another is the more straightforward Kantian approach found in O'Neill [72, 73, 74]. Rejecting the argument that the Third World has a collective 'right' to distributive justice, O'Neill develops a duty-based approach at the level of the individual. While there is a significant pragmatic component which recognizes that we cannot simply disregard existing political institutions and practices in responding to problems of economic inequalities, O'Neill's argument nevertheless points towards the need for a radical restructuring of IR.

The most prominent cosmopolitan approach is that developed by Beitz [7]. Beitz sought to extend Rawls's arguments regarding justice derived from the 'original position' to the international level – something which Rawls himself argued against. Beitz's argument is twofold. First, if representatives of states operated under the 'veil of ignorance', they would establish distributive justice with regard to resources as one of their principles. Second, global interdependence provides the appropriate conditions for the operation of an international Rawlsian 'difference principle' – that social and economic inequalities are to be arranged so that they are of greatest benefit to the least advantaged and attached to offices and positions open to all under conditions of equality of opportunity. Although he has subsequently moved away from a reliance on the condition of interdependence towards a more straightforward Kantian account of the moral personality [6], Beitz still argues for an international difference principle – and for its radical political and economic implications.

Communitarians reject the cosmopolitan emphasis on the morally autonomous pre-social individual. Instead, they argue that social institutions are constitutive of the moral individual, and therefore justice claims against others are necessarily limited to particular communities – they cannot be universalized. For communitarians, we live in a world of moral differences. This world of moral differences is self-evident in an international system marked by diverse communities embracing conflicting value systems and lacking any overarching mechanism for adjudicating between competing claims.

In its extreme realist variant, communitarianism argues that economic inequalities are simply a fact of international life which reflect differences in power [55, 104]. A more sophisticated communitarian position is found in the international society approach which suggests that the autonomy of the state calls into doubt the possibility of articulating a purposive account of justice which would be relevant and acceptable in a diverse range of political, social, economic, religious and cultural contexts. The only possible form of international justice is a procedural 'ethic of coexistence' *between* states as a basis for underpinning international order as a practical association [68]. The 'settled norms' of international society seem to rule out the idea that economic inequalities have any moral significance so that international morality is compatible with the existence of severe inequalities in international society.

There have been some attempts to move the international society approach beyond this limited account of international morality. Recognizing that the continued vitality of, and normative justification for, international society is intimately connected to the kind of justice it promotes, writers such as Bull [16] and Vincent [105] have argued that the individual and collective concerns of the Third World need to be taken seriously.

There are more subtle and sophisticated communitarian positions. Barry [4, 5] argues that although fellow citizens may have a prior moral claim, this does not necessarily preclude the requirement of justice in relations between communities. Moreover, he suggests that we need to move beyond the idea of 'justice' as 'reciprocity' to notions of justice as 'fairness' or 'impartiality'. The practical implications of this at the international level are equal access to resources, transfer systems and institutional arrangements that ensure that each state receives its fair share of global income.

Similarly, Brown [12] argues that our sense of community need not be exclusive or exclusionary. Although individuals may be constituted by their communities, they may be constituted in different degrees by different communities. This allows different levels of communal feelings, some with stronger ties and claims than others and therefore stronger justice claims than others. This allows for the possibility of a weak identification with a wider community. Thompson [103] also develops an argument regarding overlapping or 'interlocking communities' which embrace varying degrees of commitment as the basis for developing a just world order. What is interesting to note is that these communitarian arguments regarding weaker forms of identification at the international level may still entail significant practical implications for international distributive justice which are not dissimilar to those developed by cosmopolitans like Beitz.

Environmental concerns

Environmental issues are the most recent issue-area addressed by normative international theory [24, 27, 37, 39, 53]. Reflecting the lack of scientific consensus regarding the nature, causes and extent of environmental problems, the literature on the international politics of the environment is divided on the impact such concerns have on theories of IR. Some argue that they can be dealt with by traditional theory, others that they may require a softening of the doctrine of absolute sovereignty through regime theory. Still others maintain that they highlight the inadequacy of dominant theoretical perspectives and the need to develop more globalist and cosmopolitan orientations [48, 77, 84, 95].

From the communitarian perspective, environmental issues are not categorically different from any other normative concern, since there is a range of off-setting concerns which will affect individual states differentially: some will be concerned about rising sea-levels; others about desertification; others about acid rain; still others will embrace new arable land or water resources. Each of these problems requires different responses. Some will find it easier than others to adapt or intervene to deal with the local effects of these problems. But there is little likelihood of developing a universalist response to such diverse circumstances – particularly in circumstances of scientific uncertainty. Rather, states will act prudentially to protect their own national economic interests.

For cosmopolitans there is a tension between environmental concerns and the communitarian values of the system of states. The source of this tension is inherent in the nature of environmental problems: global warming, ozone depletion and acid rain, for example, are not problems which readily acknowledge or conform to the boundaries of the territorial state but affect the whole of mankind. As such, they require an orientation which emphasizes the global interconnectedness between apparently 'local' problems.

Dealing with these concerns requires a reconsideration of the principles which underpin international society, a possible restructuring of its social, political and economic institutions, as well as changes in the everyday life of individuals. In the form of 'Gaia theory' [60], they compel us to think about 'nature' not as something separated from and outside the human individual but as a totality which includes human relations. This, in turn, connects environmental concerns with the concept of inter-generational human rights and equity: the responsibility of the present population for the continued viability of the 'global commons' as the heritage of future generations.

Environmental issues are also connected to questions of distributive justice. Shue [89], for example, points to the injustice of most of the solutions proffered: having played very little part in, nor gained much from the industrialization processes which are responsible for environmental degradation, an unfair burden is being placed on the development strategies of the Third World at precisely the point where they require the use of existing resources to combat underdevelopment. Thus, environmental concerns are connected to the question of sustainable development.

Clearly, environmental concerns raise serious questions as to whether communitarian-informed normative frameworks are up to the challenges of world society. The connection between the local and the global requires the development of normative theory which is able to locate local practices and needs within a global context. In short, we are back to the familiar need to reconcile the particular with the universal.

Post-positivism and normative theory

Deploying the cosmopolitan–communitarian divide does help to structure and crystallize the debates on important issues within international relations but not without difficulties. First, the practical distinctions may be more apparent than real, depending on what type of community communitarians want to defend. Second, while the division may help to make sense of a wide body of literature, it poses the dual dangers of dichotomy and reification. Such dichotomies, as well as the approaches they delineate, have been critiqued by those working within the post-positivist turn in international theory.

The post-positivist argument brought into radical doubt the possibility of non-normative international theory. Approaches such as critical theory, postmodernism and feminism signalled a shift away from an emphasis on and prioritizing of epistemological questions to an emphasis on ontological questions. Each, in different ways, attempts to argue that the dichotomy between particularism and universalism is a false one set in motion by the Enlightenment tradition or by narrow readings of that tradition. Each attempts to takes us beyond the communitarian–cosmopolitan divide. Within these theories, it is possible to identify a number of normative orientations [10].

Explicitly or implicitly, what lies behind much of the writings in critical international theory is an effort to reinscribe the emancipatory potential within IR – both as a discipline and a social practice. Much of this work is informed by Habermas's arguments regarding communicative rationality as the basis for a discourse ethics which allows the uncovering and construction of 'truths' [8, 38, 41, 57, 58, 59, 80, 98].

Initially it might seem curious to argue that postmodernism has anything to offer by way of normative theory, given that its central claim is that there are no objective, universal standards of truth, justice or morality. But this anti-foundational perspective nevertheless provides significant scope for international morality. Indeed, it is precisely this anti-foundationalism which informs the postmodernist 'ethic of difference' without indifference [2]. It provides a basis for an 'ethic of responsibility' [113] that embraces diversity while avoiding characterizations of the 'Other' which marginalize or dehumanize. In Rorty's case, an ironic stance in a contingent world provides the conditions for a non-universalized 'ethic of solidarity' which is not limited by the boundaries of community [83]. More challenging and difficult are Nietzschean-informed arguments regarding the 'movement beyond good and evil' and the longing for a self-creating autonomy through the moment of eternal return [1, 114].

There have also been recent efforts at articulating a specifically feminist account of ethics including two excellent general readers [13, 33]. Central is Gilligan's account of feminist ethics as an 'ethic of care' which is distinct from the deontological moral reasoning of the 'ethic of justice' [36]. The 'ethic of care' is more contextual, more immersed in the details of relationships and narratives, more concerned with revealing empathy with a 'particular other'. Instead of the moral agent as a detached autonomous subject, we are offered a relational account of the moral agent as a social being embodied in a complex web of relationships.

There have been numerous efforts at extending Gilligan's arguments such as Ruddick's account of 'maternal thinking' [85] which points to a simultaneous commitment to both 'self' and 'other' in the mother–child relationship as the basis for transcending hierarchical, abstract conceptions of identity. Another, more philosophically sophisticated effort can be found in Benhabib's feminist-informed account of the 'situated self' [9]. In defending an 'interactive universalism' that is contextually sensitive and open to 'difference', her work constitutes a serious effort to move beyond the cosmopolitan–communitarian divide.

But how far do these 'post-positivist' orientations advance normative international theory? Brown [12] and Thompson [103] both argue that they are just the latest set of reworkings of communitarianism and cosmopolitanism, of the divide between particularism and universalism. This implies that they are merely extensions of the Enlightenment project, undermining their claims to have moved significantly beyond it. For others, however, they are important developments in that they offer inter-subjective rather than subjective accounts of the situated 'self', they open the space for debate, they expand the boundaries of the public sphere, legitimize marginalized voices and compel reconceptualization of the 'international'. They offer the possibility of new forms of political action, by new political actors within new political spaces which are not confined by the borders of particularist communities, but are not indifferent to them [109, 113].

Conclusion

That normative concerns are at the heart of the study of IR has become readily evident as a consequence of both real world events and the theoretical debates which have animated the discipline. But can the questions revolving around these normative concerns be resolved? Arguably not. In addressing questions of intervention, human rights, economic justice and environmental degradation we may be dealing with genuine moral dilemmas or with paradoxes in which competing ontologies clash and from which there is no Archimedean point to make a judgement. But if single, objective, 'true' answers are not possible, this does not mean that we should abandon the attempt to clarify our understanding of these dilemmas in the effort to develop practical guidelines for action.

Bibliography

1. Ansell-Pearson, K. *Nietzsche contra Rousseau: A Study of Nietzsche's Moral and Political Thought.* Cambridge, Cambridge University Press, 1991.
2. Ashley, R.K. and Walker, R.B.J. (eds) 'Speaking the Language of Exile: Dissidence in International Studies'. Special Issue, *International Studies Quarterly*, vol. 34, no. 3. 1990.
3. Barry, B. 'Humanity and Justice in Global Perspective' in J. Pennock and J. Chapman (eds) *NOMOS XXIV: Ethics, Economics and the Law.* New York, New York University Press, 1982, pp. 219–52.
4. Barry, B. *The Liberal Theory of Justice: A Critical Examination of the Principal Doctrines in 'A Theory of Justice' by John Rawls.* New York and Oxford, Clarendon Press, 1973.
5. Barry, B. *Theories of Justice.* Hemel Hempstead, Harvester Wheatsheaf, 1989.
6. Beitz, C.R. 'Cosmopolitan ideals and national sentiment'. *Journal of Philosophy*, vol. 80, no. 10, 1983, pp. 591–600.
7. Beitz, C.R. *Political Theory and International Relations.* Princeton and Guildford, Princeton University Press, 1979.
8. Benhabib, S. *Critique, Norm and Utopia: A Study of the Normative Foundations of Critical Theory.* New York, Columbia University Press, 1986.
9. Benhabib, S. *Situating the Self: Gender, Community and Postmodernism in Contemporary Ethics.* London, Routledge, 1992.
10. Bernstein, R.J. *The New Constellation: The Ethical-Political Horizons of Modernity/Postmodernity.* Cambridge, Polity Press, 1991 and Cambridge MA, MIT Press, 1992.
11. Brown, C. 'Hegel and international ethics'. *Ethics and International Affairs*, vol. 5, no. 1, 1991, pp. 73–86.
12. Brown, C. *International Relations Theory: New Normative Approaches.* Hemel Hempstead, Harvester Wheatsheaf, 1992 and New York, Columbia University Press, 1993.
13. Browning Cole, E. and Coultrap-McQuin, S. (eds) *Exploration in Feminist Ethics.* Bloomington, Indiana University Press, 1992.
14. Bull, H.N. *The Anarchical Society: A Study of World Order*, London, Macmillan and New York, Columbia University Press, 1977.
15. Bull, H.N. (ed.) *Intervention in World Politics.* Oxford, Clarendon Press, 1986.
16. Bull, H.N. 'Justice in International Relations'. *The Haughey Lectures.* Ontario, The University of Ontario, 1984.
17. Carr, E.H. *The Twenty Years Crisis, 1919-1939.* New York, Harper & Row, 1964 and London, Macmillan, 1981.
18. Cohen, M. *et al.* (eds) *War and Moral Responsibility.* Princeton and Guildford, Princeton University Press, 1974.
19. Cranston, M. *What are Human Rights?* London, Bodley Head, 1973.
20. Daniels, N. (ed.) *Reading Rawls: Critical Studies of 'A Theory of Justice'.* New York, Basic Books, 1989.
21. Donaldson, T. 'Kant's Global Rationalism' in T. Nardin and D.R. Mapel (eds) *Traditions of International Ethics.* Cambridge, Cambridge University Press, 1992, pp. 136–57.
22. Donelan, M.D. *Elements of International Political Theory.* Oxford, Clarendon Press, 1990.
23. Donnelly, J. *Universal Human Rights in Theory and Practice.* Ithaca, Cornell University Press, 1989.

24. Dower, N. (ed.) *Ethics and Environmental Responsibility*. Aldershot, Avebury, 1989.
25. Edwards, R.R. *et al.* (eds) *Human Rights in Contemporary China*. New York, Columbia University Press, 1986.
26. Ellis, A. (ed.) *Ethics and International Affairs*. Manchester, Manchester University Press in association with the Fulbright Commission, 1986.
27. Engel, J.R. and Engel, J.G (eds) *Ethics of Environment and Development: Global Challenge and International Response*. Tucson, University of Arizona Press, 1990.
28. Falk, R. *Human Rights and State Sovereignty*. New York and London, Holmes & Meier, 1981.
29. Feinberg, J. *Rights, Justice and the Bounds of Liberty*. Princeton, Princeton University Press, 1980.
30. Finnis, J. *Natural Law and Natural Rights*. Oxford, Clarendon Press, 1980.
31. Fishkin, J. 'Theories of Justice and International Relations: The Limits of Liberal Theory' in A. Ellis (ed.) *Ethics and International Affairs*. Manchester, Manchester University Press, 1986, pp. 1–12.
32. Forbes, I. and Hoffman, M. (eds) *Political Theory, International Relations and the Ethics of Intervention*. London, Macmillan, 1993.
33. Frazer, E. *et al.* (eds) *Ethics: A Feminist Reader*. Oxford, Oxford University Press, 1992.
34. Frost, M. *Towards a Normative Theory of International Relations*. Cambridge, Cambridge University Press, 1986.
35. Gewirth, A. *Human Rights: Essays on Justification and Applications*. Chicago and London, University of Chicago Press, 1982.
36. Gilligan, C. *In a Different Voice: Psychological Theory and Women's Development*. Cambridge, MA, Harvard University Press, 1982.
37. Gooden, J. 'International Ethics and the Environmental Crisis'. *Ethics and International Affairs*, vol. 4, no. 1, 1990, pp. 91–106.
38. Habermas, J. *Justifications and Application: Remarks on Discourse Ethics*. Cambridge, Polity Press, 1993.
39. Hanson, P. (ed.) *Environmental Ethics: Philosophical and Policy Perspectives*. Burnaby, Institute for Humanities/Simon Fraser University, 1986.
40. Hare, J.E. and Joynt, C.B. *Ethics and International Affairs*. London, Macmillan and New York, St. Martin's Press, 1982.
41. Hoffman, M. 'Agency, Identity and Intervention' in I. Forbes and M. Hoffman (eds) *Political Theory, International Relations and the Ethics of Intervention*. London, Macmillan, 1993, pp. 194–211.
42. Hoffman, M. 'Critical Theory and the Inter-Paradigm Debate'. *Millennium: Journal of International Studies*, vol. 16, no. 2, 1987, pp. 231–50.
43. Hoffman, M. 'Normative Approaches' in M. Light and A.J.R. Groom (eds) *International Relations: A Handbook of Current Theory*. London, Frances Pinter, 1985, pp. 27–45.
44. Hoffmann, S. *Duties Beyond Borders: On the Limits and Possibilities of Ethical International Politics*. Syracuse, Syracuse University Press, 1981.
45. Howard, R.E. *Human Rights in Commonwealth Africa*. Totowa, Rowman and Littlefield, 1986.
46. Hsiung, J.C. (ed.) *Human Rights in East Asia: A Cultural Perspective*. New York, Paragon, 1985.
47. Hurrell, A. 'Kant and the Kantian paradigm in international relations'. *Review of International Studies*, vol. 16, no. 3, 1990, pp. 183–206.

48. Hurrell, A. and Kingsbury, B. (eds) *The International Politics of the Environment: Actors, Interests and Institutions*. Oxford, Clarendon Press, 1992.
49. Jackson, R.H. *Quasi-States: Sovereignty, International Relations and the Third World*. Cambridge, Cambridge University Press, 1990.
50. Johnson, J.T. *Just War Tradition and the Restraint of War*. Princeton and Guildford, Princeton University Press, 1981.
51. Johnson, P. 'Intervention and Moral Dilemmas' in I. Forbes and M. Hoffman (eds) *Political Theory, International Relations and the Ethics of Intervention*. London, Macmillan, 1993, pp. 61–72.
52. Kant, I. *Kant's Political Writings*. translated by H.B. Nesbit, Cambridge, Cambridge University Press, 1977.
53. Kealy, D.A. *Revisioning Environmental Ethics*. Albany, State University of New York Press, 1990.
54. Kipnis, K. and Meyers, D.T. (eds) *Political Realism and International Morality*. Boulder, Westview Press, 1987.
55. Krasner, S. *Structural Conflict: The Third World against Global Liberalism*. Berkeley, University of California Press, 1985.
56. Lapid, Y. 'The Third Debate: On the Prospects of International Theory in a Post-Positivist Era'. *International Studies Quarterly*, vol. 33, no. 3, 1989, pp. 235–54.
57. Leonard, S. *Critical Theory and Political Practice*, Princeton, Princeton University Press, 1991.
58. Linklater, A. *Men and Citizens in International Theory*. second edition, London, Macmillan, 1990.
59. Linklater, A. 'The Problem of Community in International Relations'. *Alternatives*, vol. 15, no. 2, 1990, pp. 135–53.
60. Lovelock, J.E. *Gaia: A New Look at Life on Earth*. Oxford and New York, Oxford University Press, 1979.
61. Luard, E. *Human Rights and Foreign Policy*. Oxford, Pergamon Press, 1981.
62. Luper-Foy, S. (ed.) *Problems of International Justice*. Boulder and London, Westview Press, 1988.
63. Mawdudi, A'la A. *Human Rights in Islam*. Leicester, The Islamic Foundation, 1980.
64. Mayall, J. 'Non-intervention, self-determination and the "New World Order"' in I. Forbes and M. Hoffman (eds) *Political Theory, International Relations and the Ethics of Intervention*. London, Macmillan, 1993, pp. 167–76.
65. M'Baye, K. 'Human rights in Africa' in K. Vasak and P. Alston (eds) *The International Dimensions of Human Rights*. Westport, Greenwood Press, 1982, pp. 583–600.
66. McMahan, J. 'The ethics of international intervention' in A. Ellis (ed.) *Ethics and International Affairs*. Manchester, Manchester University Press, 1986, pp. 24–51.
67. Mill, J.S. 'A few words on nonintervention', *Dissertations and Discussions*, vol. 3. London, Longmans, 1873.
68. Nardin, T. *Law, Morality and the Relations of States*. Princeton and Guildford, Princeton University Press, 1983.
69. Nardin, T. 'The Problem of Relativism in International Ethics'. *Millennium: Journal of International Studies*, vol. 18, no. 2, 1989, pp. 149–61.
70. Nardin, T. and Mapel, D.R. (eds) *Traditions of International Ethics*. Cambridge, Cambridge University Press, 1992.
71. Navari, C. 'Intervention, Nonintervention and the Construction of the State' in I. Forbes and M. Hoffman (eds) *Political Theory, International Relations and the Ethics of Intervention*. London, Macmillan, 1993, pp. 43–60.

72. O'Neill, O. *Faces of Hunger: An essay on Poverty, Justice and Development.* London, Allen and Unwin, 1986.
73. O'Neill, O. 'Hunger, needs and rights' in S. Luper-Foy (ed.) *Problems of International Justice.* Boulder, Westview Press, 1988, pp. 67–83.
74. O'Neill, O. 'Transnational Justice' in D. Held (ed.) *Political Theory Today.* Oxford, Polity, 1991, pp. 276–304.
75. Pennock, J. and Chapman, J. (eds) *NOMOS XXIV: Ethics, Economics and the Law.* New York, New York University Press, 1982.
76. Poggee, T. *Realising Rawls.* Ithaca, Cornell University Press, 1989.
77. Porter, G. and Welsh Brown, J. *Global Environmental Politics.* Boulder, Westview Press, 1991.
78. Ramsey, P. *The Just War: Force and Political Responsibility.* Lanham, University Press of America and Cambridge, Cambridge University Press, 1983.
79. Rawls, J. *A Theory of Justice.* Oxford and New York, Clarendon Press, 1972.
80. Ray, L. *Rethinking Critical Theory: Emancipation in the Age of Global Social Movements.* London, Sage, 1993.
81. Renteln, A.D. *International Human Rights: Universalism vs Relativism.* London, Sage, 1990.
82. Richards, D.A. 'International Distributive Justice' in J. Pennock and J. Chapman (eds) *NOMOS XXIV: Ethics, Economics and the Law.* New York, New York University Press, 1982, pp. 275–99.
83. Rorty, R. *Contingency, Irony and Solidarity.* Cambridge, Cambridge University Press, 1989.
84. Rowlands, I. and Greene, M. (eds) *Global Environmental Change and International Relations.* London, Macmillan, 1991.
85. Ruddick, S. *Maternal Thinking: Towards a Politics of Peace.* Boston, Beacon Press, 1990.
86. Sandel, M.J. *Liberalism and the Limits of Justice.* Cambridge, Cambridge University Press, 1992.
87. Shapiro, I. *The Evolution of Rights in Liberal Theory.* Cambridge, Cambridge University Press, 1986.
88. Shue, H. *Basic Rights.* Princeton and Guildford, Princeton University Press, 1980.
89. Shue, H. 'The Unavoidability of Justice' in A. Hurrell and B. Kingsbury (eds) *The International Politics of the Environment: Actors, Interests and Institutions.* Oxford, Clarendon Press, 1992, pp. 373–97.
90. Sinaceur, M.A. 'Islamic Tradition and Human Rights' in *Philosophical Foundations of Human Rights.* Paris, UNESCO, 1986, pp. 193–225.
91. Singer, P. 'Famine, affluence and morality' in C.R. Beitz *et al.* (eds) *International Ethics.* Princeton, Princeton University Press, 1985, pp. 249–61.
92. Skinner, Q. (ed.) *The Return of Grand Theory in the Human Sciences.* Cambridge, Cambridge University Press, 1990.
93. Slater, J. and Nardin, T. 'Nonintervention and Human Rights'. *Journal of Politics,* vol. 48, no. 1, 1986, pp. 85–96.
94. Smith, M.J. 'Ethics and Intervention'. *Ethics and International Affairs,* vol. 3, no. 1, 1989, pp. 1–26.
95. Smith, P. and Warr, K. *Global Environmental Issues.* London, Hodder & Stoughton in association with the Open University Press, 1991.
96. Smith, S. 'The Forty Years Detour: The Resurgence of Normative Theory in International Relations'. *Millennium: Journal of International Studies,* vol. 21, no. 3, 1992, pp. 489–508.

97. Smith, S. *Hegel's Critique of Liberalism: Rights in Context*. Chicago, University of Chicago Press, 1989.
98. Smith, T.K. *The Role of Ethics in Social Theory: Essays from a Habermasian Perspective*. Albany, State University of New York Press, 1991.
99. Suganami, H. *The Domestic Analogy and World Order Proposals*. Cambridge, Cambridge University Press, 1989.
100. Suganami, H. 'The peace through law approach' in T. Taylor (ed.) *Approaches and Theory in International Relations*. London and New York, Longman, 1978, pp. 100–21.
101. Thomas, C. *New States, Sovereignty and Intervention*. Aldershot, Croom Helm, 1985.
102. Thomas, C. 'The Pragmatic Case Against Intervention' in I. Forbes and M. Hoffman (eds) *Political Theory, International Relations and the Ethics of Intervention*. London, Macmillan, 1993, pp. 91–103.
103. Thompson, J. *Justice and World Order: A Philosophical Inquiry*. London, Routledge, 1992.
104. Tucker, R. *The Inequality of Nations*. New York, Basic Books, 1979.
105. Vincent, R.J. *Human Rights and International Relations*. Cambridge, Cambridge University Press, 1986.
106. Vincent, R.J. 'The Idea of Rights in International Ethics' in T. Nardin and D.R. Mapel (eds) *Traditions of International Ethics*. Cambridge, Cambridge University Press, 1992, pp. 250–69.
107. Vincent, R.J. *Nonintervention and International Order*. Princeton, Princeton University Press, 1974.
108. Vincent, R.J. and Wilson, P. 'Beyond Non-Intervention' in I. Forbes and M. Hoffman (eds) *Political Theory, International Relations and the Ethics of Intervention*. London, Macmillan, 1993, pp. 122–31.
109. Walker, R.B.J. *Inside/outside: international relations as political theory*. Cambridge, Cambridge University Press, 1993.
110. Walzer, M. *Just and Unjust Wars: A Moral Argument with Historical Illustrations*. second edition, New York, Basic Books, and Harmondsworth, Penguin, 1992.
111. Walzer, M. 'The Moral Standing of States: A Reply to Four Critics'. *Philosophy and Public Affairs*, vol. 9, no. 2, 1980, pp. 209–29.
112. Walzer, M. *Spheres of Justice*. Oxford, Clarendon Press, 1985.
113. Warner, D. *An Ethic of Responsibility in International Relations*. Boulder, London, Lynne Rienner, 1992.
114. Warren, M. *Nietszche and Political Thought*. Cambridge, MA, MIT Press, 1988.
115. Wheeler, N.J. 'Pluralist or Solidarist Conceptions of International Society: Bull and Vincent on Humanitarian Intervention'. *Millennium: Journal of International Society*, vol. 21, no. 3, 1992, pp. 463–87.
116. Wicclair, M. 'Rawls and the Principle of Nonintervention' in G. Blocker and E. Smith (eds) *John Rawls's Theory of Social Justice: An Introduction*. Athens, Ohio University Press, 1980, pp. 289–308.
117. Wight, M. *International Theory: The Three Traditions*. edited by B. Porter and G. Wight, Leicester, Leicester University Press, 1992.
118. Wolfers, A. *Discord and Collaboration: Essays in International Politics*. Baltimore, Johns Hopkins University Press, 1966.

3 Gender and international relations

Margot Light and Fred Halliday

In the last 20 years gender questions have been accorded greater prominence within the social sciences. The one exception, until rather recently, has been IR. Why did IR remain immune to gender for so long?

One factor has been a prevailing insecurity about the limits and parameters of IR as a 'discipline'. IR scholars argue about the boundary between the 'international' and the 'intra-national'. In so far as they accept the category of gender, they tend to view it as an intra-national problem, irrelevant to international relations. After all, international relations has traditionally been about 'high politics', and at first sight, gender issues seem pre-eminently to concern 'low politics'. This perception has been fostered by the fact that the institutions of high politics – ministries of defence and foreign affairs – are male-dominated preserves.

The belief that gender is an inappropriate category in IR is augmented by institutional inertia: the tendency to teach what has always been taught and to confine research to 'normal science' thereby avoiding the conceptual leap required to consider new categories or concepts. Moreover, while IR has always borrowed happily from, say, philosophy and political science, it has neglected others, particularly those that end in an 'ism' and most notably feminism.

The most important reason why women have been absent from international relations, however, is the prevalent belief that international relations are 'gender neutral', that they can no more be about women than they are about men. Thus international processes are assumed to affect neither the position and role of women in society nor the relative positions of women and men. Furthermore, it is presumed that international relations are not affected by issues pertaining to women. In other words, the sphere of gender and the sphere of international relations are considered to be separate, and many scholars who support women's rights in domestic society see no connection between international relations and gender [Halliday, in 26].

It must also be said that feminists were slow to engage with IR. Primarily concerned with women's oppression, they tended to seek the causes and the remedies in inter-personal relations and in domestic society and they paid little attention to the international system. This meant that where analysis was made of gender relations, it tended to focus on the internal sphere. For example, in seeking for the origins of women's subordination, some feminists turned to existing political theories. The liberal concern for individual autonomy and freedom was easily extended to a concern for women's autonomy, equality and freedom. This was not, of course, a new concern and Mill [45], Wollstonecraft [74] and Virginia Woolf [75] are venerable classical precursors. Similarly, it was not difficult to expand the Marxist concern for the oppression of a particular class to an investigation of the subjugation of women as a group within that class, and here too there was a theoretical antecedent in Engels' analysis of the family [20]. Liberal feminists and Marxist feminists thus offer contrasting diagnoses of why women are oppressed – while liberal feminists assume that female subordination arises from customary and legal constraints which hamper women's participation in the public world, Marxist feminists see capitalism and private property as the cause of women's oppression. For both, however, gender is socially constructed and has little to do with the biological differences between the sexes.

Radical feminists, on the other hand, believe that the patriarchal system is the cause of women's oppression. They pay far more attention to biological differences than liberal and Marxist feminists; they tend not to distinguish between the public and the private and to see the underlying structure of patriarchy as determinant. Feminist psychoanalysts believe that the roots of women's oppression are embedded in the psyche, while socialist feminists are eclectic, combining several strands of theory together in an attempt to establish a specifically feminist standpoint. Postmodern feminists, by contrast, decry synthesis and believe that a unified representation of all women is an impossible task [58, 70, 78]. As Elshtain [15] points out, however, feminists of all schools of thought 'share one overriding imperative: to redefine the boundaries between the public and the private, the personal and the political'. It was some time, however, before they extended this imperative to international politics.

Although the United Nations' Decade for Women (1976–85) has been criticized for its limited practical consequences [55, 69], it served to internationalize women's concerns [48] and contributed to making the women's movement a transnational pressure group [5, Newland, in 26]. At the same time, feminists (and some male scholars) began to realize that international relations do, in fact, have gendered effects, that is they affect women and men differently, and that the task of research on gender and IR is to reveal the role of gender issues and values and to analyse the gender-specific consequences of international processes.

There are two levels at which gender and international relations can be investigated: women as a category and gender as epistemology (this level includes analyses of feminist epistemologies, feminist critiques of traditional IR concepts and feminist accounts of IR). Perhaps the easiest (because the most recognizable) level is women as a category.

Women as a category

This level of investigation of gender and IR subsumes the examination of women as international actors and as objects and victims of male dominance in the international sphere. But it also investigates why women have traditionally been absent from discourses about politics and IR. Classical political philosophers have either ignored women or assigned them to an inferior role. Socrates, Plato, Aristotle, Aquinas, Augustine, Machiavelli, Hobbes, Locke, Bentham, Rousseau and Mill, Wollstonecraft, Hegel, the Utilitarians and Marx and Engels have all been scrutinized for their treatment of women [Lange in 13, 29, 51, 52, 56]. Philosophers usually exclude women from politics by distinguishing sharply between public and private worlds and relegating women to the private domain. Elshtain [15] has explored the images and themes clustered about the public/private distinction in the work of the most important political theorists. The fundamentally dualistic nature of Western political thought which all these studies reveal, and the way in which binary oppositions tend to be cast in hierarchical terms, have profound epistemological implications and help to explain IR's silence about gender.

Women were recognized in the field of economic development earlier and more easily than in other spheres of IR, although traditional economists, too, ignored gender. According to Pujol [57], economists did not construe women as belonging in the economic sphere except as exceptions. Moreover, rational, economic man is pre-eminently masculine [25]. But there were sound practical reasons for investigating the role of women in the domestic economy and the implications of that role for bilateral and multinational aid to underdeveloped countries. It is not surprising, therefore, that much of the work on women in development is designed to be policy-relevant and that, in this field at least, advocates and practitioners interact closely with feminist scholars. Boserup's work on women and development [7] is undoubtedly seminal in this respect. First published in 1970, it revealed that the recruitment of women into the modern sector accelerated economic development, demonstrated that modern technology and cash crops often benefited men while increasing women's burden and called for improved educational opportunities for women. Boserup [in 68] has also established that industrialization affects women differently in different societies.

Although international agencies have adopted various approaches towards women in their aid policies, gender inequalities persist. The reason is partly that modernization has tended to consolidate patriarchy and expand its control, since women have inadequate access to resources and receive low wages, while men retain control of women's sexuality [44, 68]. As far as rural women are concerned, increased productivity without relief from reproductive tasks increases women's burden [38]. But persistent inequalities also result from the 'feminization of poverty' in the Third World caused by the differential effects of policies of structural adjustment [2] and the consequences for women of world recession [6]. Feminists have criticized the male bias in development policies [3, 18, 32, 76], and they have also begun to propose new policies which avoid bias by empowering women [35, 72].

But, as Moser [in 26, 49] points out, following Molyneux [46], the major
obstacle to empowering women and addressing their strategic as well as
their practical needs is the hostility of male-dominated Third World
governments. In fact, women's hopes that national independence would be
accompanied by gender equality within the state have usually been
disappointed.

Women have played an important role in the struggle for national
liberation and in many revolutionary and nationalist movements [34].
Nationalist movements have often included women's concerns in their
programmes and enticed their participation in the struggle by promising later
benefits, but they have rarely kept their promises to make fulfilment of
women's needs a priority after revolution or independence. While women
were active and highly visible in the French and Bolshevik revolutions, for
example, they did not benefit collectively from their participation [59]. In the
Third World, women often achieved legal equality, the right to vote,
education and property after independence, but the basic problems of
women's subordination were unaffected by national liberation [34]. Abdo [in
4, p. 32] maintains, 'there has yet to be a national struggle in which the
feminist agenda was compatible with the nationalist agenda'. Molyneux [46],
on the other hand, argues that there is nothing inherently contradictory
between women's emancipatory goals and other national goals; the problem
is whether gender interests are articulated into, or subordinated to, other
goals. The work of Kandiyoti [36] and the essays in [77] examine how
women affect and are affected by national and ethnic processes, while
Tretrault [in 53] constructs a theoretical framework to analyse the interaction of women, family forms and revolutionary movements.

All nationalist movements tend to subordinate women to a particular
definition of women's role in society. Where nationalism is combined with
Islamic fundamentalism, women are literally made invisible behind the veil.
The issue of women's rights has acquired a renewed salience with the
establishment of theocratic states and the rise of fundamentalist religions.
Abdo [in 4] points out that fundamentalisms, whatever their form, do not
support gender or class equality. Kandiyoti [37] argues that there are various
systems of male dominance within Islam and that women use different
strategies, or 'patriarchal bargains' to increase their security and optimize
their life options with each.

The socialist revolution promised women full equality. Moreover, it was
an internationalist project and, although international revolution in the
Marxist-Leninist sense never occurred, other socialist states based their
women's policies on the Soviet Union. Women achieved formal, legal
equality and a degree of economic independence under socialism. But they
continued to earn less than men, the higher echelons of politics, science and
economics remained male preserves and they struggled under a triple burden
as a productive obligation was added to their reproductive and domestic
functions. Disappointed with socialism, women participated in the 'velvet
revolutions' that brought an end to communism with as much optimism as
their predecessors had participated in the socialist revolution. Once again,
however, the exigencies of economic reconstruction have taken priority over

women's needs. Moreover, their participation in politics has decreased, their economic dependence on men has increased with growing unemployment and they are profoundly affected by inflation and the austerity programmes that are meant to cure it [Fischer and Munske, in 48, 11, 14].

A major debate within the field of gender and IR pertains to women and war and peace. It has generated a large theoretical literature, in particular about the central proposition that women are more peaceable than men. Many feminist theorists argue that women are, by nature and nurture, pacific. Ruddick [in 30], for example, maintains that women's alienation from war arises from the contradiction between mothering and war. Nonviolence, she believes, is a natural extension of maternal practice. As di Leonardo [40] puts it, the powerful image of the 'Moral Mother' represents the nurturant, compassionate vision of women as innately pacifist. Carrol [in 54] argues that there is a logical connection between feminism and pacifism in the liberal principle of the inalienable right to life and liberty underlying both. Elshtain [16] calls the symbol of the female noncombatant embedded in our culture 'Beautiful Soul'.

The implicit or explicit corollary of innately peaceable women is that men are inherently warmongering, at best 'Just Warriors' [16], at worst 'bully boys' [Dinnerstein, in 30], members of a 'barracks community' who make war out of fear and hostility towards the female [Hartsock, in 63]. For Enloe [22] the problem is not men *per se*, but the logical interconnection between patriarchy and militarism. Many feminist theorists point out, however, that the language of war and peace presumes a symbiosis between fighter and victim, that masculinity and femininity are complementary ideological constructions and both are used in the service of war-making. Moreover, the view that women are inherently more peaceful than men, and therefore morally superior, serves to reinforce gender stereotypes and rigid sex roles. It is also counterfactual: although there is a long historic connection between feminism and pacifism, there is an equally long history of women's complicity in war. Enloe [22] points to the many non-combatant roles women fulfil for the military, and it is also the case that women have frequently encouraged their husbands and sons to go to war. In sum, the historical record as to whether women are more pacific than men is inconclusive [Pierson, in 43; Thompson, in 54]. Boulding [in 33] cautions against simplistic gender equations; both women and men, she maintains, have the capacity for violence and for peaceableness.

One does not need to accept essentialist arguments about masculinity and femininity and war, however, to recognize the importance of their construction as complementary. Feminist theorists argue that the epistemological consequences of this dualism privilege masculine modes of thought and render an empiricist approach inadequate.

Gender as epistemology

A central claim of feminism is that political science has a 'radical deafness' to women [23]. Political and IR discourse excludes women by highlighting

certain roles, rules and events and excluding others. Its dominant epistemology is based on positivism, and the knowledge claims of positivism reflect a
particularly masculine and Western set of experiences. Moreover, it
systematically excludes the possibility that women could be knowers or
agents of knowledge [28]. Adding facts about women to bodies of
knowledge which take men as the norm will not, therefore, allow us to
understand women or to comprehend the construction of gender in IR. What
is required is a radical rethinking of traditional categories of analysis.

In one influential but contested work, Keller [39] argues that both gender
and science are socially constructed. She traces the evolution of modern
conceptions of science, asserting that the equations between mind, reason
and masculinity, and the dichotomies between mind and nature, reason and
feelings, masculine and feminine are not historically invariant. They have
ancient roots but, she claims, only became polarized in the 17th century with
the triumph of mechanical philosophy and the change in the division
between work and home required by early industrial capitalism. In effect, the
polarization produced a gender ideology. Concepts of rationality and
objectivity, and the will to dominate nature, supported both the growth of a
particular vision of science and the institutionalization of a new definition of
manhood. It is this vision of science that political science has inherited,
giving primacy to rationality and objectivity, calling for clear-cut causal
relations, exhibiting impatience with indirect approaches to knowledge and,
in the behavioural version, demanding quantitative measures.

What would distinguish a feminist epistemology from the positivism it
opposes? Harding [27, 28] elaborates three approaches. Feminist empiricism
starts from the assumption that androcentric biases can be eliminated by
strict adherence to the existing methodological norms of reason, logic,
observation, measurement, verification and falsification. But the gender of the
researcher matters: women are more likely to notice androcentric bias [78].
Harding [28] points out, however, that the researcher must be placed in the
same critical frame as the subject matter, lest her own biases shape the
results of her analyses. Feminist empiricists also argue that they enlarge the
scope of enquiry, since the issues they select to investigate reflect their
experiences as women.

Feminist standpoint theorists argue that feminist empiricism cannot avoid
culture-wide androcentric prejudices. To achieve a feminist standpoint,
feminists must see nature and social life from the point of view of women's
social experiences. A feminist standpoint requires the development of a
feminist consciousness which will give a better understanding both of the
sources of women's oppression and of the world as a whole [78]. The result
will be more complete and less distorted knowledge claims than men's
experiences [28].

The third approach, feminist postmodernism, denies the claims of both
empiricists and standpoint theorists. Postmodernists question whether there
can be a feminist epistemology and reject the idea that there is a reality apart
from the structure given to it by the knower. Postmodern feminists believe
that feminists risk reproducing the dualizing distinctions they object to in
traditional discourse. They argue that feminist theory is embedded in the

social processes it is trying to criticize. It reduces complex and changing relations to a unified, undifferentiated whole, searching for 'closure' [24]. Unless a multiplicity of women's voices are heard, feminism will itself become a hierarchical system of knowledge construction [67]. As Lovibond [41, 42] and Rosenau [60] point out, however, there is a logical inconsistency in postmodern feminism: the relativism of postmodernism and its belief that all versions of truth are equal are not easily combined with feminists' commitment to challenge objective reality and their claim that women's voices have special authority.

Whatever epistemology feminist IR theorists adopt, they set themselves a twofold task: to challenge the theories of traditional IR scholars and the concepts they use to reveal their gender biases and to produce feminist accounts and explanations of IR. Believing that the dominant IR paradigm is realism, with power as its central concept, and security its putative aim, feminist theorists have paid particular attention to these concepts. Tickner [in 26], for example, began by demonstrating the masculine bias in Morgenthau's six principles of realism, later [67] extending her analysis to the security concerns and methodology of the realist school of thought and the way it excludes women. Sylvester [in 53] sees the origins of realism's gender specificity in liberal contractarian philosophy. Whitworth [73] believes that realism would be able to incorporate the concept of gender were it not for its ontological commitment to states and states*men*. Elshtain [16] points out that realism is not the exclusive preserve of male theorists since radical feminism is indebted to its Hobbesian and Machiavellian concepts. She offers an alternative discourse on power, based on Hannah Arendt's *On Violence*.

Arendt's definition of power as the ability to act in concert frequently appears in feminist criticism of power as coercion and force [31]. Ferguson [23] argues that women participate in a web of power relations and exercise power themselves. She defines power as the ability to enable people to do what they could not otherwise do. Jaquette [in 64] points out that women are the main arbiters and enforcers of legitimate authority and have access to manipulative and persuasive power. Feminist theorists question whether power can produce security. Grant [in 26] suggests that women might have different perceptions of how to escape the security dilemma, seeking cooperation and conflict management rather than autonomous action within anarchy. Autonomy is, of course, the basis of the concept of sovereignty. Several contributors to Peterson [53] explore the masculine gender identity of the sovereign state.

Tickner [67] goes further than deconstructing the traditional concepts of international relations, offering a feminist account of national security, international political economy and ecopolitics. Sylvester [65] looks at both political economy and neorealism through feminist lenses, using feminist empiricism, standpoint and postmodernism in turn and clearly favouring postmodernism. The best proponent of a feminist standpoint, however, is Enloe. In *Does Khaki Become You?* [22] she criticizes traditional definitions of national security and goes on to analyse the roles of women 'camp followers', exploring the intersection of militarism and women's lives from a distinctive female standpoint. In *Bananas, Beaches and Bases* [21] her thesis is that traditional accounts of international politics map a landscape peopled by men (usually elite men). In her analysis of nationalist movements, diplomacy, military expansion and international debt, her landscape depicts diplomat's wives, women who work in and around military bases and women living on austerity budgets. Feminists have always argued that the personal is political. Enloe concludes that the personal is also international.

Conclusion

This survey of gender and international relations is not exhaustive: for example, it excludes the growing empirical literature on the gendered policies of international institutions, such as the EC, and on changes in international law pertaining to women. It should, however, be evident that gender has, belatedly, been recognized as having major implications for the study of IR and that this entails a radical rethinking of much of the discipline. This is now one of the most dynamic areas of IR, with consequences that have only begun to be recognized. The least that can be said is that the era of IR as that of (uncontested) masculinity is over.

Bibliography

1. Afshar, Hale (ed.) *Women, Development and Survival in the Third World.* London and New York, Longman, 1991.
2. Afshar, Hale and Dennis, Carolyne (eds) *Women and Adjustment Policies in the Third World.* London, Macmillan, 1992.
3. Allison, Helen, *et al.* (eds) *Hard Cash: Man-made Development and its Consequences.* London, Change, 1986.
4. *Alternatives*, Special issue: Feminists Write International Relations, vol. 18, no. 1, 1993.
5. Ashworth, Georgina, 'The United Nations "Women's Conference" and International Linkages in the Women's Movement' in Peter Willetts (ed.) *Pressure Groups in the Global System.* London, Pinter and New York, St. Martin's Press, 1982, pp. 125–147.
6. Benería, Lourdes and Feldman, Shelley (eds) *Unequal Burden: Economic Crises, Persistent Poverty and Women's Work.* Boulder, San Francisco and London, Westview Press, 1992.
7. Boserup, Esther *Woman's Role in Economic Development.* London, Earthscan Publications, 1989.
8. Buckley, Mary (ed.) *Perestroika and Soviet Women.* Cambridge and New York, Cambridge University Press, 1992.
9. Burguieres, Mary, 'Feminist Approaches to Peace: Another Step for Peace Studies'. *Millennium*, vol. 19, no. 1, 1990, pp. 1–18.
10. Cohn, Carol 'Sex and Death in the Rational World of Defense Intellectuals'. *Signs*, vol. 12, no. 4, summer, 1987, pp. 687–718.
11. Corrin, Chris (ed.) *Women's Changing Experience in the Soviet Union and East-Central Europe.* London, Pinter Publishers, 1991.

12. Charlton, Sue Ellen M. *Women in Third World Development.* Boulder, Westview Press, 1984.
13. Coole, Diana H. *Women in Political Theory: From Ancient Misogyny to Contemporary Feminism.* Boulder, Lynne Rienner and Hemel Hempstead, Harvester Wheatsheaf, 1993 (second edition).
14. Einhorn, Barbara *Cinderella Goes to Market: Citizenships, Gender and the Women's Movement in East Central Europe.* London, Verso, 1993.
15. Elshtain, Jean Bethke *Public Man, Private Woman: Women in Social and Political Thought.* Oxford, Martin Robertson, 1981.
16. Elshtain, Jean Bethke *Women and War.* Brighton, Harvester Press and New York, Basic Books, 1987.
17. Elshtain, Jean and Tobias, Sheila (eds) *Women: Militarism and War: Essays in History, Politics and Social Theory,* Totowa, Rowman & Littlefield, 1990.
18. Elson, Diane *Male Bias in the Development Process.* Manchester, Manchester University Press, 1991.
19. Elson, Diane and Pearson, Ruth *Women's Employment and Multinationals in Europe.* London, Macmillan, 1989.
20. Engels, F. *The Origin of the Family, Private Property and the State.* London, Lawrence & Wishart, 1972 and New York, Viking Penguin, 1986.
21. Enloe, Cynthia *Bananas, Beaches and Bases: Making Feminist Sense of International Politics.* London, Pandora Books, 1989.
22. Enloe, Cynthia *Does Khaki Become You? The Militarisation of Women's Lives.* London, Pluto, 1983.
23. Ferguson, Kathy E. 'Male-Ordered Politics: Feminism and Political Science' in Terence Ball (ed.) *Idioms of Inquiry: Critique and Renewal in Political Science.* Albany, State University of New York Press, 1987, pp. 209–29.
24. Flax, Jane 'Postmodernism and Gender Relations in Feminist Theory'. *Signs,* vol. 12, no. 4, 1987, pp. 621–43.
25. Folbre, Nancy and Hartmann, Heidi 'The Rhetoric of Self-Interest: Ideology and Gender in Economic Theory' in Arjo Klamer, Donald McCloskey and Robert M. Solow (eds) *The Consequences of Economic Rhetoric.* Cambridge and New York, Cambridge University Press, 1988, pp. 184–203.
26. Grant, R. and Newland, K. (eds) *Gender and International Relations.* Milton Keynes, Open University Press and Bloomington and Indianapolis, Indiana University Press, 1991.
27. Harding, Sandra *The Science Question in Feminism.* Milton Keynes, Open University Press and Ithaca, Cornell University Press, 1986.
28. Harding, Sandra (ed.) *Feminism and Methodology: Social Science Issues.* Milton Keynes, Open University Press and Bloomington and Indianapolis, Indiana University Press, 1987.
29. Harding, Sandra and Hintikka, Merrill B. (eds) *Discovering Reality: Feminist Perspectives on Epistemology, Metaphysics, Methodology, and the Philosophy of Science.* Dordrecht, Boston and London, D. Reidel Publishing, 1983.
30. Harris, Adrienne and King, Ynestra (eds) *Rocking the Ship of State: Towards a Feminist Peace Politics.* Boulder, San Francisco and London, Westview Press, 1989.
31. Hartsock, Nancy C.M. *Money, Sex and Power: Towards a Feminist Historical Materialism.* London and New York, Longman, 1983.
32. *International Studies Notes,* Special Issue: Women and Development. vol. 14, no. 3, 1989.
33. Isaksson, Eva (ed.) *Women and the Military System.* New York, London, Toronto, Sydney, Tokyo, Wheatsheaf, 1988.

34. Jayawardena, Kumari *Feminism and Nationalism in the Third World.* London and Atlantic Highlands, Zed Books, 1986.
35. Kabeer, Naila *Rethinking Development from a Gender Perspective: Contributions to a Feminist Economics.* London, Verso, 1992.
36. Kandiyoti, Deniz 'Identity and its Discontents: Women and the Nation'. *Millennium,* vol. 20, no. 3, 1991, pp. 429–43.
37. Kandiyoti, Deniz 'Islam and Patriarchy: A Comparative Perspective' in Nikki R. Keddie and Beth Baron (eds) *Women in Middle Eastern History: Shifting Boundaries in Sex and Gender.* New Haven and London, Yale University Press, 1992, pp. 23–42.
38. Kandiyoti, Deniz 'Women and Rural Development Policies: the Changing Agenda'. *Development and Change,* vol. 21, no. 1, 1990, pp. 5–22.
39. Keller, Evelyn Fox *Reflections on Gender and Science.* New Haven and London, Yale University Press, 1985.
40. Leonardo, Micaela di 'Morals, Mothers and Militarism: Anti-militarism and Feminist Theory'. *Feminist Studies,* vol. 11, no. 3, 1985, pp. 599–617.
41. Lovibond, Sabina 'Feminism and Postmodernism'. *New Left Review,* no. 178, November–December, 1989, pp. 5–28.
42. Lovibond, Sabina 'Feminism and Pragmatism: A Reply to Richard Rorty'. *New Left Review,* no. 193, May–June, 1992, pp. 56–74.
43. MacDonald, Sharon, Holden, Pat and Ardener, Shirley (eds) *Images of Women in Peace and War: Cross-Cultural and Historical Perspectives.* London, Macmillan, 1987 and Madison, Wisconsin University Press, 1988.
44. Mies, Maria *Patriarchy and Accumulation on a World Scale: Women in the International Division of Labour.* London and Atlantic Highlands, Zed Books, 1985.
45. Mill, J.S. 'The Subjection of Women' in S. Collini (ed.) *J.S. Mill, On Liberty and other writings.* Cambridge and New York, Cambridge University Press, 1989, pp. 117–217.
46. Molyneux, Maxine, 'Mobilisation without Emancipation? Women's Interests, The State, and Revolution in Nicaragua'. *Feminist Studies,* vol. 11, no. 2, 1985, pp. 227–54.
47. Momsen, Janet *Women and Development in the Third World.* London and New York, Routledge, 1991.
48. Morgan, Robin (ed.) *Sisterhood is Global: The International Women's Movement Anthology.* Garden City, Anchor Press/Doubleday, 1984.
49. Moser, Caroline O.N. *Gender Planning and Development: Theory, Practice and Training.* London and New York, Routledge, 1993.
50. Muir, Kate *Arms and the Woman.* London, Sinclair-Stevenson, 1992.
51. Nye, Andrea *Feminist Theory and the Philosophies of Man.* London, New York and Sydney, Croom Helm, 1988.
52. Okin, Susan Moller *Women in Western Political Thought.* London, Virago, 1980 and Princeton, Princeton University Press, 1979.
53. Peterson, V. Spike (ed.) *Gendered States: Feminist (Re)Visions of International Relations Theory.* Boulder and London, Lynne Rienner, 1992.
54. Pierson, Ruth Roach (ed.) *Women and Peace: Theoretical, historical and practical perspectives.* London, New York and Sydney, Croom Helm, 1987.
55. Pietila, Hikkla and Vickers, Jeanne *Making Women Matter: The Role of the United Nations.* London and Atlantic Highlands, Zed Books, 1990.
56. Pitkin, Hanna F. *Fortune is a Woman: Gender and Politics in the Thought of Niccolo Machiavelli.* Berkeley, Los Angeles and London, University of California Press, 1984.

57. Pujol, Michèle *Feminism and Anti-Feminism in Early Economic Thought.* Aldershot, Edward Elgar, 1992.
58. Randall, Vicky *Women and Politics: An International Perspective.* London, Macmillan and Chicago, University of Chicago Press, 1987 (second edition).
59. Reynolds, Siân (ed.) *Women, State and Revolution. Essays on Power and Gender in Europe since 1789.* Brighton, Wheatsheaf and Amherst, University of Massachusetts Press, 1986.
60. Rosenau, Pauline Marie *Post-Modernism and the Social Sciences: Insights, Inroads and Intrusions.* Princeton, Princeton University Press, 1992.
61. Sen, Gita and Grown, Caren (eds) *Development, Crises and Alternative Visions: Third World Women's Perspectives.* London, Earthscan, 1988 and New York, Monthly Review Press, 1987.
62. Stiehm, Judith *Arms and the Enlisted Woman.* Philadelphia, Temple University Press, 1989.
63. Stiehm, Judith Hicks (ed.) *Women and Men's Wars.* London, Pergamon, 1983.
64. Stiehm, Judith Hicks (ed.) *Women's Views of the Political World of Men.* Dobbs Ferry, Transnational Publishers, 1984.
65. Sylvester, Christine 'The Emperors' Theories and Transformations: Looking at the Field Through Feminist Lenses' in Dennis C. Pirages and Christine Sylvester (eds) *Transformations in the Global Political Economy.* London, Macmillan and New York, St. Martin's Press, 1988, pp. 230–53.
66. Sylvester, Christine 'Some Dangers in Merging Feminist and Peace Projects'. *Alternatives,* vol. 12, no. 4, October, 1987, pp. 493–509.
67. Tickner, J. Ann *Gender in International Relations: Feminist Perspectives on Achieving Global Security.* New York, Columbia University Press, 1992.
68. Tinker, Irene (ed.) *Persistent Inequalities: Women and World Development.* New York and Oxford, Oxford University Press, 1990.
69. Tinker, Irene and Jaquette, J. 'UN Decade for Women: Its Impact and Legacy'. *World Development,* vol. 15, no. 3, 1987, pp. 419–27.
70. Tong, Rosemarie *Feminist Thought: A Comprehensive Introduction.* London, Unwin Hyman and Boulder, Westview Press, 1989.
71. Vickers, Jeanne *Women and the World Economic Crisis.* London and Atlantic Highlands, Zed Press, 1991.
72. Waring, Marilyn *If Women Counted: A New Feminist Economics.* London, Macmillan and San Francisco, Harper & Row, 1988.
73. Whitworth, Sandra 'Gender in the Inter-Paradigm Debate'. *Millennium,* vol. 18, no. 2, 1989, pp. 265–72.
74. Wollstonecraft, Mary *A Vindication of the Rights of Women.* Harmondsworth, Penguin, 1992.
75. Woolf, Virginia *The Three Guineas.* Oxford, Oxford University Press, 1992, pp. 151–433.
76. Young, Kate *et al.* (eds) *Of Marriage and the Market: Women's Subordination Internationally and its Lessons.* London and New York, Routledge & Kegan Paul, 1984 (second edition).
77. Yuval-Davis, Nira and Anthias, Floya (eds) *Woman-Nation-State.* London, Macmillan and New York, St. Martin's Press, 1989.
78. Zalewski, Marysia 'Feminist Theory and International Relations' in Mike Bowker and Robin Brown (eds) *From Cold War to Collapse: Theory and World Politics in the 1980s.* Cambridge, Cambridge University Press, 1993, pp. 115–44.

4 Critical theory and postmodernism in international relations

Chris Brown

Introduction

'Critical theory' and 'postmodernism' are ambiguous terms. Cox, in a seminal essay, defines critical theory as theory which stands apart from and challenges the existing order [27], but many normative theorists (see Chapter 2) not usually thought of as critical theorists produce 'critiques' of this kind. Hoffman [52] endorses Cox but also links critical theory more specifically to the Frankfurt School and Jürgen Habermas. Similarly, Coker [22] uses postmodern largely as a periodizing term while Der Derian and Shapiro [35] link postmodern international relations to literary theory and anti-analytical (largely Continental) philosophy. Ashley [9] uses postmodernism as a synonym for poststructuralism, not something that would be acceptable in Paris, while Connolly [26] and, in a later work, Der Derian [40] employ 'late modern' instead of postmodern (late for what?) Are postmodernists *critical* theorists? Yes, in the broad sense of the term, in that they certainly challenge the existing order but not necessarily in any more specific sense. While Rengger and Hoffman [80], in their subtitle, use 'Critical Theory' as a generic term which clearly includes postmodern approaches, earlier papers by Rengger [77, 78, 79] undermine this usage, and the undoubted critical theorist Habermas's recent work is explicitly and strongly *anti*-postmodernist [48].

Clearly, it is necessary to stipulate meanings for these terms, and the best way to do this is by examining the broader intellectual context out of which all these approaches emerged. Such a strategy of enquiry is true to one of the few positions common to *all* varieties of critical theory and postmodernism, namely a refusal to treat academic International Relations (IR) as a separate discourse with its own distinctive concepts and rhetorical strategies. Such a belief in the need to place IR within a wider context is held in common with many normative theorists [18], but a further common feature of the authors discussed here, not shared with other normative writers, is the belief that post-Enlightenment Western thought is in crisis. Before returning to the specifically international dimension of critical theory and postmodernism, it may be helpful to outline briefly the different ways in which these writers characterize this crisis and their different reactions to it.

The Enlightenment Project in danger?

What was the 'Enlightenment Project'? A long story here has to be cut very short and complex ideas reduced to bumper-sticker dimensions; the Enlightenment Project was no less than the liberation of humanity. Light is to replace darkness – prejudice, custom and unchallengeable authority – by the power of reason, the application of scientific knowledge and, most of all, by a willingness to think for one's self. Thus, in Kant's terms, Enlightenment is humanity's emergence from its 'self-incurred immaturity' – self-incurred because of a lack of resolution and courage [76, p. 54]. Dare to know, and the truth will set you (us) free: this is the essential claim of the Enlightenment, and the desire for rational autonomy has inspired radical, progressive, 'left' thought for two centuries – whether in the guise of liberalism, Marxism or social democracy; it has been an essential feature of the changes which have created 'modernity'. But can this project for rational change be, itself, rationally justified?

Kant, of course, directed his *Critiques* to exactly this problem, and already by the early 19th century Hegel had historicized the idea of rationality [95], but none the less, for much of the rest of that century, and the first part of our own, the Enlightenment Project flourished. The Victorians, Marx and Darwin, produced two of the grandest narratives of liberation and progress, and even when Freud uncovered the dark side of human nature and revealed limits to rational autonomy, his achievement was based on what he saw as solidly rational and scientific procedures. However, by the time Freud wrote, an earlier, and greater, psychologist, Friedrich Nietzsche, had already prefigured many of the critiques of Enlightenment that would dominate the next hundred years.

Nietzsche's account of the 'Last Men' in the Prologue to *Thus Spake Zarathustra* [71], is a poetic, dystopian vision of a world dehumanized by the triumph of rationality – a theme taken up in Weber's metaphor of reason as an 'iron cage' [116] – while his 'perspectivist' critique of positivist epistemology [70] with its insistence that physics is 'only an interpretation and arrangement of the world . . . and not an explanation' (p. 26) clearly anticipates many of the themes of the philosophy of science of the late 20th century. But, perhaps most central, is Nietzsche's insistence that the 'death of God' has fundamentally changed European life and thought. Here is an early, but very clear, exploration of 'antifoundationalism' – the belief that there are no grounds for belief, no foundations for knowledge. This is a position that has taken many forms over the last century, from James's pragmatist definition of truth as 'that which is good in the way of belief' [56, p. 215] to the structuralist proposition that meaning emerges in the relationship between signifiers rather than by reference to the signified [42] and Derrida's poststructuralist dictum that 'there is nothing outside the text' [41]. In the absence of foundations, the idea of 'representation' itself becomes suspect [88]; instead of representations we have simulation and 'simulacra' – a 'hyperreal' world of self-reflecting signs, models of nothing other than themselves [11].

What this all-too-brief account is describing is a crisis in Western thought. What most of these critics have in common is the belief that the dominant trend of 19th and early 20th century thought is leading to disaster; far from delivering liberation, the Enlightenment Project – or a perverted version thereof – is bringing dehumanization. The work of the greatest thinkers among these critics – Nietzsche and Heidegger [51] – is overlaid by a sense of danger, hovering on the edge of despair, and falling over the edge in the cultural pessimism of writers such as Adorno and Horkheimer [1].

In the face of this situation there are two characteristic reactions, out of which the beginnings of a classification can emerge. On the one hand, there are those who are unwilling to abandon the Enlightenment Project even though they realize that it can no longer be defended in the old way. Let us call this the approach of 'Critical Theory' (capitalized to distinguish this from looser usages) – a term used by some of the most famous such thinkers, each word of which counts; these writers wish to produce 'critiques' and 'theory', linking themselves thereby with Kant and his successors. On the other hand, there are those who *are* willing to abandon the Enlightenment Project, the 'metanarratives' it generated [69], and the monologic account it offered of rationality and science [10] and who look to think and live without these foundations. Call this 'postmodernism' – using 'modern' as shorthand for the Enlightenment version of modernity, and avoiding the word 'theory' because the aspiration to create theory is part of the old order. This is not a foolproof classification – there are significant writers who hover between these two approaches, as will be apparent – but it offers a useful starting point and a basis upon which it is possible to approach the more specifically IR literature.

Critical Theory and international relations

The aim of Critical Theory is the 'restructuring of social and political theory' [13] which involves both challenging positivist approaches to social science and proposing alternatives. Taylor [95] challenges positivism in the name of 'interpretation', drawing on hermeneutics, but the most influential critical social theorist is Jürgen Habermas whose work grows out of the Institute of Social Research at Frankfurt. The Frankfurt School [58] was originally Marxist in inspiration, but, doubtless partly as a result of its post-1933 exile, its later work was infused with a very unMarxist pessimism about the prospects for progressive social change [1]. Habermas has built on Frankfurt Critical Theory but has left behind both its residual Marxism and its cultural despair.

His later work has focused on 'discourse ethics' [49] and theories of truth, explicitly directed against the 'neoconservatives' of postmodernism [48], but his earlier work was epistemological and explored the relationship between knowledge and human interests [47]. He identifies three 'knowledge-constitutive interests': in prediction and control, met by the **empirical-analytical** sciences; in the understanding of meaning, met by the **historical-hermeneutic** sciences; and in freedom from domination, emancipation and the achievement of rational autonomy, met by **Critical Theory**. It is this last category that is specific to Habermas and which has been highly influential in so far as it seems to promise an escape route from both status-quo oriented positivistic social science and apolitical hermeneutics.

Habermas's emancipatory project has been explicitly applied to IR by a number of authors. Cox [27] uses some Habermasian ideas but refers to him by name only in passing. The most extensive employment of Habermas comes in a much-cited essay by Hoffman [52] which links Habermas's work to the so-called 'inter-paradigm debate' in IR, with the promise that Critical Theory will be the next stage – or possibly a fourth paradigm – in international theory. The possibility that this might indeed be the case is endorsed by Linklater [68] who, in his own major study *Beyond Realism and Marxism* [67], employs Habermas as one of his sources.

The problem with this aspiration is that once one gets beyond programmatic statements to actual theoretical work, it becomes difficult to distinguish Critical Theory from other varieties of progressive social thought. Thus, Hoffman's cosmopolitan ethics [54] are difficult to distinguish from those generated by Beitz [12], Shue [92] or Onuf [72], the first two of whom, at least, are Critical Theorists only in the sense that they are critical of the existing order. The radical political economy espoused by Cox [27, 28, 30] Alker and Biersteker [2] and Linklater [67] may be post-Marxist in the sense that it no longer rests on the positivist epistemology of classic Marxist theories of imperialism, but in *content* it is, clearly, closely related to traditional Marxism, a point made more generally with respect to Critical IR by Kubálková and Cruickshank [64] and, effectively, acknowledged by Cox in a later postscript to his most famous article [29].

It is not surprising that Critical Theory merges with a wider 'progressive' literature – the aim is to recast, rather than to abandon, the Enlightenment Project, and it follows that the substantive work Critical Theorists produce is unlikely to differ dramatically from that of those who do not share the view that such a recasting is required. The values of the Enlightenment remain the same, whether held by those with an uncomplicated belief in emancipation and rational autonomy or not. The most distinctive feature of Critical IR theory lies in its programmatic self-justification, and this becomes of particular importance not in contest with conventional Enlightenment thought but with respect to *critics* of the Enlightenment Project.

Originally these critics were from the right, but today they are as likely to be found on the postmodern wing of modern social theory. Thus, Habermas's attempt to find a rational grounding for ethics in the 'ideal-speech situation' [49] has been criticized for its foundationalism by Rorty [81] and for its unwillingness to recognize the essential ambiguity of social communications by Connolly [24]. Habermas's own assaults on postmodernism have been referred to above [48]; Taylor's attack on Foucault [97] and his subsequent exchange with Connolly [23, 98] is on similar lines. Specifically in IR, Linklater defends the idea of theory against postmodern critics [68], and many of the issues involved are clarified in an exchange between Rengger [77] and Hoffman [53]. These discussions are of great value – there are, of course, critics of postmodernism who are not Critical Theorists (see below), but a major advantage possessed by the latter is that they generally have a good grasp of the nature of their opponent's aims precisely because they share with them a sense of the futility of the defences of modernist rationality offered by traditional supporters of the Enlightenment Project. Although they disagree as to prognosis, both sides agree that there is a crisis in Western thought. However, valuable though these debates are, they do not add to the store of new ideas with which to restock IR theory, and, for the time being, it seems that the postmodern reaction to the crisis of the Enlightenment is a more likely source of innovation.

Postmodernism and international relations theory

On the definition stipulated here, postmodern thinking rejects the aim of unified, integrated theory, that is the 'metanarratives' and 'depth metaphors' with which thinkers such as Freud and Marx have attempted to relate surface phenomena to deeper underlying causes. This is quite a restrictive definition – it would, for example, exclude the work of Harvey [50] and Jameson [57], both of whom employ some postmodern notions which they relate back to changes in the overall mode of production of post-industrial society, thus re-introducing a metanarrative, albeit one which says that metanarratives are no longer possible. None the less, the postmodernist work that meets this definition is still extensive and, predictably, difficult to classify; there are no figures who play the role that Habermas plays within Critical Theory. There is a 'school' of postmodernist IR scholars in the United States in the sociological sense of a group who communicate among themselves, cluster around senior figures such as Richard Ashley and William Connolly and publish together [6, 35], but the degree to which there is a school in the intellectual sense of the term is much more limited. Thus, what follows is necessarily somewhat diffuse and ill-defined, consisting of references to prominent individual thinkers and important general themes, without any attempt to integrate this account into a coherent, but thereby unpostmodernist, narrative.

One distinction that is useful is between programmatic articles about what postmodernist work *might* look like, or *should* look like, and actual attempts to deliver the goods. There are a great many of the former, such as Lapid's accounts of the 'Third Debate' [65, 66] and supporting texts by Biersteker [14] and George [45] and the introductory essays by Der Derian [36] and Shapiro [87] to their *International/Intertextual* collection. However, the two most influential programme articulators have been Richard Ashley and R.B.J.Walker. Ashley's early work was a more or less conventional study in the scientific mould, but he first came to prominence with his highly influential attack on 'neorealism' [3, 59]. This was influenced by Bourdieu

[16] and, in form, by E.P. Thompson [99], and in terms of this chapter was clearly 'Critical' rather than 'postmodern'. Articles on geopolitics [4] and the 'anarchy problematique' [5] were clearly moving in a postmodern direction but, equally clearly, still related to a pre-Morgenthauian, practice-oriented realism. The evolution of his thought up to this point is traced in Waever [104]. The first fully postmodern Ashleyan work is his deconstruction of Waltz [9] in Der Derian and Shapiro [35].

Walker's evolution is not dissimilar. His early papers and collections on social movements [105, 106, 107] emerge from the World Order Models Project tradition and, like WOMP, are clearly modernist and 'Critical' rather than postmodern. However, his later critiques of realism and sovereignty [108, 109, 111, 112, 113], and examinations of the relationship of political theory to international theory [110, 114], have been increasingly postmodern in orientation. In 1990, Ashley and Walker together edited a rather incongruously titled Special Issue of International Studies Quarterly [6] and their two, jointly authored, chapters in this volume [7, 8] set out the clearest account available of the postmodern project, or rather, refusal to have a project, in IR – reinforced by a similarly intentioned paper by George and Campbell [46].

Der Derian has also produced programmes [34, 36] but, more significantly, the most substantial body of postmodernist writings in IR. His Foucauldian genealogy of diplomacy [32, 33] was the first full-length postmodernist study in IR and is still the best, richly suggestive in its intertextually eclectic range of sources. His more recent work applies Baudrillard's notion of simulation and the 'hyperreal' [11], and Virilio's ideas on speed and politics [101, 102] to what he calls 'antidiplomacy' in a series of papers [37, 38, 39] collected and amplified in Antidiplomacy [40]. Shapiro, Der Derian's co-author and associate, drawing on similar post-structural sources has produced a major account of the crisis of represen-tation [88] and a number of studies concentrating on the literature and politics interface [86, 89, 90], collected in Reading the Postmodern Polity [91].

One of the major applications of postmodern IR has been in the area of security studies. Der Derian's antidiplomacy clearly is relevant, as is Shapiro's study of strategic discourse [89], while Klein has produced a number of studies of NATO examining the textual strategies that organization has employed to define the threats to its security [61, 62, 63]. Dalby [31] follows a similar line. Much of this is interesting, although perhaps not as far away from the radical end of the security studies' profession (see, for example, Booth [15]) as its authors seem to think. However, the most impressive work in this area is that of Campbell [20, 21]. Writing Security – an examination of the constitutive role of foreign policy in establishing a US identity – is genuinely original in its combination of postmodernist criticism with a firm grasp of the conventional literature. Reversal of the traditional view that the international relations of a state are a function of its domestic constitution is a feature of a number of recent postmodern studies of sovereignty [44, 90, 111, 113] and intervention [115].

Security studies often focus on the role of the 'other' in the constituting of the polity, and the general theme of identity and difference is important to postmodern IR. In the work of Connolly [24, 26] drawing on, in particular, Foucault [75], this theme becomes the basis for a positive critique, as opposed to the negativism of Ashley's deconstructions [25, 9]. Much contemporary feminist writing on international relations is influenced by postmodernist notions of difference – see [43, 73, 94] and Chapter 3 in this volume. Bakhtin's notion of 'dialogism' [10] – the replacement of mono-logical narrative by changing perspectives none of which are given privileged status – has already provoked a remarkable study of the clash of cultures by Todorov [100] which, as this theme comes to occupy centre-stage in contemporary IR, will be of increasing importance. Already some of the best studies of non-Western/Western relations are laced with postmodernist formulations – as in Piscatori on the Salman Rushdie affair [74]. One of the supposed achievements of the Enlightenment was the universality of its thought, its claim to be able to understand itself and other realms of thought in its own, privileged terms. Postmodernism's abandonment of this claim may have undesirable side effects – although Rorty argues that it is possible to defend the positive side of Enlightenment from the perspective of a liberal ironism [81] – but it may make possible genuine dialogue with other cultures by recognizing the category 'different but equal' [17, 19].

Criticisms and conclusions

As yet, there is little critical literature on postmodernism in IR, apart from the debate between Critical Theory and postmodernism referred to above and the criticisms postmodernists have of each other [85, 25, 103]. Spegele's study of Ashley [93] is pioneering. Brown [18] is one of the only general studies of normative IR theory to have a substantial section on post-modernism. The collection by Rengger and Hoffman [80] is one of the few to cover Critical Theory and postmodernism and to have papers by both critics and adherents. Keohane's well publicized call for postmodernists to develop a 'research programme' of their own is, in effect, an invitation for them to stop being postmodernist [60]. Pauline Rosenau's attacks on postmodernism [82, 83, 84] are based on a knowledge of the field which is impressively extensive but, curiously, seems to miss the basic point that postmodernists experience the crisis of Western thought as a source of *danger*. In common with Keohane, Rosenau mistakes the sense of fun displayed by writers such as Der Derian for an underlying and irresponsible frivolity which is not, in fact, present. On the contrary, this is a deeply serious body of work; the paradoxes of relativism, of simultaneously denying and presupposing truth stem from a desire to resist closure. In the words of Connolly, 'the postmodernist thinks within the code of paradox because only attentiveness to paradox can loosen the hold monotonic standards of identity have over life in the late-modern age' [25, p. 339]. It remains to be seen which areas of postmodernist discourse will survive and flourish. Constructive criticism has a role to play here, but for the most part 'wait and see' is the best policy.

Bibliography

1. Adorno, T. W. and Horkheimer, M. *Dialectic of Enlightenment*. London, Verso, 1979.
2. Alker, Hayward and Biersteker, Thomas J. 'The Dialectics of World Order: Notes for a Future Archeologist Of International Savoir Faire'. *International Studies Quarterly*, vol. 28, no. 2 (Spring 1984), pp. 225–86.
3. Ashley, Richard K. 'The Poverty of Neorealism'. *International Organization*, vol. 38, no. 2 (Spring 1984), pp. 225–86.
4. Ashley, Richard 'The Geopolitics of Geopolitical Space'. *Alternatives*, vol. 12 (October 1987), pp. 403–34.
5. Ashley, Richard K. 'Untying the Sovereign State: A Double Reading of the Anarchy Problematique'. *Millennium: Journal of International Studies*, vol. 17, no. 2 (Summer 1988), pp. 227–62.
6. Ashley, Richard and Walker, R.B.J. (eds) 'Speaking the Language of Exile: Dissidence in International Studies'. Special Issue *International Studies Quarterly*, vol. 34, no. 3 (September 1990).
7. Ashley, Richard and Walker, R.B.J. 'Speaking the Language of Exile: Dissident Thought in International Studies'. Special Issue *International Studies Quarterly*, vol. 34, no. 3 (September 1990), pp. 259–68.
8. Ashley, Richard and Walker, R.B.J. 'Reading Dissidence/Writing the Discipline: Crisis and the Question of Sovereignty in International Studies'. Special Issue *International Studies Quarterly*, vol. 34, no. 3 (September 1990), pp. 367–416.
9. Ashley, Richard K. 'Living on Borderlines: Man, Poststructuralism, and War' in J. Der Derian and M. Shapiro (eds) *International/Intertextual Relations: Postmodern Readings in World Politics*. Lexington, Lexington Books, 1989, pp. 259–321.
10. Bakhtin, Mikail M. *The Dialogic Imagination: Four Essays*. M. Holoquist (ed.) translated by C. Emerson, C. and M. Holoquist, Austin, University of Texas Press, 1981.
11. Baudrillard, Jean *Selected Writings*. Mark Poster (ed.), Cambridge, Polity Press, 1988.
12. Beitz, Charles R. *Political Theory and International Relations*. Princeton, Princeton University Press, 1979.
13. Bernstein, Richard J. *The Restructuring of Social and Political Theory*. London, Methuen, 1979 and Pittsburgh, University of Pennsylvania Press, 1978.
14. Biersteker, Thomas J. 'Critical reflections on Post-Positivism in International Relations'. *International Studies Quarterly*, vol. 33, no. 3 (September 1989), pp. 63–7.
15. Booth, Ken 'Security and Emancipation'. *Review of International Studies*, vol. 17, no. 4, (October 1991), pp. 313–26.
16. Bourdieu, Pierre *Outline of a Theory of Practice*. translated by R. Nice, Cambridge, Cambridge University Press, 1977.
17. Brown, Chris 'The Modern Requirement? Reflections on Normative International Theory in a Post-Western World'. *Millennium: Journal of International Studies*, vol. 17, no. 2 (Summer 1988), pp. 339–48.
18. Brown, Chris *International Relations Theory: New Normative Approaches*. Harvester, Hemel Hempstead, 1992 and New York, Columbia University Press, 1993.
19. Brown, Chris '"Turtles All the Way Down": Antifoundationalism, Critical Theory and International Relations' in N.J. Rengger and M. Hoffman (eds)

Beyond the Inter-Paradigm Debate. Hemel Hempstead, Harvester Wheatsheaf, forthcoming.

20. Campbell, David 'Global Inscription: How Foreign Policy Constitutes the United States'. *Alternatives*, vol.15, no. 3 (Summer 1990), pp. 263–86.

21. Campbell, David *Writing Security: United States Foreign Policy and the Politics of Identity.* Manchester, Manchester University Press and Minneapolis, University of Minnesota Press, 1992.

22. Coker, Christopher 'Postmodernity and the end of the Cold War; has war been disinvented?'. *Review of International Studies*, vol. 18, no. 3 (July 1992), pp. 189–98.

23. Connolly, William E. 'Taylor, Foucault and Otherness'. *Political Theory*, vol. 13, no. 3 (August 1985), pp. 365–76.

24. Connolly, William E. *Politics and Ambiguity.* Madison, Wisconsin University Press, 1987.

25. Connolly, William E. 'Identity and Difference in Global Politics' in J. Der Derian and M. Shapiro (eds) *International/Intertextual Relations.* Lexington, Lexington Books, pp. 323–42.

26. Connolly, William E. *Identity/Difference: Democratic Negotiations of Political Paradox.* Ithaca, Cornell University Press, 1991.

27. Cox, Robert 'Social Forces, States and World Order'. *Millennium: Journal of International Studies*, vol.10, no. 2 (Summer 1981), pp. 126–55.

28. Cox, Robert 'Gramsci, Hegemony and International Relations'. *Millennium: Journal of International Studies*, vol. 12, no. 2 (Summer 1983), pp. 162–75.

29. Cox, Robert, 'Postscript 1985' in R.O. Keohane (ed.) *Neorealism and its Critics.* New York, Columbia University Press, 1986, pp. 239–49.

30. Cox, Robert *Production Power and World Order: Social Forces in the Making of History.* New York, Columbia University Press, 1987.

31. Dalby, Simon 'Geopolitical Discourse: The Soviet Union as Other'. *Alternatives*, vol. 13, no. 4 (1988), pp. 415–42.

32. Der Derian, James *On Diplomacy: A Genealogy of Western Estrangement.* Blackwell, Oxford, 1987.

33. Der Derian, James 'Mediating Estrangement: A Theory for Diplomacy'. *Review of International Studies*, vol. 13, no. 2 (April 1987), pp. 91–110.

34. Der Derian, James 'Introducing Philosophical Traditions in International Relations'. *Millennium: Journal of International Studies*, vol. 17, no. 2 (Summer 1988), pp. 89–193.

35. Der Derian, James and Shapiro, Michael J. (eds) *International/Intertextual Relations: Postmodern Readings in World Politics.* Lexington, Lexington Books, 1989.

36. Der Derian, James 'The Boundaries of Knowledge and Power in International Relations' in J. Der Derian and M. Shapiro (eds) *International/Intertextual Relations.* Lexington, Lexington Books, 1989, pp. 3–10.

37. Der Derian, James 'Spy vs. Spy: The Intertextual Power of International Intrigue' in J. Der Derian and M. Shapiro (eds) *International/Intertextual Relations.* Lexington, Lexington Books, 1989, pp. 163–87.

38. Der Derian, James 'The (S)pace of International Relations: Simulation, Surveillance and Speed' in Richard Ashley and R.B.J. Walker (eds) Special Issue *International Studies Quarterly*, vol. 34, no. 3 (September 1990), pp. 295–310.

39. Der Derian, James 'S/N: International Theory, Balkanisation and the New World Order'. *Millennium: Journal of International Studies*, vol. 20, no. 3 (Winter 1991), pp. 485–506.

40. Der Derian, James *Antidiplomacy: Spies, Terror, Speed and War*. Cambridge, MA and Oxford, Blackwell, 1992.

41. Derrida, Jacques *Of Grammatology*. Baltimore and London, Johns Hopkins University Press, 1976.

42. Descombes, Vincent *Modern French Philosphy*. Cambridge, Cambridge University Press, 1980.

43. Elshtain, Jean Bethke 'Freud's Discourse of War/Politics' in J. Der Derian and M. Shapiro (eds) *International/Intertextual Relations*. Lexington, Lexington Books, 1989, pp. 49–67.

44. Elshtain, Jean Bethke 'Sovereignty, Identity, Sacrifice'. *Millennium: Journal of International Studies*, vol. 20, no. 3 (Winter 1991), pp. 395–406.

45. George, Jim 'International Relations and the Search for Thinking Space: Another View of the Third Debate'. *International Studies Quarterly*, vol. 33, no. 3 (1989), pp. 269–93.

46. George, Jim and Campbell, David 'Patterns of Dissent and the Celebration of Difference: Critical Social Theory and International Relations' in Richard Ashley and R.B.J. Walker (eds) Special Issue *International Studies Quarterly*, vol. 34, no. 3 (September 1990), pp. 269–93.

47. Habermas, Jürgen *Knowledge and Human Interests*. London, Heinemann and Boston, Beacon, 1972.

48. Habermas, Jürgen *The Philosophical Discourses of Modernity*. Cambridge, Polity Press, 1987.

49. Habermas, Jürgen *Moral Consciousness and Communicative Action*. Cambridge, Polity Press, 1990.

50. Harvey, David *The Condition of Postmodernity: An Enquiry Into the Origins of Cultural Exchange*. Oxford, Blackwell, 1989.

51. Heidegger, Martin *Basic Writings*. San Francisco, Harper & Row, 1977.

52. Hoffman, Mark 'Critical theory and the Inter-Paradigm Debate'. *Millennium: Journal of International Studies*, vol. 16, no. 2 (Summer 1987), pp. 231–49.

53. Hoffman, Mark 'Conversations on Critical International Relations Theory'. *Millennium: Journal of International Studies*, vol. 17, no. 1 (Spring 1988), pp. 91–5.

54. Hoffman, Mark 'Cosmopolitanism and Normative International Theory'. *Paradigms*, vol. 2, no. 1 (1988), pp. 60–75.

55. Hoffman, Mark 'Restructuring, Reconstruction, Reinscription, Rearticulation: Four Voices in Critical International Theory'. *Millennium: Journal of International Studies*, vol. 20, no. 2 (Summer 1991), pp. 69–185.

56. James, William *Selected Papers on Philosophy*. London, Dent, 1917.

57. Jameson, Frederic *Postmodernism, or, The Cultural Logic of Late Capitalism*. London, Verso, 1971.

58. Jay, Martin *The Dialectical Imagination: A History of the Frankfurt School and the Institution of Social Research, 1923–1950*. Boston, Little Brown and London, Heinemann, 1973.

59. Keohane, Robert O. (ed.) *Neorealism and its Critics*. New York, Columbia University Press, 1986.

60. Keohane, Robert O. 'International Institutions: Two Approaches'. *International Studies Quarterly*, vol. 32, no. 4 (1988), pp. 379–96.

61. Klein, Bradley S. 'After Strategy: The Search for a Post-Modern Politics of Peace'. *Alternatives*, vol. 13, no. 3 (July 1988), pp. 293–318.

62. Klein, Bradley S. 'The Textual Strategies of the Military: Or Have You Read Any Good Defense Manuals Lately?' in J. Der Derian and M. Shapiro (eds) *International/Intertextual Relations*. Lexington, Lexington Books, 1989, pp. 97–112.

63. Klein, Bradley S. 'How the West Was Won: Representational Politics of NATO' in Richard Ashley and R.B.J. Walker (eds) Special Issue *International Studies Quarterly*, vol. 34, no. 3 (September 1990), pp. 311–26.

64. Kubálková, V. and Cruickshank, A.A. 'The "New Cold War" in "critical international relations studies"'. *Review of International Studies*, vol. 12, no. 3 (July 1986), pp. 63–185.

65. Lapid, Yosef '*Quo Vadis* International Relations? Further Reflections on the "Next Stage" of International Theory'. *Millennium: Journal of International Studies*, vol. 18, no. 1 (Spring 1989), pp. 77–88.

66. Lapid, Yosef 'The Third Debate: On the Prospects of International Theory in a Post-Positivist Era'. *International Studies Quarterly*, vol. 33, no. 3 (1989), pp. 235–54.

67. Linklater, Andrew *Beyond Realism and Marxism: Critical Theory and International Relations*. Basingstoke, Macmillan and New York, St. Martin's Press, 1990.

68. Linklater, Andrew 'The Question of the Next Stage in International Relations Theory: A Critical-Theoretical Point of View'. *Millennium: Journal of International Studies*, vol. 21, no. 1 (Spring 1992), pp. 77–98.

69. Lyotard, J-F. *The Postmodern Condition: A Report on Knowledge.* translated by G. Bennington and B. Massumi, Manchester, Manchester University Press, 1984.

70. Nietzsche, Friedrich *Beyond Good and Evil.* translated by R.J. Hollingdale, Harmondsworth, Penguin, 1971.

71. Nietzsche, Friedrich *Thus Spake Zarathustra.* translated by R.J. Hollingdale, Penguin, Harmondsworth, 1971.

72. Onuf, Nicholas Greenwood *World of Our Making: Rules and Rule in Social Theory and International Relations.* Columbia, University of South Carolina Press, 1989.

73. Peterson, V. Spike (ed.) *Gendered States: Feminist (Re)Visions of International Relations Theory.* Boulder, Lynne Rienner, 1992.

74. Piscatori, James 'The Rushdie Affair and the Politics of Ambiguity'. *International Affairs*, vol. 66, no. 4 (October 1990), pp. 767–89.

75. Rabinow, Paul (ed.) *The Foucault Reader.* Harmondsworth, Penguin, 1986.

76. Reiss, Hans J. *Kant's Political Writings.* Cambridge, Cambridge University Press, 1970.

77. Rengger, N.J. 'Going Critical? A Response to Hoffman'. *Millennium: Journal of International Studies*, vol. 17, no. 1, (Spring 1988), pp. 81–9.

78. Rengger, N.J. 'Incommensurability, International Theory, and the Fragmentation of Western Political Culture' in J. Gibbins (ed.) *Contemporary Political Culture: Politics in a Postmodern Age.* London, Sage, 1989, pp. 237–50.

79. Rengger, N.J. 'The Fearful Sphere of International Relations'. *Review of International Studies*, vol. 16, no. 4 (October 1990), pp. 361–8.

80. Rengger, N.J. and Hoffman, Mark (eds.) *Beyond the Inter-Paradigm Debate: Critical Theory and International Relations.* Hemel Hempstead, Harvester Wheatsheaf, forthcoming.

81. Rorty, Richard *Contingency, Irony and Solidarity.* Cambridge, Cambridge University Press, 1989.

82. Rosenau, Pauline 'Once Again into the Fray: International Relations Confronts the Humanities'. *Millennium: Journal of International Studies*, vol. 19, no. 1 (Spring 1990), pp. 83–110.

83. Rosenau, Pauline 'Internal Logic, External Absurdity: Post Modernism in Political Science'. *Paradigms*, vol. 4, no. 1 (1990), pp. 39–57.

84. Rosenau, Pauline M. *Postmodernism and the Social Sciences: Insights, Inroads and Intrusions*. Princeton, Princeton University Press, 1991.
85. Roy, Ramashray, Walker, R.B.J. and Ashley, Richard 'Dialogue: Towards a Critical Social theory of International Politics'. *Alternatives*, vol. 13, no. 1 (January 1988), pp. 77–102.
86. Shapiro, Michael J. and Neubauer, Dean 'Spatiality and Policy Discourse: Reading the Global City'. *Alternatives*, vol. 14, no. 3 (July 1989), pp. 301–25.
87. Shapiro, Michael J. 'Textualising Global Politics' in J. Der Derian and M. Shapiro (eds) *International/Intertextual Relations*. Lexington, Lexington Books, 1989, pp. 11–22.
88. Shapiro, Michael *The Politics of Representation: Writing Practices in Biography, Photography, and Policy Analysis*. Madison, University of Wisconsin Press, 1987.
89. Shapiro, Michael J. 'Strategic Discourse/Discursive Strategy: The Representation of "Security Policy" in the Video Age' in Richard Ashley and R.B.J. Walker (eds) Special Issue *International Studies Quarterly*, vol. 34, no. 3 (September 1990), pp. 327–40.
90. Shapiro, Michael J. 'Sovereignty and Exchange in the Orders of Modernity'. *Alternatives*, vol. 16, no. 4, 1990, pp. 447–77.
91. Shapiro, Michael J. *Reading the Postmodern Polity*. Minneapolis, University of Minnesota Press, 1992.
92. Shue, Henry *Basic Rights*. Princeton, Princeton University Press, 1980.
93. Spegele, Roger D. 'Richard Ashley's Discourse for International Relations'. *Millennium*, vol. 21, no. 2, 1992, pp. 147–82.
94. Sylvester, Christine *Feminist Theory and International Relations in a Postmodern Era*. Cambridge, Cambridge University Press, 1992.
95. Taylor, Charles *Hegel*. Cambridge, Cambridge University Press, 1975.
96. Taylor, Charles 'Interpretation and the Sciences of Man'. *Review of Metaphysics*, vol. 25, no. 1, 1971, pp. 3–51.
97. Taylor, Charles 'Foucault on Freedom and Truth'. *Political Theory*, vol. 12, no. 2, 1984, pp. 152–83.
98. Taylor, Charles 'Connolly, Foucault and Truth'. *Political Theory*, vol. 13, no. 3, 1985, pp. 377–85.
99. Thompson, E.P. *The Poverty of Theory*. Merlin, London, 1978.
100. Todorov, Tzvetan *The Conquest of America*. New York, HarperCollins, 1985.
101. Virilio, Paul and Lotringer, Sylvere *Pure War*. New York, Semiotext(e). Foreign Agents Series, 1983.
102. Virilio, Paul *Speed and Politics: An Essay in Dromology*. New York, Semiotext(e). Foreign Agents Series, 1986.
103. Waever, Ole *Beyond the Beyond of Critical International Theory*. Centre for Peace and Conflict Research, Copenhagen, 1989.
104. Waever, Ole *Tradition and Transgression in International Relations: A Post-Ashleyan Position*. Centre for Peace and Conflict Research, Copenhagen, 1989.
105. Walker, R.B.J. *Culture, Ideology and World Order*. Boulder and London, Westview Press, 1984.
106. Walker, R.B.J. 'Culture, Discourse, Insecurity'. *Alternatives*, vol. 11, no. 4, 1986, pp. 485–504.
107. Walker, R.B.J. 'Realism, Change, and International Political Theory'. *International Studies Quarterly*, vol. 31, no. 1, 1987, pp. 65–86.
108. Walker, R.B.J. 'History and Structure in the Theory of International Relations'. *Millennium: Journal of International Studies*, vol. 18, no. 2, 1989, pp. 163–83.

109. Walker, R.B.J. and Mendlovitz, S.H. (eds) *Contending Sovereignties: Redefining Political Community.* Boulder and London, Lynne Rienner, 1990.
110. Walker, R.B.J. '*The Prince* and "The Pauper": Tradition, Modernity and Practice in the Theory of International Relations' in J. Der Derian and M. Shapiro (eds) *International/Intertextual Relations.* Lexington, Lexington Books, 1989, pp. 25–48.
111. Walker, R.B.J. 'Security, Sovereignty, and the Challenge of World Politics'. *Alternatives,* vol. 15, no. 1, 1990, pp. 3–28.
112. Walker, R.B.J. 'On the Spatiotemporal Conditions of Democratic Practice'. *Alternatives,* vol. 16, no. 2, 1991, pp. 243–62.
113. Walker, R.B.J. 'State Sovereignty and the Articulation of Political Space/Time'. *Millennium: Journal of International Studies,* vol. 20, no. 3, 1991, pp. 445–61.
114. Walker, R.B.J. *Inside/Outside: International Relations as Political Theory.* Cambridge University Press, Cambridge, 1992.
115. Weber, Cynthia 'Reconsidering statehood: examining the sovereignty/intervention boundary'. *Review of International Studies,* vol. 18, no. 3, 1992, pp. 199–216.
116. Weber, Max *The Protestant Ethic and the Spirit of Capitalism.* Unwin Hyman, London, 1989 (20th impression).

5 The end of international relations?

John W. Burton and Tarja Väyrynen

Over the past 15 years there have been major changes both in world society, and also, importantly, in theories and thinking about it.

The United Nations and changes in the world society

The most far-reaching change is the exponential increase both in the number of states and also in other separate entities (ranging from collectivities or sets of individuals to international coalitions and organizations) that make up the world society [10, 26]. When the United Nations was formed in 1945 there were some 50 member states. Now there are more than three times as many.

Even so, many ethnic and other identity groups feel unrepresented by the state authorities that claim jurisdiction over them. In due course these new entities will challenge the legitimacy of the United Nations if it and its members fail to adjust to these altering circumstances. The United Nations [79, 89, 81] is an organization of states, comprising those that were formed as a result of frontier expansion and, in more recent times, those formed as the result of the end of colonialism and the establishment of independent states.

However formed, most existing states contain several different tribal, religious, ethnic or other identity groups, each of which (for reasons to be discussed) seeks its own recognition and autonomy [41]. Thus there is now a priority, shared by almost all, for UN members to work together to preserve their present constitutions and boundaries against secession movements and the internal conflicts that are engendered when secession is resisted.

Demands for autonomy

Much traditional thought exhibits an inherent assumption that societies are integrated social and political units, and if they are not, then authorities must make them so. Thus race and culture should not prevent societies from being integrated: multi-ethnic and multi-cultural societies should not be treated as special cases. This view, however, has not attached sufficient importance to ethnic and cultural differences, the sense of insecurity experienced by minorities and consequent demands for autonomy [21]. Moreover, the commitment to preserving integration has led to extreme measures. Cyprus, an island divided by war when all attempts at unification failed, has had UN peace-keeping forces for three decades whose presence is based on the assumption that the two factions in this former state and member of the UN will one day be brought together. If the *de facto* position had been accepted years ago and two separate autonomies recognized, they could have been helped at far less cost to work out positive functional arrangements between them [52]. Problems in Europe, Africa and Asia persist because such defensive reactions to demands for autonomy have become a norm in the global society.

Examples such as Cyprus and Northern Ireland demonstrate that the ideology of an integrated nation-state is too restrictive, and that it may prevent conflict resolution based on an alternative view of integration through separation. Integration does not inevitably preserve cultural and consensual values. Often the opposite is the case. Given the failure of integration, therefore, it can be argued that separation promotes a sense of security from which subsequently there can be cooperative transactions in areas of common interest. Functional arrangements, which are negotiated by officials who act as specialists in respect of particular administrative areas, are usually more efficient and professional than arrangements made by political representatives operating in an adversarial structure. Since this type of functional relationship does not impinge on ethnic issues, it can promote cooperation in common problems [23, 20, 53, 72, 73].

The heritage of colonialism

Why are demands for autonomy resisted? Defensive reactions have their historical roots in colonialism. When colonialism ended, the new authorities claimed and defended the colonial boundaries which they had inherited. While they themselves had sought independence, they were not prepared to grant it to minorities (and sometimes weaker majorities) within their territories. Thus the Organization of African Unity laid down that existing political boundaries should be maintained. But these had been based on colonial expansionism, rather than on the preserves of tribal or ethnic entities, and many political boundaries cut through such natural boundaries. These post-colonial authorities are now under threat just as the former colonial powers were, a threat made possible by new forms of communication and the general availability of weapons.

From another point of view, however, many post-colonial authorities are under threat because they are not legitimized, that is, their authority is not derived from those over whom it is exercised, even though the authorities may be 'legal'. It has often been the case that authorities recognized as legal have difficulty in maintaining effective control without the employment of at least some force. This is particularly the case in multi-ethnic and culturally divided societies where legal authority cannot always exercise political control over all peoples and, therefore, employs force. Legitimized relationships, on the other hand, stress the reciprocal nature of relations with authorities, the support given in return for the services they render and respect for legal norms when these are legitimized norms. An erosion of authority – that is, a challenge to effective control – is, therefore, a symptom and precondition of conflict [18, 20, 22].

Post-colonial defensive positions cannot be maintained in the longer term. There will be hundreds of new autonomies. But because there is still a consensus among existing states that boundaries should be preserved, little thought has been given to the forms these autonomies might take: separate nations (the Czech Republic and Slovakia), autonomies with some special functional relationships with previous authorities (French Canadians), or some other. South Africa is struggling to find an alternative to the one-person–one-vote definition of democracy which the more numerous ANC understandably demands. The end result (after much violence), must be, as in Cyprus, Sri Lanka and elsewhere, some constitutional means of satisfying the demands of minorities for separate identity and recognition. A minority status in a legislature, or even a veto provision, does not necessarily do this, as the Cyprus experience demonstrates.

Diplomacy

There are many far-reaching consequences of the global changes in the number of units in the international system. Given some hundreds of separate nations or autonomies of one kind or another, old forms of diplomacy in which representatives are exchanged become impossible, especially for small entities. What should have happened years ago when communications made possible a dramatic change in the relationships among countries must now happen: direct communication between authorities and an end to costly 'diplomatic representatives' abroad. This will have many advantages. It will help small autonomies to free themselves from the military, intelligence and other subversive influences that larger units have been able to exercise over smaller ones through the activities of persons who are misleadingly given the title of diplomatic representatives. Larger units may, however, resist changes in the forms of diplomacy because small entities benefit more than the big ones from direct communication between authorities.

Indeed, these developments are already beginning to eliminate the power approach to international relations. There must be far greater recognition of values attached to independence and to cultural requirements. These could include forms of protection of industries designed to promote diversity. The

United States' 'new world order', in which smaller members are required to adopt policies that happen to suit the larger ones even though these larger ones do not in fact adopt them, will not be able to withstand the drive for independence and development that is now under way [60].

Domestic policies

A second major change in the world society is domestic in origin. Galbraith [46] has described the 'culture of contentment' and its consequences. Members of the global society, whatever developmental status they might have, will experience increasing violence as a result of domestic policies (such as privatization, de-regulation, support to private enterprise at the expense of the wider community in times of recession) which favour the 'middle-class' and ignore the 'under-class'. Let us note that both of these terms can be applied internationally as well as domestically, implying higher levels of global conflict and violence. Indeed, it is becoming clear that in this and other respects international relations and foreign policies are a spill-over of domestic policies. Domestic policies, in turn, reflect political structures and management of political affairs. Moreover, domestic system failings and their political manifestations are a symptom of a failure to satisfy human needs such as identity and participation and of a lack of legitimization of authority [23]. Unless the culture of contentment is eliminated domestically and internationally, societies and the global society will become more and more disrupted, finally threatening the contented and civilization generally. To the extent that war is triggered by domestic problems, this culture of contentment represents a major threat to world peace.

The inadequacy of the power frame

This brings us to the third change, the change in theories and in thinking about IR. The power frame, once described as 'political realism', must now be seen as wholly unrealistic and policies based on it as seriously dysfunctional. Military defeats of great powers by small powers have shown that there are influences at work more powerful than economic and military power [66]. Since theoretical and intellectual frames are, to some degree, self-fulfilling and self-perpetuating, they help to create the reality with which we have to deal. For example, if we accept the power frame, we select empirical data which serve it and, moreover, reject data which challenge the frame [11]. The power frame has led to dysfunctional policies because it has not taken into account human attributes and the behavioural reasons why conflicts exist.

In recent histories of Australian military and diplomatic affairs [40, 49, 68] authors adopted a power framework, for they traced out in detail the prolonged diplomatic negotiations that led to fighting 'rebels' in Malaysia and to the Vietnam war. But these same historians had difficulty reporting an alternative point of view which had been canvassed some years earlier. They referred to it, as if in passing, as a somewhat strange and ill-informed approach. It was an approach which assumed that what had happened in Indonesia, Malaysia, and Indo-China was evidence of post-colonial, and post-Japanese occupation independence movements. They offered neither an expansionist threat nor, as independence movements, a Communist threat, since they would resist both Western and Eastern intervention.

Events have proved this perspective to be valid. Vietnam and Korea demonstrated the existence of a 'power' far greater than military and economic power. But it still seems difficult for those within a power frame to interpret empirical data accordingly. The Iraq war was fought as a result of interpretations of data within this same power frame. A senior State Department official confessed total surprise by the need for war, having assumed that threat and deterrence would deter. There seemed to be no knowledge of, or understanding of, the ethnic and associated problems facing Iraq and the consequences of past great-power interventions in the region.

In science, as Kuhn [61] has noted, there is, at any time, a wide professional consensus. However, paradigms change: a switch between paradigms takes place through intellectual revolutions when situations occur that clearly cannot be explained within an existing intellectual frame. In terms of theory formation and hypothesis testing, Peirce [64] has argued, unlike Popper [75] and Lakatos [62], that the original personal hypothesis of the investigator is of important scientific significance. According to Peirce, even the most tentative hypothesis or conjecture is selected by a rational procedure. His approach, called abduction or retroduction, emphasizes the need to go back and find out how hypotheses have been reached. This is important, for rarely can there be realistic testing in politics. Thus, the original personal hypothesis, and the deductions flowing from it, are fundamental for the behavioural sciences.

The need for a shift in thinking

The power frame is of necessity giving way to a frame that takes into account human attributes that power politics always ignored. Independence movements, the need for ethnic recognition, like problems of street gangs, cannot be contained. There are human elements here that have to be addressed both at the local and international level.

However, even at the local level, academics and officials find it difficult to move from a power frame that ignores all behavioural elements to one which includes the human needs and drives that lead to conflict. They do not seem to be able to take into account the costs and consequences of ignoring these human elements. Unemployment, alienation, an absence of adequate and relevant educational opportunities, and other conditions that deny identity do not fit into the traditional power frame that requires people to adapt to institutions and not the other way around. Even psychiatrists, having no influence on the social environment, are primarily concerned with helping people to adjust to the institutions and norms of society.

Traditional behavioural disciplines cannot cope with these emerging circumstances. Economics is now seen as destructive of societies when theories and policies, designed to maintain existing institutions and the 'culture of contentment', lead to unemployment, poverty, violence and social disruption. It would suit developed economies if there were no tariffs; but protection could well be important to less-developed economies as a means of promoting diversity and quality of life. Political science, in its defence of outmoded concepts and institutions, again is oriented towards the defence of the powerful: 'democracy' is defined as one-person–one-vote, and adversarial party parliamentary systems are the advocated processes, even in societies in which there are minorities not thereby represented.

Human needs

What would the move from the power frame to a frame which takes into account human attributes mean? Many scholars have argued that greater emphasis has to be paid to the individual and to personal needs such as identity, recognition and participation [13, 22, 27, 30, 32, 38, 45, 47, 48, 63, 67, 78]. As Sites [77] has noted, it is the individual usually acting through an identity group who has effective power, not authorities. Thus, the focus needs to be shifted from the state as a unit of analysis to the individual as purposeful actor [1, 2]. Such a new paradigm or intellectual frame takes as its starting-point human needs and their satisfaction: there are needs of individual development and control that will be pursued, regardless of consequences. The integration of multi-ethnic societies often means that the underlying needs and values are submerged by majority (and sometimes minority) dominance and control. In some rare cases the higher valued human needs are to a large degree satisfied and are not, therefore, seen to be in competition with nationalism. Once altered circumstances threaten those more fundamental needs, loyalty is to the identity group, not to the state, and needs will be pursued even at the cost of social disruption and personal disorientation. However, conflict is not inevitable because the needs being pursued are not necessarily in short supply.

It is important to differentiate between interests, values and needs. Interests are negotiable, can be bargained over, can be altered and traded. Values are cultural and are less subject to change and negotiation. Needs, however, are not for trading. No power bargaining, no judicial processes, no mediation, no negotiation techniques can alter the importance attached to needs. Therefore, traditional means of conflict settlement may be appropriate when only interests are at stake; but they are unlikely to be relevant or effective when needs are at issue. This is a reconceptualization of conflict, and it has implications for conflict resolution which copes with failed institutions, processes and policies. In other words, conflict settlement needs to be differentiated from resolution [5, 7, 8]. For example, 'Alternative Dispute Resolution' is an alternative to court procedures but not an alternative in basic approaches since it works at the level of interests, not needs. Similarly, negotiations to reduce levels of armaments are not an alternative to discredited deterrence strategies [16, 28].

Conflict resolution and problem-solving

One response to failed institutions, processes and policies has been described in the evolving literature on conflict resolution and problem-solving [3, 4, 14, 19, 25, 50, 69, 70, 71]. This literature adopts a problem-solving approach which is analytical, in which the non-judgemental and neutral third party assists, but does not put forward proposals, and in which options that satisfy both parties are explored. Necessarily, these are inter-active processes that enable accurate definitions of situations, and reliable assessments of costs and consequences of policies, before decisions are taken [15, 33, 34, 35, 36, 37, 42, 43, 44, 53, 54, 55, 57, 58, 59, 65, 82]. It is a literature that cuts across all social levels and all disciplines [17, 38, 39, 76, 83]. It implies the need to adjust existing adversarial institutions, such as courts and party-political parliamentary systems, and to ensure an analytical approach to problem-solving. It implies, therefore, a radical change in education and in training in management and in decision-making skills [29, 56].

The shift from conflict settlement to resolution also implies conflict prevention [20] which is concerned with longer-term policy rather than with procedures. There is the same costing of options to be assessed as in facilitated conflict resolution but in different time-frames. In prevention there is the same problem of parties and issues, but in this case the parties are not specific ones, but total societies, and the issues are the far broader issues of common good and of political interests and ideologies. Prevention, doing something about problems before they cause conflict, presupposes prediction. When we look to prediction as a step toward provention, we are involved in discovering the causal factors that must be dealt with. The knowledge of what to look for, the discovery of what conditions provoke the behaviour to be prevented, require an adequate theory of human and societal behaviour, including a reliable theory of conflict and conflictual behaviour. Needs theory is vital because it provides us with an explanation of societal behaviour in general and, in particular, of conflictual behaviour. It provides us, therefore, with the basis of prediction. Needs theory that directs attention to the need to adjust systems to people, rather than the other way around, provides a predictive base that points to the necessity to alter environments and conditions as the means of provention.

The evolution of conflict resolution, problem-solving and conflict prevention theories and practices is not stimulated by some well-meaning intent or belief system. It is an inevitable development once the real political realities are included in decision-making, in particular the human needs that give rise to protest, rebellion, secession and violence. There can be no power outcome to ethnic conflicts or to management conflicts that stem from a failure to acknowledge and cater to human needs. The future of civilization is at stake. No amount of military power can contain drives toward the fulfilment of human needs of identity and recognition and the enduring security of these goals.

Future of international relations

The question that must be posed is: what ought the purpose or goal of IR to be? Presumably the answer to this question is the exploration of approaches, institutions and policies that avoid conflict which destroys peoples, the environment and scarce resources, and positively, through productive relationships, promotes the quality of life [6]. If this definition of goals were accepted, then what would be the content of the subject?

There are four separate areas: the history of thought, and in particular recent paradigm shifts; contemporary theory, with a focus on the shift from an institutional frame to a behavioural one that is now required in all social disciplines; means of dealing with ethnicity and related problems inherited from the past; and national foreign economic and political policies, and defence policies, including the ways in which all are influenced and determined by domestic considerations [9, 12, 31, 51, 74].

With the possible exception of the first, none of these areas can be dealt with as though IR was a separate subject: they all touch on political philosophy generally and on political science. Conflict resolution has developed as a separate discipline, but that is only because other behavioural disciplines ignored the human factor. Once the human factor is incorporated into thinking, conflict resolution should be phased out. So, too, perhaps should IR be phased out. As countries become identity units and not nation-states, the study of their nature and of their relationships would necessarily be part of all other disciplines. The training and study that is required is in decision-making but within a behavioural and problem-solving frame. Such training and research applies to all system levels: decision-making at the industrial level and decision-making at the international level are no different.

Bibliography

1. Alger, C.F. 'Bridging the Micro and the Macro in International Relations Research'. *Alternatives*, vol. 10, no. 3, Winter 1984–5, pp. 319–44.
2. Alger, C.F. 'Role of People in the Future Global Order'. *Alternatives*, vol. 4, no. 2, 1978, pp. 233–62.
3. Avruch, K. and Black, P.W. 'A Generic Theory of Conflict Resolution'. *Negotiation Journal*, vol. 3, no. 1, 1987, pp. 87–100.
4. Avruch, K. and Black, P.W. 'Ideas of Human Nature in Contemporary Conflict Resolution Theory'. *Negotiation Journal*, vol. 6, no. 3, 1990, pp. 221–8.
5. Azar, E.E. *The Management of Protracted Social Conflict*. Aldershot, Dartmouth and Brookfield, Gower, 1990.
6. Azar, E.E. 'Peace Amidst Development: A Conceptual Agenda for Conflict and Peace Research'. *International Interactions*, vol. 6, no. 2, 1979, pp. 123–43.

7. Azar, E.E. and Burton, J.W. (eds) *International Conflict Resolution: Theory and Practice*. Brighton, Wheatsheaf and Boulder, Lynne Rienner, 1986.
8. Azar, E.E. and Chung In Moon 'Managing Protracted Social Conflicts in the Third World: Facilitation and Development Diplomacy'. *Millennium: Journal of International Studies*, vol. 15, no. 3, 1986, pp. 393–406.
9. Banks, M. 'Bucking the System: A Peace Researcher's Perspective on the Study of International Relations' in H.C. Dyer and L. Mangasarian (eds) *The Study of International Relations: The State of the Art*. London, The Macmillan Press (in association with *Millennium: Journal of International Studies*), 1989, pp. 366–74.
10. Banks, M. (ed.) *Conflict in World Society, A New Perspective on International Relations*. Brighton, Wheatsheaf and New York, St. Martin's Press, 1984.
11. Banks, M. 'The International Relations Discipline: Asset or Liability for Conflict Resolution?' in E.E. Azar and J.W. Burton (eds) *International Conflict Resolution, Theory and Practice*. Sussex, Wheatsheaf Books and Boulder, Lynne Rienner, 1986, pp. 5–27.
12. Banks, M. 'Where Are We Now?'. *Review of International Studies*, vol. 11, no. 3, 1985, pp. 215–33.
13. Bay, C. 'Politics and Pseudopolitics: A Critical Evaluation of Some Behavioral Literature'. *The American Political Science Review*, vol. LIX, no. 1, 1965, pp. 39–51.
14. Bendahmane, D.B. and McDonald, J.W. (eds) *Perspectives on Negotiation, Four Case Studies and Interpretations*. Washington, DC, Foreign Service Institute, US Department of State, 1986.
15. Bercovitch, J. *Social Conflicts and Third Parties: Strategies of Conflict Resolution*. Boulder, Westview Press, 1984.
16. Berman, M.R. and Johnson, J.E. (eds) *Unofficial Diplomats*. New York, Columbia University Press, 1977.
17. Blake, R.R., Shepard, H.A. and Mouton, J.S. *Managing Intergroup Conflict in Industry*. Houston, Gulf Publishing Company, 1964.
18. Burns, J.M. 'Wellsprings of Political Leadership'. *The American Political Science Review*, vol. LXXI, no. 1, 1977, pp. 266–75.
19. Burton, J.W. *Conflict and Communication: The Use of Controlled Communication in International Relations*. London, Macmillan, 1969.
20. Burton, J.W. *Conflict: Resolution and Provention*. London, Macmillan, 1990.
21. Burton, J.W. *Dear Survivors*. London, Frances Pinter, 1982.
22. Burton, J.W. *Deviance, Terrorism and War*. New York, St. Martin's Press and Oxford, Martin Robertson, 1979.
23. Burton, J.W. *Global Conflict: The Domestic Sources of International Crisis*. Brighton, Wheatsheaf and College Park, Center for International Development, University of Maryland, 1984.
24. Burton, J.W. *Peace Theory: Preconditions of Disarmament*. New York, Alfred A. Knopf, 1962.
25. Burton, J.W. *Resolving Deep-Rooted Conflict, A Handbook*. London and New York, University Press of America, 1987.
26. Burton, J.W. *World Society*. Cambridge, Cambridge University Press, 1972.
27. Burton, J.W. (ed.) *Conflict: Human Needs Theory*. London, Macmillan and New York, St. Martin's Press, 1990.
28. Burton, J.W. and Dukes, F. *Conflict: Practices in Management, Settlement and Resolution*. London, Macmillan and New York, 1990.
29. Burton, J.W. and Rubenstein, R. 'Courts, Alternative Dispute Resolution and Conflict Resolution'. *Paradigms*, vol. 2, no. 1, 1988, pp. 56–9.

30. Burton, J.W. and Sandole, D.J.D. 'Generic Theory: The Basis of Conflict Resolution'. *Negotiation Journal*, vol. 2, no. 4, 1986, pp. 333–44.
31. Burton, J.W. and Dukes, F. (eds) *Conflict: Readings in Management and Resolution*. London, Macmillan, 1990.
32. Coate, R.A. and Rosati, J.A. (eds) *The Power of Human Needs in World Society*. Boulder and London, Lynne Rienner, 1988.
33. Cohen, S.P., Kelman, H.C., Miller, F.D. and Smith, B.L. 'Evolving Intergroup Techniques for Conflict Resolution: An Israeli-Palestinian Pilot Workshop'. *Journal of Social Issues*, vol. 33, no. 1, 1977, pp. 165–89.
34. de Reuck, A. 'Controlled Communication: Rationale and Dynamics'. *The Human Context*, vol. VI, no. 1, 1974, pp. 64–80.
35. de Reuck, A. 'A Theory of Conflict Resolution by Problem-Solving'. *Man, Environment, Space and Time*, vol. 3, no. 1, 1983, pp. 53–69. (Also in J.W. Burton and F. Dukes (eds) *Conflict: Readings in Management and Resolution*. London, Macmillan, 1990, pp. 183–98.)
36. Diamond, L. and McDonald, J.W. (eds) *Multitrack Diplomacy: A System Guide and Analysis*. Grinnell, Iowa Peace Institute, 1991.
37. Doob, L.W. (ed.) *Resolving Conflict in Africa: The Fermeda Workshop*. New Haven and London, Yale University Press, 1970.
38. Doyal, L. and Gough, I. *A Theory of Human Needs*. London, Macmillan, 1991.
39. Dryzek, J.S. *Discursive Democracy: Politics, Policy, and Political Science*. Cambridge, Cambridge University Press, 1990.
40. Edwards, P.G. *Crises & Commitments: The Politics and Diplomacy of Australia's Involvement in Southeast Asian Conflicts 1948–1965*. London and North Sydney, Allen Unwin in Association with the Australian War Memorial, 1992.
41. Enloe, C. *Ethnic Conflict and Political Development*. Boston, Little, Brown and Company, 1973.
42. Fisher, R.J. 'Third Party Consultation: A Method for the Study and Resolution of Conflict'. *Journal of Conflict Resolution*, vol. XVI, no. 1, 1972, pp. 67–94.
43. Fisher, R.J. 'Third Party Consultation as a Method of Intergroup Conflict Resolution, A Review of Studies'. *Journal of Conflict Resolution*, vol. 27, no. 2, 1983, pp. 301–34.
44. Fisher, R.J. and Keashly, L. 'The Potential Complementarity of Mediation and Consultation within a Contingency Model of Third Party Intervention' in Special Issue of *Journal of Peace Research*, vol. 28, no. 1, 1991, pp. 29–42.
45. Fitzgerald, R. (ed.) *Human Needs and Politics*. Oxford and New York, Pergamon Press, 1977.
46. Galbraith, J.K. *The Culture of Contentment*. Boston, Houghton Mifflin Company and London, Sinclair-Stevenson, 1992.
47. Galtung, J. 'Twenty-Five Years of Peace Research: Ten Challenges and Some Responses'. *Journal of Peace Research*, vol. 22, no. 2, 1985, pp. 141–58.
48. Galtung, J. 'Violence, Peace, and Peace Research'. *Journal of Peace Research*, vol. 6, no. 3, 1969, pp. 167–91.
49. Grey, J. *A Military History of Australia*. Cambridge, Cambridge University Press, 1990.
50. Groom, A.J.R. 'No Compromise: Problem-Solving in a Theoretical Perspective'. *International Social Science Journal*, vol. XLIII, no. 1, 1991, pp. 77–86.
51. Groom, A.J.R. 'Paradigms in Conflict: The Strategist, the Conflict Researcher and the Peace Researcher'. *Review of International Studies*, vol. 14, no. 2, 1988, pp. 97–115.

52. Groom, A.J.R. 'The Process of Negotiation: 1974–1993' in C.H. Dodd (ed.) *The Political, Social and Economic Development of Northern Cyprus*. Huntingdon, Eothen Press, 1993, pp. 15–45.
53. Groom, A.J.R. and Taylor, P. (eds) *Functionalism: Theory and Practice in International Relations*. London, University of London Press, 1975.
54. Hill, B. 'An Analysis of Conflict Resolution Techniques, From Problem-Solving Workshop to Theory'. *Journal of Conflict Resolution*, vol. 26, no. 1, 1982, pp. 109–38.
55. Hoffman, M. 'Third-Party Mediation and Conflict-Resolution in the Post-Cold War World' in J. Baylis and N.J. Rengger (eds) *Dilemmas of World Politics*. Oxford, Clarendon Press, 1992, pp. 261–86.
56. Kelman, H.C. 'On the History and Development of Peace Research: Personal Reflections' in J. Nobel (ed.) *The Coming of Age of Peace Research*. Groningen, Styx Publications, 1991, pp. 25–37.
57. Kelman, H.C. 'The Problem-Solving Workshop in Conflict Resolution' in R.L. Merritt (ed.) *Communication in International Politics*. Chicago, University of Illinois Press, 1972, pp. 168–204.
58. Kelman, H.C. and Cohen S.P. 'The Problem-Solving Workshop: A Social-Psychological Contribution to the Resolution of International Conflicts'. *Journal of Peace Research*, vol. XIII, no. 2, 1976, pp. 79–90.
59. Kelman, H.C. and Cohen, S.P. 'Reduction of International Conflict: An Interactional Approach' in W.G. Austin and S. Worchel (eds) *The Social Psychology of Intergroup Relations*. Monterey, Brooks/Cole Publishing Company, 1979, pp. 288–303.
60. Kostakos, G., Groom, A.J.R., Morphet, S. and Taylor, P. 'Britain and the New UN Agenda: Towards Global Riot Control?'. *Review of International Studies*, vol. 17, no. 1, 1991, pp. 95–105.
61. Kuhn, T.S. *The Structure of Scientific Revolutions*. Chicago and London, University of Chicago Press, 1970, second edition.
62. Lakatos, I. and Musgrave, A. (eds) *Criticism and the Growth of Knowledge*. Cambridge, Cambridge University Press, 1970.
63. Lederer, K. (ed.) *Human Needs: A Contribution to the Current Debate*. Cambridge, MA, Oelgeschlager, Lager, Gunn & Hain & Königstein/Ts, Verlag Anton Hain, 1980.
64. Levi, I. 'Induction as Self Correcting According to Peirce' in D.H. Mellor (ed.) *Science, Belief, and Behaviour*. Cambridge and New York, Cambridge University Press, 1980, pp. 127–40.
65. McDonald, J.W. and Bendahmane, D.B. (eds) *Conflict Resolution: Track Two Diplomacy*. Washington DC, Foreign Service Institute, US Department of State, 1987.
66. Mack, A.J. 'Why Big Nations Lose Small Wars'. *World Politics*, vol. XXVII, no. 2, 1975, pp. 175–200.
67. Maslow, A.H. *Motivation and Personality*. New York, Harper & Row, 1987, third edition.
68. Milner, A.C. and Wilson, T. (eds) *Australian Diplomacy: Challenges and Options for the Department of Foreign Affairs*. Canberra, Australian Institute of International Affairs, 1986.
69. Mitchell, C.R. 'Classifying Conflicts: Asymmetry and Resolution'. *The Annals of the American Academy of Political and Social Science*, vol. 518, 1991, pp. 23–38.
70. Mitchell, C.R. *Peacemaking and the Consultant's Role*. Farnborough, Hampshire, Gower, 1981.

71. Mitchell, C.R. *The Structure of International Conflict.* London, Macmillan and New York, St. Martin's Press, 1989.
72. Mitrany, D.A. *The Functional Theory of Politics.* London, Martin Robertson, 1975.
73. Mitrany, D.A. *Working Peace System.* Chicago, Quadrangle Books, 1966.
74. Olson, W.C. and Groom, A.J.R. *International Relations Then and Now: Origins and Trends in Interpretation.* London, Routledge, 1992.
75. Popper, K.R. *The Poverty of Historicism.* London, Routledge & Kegan Paul, 1960 and New York, Harper & Row, 1977.
76. Sandole, D.J.D. and Sandole-Staroste, I. (eds) *Conflict Management and Problem Solving: Interpersonal to International Applications.* London, Frances Pinter and New York, New York University Press, 1987.
77. Sites, P. *Control: The Basis of Social Order.* New York, Dunellen Publishing Co., 1973.
78. Springborg, P. *The Problem of Human Needs and the Critique of Civilisation.* London, George Allen & Unwin, 1981.
79. Taylor, P. and Groom, A.J.R. (eds) *International Institutions at Work.* London, Pinter and New York, St. Martin's Press, 1988.
80. Taylor, P. and Groom, A.J.R. (eds) *Global Issues in the United Nations' Framework.* Basingstoke, Macmillan, 1989.
81. Taylor, P. and Groom, A.J.R. *The United Nations and the Gulf War, 1990–91: Back to the Future.* London, The Royal Institute of International Affairs (RIIA Discussion Paper, no. 38), 1992.
82. *UNITAR Research Reports, no. 1.* L.W. Doob (ed.) 'Social Psychological Techniques and the Peaceful Settlement of International Disputes'. New York, UNITAR, 1970.
83. Wedge, B. 'A Psychiatric Model for Intercession in Intergroup Conflict'. *Journal of Applied Behavioral Science,* vol. 7, no. 6, 1971, pp. 733–61.

6 From world politics to global governance – a theme in need of a focus

A.J.R. Groom and Dominic Powell

In hindsight, the period around 1960 marks an evolution in world politics wherein the concept of global governance has become increasingly relevant. World politics concerned, and still concerns, issues which may touch all or substantial parts of the globe but do not necessarily so. The Second World War, for example, is rightly thus termed, but it was not a global war. Global governance concerns the identification and management of those issues which necessarily have an impact on all parts of the globe. The growth of issues of global governance is a characteristic of our times. But global governance has an amorphous quality so that there is, as yet, no conception of a whole. In short, global governance is a theme in need of a focus.

The growth of issues of global governance can be seen in a variety of clearly interactive dimensions which are not yet adequately conceptualized. It is evident, for example, that no part of the globe could escape from the consequences of a nuclear war since radioactive fallout or nuclear winter would afflict everyone everywhere. The global ramifications of a nuclear war became evident around 1960 after Sputnik heralded the age of space in military terms, and nuclear warheads were deliverable with high degrees of accuracy to any quarter of the globe.

It was much the same in the global economy. By 1960 both Western Europe and Japan had recovered from the ravages of the Second World War. New arrangements were necessary so that the global economy could be managed as a whole and the lessons of the 1930s learned. Hence the establishment of the OECD, which joined the IMF, the World Bank group and the GATT as the principal instruments of global economic governance; a governance which has now been extended to the former socialist economies.

Around 1960 the communications revolution began to make itself more keenly felt. Radio had long been a powerful political tool and it remained important, but the impact of television had begun to have an influence in a myriad of ways. Moreover, the advent of cheap mass transport on a global scale was such that not only were the middle classes of the North able to take advantage of the possibilities of greater mobility but also the poor of the South, as they began to migrate in increasing numbers towards Western Europe and North America. The reactions to these movements have been the piecemeal institution of a global *apartheid* where the principle of free movement is denied when people in their masses are able to take advantage of it. Restrictive entry to Britain for Commonwealth citizens began in 1962. The door to the United States had for long been partially closed.

Of the 51 founder member states of the United Nations, only a handful were African or Asian. Beginning with Ghana in 1957, the process of decolonization in Anglophone and Francophone Africa swept the continent except for its southern reaches. Likewise in Asia, after the independence of the sub-continent other areas achieved independence or political emancipation, often at fearful cost in life and resources. By the 1960s Asia was largely its own political master. The process was gentler in the Caribbean and the Pacific. Colonialism was dead in its 19th-century form, but structural domination was ever more evident – giving rise to demands for a New International Economic Order, the quest for which enlivened global politics in the 1960s and 1970s.

The 1960s also saw a heightened awareness of environmental questions and ecological issues. This period culminated in the widely discussed studies of the Club of Rome [40] and a major global environmental conference in Stockholm in 1972 under the auspices of the United Nations but with a highly significant participation of non-governmental actors [61]. Moreover, while the growth of a global system of transactions leading to an increased movement of goods, services, ideas and people had many beneficial effects, it also facilitated the spread, as well as the cure, of diseases. Smallpox was eliminated, but AIDS is a modern version of the Great Plague.

In this new world, where differences of degree were beginning to be conceptualized as differences of kind, the notion of common interest took on a new meaning. It was becoming increasingly evident that those who did not hang together would surely hang separately. There was a growing realization that an element of community interest was inseparable from self-interest. Moreover, if societal dues were not paid by the small and the weak, they could be excluded from societal benefits; but if they were not paid by the strong, the system would collapse. This raised issues of the global commons or collective goods [68]. For the study of IR, it took the subject back to its fundamentals. What was the basic unit of analysis? What was the global agenda? Was the world characterized by a harmony or conflict of global interests? This range of issues was encapsulated neatly by Cox [10] when he referred to the contemporary world as being post-Westphalian, post-hegemonic and post-globalization. If, as the empirical evidence suggests, Cox is correct, analysts must turn to theories of global and regional integration and disintegration, sovereignty and security, the environment and ecology, as well as to all manner of structural approaches as they seek to give a focus and content to a heightened need for global governance.

Integration theory, the European Community and the UN

In this volume's predecessor [36] these questions were broached timidly in the chapter on integration and disintegration. An effort was made to group the literature around the themes of intergovernmental cooperation, rebuilding the state system as in the EC, building beyond the state system, for example through transnational agreements, and by building down through various modes of subsidiarity or disintegration. This framework has been given fuller exposition in Groom and Taylor [24]. Taylor has addressed these conceptual issues in a major analysis of the EC and the UN [60], and Groom has done likewise in a monograph on the EC [23]. It is surprising that the now European Union (EU) has not excited a greater degree of theorization since it represents a major organized change in the existing state system from which lessons may be learned for global governance. Yet despite an heroic period of theorizing in the 1950s and 1960s led ably by scholars from the United States, the important changes in recent years in the Community such as the Single Act and the Treaty of Maastricht have not inspired a new age of theorizing. Birley and Mattli's [4] application of neo-functionalist theory to the European Court, some of the essays in Kelstrup [29], Sbragia's study [58] and Keohane and Hoffmann's volume [31] are informed by theory and worthy of note. On issues of natural resources and the environment, Young combines a perceptive conceptual analysis fused with empirical research in his analytical application of regime theory [69].

Descriptive studies of the UN are beyond the remit of this volume. However, some writers have raised the question of the UN system as a means of global governance. Bertrand, a former member of the UN's Joint Inspection Unit, has made good use of his experience, first in producing a major report on the UN system [62], and then in the forward-looking essay which calls for a Third Generation World Organization which would be part of a programme for peace, broadly defined [3]. It is not surprising that some veteran WOMPers (World Order Models Project) – Falk, Kim and Mendlovitz [18] – have also addressed such questions in a collection of 41 republished essays. These reflect their concern with world order values including social justice, the environment, disarmament and participatory processes in global decision-making. One of the late Evan Luard's [37] last books also deals with these issues.

Most of these writings are evolutionary in tone as is a more general literature which is recognizably IR, whether it is overtly conceptual or more empirical. For example, Ferguson and Mansbach [20] explored *The State, Conceptual Chaos and the Future of International Relations Theory*, the history of which was chronicled from the 19th century in some detail by Olson and Groom [49] and in longer historical perspectives by Knutsen [34]. In their analysis of contemporary IR theory, Olson and Groom reflected the now conventional interparadigm debate of realists, pluralists and structuralists. This triptych was also used by McKinlay and Little [39] in their analysis of *Global Problems and World Order*. As the issues of global governance came to the fore, all began increasingly to be concerned with normative theory, a theme also treated by Brown [8]. The literature of the last five years has laid the groundwork for a discussion of global governance and world order as a principal item on the conceptual agenda for the mid-1990s.

Global governance and world order: sovereignty and security

The notion of global governance and world order does not yet have a clear focus in the IR literature. Aspects of it are treated in other chapters, notably those concerned with development, feminism, human rights and identity as well as other human needs. Such issues require to be moulded into a whole which also includes an analysis of contemporary ideas of sovereignty, security and global governance, defined in the broadest of terms, together with environmental issues. Beyond this there is the primarily empirical agenda of global riot control which deals with disarmament (both conventional and nuclear), refugees, migration, drugs, terrorism, development issues as well as many items on the environmental agenda. At present these are broached piecemeal, largely because there is no conceptual framework which would permit an holistic approach. The rest of this decade therefore bids fair to heralding a new period of heroic conceptualization.

It is hardly surprising that the question of the nature of sovereignty in the contemporary world should be a topic high both on the practical and academic agendas. From the practical point of view, the growth of complex interdependence and the issues of global governance point to the inadequacies of the concept both as a practical guide for policy and as an analytical tool. If the world was ever state-centric, it can hardly be so now, and governments find it difficult to provide those twin elements of legitimacy – security for their citizens and a stable economy – in the face of a turbulent world. Yet analytically the state system is still treated with great reverence by IR scholars.

The debate on whether the Treaty of Maastricht, and indeed the whole of the concept of European Union, transgresses the pristine purity of sovereignty can be answered with the response that it does and it does not. The chief characteristic of the EU is the joint management of pooled sovereignty by a consociation of governmental élites in the context of a process which is also building down by extending the principle of subsidiarity to regions, building across with transnational ties and building beyond through a network of association agreements linking the Union with all parts of the world. Such a process is not at all federal, but it does exemplify the way in which sovereignty must be reconsidered as it is transformed from the sovereign's command to the legitimized exercise of sectoral or regional authority.

It may well be that the conceptions of sovereignty exemplified by the European state system which emerged in its final modern form in the Treaty of Westphalia in 1648 are an anomaly. The previous Christian Commonwealth of Europe was an intriguing mixture of feudal lords, independent cities, bishoprics, petty princes, Holy Roman Empires and the like. Elsewhere in the world similar phenomena were evident, whether in pre-British and British India, the Ottoman Empire or the Chinese Middle Kingdom. We seem to be returning to such fructuous diversity. Jackson's book on *Quasi-States* [27] broaches, from a different point of view, its consequences.

It is, however, remarkable that the IR literature on sovereignty is not more plentiful. IR, as a discipline, was founded on the basic difference between intra-state and inter-state politics. If that distinction is found to be wanting then the disciplinary foundations of some conceptions of IR collapse and, with them, the university administrative structure. This is not a particular worry of those who espouse world society approaches, or structural approaches, but it is a serious threat for realists of all hues since sovereignty is a fundamental concept for their approach. Its now anomalous nature and the doubt regarding its appropriateness as the foundation for the discipline may inhibit them from writing about it. Nevertheless a good comprehensive survey of recent writing in this area has been provided by Onuf [47], and Walker [64, 65] has written provocatively on the subject in the historical context of the development of political theory.

The question of sovereignty is closely linked with that of security; IR was conceived from the beginning as being about the causes of war and the conditions of peace between states. In this sense world order and global governance have always been central issues. However, Booth's chapter suggests that the agenda is changing rapidly. Security is now seen as a much broader concept, perhaps best conceptualized in a context of world order and global governance. Dalby [12] has provided an extensive and good bibliography of books and articles, some well known, others less familiar, on the dilemmas of the post-Cold War security discourse.

The question of global governance has also excited some of the leading scholars of the senior generation. Falk [17] rejects 'Disneyland post-modernism' . . . 'for rooted Utopianism'. He follows those, such as Mishra, who earlier described non-alignment in terms similar to Falk's 'Highway D5', that is democracy, demilitarization, dealignment–depolarization, democratization and development. As one student put it, Falk is 'loopy, but trying not to be', in that he recognizes the inherent trip wires in being concerned with normative issues at a fundamental level. Rosenau finds the current trend a strong vindication of his earlier writing as he comments on *Turbulence in World Politics* in the context of change and continuity [55]. His contribution reflects a return to that multicentric world which, along with Burton and Mitrany, he was one of the first to identify and to conceptualize. Rosenau's judiciously chosen volumes edited with Czempiel [11, 54] are useful companion pieces. Finally, of the senior figures, North [46] has developed further his ideas of lateral pressure with its theory of war based on expansion, growth and conflict of interest. It is a conceptual framework that is intended to link four levels of analysis – the individual, the state, the international and the global. It serves, too, as a link to recent essays in peace research [63], many of them overtly normative. One fertile source for such issues is the journal *Alternatives*. But what of the new agenda, particularly that concerned with the environment and ecology?

The Environment and ecology

Much of the work on green issues consists of accounts of environmental diplomacy and assessments of how the negotiated initiatives are working. Benedick [2], Carroll [9], Matthews [38], Ostrom [50], Porter and Brown [53], Rowlands and Greene [57], and Young [69] are all concerned with environmental 'management' or regimes. Other literature on ecology goes further and calls into question whether the interstate system as it currently functions can address adequately the environmental and developmental crises of the contemporary world. The deep ecologists, especially, tend to see the crisis as the logical culmination of a series of wrongheaded institutionalized attitudes towards our interaction with the environment. They attack the modern state both directly (Bookchin [7, 6] – not so much a 'deep ecologist' as an anarchist 'social ecologist') and indirectly. The development–environment crises are closely linked and are treated by Adams [1], Daly and Cobb [13], Engel and Engel [15], Kothari [35], Nandy [45] and Pearce et al. [51]. A strong theme in both the green literature and the development literature is the inappropriateness of Western models of development not only for the underdeveloped world but for the planet as a whole.

The perceived seriousness of the environmental crisis and the development crisis, each with transboundary implications for neighbouring states both close and distant, is one factor stimulating reconceptualizations. Dalby [12], many of the WOMPers, as well as Klare and Thomas [33] all bring the environment into security. Increased concern with social movements lead some, for example Mendlovitz and Walker [41], to envisage a global civic culture of sorts, with grass-roots organizations leading the way. While serious problems are not being met by the state, others such as Walker [65, 66], Rosenau [54, 55] and Falk [17], are attempting to do something about them, not least at the analytical level.

Structural approaches

Deep ecology now has a growing prominence among the structural approaches to IR, but it is not alone. Political geography, as noted elsewhere, has returned to the mainstream and the economic approaches remain salient. Cox's [10] writing and his rehabilitation of Gramsci are seminal. Wallerstein's [68] recent excellent set of essays, Geopolitics and Geocultures, begins with a stimulating analysis of the lessons of the 1980s. On the other hand, the essays in Featherstone's volume on global culture [19] are critical of Wallerstein's world systems theory and emphasise research on ethnicity and subnationalisms. These themes are developed in Chapters 5 and 13, as well as in the excellent volume by Heraclides [25] and Bloom's stimulating analysis of linkages of personal identity, national identity and international relations [5].

Neo- or structural realists conceive global structure in political terms as the balance of power or global hegemonic leadership. They acknowledge that actors frequently have to take the political structure as given, but stress that it is manipulable by the actors in concert. Fundamental structuralists, on the other hand, acknowledge the autonomy and independence of structural factors. The neorealist position has been summarized cogently by the contributors to Keohane's [32] volume, and others have also insisted on the importance of *Bringing the State Back In* [16], although not convincingly since in their conception the state appears to be more a battlefield between contending social groups or a tool to be used by the victor than an autonomous independent actor. In the state-centric approach to global management, Kennedy's popular account of *The Rise and Fall of the Great Powers* [30] is an historical vulgarization of the power cycle which receives a political scientist's interpretation in Doran's [14] analysis of the new imperatives of high politics at this century's end. This suggests a consideration of long cycles of which George Modelski is the acknowledged master [42, 43, 44]. He has now fused cycles of world political leadership with economic cycles, while at the same time recognizing, if not incorporating, cultural factors. His analysis is open ended for our times, since he does not say that the decline of the United States will lead necessarily to a world war or that a new state must take up the reins of global leadership. Rather the cycle may evolve into a consortium in which leadership is exercised by different states or groupings in different dimensions without the catastrophic effects of a global war. Modelski's work and the parallel comments of Goldstein [21] and Rosecrance [56] offer an intriguing pathway to the future.

Conclusion

Where does the focus of all this lie? This survey of the global governance literature is necessarily eclectic since there is no clear thread uniting the notions of ecology, global issues and structural factors – geographical, political, economic and cultural – with questions of global governance. An unfortunate bifurcation between IR broadly defined and green politics has emerged. Moreover, it is vital to remember that at the centre of it all is the individual. Can we evolve adequate procedures for global governance that can accommodate individual human needs in a framework of global issues seen in long historical perspective? The challenge is great but if it is not met, the future will be bleak indeed.

Bibliography

1. Adams, W.M. *Green Development*. London, Routledge, 1990.
2. Benedick, Richard Elliot *Ozone Diplomacy: New Directions in Safeguarding the Planet*. Washington DC, WWF, 1991.
3. Bertrand, Maurice *The Third Generation World Organization*. Dordrecht, M Martinus Nijhoff, 1989.
4. Birley, Anne-Marie and Mattli, Walter 'Europe before the Court'. *International Organization*, vol. 47, no. 1, Winter 1993, pp. 41–76.

5. Bloom, William *Personal Identity, National Identity, and International Relations.* Cambridge, Cambridge University Press, 1990.
6. Bookchin, Murray *Remaking Society: Pathways to a Green Future.* Boston, South End, 1990.
7. Bookchin, Murray *The Ecology of Freedom.* Palo Alto, Cheshire, 1982.
8. Brown, Seyom *International Relationships in a Changing Global System.* Boulder, Westview, 1992.
9. Carroll, John E. (ed.) *International Environmental Diplomacy: the management and resolution of transfrontier environmental problems.* Cambridge, Cambridge University Press, 1990.
10. Cox, Robert *Production, Power and World Order: Social Forces in the Making of History.* New York, Columbia University Press, 1987.
11. Czempiel, Ernst-Otto and Rosenau, J. *Global Change and Theoretical Challenges: Approaches to World Politics for the 1990s.* Lexington, Lexington Books, 1989.
12. Dalby, Simon 'Security, Modernity, Ecology: The Dilemmas of Post-Cold War Security Discourse'. *Alternatives*, vol. 17, no. 1, Winter 1992, pp. 95–134.
13. Daly, H. and Cobb, J.B. *For the Common Good: Redirecting the Economy towards Community, the Environment and a Sustainable Future.* Boston, Beacon Press, 1989.
14. Doran, Charles F. *Systems in Crisis*, Cambridge, Cambridge University Press, 1991.
15. Engel, J. Robert and Engel Joan Gibb (eds) *Ethics of Environment and Development.* London, Belhaven, 1990.
16. Evans, Peter, Rueschemeyer, D. and Skocpol, T. (eds) *Bringing the State Back In.* Cambridge, Cambridge University Press, 1985.
17. Falk, R. *Explorations at the End of Time.* Philadelphia, Temple University Press, 1992.
18. Falk, R., Kim, S. and Mendlovitz, S. *The UN and a Just World Order.* Boulder, Westview, 1991.
19. Featherstone, Mike (ed.) *Global Culture: Nationalism, Globalization and Modernity.* London, Sage, 1991.
20. Ferguson, Yale H. and Mansbach, Richard W. *The State, Conceptual Chaos and the Future of International Relations Theory.* Boulder, Lynne Rienner, 1989.
21. Goldstein, Joshua *Long Cycles.* New Haven, Yale University Press, 1988.
22. Gosovic, Branislav *The Quest for World Environment Cooperation: The Case of the UN Global Monitoring System.* London, Routledge, 1992.
23. Groom, A.J.R. *The European Community in Context.* Canberra, Australian National University, 1992.
24. Groom, A.J.R. and Taylor, Paul (eds) *Frameworks for International Cooperation.* London, Pinter, 1990.
25. Heraclides, Alexis *The Self-determination of Minorities in International Politics.* London, Frank Cass, 1991.
26. Hurrell, Andrew and Kingsbury, Benedict (eds) *The International Politics of the Environment.* Oxford, Clarendon Press, 1992.
27. Jackson, Robert H. *Quasi-States: Sovereignty, International Relations and the Third World.* Cambridge, Cambridge University Press, 1990.
28. Käkönen, Jyrki *Perspective on Environmental Conflict and International Politics.* London, Pinter, 1992.
29. Kelstrup, Morten (ed.) *European Integration and Denmark's Participation.* Copenhagen, Copenhagen Political Studies Press, 1992.
30. Kennedy, Paul *Rise and Fall of the Great Powers.* London, Unwin Hyman, 1988.

31. Keohane, Robert O. and Hoffmann, Stanley (eds) *The New European Community*. Boulder, Westview, 1991.
32. Keohane, Robert (ed.) *Neorealism and its Critics*. New York, Columbia University Press, 1986.
33. Klare, Michael and Thomas, D.C. (eds) *World Security*. New York, St. Martin's Press, 1991.
34. Knutsen, Thorbjörn *A History of International Relations Theory*. Manchester and New York, Manchester University Press, 1992.
35. Kothari, R. *Rethinking Development: In Search of Humane Alternatives*. Delhi, Ajanta, 1989.
36. Light, Margot and Groom, A.J.R. (eds) *International Relations: A Handbook of Current Theory*. London, Pinter, 1985.
37. Luard, E. *International Society*, Basingstoke, Macmillan, 1990.
38. Matthews, Jessica Tuchman (ed.) *Preserving the Global Environment: The Challenge of Shared Leadership*. New York, W.W. Norton, 1990.
39. McKinlay, R.D. and Little, Richard *Global Problems and World Order*. London, Pinter, 1986.
40. Meadows, Donella H. *et al. The Limits to Growth*. London, Pan, 1974.
41. Mendlovitz, S. and Walker, R.B.J. (eds) *Towards a Just World Peace: Perspectives from Social Movements*. London, Butterworths, 1987.
42. Modelski, George *Long Cycles in World Politics*. London, Macmillan, 1988.
43. Modelski, George *Seapower in Global Politics 1494–1993*. London, Macmillan, 1988.
44. Modelski, George *Long Cycles*. Boulder, Lynne Rienner, 1987.
45. Nandy, Ashis *Science, Hegemony and Violence*. New Delhi, Oxford University Press, 1989.
46. North, Robert C. *War, Peace, Survival: Global Politics and Conceptual Synthesis*. Boulder, Westview, 1990.
47. Onuf, Nicholas Greenwood 'Sovereignty: Outline of a Conceptual History'. *Alternatives*, vol. 16, no. 4, Fall 1991, pp. 425–46.
48. Olsen, Mancur *The Logic of Collective Action*. Cambridge, Harvard University Press, 1971.
49. Olson, William C. and Groom, A.J.R. *International Relations Then and Now*. London, Routledge, 1992.
50. Ostrom, Elinor *Governing the Commons: The Evolution of Institutions for Collective Action*. Cambridge, Cambridge University Press, 1990.
51. Pearce, D., Markandya, A. and Barbier, E.B. *Blueprint for a Green Economy*. London, Earthscan, 1989.
52. Peterson, V. Spike (ed.) *Gendered States: Feminist (Re)Visions of International Relations Theory*. Boulder, Lynne Rienner, 1992.
53. Porter, Gareth and Brown, Janet Walsh *Global Environment Politics*. London, Westview, 1991.
54. Rosenau, J. and Czempiel, Ernst-Otto (eds) *Governance without Government: Order and Change in World Politics*. Cambridge, Cambridge University Press, 1992.
55. Rosenau, J. *Turbulence in World Politics: a Theory of Change and Continuity*. New York, Harvester Wheatsheaf, 1990.
56. Rosencrance, Richard 'Long cycle theory and International Relations'. *International Organization*, vol. 41, no. 2, Spring 1987, pp. 283–301.
57. Rowlands, Ian H. and Greene, Malory (eds) *Global Environmental Change and International Relations*. London, Macmillan, 1992.
58. Sbragia, Alberta *Europolitics*. Washington DC, Brookings, 1992.

59. Suganami, H. *The Domestic Analogy and World Order Proposals.* Cambridge, Cambridge University Press, 1989.
60. Taylor, Paul *International Organization in the Modern World.* London, Pinter, 1993.
61. Taylor, Paul and Groom, A.J.R. (eds) *Global Issues in the United Nations Framework.* London, Macmillan, 1989.
62. Taylor, Paul and Groom, A.J.R. (eds) *International Institutions at Work.* London, Pinter, 1988.
63. Väyrynen, R., Senghaas, D. and Schmidt, Christian (eds) *The Quest for Peace: Transcending Collective Violence and War Among Societies, Cultures and States.* London, Sage, 1987.
64. Walker, R.B.J. *Inside/Outside: international relations as political theory.* Cambridge, Cambridge University Press, 1993.
65. Walker, R.B.J. and Mendlovitz, Saul (eds) *Contending Sovereignties: Redefining Political Community.* Boulder, Lynne Rienner, 1990.
66. Walker, R.B.J. *One World, Many Worlds.* Boulder, Lynne Rienner, 1988.
67. Wallerstein, Immanuel *Geopolitics and Geoculture.* Cambridge, Cambridge University Press, 1991.
68. Wallerstein, Immanuel *Geopolitics and Geocultures: Essays on the Changing World Systems.* Cambridge, Cambridge University Press, 1991.
69. Young, Oran R. *International Cooperation: Building Regimes for National Resources and the Environment.* Ithaca, Cornell University Press, 1989.

Part 2
Partial theories in international relations

7 Foreign policy analysis
Margot Light

In some respects, Foreign Policy Analysis (FPA) is firmly within the realist paradigm. It assumes a state-centric international political system, and, although it acknowledges that there are other actors within that system, it primarily focuses on the transactions which take place between states or which concern, on one side at least, a government acting on behalf of the state. In other respects, however, FPA diverges from realism. Realists, for example, assume that the relations between states are motivated by the pursuit of power. Foreign policy analysts accept that power relations are important and that force (threatened, used or simply implicit) is a major instrument of foreign policy. But they are also interested in other types of relations and in other policy instruments. Moreover, while realists assume that the state is a unitary actor, many foreign policy analysts open up the 'black box' of the state to examine the various units that make up its decision-making apparatus. They believe that policy can often be explained by the way the units relate to one another. Finally, realists assume that the state is a rational actor, whereas rationality is a contested concept in FPA. Indeed, a great deal of FPA research is concerned with seeking an explanation for seemingly irrational foreign policy decisions.

Perhaps because FPA does not fit squarely within the realist, world society or structuralist paradigms, it is frequently criticized by IR theorists. This chapter will begin by examining and countering their criticisms. The discussion which follows concentrates almost entirely on work which has been published since 1985 (a discussion of earlier work can be found in [59]). For analytical convenience, the field has been divided into three categories: domestic politics, middle-range theories and comparative foreign policy (CFP), using part of a typology initially employed by Smith [137]. The chapter ends by considering tendencies which do not fall easily into any typology.

In defence of foreign policy analysis

It is not unusual to hear grumbling in academic departments that FPA is unworthy of the status of a compulsory subject for an IR degree. The nature

of the objection depends upon the interests of the complainant: 'grand'
theorists maintain that FPA is devoid of theory; it is simply diplomatic
history. Both diplomatic historians and IR traditionalists disagree,
complaining that foreign policy analysts concentrate on political process at
the expense of policy outcome and accusing them of 'scientism'.
Methodological purists, on the other hand, believe that FPA methodology
is insufficiently rigorous, while international system theorists argue that by
focusing on the inner workings of the state, foreign policy analysts get the
level of analysis wrong and study politics, not international relations.

An added complaint, not always *sotto voce*, is that theoretical research in
FPA relies heavily on American foreign policy for its empirical data – a
tribute, nevertheless, to the relatively easy accessibility of information about
American political processes and policy.

Foreign policy analysts have also become their own trenchant critics. Some
of their self-doubt arises from disappointment that the subject did not
produce the all-encompassing IR theory its early proponents assumed would
ensue if the 'black box' or 'billiard ball' was opened and investigated.
Others, influenced by the post-behavioural rejection of positivism, question
their early enthusiasm for quantitative methods, while many agree that
excessive concentration on processes taking place within the state has made
them underestimate the systemic constraints that limit the autonomy of
policy makers. These criticisms, self-criticisms and assessments of the
achievements of FPA can be found in articles and chapters discussing the
state of the art of IR or FPA [for example, Chapter 7 in 33, 56, 74, 136,
137].

Nevertheless, while FPA is not coterminous with IR, there could be no
IR without FPA. It would be difficult, for example, to envisage an
international *system* unless there were external relations. A system assumes
more than units enclosed by a boundary; it also presupposes that there are
interactions between the units. And the official relations that take place
between the units of the international system constitute foreign policy. FPA
is the study of those transactions, the domestic circumstances that produce
them, the effect on them of the system and its structures and their
influence on the system. Many of the theoretical issues which are raised in
this book are significant in part because of the effect that they have on
foreign policy.

As a subject of study, FPA is invaluable both because it is a 'bridging
discipline' [55, p. 1], connecting together the diverse issues that students deal
with under separate headings in other subjects, and because it translates
abstract theory into concrete problems. Furthermore, by concentrating on the
interface between the state and the state system, FPA links the micro level of
politics with the macro level of the international system. And, since it is
eclectic and interdisciplinary, it connects IR to other social sciences. Finally,
some of its insights have become part of the conventional discourse of IR,
and some of the questions it has been unable to answer have become the
more general puzzles of IR theory. FPA, therefore, continues to be taught
widely and research proliferates.

Domestic politics

Perhaps the most widely known conceptualization of how foreign policy decisions are made is bureaucratic politics. Allison's *Essence of Decision* [1] is the classic work in which this model, and the rational actor and organizational process models, is described. Few IR books have generated more debate or been the subject of more criticism. Yet many of Allison's original insights have become the truisms of FPA, terms which he coined have entered the IR vocabulary, and his work continues to provoke discussion. Allison's adaptation of the model to foreign policy decision-making has been questioned [56], his model has been tested [6], adapted [60, 91] and used by other scholars [89]. None of the adaptations have produced a single, definitive policy-making model, but they invariably produce interesting new insights into the way that decisions are made. Hilsman, for example, proposes a 'political process' model [60] to explain defence and foreign policy making. He suggests that although policy is made by a variety of people working through different institutions (power centres) with disparate motives and diverse views about means, these power centres share some goals. Thus conflict over policy is accompanied by persuasion, compromise and consensus building. He applies his model to seven different case studies, providing a useful investigation of American foreign policy in the process. Strong [145] compares Kissinger's academic views on bureaucracy with his behaviour during his years in office. Those who have forgotten the classical theories of bureaucracy will find Beetham's short book [5] very useful.

Continuing interest in the politics of competing bureaucracies and the attendant effect on foreign policy in the Allison mode has been paralleled by investigation of more general questions of the impact of domestic politics on foreign policy. The conventional belief was that the foreign policy of authoritarian states tends to be more predictable and stable and, at the same time, more flexible than that of democratic states in which publics are resistant to innovation but not averse to imposing sudden change on their governments. However, studies suggesting that public opinion is, for the most part, indifferent to foreign policy and that, in any case, even in a democracy foreign policy tends to be the business of the executive branch of government seemed to contradict the conventional view that authoritarian systems were 'better' at foreign policy. In the post-Cold War world, where more and more countries are switching from authoritarianism to democracy, the effect of domestic politics on foreign policy acquires more than mere theoretical significance: the conventional view suggests that the end of the Cold War will result in a less predictable international system and not just for the usual reason given – that a bipolar balance of power is more stable than a multipolar balance.

Recent studies on domestic politics and foreign policy [26, 42, 46, 91, 96, 119, 121] have been as inconclusive about the effects of democracy on foreign policy as earlier research. While the findings of the various contributors to Skidmore and Hudson's collection [134] suggest that domestic publics rarely play an important role in foreign policy formulation, the editors point out that even in cases where they are thought to be influential, it is extremely difficult to establish causality (would the policy have been adopted even if the societal group had not exerted pressure?) or to discover the relative importance of group influences compared to other factors affecting the choice of policy. Although the effect of interest groups on foreign policy continues to engage analysts [40], Hinckley (arguing that public opinion does have a perceptible influence on national security decisions) suggests that the information revolution has eroded the importance of interest groups: the flow of information direct to individuals has increased, and the function of interest groups to inform and aggregate opinion is consequently diminished [61]. Examining a longer period of history, Holmes [66] agrees that public opinion, in the form of foreign policy mood, is an important input into American foreign policy. Auerbach [2] looks at strategies employed by decision makers to win public support for 'turning point' decisions.

In a closely argued book defending the effects of democracy on foreign policy [112], Nincic defines a democratic foreign policy as one that reflects the preferences of the national community it is meant to serve and argues that the resultant policy of 'principled pragmatism' is likely to be stable and coherent. Nincic bases his argument entirely on the United States, but the change to democracy in East and Central Europe provides a number of opportunities to test his thesis. Unfortunately, East European democratization occurred too late to be included in the collection by Boyd and Hopple on political change and foreign policy [11]. When other foreign policy analysts turn their attention to the post-socialist world, however, they will be able to use the frameworks suggested by Hermann [54] and Holsti [67] or Goldmann's very complex theory of change and stability [41] to study domestic change and foreign policy re-orientation.

The freedom to choose one foreign policy action over another is affected not just by internal political structures and processes but also by the effects on the domestic political process of external constraints. As a result of the recognition that the number of conventional conflicts in the international system had increased rather than diminished since the invention of nuclear weapons, the geopolitical fatalism of nuclear deterrence (the belief that nuclear weapons rendered geography irrelevant) has been replaced by a renewed interest in geopolitics in recent years (see Chapter 12). Although much of the published work is interesting but only peripherally relevant to foreign policy analysts [116, 132], Parker's study of the geopolitics of domination [118] echoes the Sprouts' distinction between the operational and psychological environments and suggests how geopolitical factors might influence perceptions of the outside world. Sloan [135] argues that geopolitics has a 'conditioning influence' on US strategic policy since it affects the perceptions of decision makers. Douglas [in 117] proposes an agenda for the geographical investigation of inter-state conflict.

There are other external constraints on foreign policy that have little to do with geography. In a detailed empirical study, Geldenhuys compares the predicament of states that exist in enforced isolation from the international system [37], while Jackson [76] examines the prospects, and the consequences for the international system, of 'quasi-states', that is, states to whom the trappings of external sovereignty have been ascribed despite their lack of the usual features of internal sovereignty and legitimacy.

Middle-range theories

The psychological attributes of individual leaders and groups and the significance of perception have long been important aspects of FPA. Much of the recent work which falls into the category of middle-range theories continues this line of investigation. Useful surveys of past research on perception, personality and the effect of the psychology of groups on foreign policy appear in Singer and Hudson's collection of essays on political psychology [133].

Earlier work on leadership was concerned with the personality of individual leaders and this line of enquiry has continued [22, 26, 75, Chapter 5 in 133]. Hoffmann [62] argues that concentration on how structures shape policies may lead to an underestimation of the role of leadership. Post [120], on the other hand, is concerned with the mental and physical health of leaders and the effect of ill health on policy. To establish how the American presidency has evolved, Greenstein, a pioneer of studies of leadership, has made a comparative analysis of nine US presidents since 1933 [45]. But his attention, and that of other scholars in the field, has shifted to a more overtly normative concern with the way in which leaders can obtain the best advice from those that surround them.

Burke and Greenstein [15], for example, compare and contrast Eisenhower's decision not to intervene in Vietnam in 1954 with Johnson's 1965 decision to intervene. They conclude, rather surprisingly, that the former's formal advisory system worked rather better than the informal arrangements preferred by Johnson. They suggest that 'multiple advocacy' (a technique developed by Alexander George whereby advisers compete for their preferred options) can curb the negative effects of small group dynamics (for example, group think) and ameliorate defective advisory processes. Multiple advocacy can, however, produce paralysis of action resulting from too much choice. Moens, who has tested multiple advocacy on the foreign policy decision making of the Carter administration [106], maintains that the technique failed when Brzezinski became an actor rather than the organizer of the process. In other words, if multiple advocacy is to work, there must be a coordinator to help the decision maker choose among options. The late lamented Janis also became concerned about 'good' decision-making [52, 53], while Orbovich and Molnar [in 133] construct models of various advisory processes.

The phenomenon of foreign policy that has most preoccupied analysts is international crisis. Their primary normative concern is to establish how crisis can be avoided or at least managed to prevent escalation and war. Janis concentrates on 'good' decision-making, defined as 'vigilant problem solving', as the essential prerequisite [77], while George proposes seven operational principles of crisis management [38]. He links his analysis of inadvertent war (a war neither side wanted or expected) with the role that crisis management can play in preventing it, contrasting six successfully managed crises with five inadvertent wars. In an interesting and topical epilogue, he defines the second Gulf War as an inadvertent war and discusses why crisis management failed. Unlike Janis and George, Lebow does not believe that there is a key to crisis management or the achievement of national security, at least with regard to a nuclear crisis between the two superpowers [92]. He argues that as long as force structures, doctrines and targets remain unchanged, the best that can be expected is a reduction in crisis instability. He implies that the fact that nuclear catastrophe has been avoided is a matter of luck rather than management and Dixon [29] would certainly agree with his view. As Brecher and Wilkenfeld point out [12], however, in direct confrontation with the United States the Soviet Union almost always backed off, thereby reducing crisis instability. Since Lebow's three requirements for national security have now occurred, Janis's good decision-making and George's seven principles of crisis management have presumably acquired a new salience in American–Russian relations.

The International Crisis Behavior Project has produced a number of decision-making studies over the years that have become classics of FPA. The project is now complete, and the results have been published in three volumes. Two of the volumes [13] give profiles of the most crisis-active states between 1929 and 1979, summaries of 278 different crises and the major findings of the survey. The third [12] presents the findings of the project in an integrated and systematic form.

Whether or not they are dealing with a foreign policy crisis, what advisers advocate and what policy makers decide depend to a large extent on how they perceive their own countries and the outside world, as well as their perceptions of the past, the values they hold and how they process the information they receive. Foreign policy analysts have always distinguished between the psychological and the operational environments of decision-making. Recent studies, however, have turned to the problem of belief systems [98, 125] and ideology [20] and how they affect policy, the role of history in decision-making and whether and how decision makers learn and process information, whether from past history or from more recent experience.

It seems common sense that the past affects the way the present is perceived. After all, individuals could not learn unless their past experiences guided their responses. But analysts argue about the use, abuse and usefulness of history in foreign policy decision-making. Fry [34] argues that statesmen use history habitually as an aid. Hill [58] would not disagree, but he distinguishes among legacies from the past that have been so deeply internalized that they are ineradicable, those which, although profound, can still be transformed with difficulty and those from the less closely held past, which constrains choice in a more limited way. In *The Lessons of History* Howard [69] denies that history teaches any lessons, since 'the past is infinitely various' (p. 11). In a later essay, however, he argues that 'only a knowledge of the past enables us to fully understand the present' (p. 188). But the history of foreign policy is replete with examples of leaders learning the wrong lessons from history. Warning against easy analogies and insisting that presumptions must always be questioned, Neustadt and May [109] offer decision makers a primer on how to know the past.

Der Derian [27] would probably reject their primer since he argues that traditional theorists (by which he means those who are not postmodernists) abuse history by projecting the present on the past. Vertzberger, on the other hand, recommends the Neustadt and May rules as a means of ensuring that history is not abused [Chapter 6 in 151]. He is not only concerned that leaders should learn the correct lessons of history, since the question he poses is why decision makers make mistakes even when all the information they need is available [151]. To broach this question, he examines the effect of perception and misperception on information processing, the trade off that frequently takes place between efficiency and accuracy and the impact of personality and societal-cultural factors on the quality of information processing. He concludes his interesting study by suggesting how the potential negative consequences of faulty processing can be limited.

Insisting that the 'correct' lessons of the past must be learned, considering how decision makers' techniques of information processing can be improved, devising better structures of conflict management and ensuring that the best possible advice is available to decision makers all indicate a normative concern for 'good' foreign policy management. But there are also underlying implications that rationality is an attainable and sufficient aspiration and that decision makers are untrammelled by the structures within which they operate.

On rationality, Ferguson and Mansbach [Chapter 6, 33] argue that cognitive approaches are interesting but cannot serve as the basis for theory because cognitive behaviour varies not only between people and institutions but also between decisions. Without the assumption of bounded rationality, therefore, FPA is doomed to turn from scientific analysis to idiosyncratic narrative. Some studies of perception are, however, based on assumptions of bounded rationality [see, for example, Chapters 2 and 3 in 133]. Moreover, critics have pointed out that although bureaucratic politics is intended to debunk the idea of a unitary rational decision maker, the bargaining between and within bureaucracies posited by the model implicitly assumes rationality.

The second problem, the relationship of agency to structure, is one of the central issues of IR. To quote Carlsnaes [19], as far as FPA is concerned, 'the question is how to conceptualize interstate behaviour in terms of both human choice and social determination' (p. 256). Wendt [159] approaches the problem through Giddens's structuration theory. Carlsnaes argues that the simultaneous duality of Giddens's theory makes it impossible to apply in practice. He attempts to resolve the problem by positing a reciprocal interplay over time between agency and structure: actions are not only causally affected by structures (which both constrain and enable) but they themselves subsequently affect structures.

Hollis and Smith [64, 65] invoke the notion of role (a term also used by Walker [154] in a more restricted meaning) to deal with the relationship between agency and structure and to improve both the rational actor and the bureaucratic politics models. Roles operate within structures, acting as constraints and enablements. But they contain an area of indeterminacy and they are inconsistent, thus leaving room for personal qualities of judgement and skill. The question of the interaction of agency and structure represents the intersection of social science and international relations theory with the theory of foreign policy. It is a problem which will continue to preoccupy both IR theorists and foreign policy analysts.

Comparative foreign policy

Comparative foreign policy (CFP) is the field of FPA that has been most subject to criticism and self-criticism. While its critics do not expect it to make much progress [Chapter 7 in 33], its defenders give examples of how CFP efforts at theory building could form the basis for more comprehensive theories [Chapter 1 in 55]. Whether one is a detractor or defender of CFP, cross-national events data and other comparative collections provide a rich mine for the future use of IR and FPA theorists. The findings of the International Crisis Behavior Project [13] represent one example.

There are a great number of foreign policy analysts who are less concerned with scientific rigour (in the sense of producing testable hypotheses) than those who classify their work as CFP but whose research is distinctly comparative and rigorous. Geldenhuys's work on isolated states [37], for example, or Jackson's notion of quasi-states [76] are based on comparative studies. Other scholars have grouped together various types of states to investigate aspects of their foreign policies. The foreign and defence policies of Third World states and new states have been examined, for example [16, 79, 146], and the particular problems of small states have been investigated [51, 80, 82, 131]. There are also interesting cross-national studies of particular types of policy [28, 35, 107]. Whatever the future fate of CFP, this kind of comparative foreign policy is unlikely to disappear.

FPA in a changing world

It is a truism of FPA that whereas in previous centuries foreign policy consisted almost entirely of 'high' politics, it now embraces 'low' politics. Economic instruments of foreign policy have become at least as important as diplomacy and force. Increasingly it has become difficult to separate foreign policy from domestic politics. Nor are governments and the states they represent any longer the sole actors in the international system. While this does not imply that governments no longer conduct foreign policy, it is clear that interdependence, concern about global problems and permanent membership of alliances, regional and international organizations mean that governments are no longer free arbiters of the policies of their states. Thus there is a steady erosion of a separate concept of foreign policy and a consequent undermining of FPA as a discrete field of investigation.

On the other hand, the demise of the territorial state has not occurred, and the number of new states joining the international system has increased markedly in the last five years. Foreign policy, therefore, has both changed and expanded. Rather than undermining FPA, these new phenomena represent the expanding range of concerns that are relevant to the subject. In addition to the matters they have traditionally investigated, therefore, foreign policy analysts now need to consider the implications of international political economy [39, 114, 143, 144] for foreign policy and to consider how interdependence [83, 87] or membership of regional organizations [32, 93, 127, 149] affect the independent conduct of foreign policy. Since new states are appearing at the same time as demands for autonomy are increasing in old ones, the potential for foreign policy-making in subnational units is of great consequence [72, 103]. The global system may, in some respects, enjoy governance without government [126], but foreign policy, and therefore FPA, will remain relevant to the international system and to IR for the foreseeable future.

Bibliography

1. Allison, Graham T. *Essence of Decision*. Boston, Little, Brown, 1971.
2. Auerbach, Yehudit 'Legitimation for turning point decisions in foreign policy: Israel vis-à-vis Germany 1952 and Egypt 1977'. *Review of International Studies*, vol. 15, no. 4, 1989, pp. 329–40.
3. Azzam, Maha 'The Gulf Crisis: perceptions in the Muslim world'. *International Affairs*, vol. 67, no. 3, 1991, pp. 473–85.
4. Barston, R.P. *Modern Diplomacy*. London, Longmans, 1988.
5. Beetham, David *Bureaucracy*. Milton Keynes, Open University Press, 1987.
6. Bendor, Jonathan and Hammond, Thomas H. 'Rethinking Allison's Models'. *American Political Science Review*, vol. 86, no. 2, June, 1992, pp. 301–22.
7. Berridge, G.R. and Young, John W. 'What is a Great Power?' *Political Studies*, vol. XXXVI, no. 2, June, 1988, pp. 224–34.
8. Betts, Richard K. *Nuclear Blackmail and Nuclear Balance*. Washington, DC, Brookings, 1987.
9. Betts, Richard and Levite, Ariel 'Intelligence and Strategic Surprise'. *International Studies Quarterly*, vol. 33, no. 3, September, 1989, pp. 329–49.
10. Bloom, William *Personal Identity, National Identity and International Relations*. Cambridge and New York, Cambridge University Press, 1990.
11. Boyd, Gavin and Hopple, Gerald W. (eds) *Political Change and Foreign Policies*, London, Frances Pinter, 1987.
12. Brecher, Michael and Wilkenfeld, Jonathan *Crisis, Conflict and Instability*, Oxford and New York, Pergamon Press, 1989.
13. Brecher, Michael, Wilkenfeld, Jonathan and Moser, Sheila *Crises in the Twentieth Century*, Vol. I: *Handbook of International Crises*, Vol II: *Handbook of Foreign Policy Crises*. Oxford and New York, Pergamon Press, 1988.
14. Breslauer, George W. and Tetlock, Philip E. (eds) *Learning in US and Soviet Foreign Policy*. Boulder and Oxford, Westview Press, 1991.
15. Burke, John P. and Greenstein, Fred *How Presidents Test Reality: Decisions on Vietnam 1954 and 1965*. New York, Russell Sage Foundation, 1989.
16. Calvert, Peter *The Foreign Policy of New States*. Brighton, Wheatsheaf, 1986.
17. Camilleri, J.A. and Falk, Jim *The End of Sovereignty? The Politics of a Shrinking and Fragmenting World*. London, Edward Elgar, 1992.
18. Campbell, David *Writing Security: United States Foreign Policy and the Politics of Identity*. Manchester, Manchester University Press, 1992.

19. Carlsnaes, Walter 'The Agency–Structure Problem in Foreign Policy Analysis'. *International Studies Quarterly*, vol. 36, no. 3, September, 1992, pp. 245–70.
20. Carlsnaes, Walter *Ideology and Foreign Policy: Problems of Comparative Conceptualization*. Oxford, Blackwell, 1986.
21. Clarke, Michael and White, Brian (eds) *Understanding Foreign Policy: The Foreign Policy Systems Approach*. Aldershot and Brookfield, Edward Elgar, 1989.
22. Clarke, Peter *A Question of Leadership: Gladstone to Thatcher*. London, Hamish Hamilton, 1991.
23. Cohen, Raymond *Theatre of Power: the Art of Diplomatic Signalling*. London, New York, Longmans, 1987.
24. Cohen, Yoel 'News Media and the News Department of the Foreign and Commonwealth Office'. *Review of International Studies*, vol. 14, no 2, 1988, pp. 117–31.
25. Cox, Andrew and Kirby, Stephen *Congress, Parliament and Defence: The Impact of Legislative Reform on Defence Accountability in Britain and America*. London, Macmillan, 1986.
26. Crabb Jr, Cecil V. and Mulcahy, Kevin V. *Presidents and Foreign Policy-Making: from FDR to Reagan*. Baton Rouge and London, University of Louisiana Press, 1986.
27. Der Derian, James *On Diplomacy: A Genealogy of Western Estrangement*. Oxford and New York, Basil Blackwell, 1987.
28. Dillon, G.M. (ed.) *Defence Policy-Making: A Comparative Analysis*. Leicester, Leicester University Press, 1988.
29. Dixon, Norman *Our Own Worst Enemy*, London, Cape, 1987.
30. Domke, William K., Eichenberg, Richard C. and Kelleher, Catherine M. 'Consensus Lost? Domestic Politics and the "Crisis" in NATO'. *World Politics*, vol. XXXIX, no. 3, April, 1987, pp. 382–407.
31. Doxey, Margaret P. *International Sanctions in Contemporary Perspective*. London, Macmillan, 1987.
32. Edwards, Geoffrey and Regelsberger, Elfriede (eds) *Europe's Global Links: The European Community and Inter-Regional Cooperation*. London, Pinter, 1990.
33. Ferguson, Yale H. and Mansbach, Richard W. *The Elusive Quest: Theory and International Politics*. Columbia, University of South Carolina Press, 1988.
34. Fry, Michael (ed.) *History, the White House and the Kremlin: Statesmen as Historians*. London, Pinter Publishers, 1991.
35. Gaenslen, Fritz 'Culture and Decision-Making in China, Japan, Russia and the United States'. *World Politics*, vol. XXXIX, no. 1, October, 1986, pp. 78–103.
36. Garthoff, Raymond L. *Reflections on the Cuban Missile Crisis*, revised edition, Washington DC, Brookings, 1989.
37. Geldenhuys, Deon *Isolated States: A Comparative Analysis*. Cambridge and New York, Cambridge University Press, 1990.
38. George, Alexander L. (ed.) *Avoiding War: Problems of Crisis Management*. Boulder and Oxford, Westview Press, 1991.
39. Gilpin, Robert *The Political Economy of International Relations*. Princeton, Princeton University Press, 1987.
40. Goldberg, D.H. *Foreign Policy and Ethnic Interest Groups: American and Canadian Jews Lobby for Israel*. New York and London, Greenwood, 1990.
41. Goldmann, K. *Change and Stability in Foreign Policy: The Problems and Possibilities of Detente*. London, Harvester Wheatsheaf and Princeton, Princeton University Press, 1988.

42. Goldmann K., Berglund S. and Sjöstedt G. *Foreign Policy and Democracy: The Case of Sweden*. Aldershot and Brookfield, Gower Publishing, 1986.
43. *Government and Opposition*, vol. 28, no. 2, Spring, 1993. Special issue on 'Globalisation: the interweaving of foreign and domestic policy making'.
44. Gray, Colin *The Geopolitics of Super power*. Lexington, University Press of Kentucky, 1988.
45. Greenstein, Fred (ed.) *Leadership in the Modern Presidency*. Cambridge, MA and London, Harvard University Press, 1988.
46. Hagan, Joe D. *Political Opposition and Foreign Policy in Comparative Perspective*. Boulder and London, Lynne Rienner, 1992.
47. Halliday, Fred *Revolution and Foreign Policy: The Case of South Yemen 1967–87*. Cambridge and New York, Cambridge University Press, 1990.
48. Handel, Michael *War, Strategy and Intelligence*. London and Totowa, Frank Cass, 1989.
49. Handel, Michael (ed.) *Leaders and Intelligence*. London, Frank Cass, 1989.
50. Hanson, Philip *Western Economic Statecraft in East–West Relations: Embargoes, Sanctions, Linkage, Economic Warfare and Detente*. Chatham House Papers 40, London and New York, Routledge and Kegan Paul for RIIA, 1988.
51. Harden, Sheila (ed.) *Small is Dangerous: Micro-states in a Macro World*. London, Frances Pinter, 1985.
52. Herek, Gregory M., Janis, Irving L. and Huth, Paul 'Decision-Making during the Cuban Missile Crisis: Major Errors in Welch's Reassessment'. *Journal of Conflict Resolution*, vol. 33, no. 3, September, 1989, pp. 446–59.
53. Herek, Gregory M., Janis, Irving and Huth, Paul 'Decision-making during International Crises: Is Quality of Process Related to Outcome?'. *Journal of Conflict Resolution*, vol. 31, no. 2, June, 1987, pp. 203–26.
54. Hermann, Charles F. 'Changing Course: When Governments Choose to Re-direct Foreign Policy'. *International Studies Quarterly*, vol 34, no 1, March, 1990, pp. 3–21.
55. Hermann, Charles F., Kegley Jr, Charles W., Rosenau, James N. (eds) *New Directions in the Study of Foreign Policy*. London and Boston, Allen & Unwin, 1987.
56. Hermann, Margaret G. and Charles, F. 'Who Makes Foreign Policy Decisions and How: An Empirical Enquiry'. *International Studies Quarterly*, vol 33, no. 4, December, 1989, pp. 361–87.
57. Hibbert, Reginald, 'Intelligence and Policy'. *Intelligence and National Security*, vol 5, no 1, January, 1990, pp. 110–28.
58. Hill, Christopher 'The Historical Background: Past and Present in British Foreign Policy' in Michael Smith, Steve Smith, Brian White (eds) *British Foreign Policy: Tradition, Change and Continuity*. London and Boston, Unwin Hyman, 1988, pp. 25–49.
59. Hill, Christopher and Light, Margot 'Foreign Policy Analysis' in Margot Light and A.J.R. Groom (eds) *International Relations: A Handbook of Current Theory*. London, Frances Pinter and Boulder, Lynne Rienner, 1985, pp. 156–73.
60. Hilsman, Roger *The Politics of Policy Making in Defense and Foreign Affairs: Conceptual Models and Bureaucratic Politics*. Englewood Cliffs, Prentice Hall, 1987.
61. Hinckley, Ronald H. *People, Polls, and Policymakers: American Public Opinion and National Security*. New York, Lexington and Oxford, Maxwell Macmillan International, 1992.
62. Hoffmann, Stanley 'The case for leadership'. *Foreign Policy*, no. 81, Winter, 1990-1, pp. 20–38.

63. Hogan, Michael J. and Paterson, Thomas G. *Explaining the History of American Foreign Relations*. Cambridge and New York, Cambridge University Press, 1991.
64. Hollis, Martin and Smith, Steve *Explaining and Understanding International Relations*. Oxford, Clarendon Press and New York, Oxford University Press, 1991.
65. Hollis, Martin and Smith, Steve 'Roles and Reasons in Foreign Policy Decision-Making'. *British Journal of Political Science*, vol. 16, no. 3, 1986, pp. 269–86.
66. Holmes, Jack E. *The Mood/Interest Theory of American Foreign Policy*. Lexington, University Press of Kentucky, 1985.
67. Holsti, K.J. *Change in the International System: Essays on the Theory and Practice of International Relations*. Aldershot and Brookfield, Edward Elgar, 1991.
68. Holsti, K.J. *International Politics: A Framework for Analysis*, sixth edition, Englewood Cliffs, Prentice Hall International, 1992.
69. Howard, Michael *The Lessons of History*. Oxford, Clarendon Press, 1991.
70. Ifestos, Panayiotis *European Political Cooperation: Toward a Framework of Supranational Diplomacy?* Aldershot and Brookfield, Avebury, 1987.
71. Inada, Juichi 'Japan's Aid Diplomacy: Economic, Political or Strategic'. *Millennium*, vol 18, no. 3, Winter, 1989, pp. 399–414.
72. *International Journal*, vol. XLI, no. 3, Summer, 1986. Special Issue on 'Foreign Policy in Federal States'.
73. *International Security*, vol. 17, no. 4, Spring, 1993; articles on 'Primacy and its Discontents' by Christopher Layne, Robert Jervis and Samuel Huntington, pp. 5–83.
74. *International Studies Notes*, vol. 13, no. 2, Spring, 1987. Special issue on 'The Comparative Study of Foreign Policy'.
75. Ionescu, Ghiţa *Leadership in an Interdependent World: the Statemanship of Adenauer, de Gaulle, Thatcher, Reagan and Gorbachev*. Harlow, Longman and Boulder, Westview Press, 1991.
76. Jackson, Robert *Quasi-States: Sovereignty, International Relations and the Third World*. Cambridge and New York, Cambridge University Press, 1990.
77. Janis, Irving L. *Crucial Decisions: Leadership in Policy-Making and Crisis Management*. London, Collier Macmillan and New York, Free Press, 1989.
78. Jeffreys-Jones, Rhodri *The CIA and American Democracy*. New Haven and London, Yale University Press, 1989.
79. Job, Brian L. (ed.) *The Insecurity Dilemma: National Security of Third World States*. Boulder and London, Lynne Rienner, 1992.
80. *Journal of Commonwealth and Comparative Politics*, vol. XXXI, no. 2, July, 1993. Special issue on 'Size and Survival: The Politics of Security in the Caribbean and the Pacific', Paul Sutton and Anthony Payne (eds).
81. Karsh, Efraim 'Military Power and Foreign Policy Goals: The Iran–Iraq War Revisited'. *International Affairs*, vol. 64, no. 1, Winter, 1987–8, pp. 83–95.
82. Karsh, Ephraim, *Neutrality and Small States: The European Experience in World War II and Beyond*. London and New York, Routledge, 1988.
83. Karvonen, Lauri and Sundelius, Bengt 'Interdependence and Foreign Policy Management in Sweden and Finland'. *International Studies Quarterly*, vol 34, no. 2, June, 1990, pp. 211–27.
84. Karvonen, Lauri and Sundelius, Bengt *Internationalization and Foreign Policy Management*, Aldershot and Brookfield, Gower, 1987.
85. Kennedy, Paul *The Rise and Fall of the Great Powers: Economic Change and Military Conflict from 1500 to 2000*. Boston, Random House and London, Unwin Hyman, 1988.

86. Keohane, Robert, and Nye, Joseph 'Power and Interdependence Revisited'. *International Organisation*, vol. 41, no. 4, Autumn, 1987, pp. 725–53.

87. Keohane, Robert, and Nye, Joseph *Power and Interdependence: World Politics in Transition*, second edition, Boston, Little, Brown, 1989.

88. Kolodziej, Edward *Making and Marketing Arms: The French Experience and its Implications for the International System* Princeton, Princeton University Press, 1987.

89. Kozak, David C. and Keagle, James M. (eds) *Bureaucratic Politics and National Security: Theory and Practice.* Boulder and London, Lynne Rienner, 1988.

90. Lamborn, Alan *The Price of Power: Risk and Foreign Policy in Britain, France and Germany.* London and Boston, Unwin Hyman, 1991.

91. Lamborn, Alan and Mumme, Stephen *Statecraft, Domestic Politics and Foreign Policy-Making: The El Chamizal Dispute.* Boulder and London, Westview, 1988.

92. Lebow, Richard Ned *Nuclear Crisis Management: A Dangerous Illusion.* Ithaca and London, Cornell University Press, 1987.

93. Leifer, Michael *ASEAN and the Security of South-East Asia.* London, Routledge, 1989.

94. Levy, Jacks 'Organizational Routines and the Causes of War'. *International Studies Quarterly*, vol. 30, no. 2, June, 1986, pp. 193–222.

95. Leyton-Brown, David (ed.) *The Utility of International Economic Sanctions.* London, Croom Helm, 1987.

96. Lian, Bradley and O'Neal, John R. 'Presidents, the Use of Military Force and Public Opinion'. *Journal of Conflict Resolution*, vol. 37, no. 2, June, 1993, pp. 277–300.

97. Lindsay, James M. 'Trade Sanctions as Policy Instruments: A Re-Examination'. *International Studies Quarterly*, vol. 30, no. 2, June, 1986, pp. 153–73.

98. Little, Richard and Smith, Steve (eds) *Belief Systems and International Relations.* Oxford and New York, Basil Blackwell in association with British International Studies Association, 1988.

99. Luard, Evan *The Blunted Sword: The Erosion of Military Power in Modern World Politics.* London, I.B. Tauris, 1988.

100. Macridis, Roy C. (ed.) *Foreign Policy in World Politics: States and Regions,* eighth edition, Englewood Cliffs and London, Prentice Hall International, 1992.

101. Maoz, Zeev 'Framing the National Interest: The Manipulation of Foreign Policy Decisions in Group Settings'. *World Politics*, vol. 43, no. 1, October, 1990, pp. 77–110.

102. Mastanduno, Michael, Lake, David and Ikenberry, G. John 'Toward a Realist Theory of State Action'. *International Studies Quarterly*, vol 33, no. 4, December, 1989, pp. 457–74.

103. Michelmann, Hans J. and Soldatos, Panayotis (eds) *Federalism and International Relations: The Role of Subnational Units.* Oxford and New York, Oxford University Press, 1990.

104. Minogue, K. and Biddiss, M. (eds) *Thatcherism: Personality and Politics.* London, Macmillan, 1987.

105. Mitchell, J. *International Cultural Relations,* London and Boston, Allen & Unwin in association with the British Council, 1986.

106. Moens, Alexander, *Foreign Policy under Carter: Testing Multiple Advocacy Decision-Making.* Boulder and Oxford, Westview Press, 1990.

107. Murray, Douglas J. and Vioti, Paul R. (eds) *The Defense Policies of Nations: A Comparative Study,* second edition, Baltimore and London, Johns Hopkins University Press, 1989.

108. Nau, Henry (ed.) *Domestic Trade Politics and the Uruguay Round*. New York, Columbia University Press, 1989.
109. Neustadt, Richard E. and May, Ernest R. *Thinking in Time: the Uses of History for Decision-Makers*. London, Collier Macmillan and New York, Free Press, 1986.
110. Newsom, David D. (ed.) *Diplomacy under a Foreign Flag: When Nations Break Relations*. London, Hurst & Co. and New York, St. Martin's Press, 1990.
111. Newsom, David (ed.) *Private Diplomacy with the Soviet Union*. Lanham and London, University Press of America, 1987.
112. Nincic, Miroslav *Democracy and Foreign Policy: The Fallacy of Political Realism*. New York and Oxford, Columbia University Press, 1992.
113. Nye, Joseph *Bound to Lead: The Changing Nature of American Power*. New York, Basic Books, 1990.
114. O'Brien, Richard *Global Financial Integration: The End of Geography*. London, Pinter Publishers for the RIIA, 1992.
115. Olson, William 'The US Congress: an independent force in world politics?'. *International Affairs*, vol. 67, no. 3, 1991, pp. 547–63.
116. O'Sullivan, Patrick *Geopolitics*. London, Croom Helm, 1986.
117. Pacione, Michael (ed.) *Progress in Political Geography*. London and Dover NH, Croom Helm, 1985.
118. Parker, Geoffrey *The Geopolitics of Domination*. London and New York, Routledge, 1988.
119. Pfetsch, Frank R. *West Germany: Internal Structures and External Relations: The Foreign Policy of the Federal Republic of Germany*. New York and London, Praeger, 1988.
120. Post, Jerrold M. and Robins, Robert S. *When Illness Strikes the Leader: The Dilemma of the Captive King*. New Haven and London, Yale University Press, 1993.
121. Putnam, Robert D. 'Diplomacy and Domestic Politics: the Logic of Two-Level Games'. *International Organization*, vol. 42, no. 3, Summer, 1988, pp. 427–60.
122. Raboy, Marc and Dagenais, Bernard (eds) *Media, Crisis and Democracy: Mass Communication and the Disruption of Social Order*. New York and London, Sage, 1992.
123. Roberts, Jonathan *Decision-Making during International Crises*. Basingstoke, Macmillan, 1988.
124. Rohrlich, Paul Egan 'Economic Culture and Foreign Policy: the cognitive analysis of economic policy making'. *International Organisation*, vol. 41, no. 1, Winter, 1987, pp. 61–92.
125. Rosati, Jerel *The Carter Administration's Quest for Global Community: Beliefs and their Impact on Behavior*. Columbia, University of South Carolina Press, 1987.
126. Rosenau, James and Czempiel, Ernst-Otto (eds) *Governance without Government: Order and Change in World Politics*. Cambridge and New York, Cambridge University Press, 1992.
127. Sandwick, John A. (ed.) *The Gulf Co-operation Council: Moderation and Stability in an Interdependent World*. Boulder, Westview for American–Arab Affairs Council, distributed in the UK by Mansell Publishing Ltd., 1987.
128. Sayigh, Yezud 'The Gulf Crisis: why the Arab regional order failed'. *International Affairs*, vol. 67, no. 3, 1991, pp. 487–507.
129. Schlesinger Jr, Arthur M. *The Cycles of American History*. Boston, Houghton Mifflin, 1986 and London, Deutsch, 1987.

130. Scholte, Jan Aarte *International Relations of Social Change*. Milton Keynes and Philadelphia, Open University Press, 1993.
131. Sharp, Paul 'Small State Foreign Policy and International Regimes'. *Millennium*, vol 16, no. 1, Spring, 1987, pp. 55–72.
132. Short, John R. *An Introduction to Political Geography*, second edition, London and New York, Routledge, 1993.
133. Singer, Eric and Hudson, Valerie (eds) *Political Psychology and Foreign Policy*. Boulder and Oxford, Westview Press, 1992.
134. Skidmore, David and Hudson, Valerie M. (eds) *The Limits of State Autonomy: Societal Groups and Foreign Policy Formulation*. Boulder and Oxford, Westview Press, 1993.
135. Sloan, G.R. *Geopolitics in United States Strategic Policy 1890–1987*. Hemel Hempstead, Harvester Wheatsheaf, 1988.
136. Smith, Steve 'Foreign Policy Analysis and International Relations'. *Millennium: Journal of International Studies*, Special Issue on 'The Study of International Relations', vol. 16, no. 2, Summer, 1987, pp. 345–8.
137. Smith, Steve 'Theories of Foreign Policy: An Historical Overview'. *Review of International Studies*, vol. 12, no. 1, January, 1986, pp. 13–29.
138. Snyder, Jack *Myths of Empire: Domestic Politics and International Ambition*. Ithaca and London, Cornell University Press, 1991.
139. Sofer, Sasson 'Old and New Diplomacy: a Debate Revisited'. *Review of International Studies*, vol. 14, no. 3, July, 1988, pp. 195–211.
140. Stein, J.G. 'International Co-operation and Loss Avoidance: Framing the Problem'. *International Journal*, vol. XLVII, no. 2, Spring, 1992, pp. 202–34.
141. Steiner, Zara, 'Decision-Making in American and British Foreign Policy: An Open and Shut Case'. *Review of International Studies*, vol 13, no. 1, 1987, pp. 1–18.
142. Stohl, Michael and Lopez, George A. (eds.) *Terrible beyond Endurance: The Foreign Policy of State Terrorism*. New York and London, Greenwood, 1988.
143. Stopford, John M. and Strange, Susan with John S. Henley *Rival States, Rival Firms: Competition for World Market Shares*. Cambridge and New York, Cambridge University Press, 1991.
144. Strange, Susan, *States and Markets: An Introduction to International Political Economy*. London, Pinter Publishers, 1988.
145. Strong, Robert J. *Bureaucracy and Statesmanship: Henry Kissinger and the Making of American Foreign Policy*, The Credibility of Institutions, Policies and Leadership, Vol. 9. Lanham and London, University Press of America, 1987.
146. Thomas, Caroline *In Search of Security: The Third World in International Relations*. Brighton, Wheatsheaf and Boulder, Lynne Rienner, 1987.
147. Thompson, Kenneth, W. (ed.) *Paper on Presidential Transitions and Foreign Policy*, 3 Vols. Lanham and London, University Press of America, 1986.
148. Treverton, Gregory *Covert Action: The CIA and the Limits of American Intervention in the Post-War World*. New York, Basic Books, 1987 and London, Tauris, 1988.
149. Troxler, Nancy 'The Gulf Co-operation Council: The Emergence of an Institution'. *Millennium*, vol. 16, no. 1, Spring, 1987, pp. 1–19.
150. Twiggs, Joan *The Tokyo Round of Multi-lateral Trade Negotiations: A Case-Study in Building Domestic Support for Diplomacy*. Lanham and London, University Press of America, 1987.
151. Vertzberger, Yaacov Y.I. *The World in their Minds: Information Processing, Cognition and Perception in Foreign Policy Decisionmaking*. Stanford, Stanford University Press, 1990.

152. Vincent, R.J. 'Human rights in foreign policy' in his *Human Rights and International Relations*. RIIA and Cambridge University Press, 1986, pp. 129–52.
153. Walker, R.B.J. and Mendlovitz, Saul H. (eds) *Contending Sovereignties: Redefining Political Community*. Boulder and London, Lynne Rienner, 1990.
154. Walker, Stephen G. (ed.) *Role Theory and Foreign Policy Analysis*. Durham, Duke University Press, 1987.
155. Wallace, William 'Foreign policy and national identity in the United Kingdom'. *International Affairs*, vol. 67, no. 1, 1991, pp. 65–80.
156. Wallace, William 'What price independence? Sovereignty and interdependence in British politics'. *International Affairs*, vol. 62, no. 3, Summer, 1986, pp. 367–89.
157. Wallis, Roger and Baran, Stanley *The Known World of Broadcast News: International News and the Electronic Media*. London and New York, Routledge, 1990.
158. Wardlaw, Grant 'Terror as an Instrument of Foreign Policy' in David C. Rapoport (ed.) *Inside Terrorist Organizations*. London, Cass, 1988, pp. 237–59.
159. Wendt, Alexander E. 'The Agent–Structure Problem in International Relations Theory'. *International Organization*, vol. 41, no. 3, Summer, 1987, pp. 335–70.
160. Ziegler, Charles E. *Foreign Policy and East Asia: Learning and Adaptation in the Gorbachev Era*. Cambridge and New York, Cambridge University Press, 1993.

8 Strategy
Ken Booth

From the perspective of 1994 we can see the whole history of academic strategic studies. It falls into three distinct parts: early strategic studies, from the first atomic bomb to the 'massive retaliation' debate (1945–55); the period of high strategic theory (1956–85) when the subject became a major subfield within international relations; and finally – and conveniently for this survey – the period of late strategic studies, defined by the Gorbachev era (1985–91). In Gramscian terms this last period could be seen as an 'interregnum', when the old was dying, the new could not yet be born and there existed a great diversity of morbid symptoms [18].

Pre-nuclear strategy

Throughout history strategy was always an expanding phenomenon, both conceptually and in practice. In ancient times the word simply meant a commander's 'plan for battle'; it then evolved into 'the art of war', and by the 19th century into a country's whole disposition for war whether in peacetime or during periods of conflict; by the middle of the 20th century, strategy and external policy were seen frequently as synonymous in the industrial world, and the consequence of major conflict risked being coterminous with the destruction of civilization in the northern hemisphere.

Strategy relates military means and political ends, in both war and peace. Accordingly, strategic studies is concerned with understanding and explaining the military dimensions of international relations; this involves the study of the ends and means of strategy, the threat and use of military force, the prevention and conduct of war and the societal effects of strategy. As a developing subfield of IR strategic studies fitted comfortably into the dominating realist (and then neorealist) perspective.

Clearly, strategy as a major business of states long preceded its systematic academic study. For most of history, writing about strategy was confined to occasional chroniclers of war and, even rarer, theorists. A handful of these writers have now achieved 'classic' status; a short-list, in chronological order, includes Sun Tzu, Thucydides, Machiavelli, Clausewitz, Mahan, Douhet and Liddell Hart [84, 202, 130, 42, 132, 51, 122]. For many years the only exegesis on the theorists of modern strategy was Earle's collection [54]; in 1986 a new and substantially revised edition was published by Paret [161]. A brief overview is provided by Booth [16].

Early strategic studies, 1945–55

Academic strategic studies dates from the almost simultaneous occurrence of the nuclear revolution and the Cold War. These events established the context for the subject for the next 40 years. The most significant theoretical work during the subject's first decade, appearing within a year of the dropping of atomic bombs on Japan, was edited and partly written by Brodie [22]. *The Absolute Weapon*, and particularly Brodie's own chapters, has claim to be the foundation of the theory of nuclear deterrence which came to be regarded as the conceptual jewel in the crown of strategic studies.

Much of the strategic writing in the West in the early postwar years had a rather undeveloped tone; that in the Soviet Union, imprisoned by Stalinist orthodoxy, was even cruder. The main ideas of the time, about offence and defence, deterrence and aggression, massive retaliation and limited war, and surprise attack and arms racing are traced in Freedman's standard work, a new edition of which appeared in 1989 [63].

High strategic theory 1956–85

During the three decades of high strategic theory, new standards of analysis and productivity were established, and new levels of strategic rationality appeared to have been attained. The first ten years, which Garnett labelled the 'golden age', were clearly the most creative, characterized by theoretical development in nuclear deterrence, arms control, crisis management and limited war [69]. The theories, concepts and defence policies which shaped these years are described and explained at length in the successive editions of Baylis *et al.* [4]; a brief survey is offered by Groom [85]. The archetypal strategist of this period was civilian, American and male, and their work was characterized by a certain intellectual hubris [159].

There were, nevertheless, several distinctive contributions to the expanding literature from the much smaller group of Australian, British, French and Soviet strategists. The policy concerns and conceptual developments of these years can be traced in Freedman [62] and Gray [79]; extended essays on the key theorists of nuclear strategy are in Baylis and Garnett [5]; and Herken places the US thinkers in historical context [92] as Kaplan had a few years earlier [105]. Outside the nuclear and Cold War preoccupations, the main theoretical interest was in revolutionary warfare and how to counter it. Significant contributions, respectively, were by Mao Tse-tung [133] and Thompson [201].

The 'golden age' provoked a critical reaction from the developing field of peace research in general and Green [82] and Rapoport [168] in particular. The 'new strategists' were criticized for their methodology, their scholarly conduct, their understanding of the 'real world' and their moral standpoint. Later, they were criticized for their ingrained ethnocentrism [12].

After the mid-1960s there was a 15-year period in which the Cold War eased into an unrelaxed era of *détente*, during which the ideas of the 'golden age' were refined and elaborated. Work done in area studies, history and political psychology was incorporated into strategic theory. The contributions of Brodie and Jervis were particularly important [23, 100]. Mearsheimer, Posen and Snyder led the way in applying new strategic concepts to historical case studies [143, 165, 185].

With the outbreak of the new Cold War at the end of the 1970s, strategic issues returned to the top of the political agenda. The most contentious debates focused on the issues of limited nuclear war, prevailing strategies, nuclear winter, ballistic missile defence and nuclear blackmail. The agenda of these years was set by the 'strategic fundamentalists' of the Reagan administration [14]. Some of their extraordinary ideas were captured, while they were still fresh, by Scheer [172].

The most creative thinking in the strategy-saturated first half of the 1980s did not emerge from the established strategic studies' community but from a growing school of thought which attracted the label of 'alternative' security thinkers. Ideas about common security, non-offensive defence, a nuclear freeze, military confidence-building, democracy and disarmament, *détente* from below and alternative security orders emerged. Key contributors were Afheldt, Forsberg, Kaldor and Palme [148]. By the mid-1980s the golden age strategic studies paradigm was under increasing strain; this, together with the Gorbachev revolution in the Soviet Union helped to create the conditions for strategic studies' postmodern moment, when the subject's modernist principles and preoccupations were challenged but not (yet?) overthrown.

Late strategic studies, 1985–91

In the second half of the 1980s academic strategic studies lost its real world context: alternative security ideas captured the Kremlin, arms control performance outran what was being negotiated, bipolar confrontation was giving way to multilateral conflict resolution, a 'superpower' was abdicating and nuclear strategy seemed irrelevant to the revolutions taking place in world politics. Furthermore, even students of strategy could no longer be immune to the doubts of the 'dividing discipline' [95] and the growing criticism of the paradigm represented by Westphalia, Machiavelli and Clausewitz. During these confused years individual strategic analysts might have known where they were going but strategic studies did not.

Few books on strategy written between 1985 and 1991 are likely to be accorded landmark status. Nevertheless, these were fascinating years, and the attempts of writers to make sense of them exhibited a generally higher level of political and methodological sophistication than had usually been the case in the 'golden age'.

(a) Approaches and methodology

In the late 1980s a vigorous debate began (which has not yet run its course) about the boundaries of strategic studies. Crucial in this regard was Buzan's *People, States & Fear*, [30]. 'Security' had always been the transcendent value in strategic studies, but it was an essentially unexplored concept. Buzan discussed its meaning and implications with subtlety, and himself argued for an holistic conception. Others responded to his agenda-setting and thereby helped to create a syllabus for a new 'security studies' which a growing number of writers believed should encompass the narrower notion of 'strategic studies' [19, 46, 114, 155, 182, 208].

Within the traditional boundaries of strategic studies a number of general works were published. Buzan wrote an *Introduction to Strategic Studies*, in which he defined the subject as the military technological variable within international relations [28]. Baylis and his collaborators updated and expanded *Contemporary Strategy*, attempting to describe and analyse the most important strategic concepts and theories on the brink of the Gorbachev revolution [4]. Clark wrote a helpful philosophical introduction to waging war – an outcome most strategists in the nuclear age tried to avoid [41] – while Ceadel provided a thoughtful categorization of the way people think about defence [35]. Luttwak, who in the early 1980s had written books emphasizing Soviet power and US weakness, published a general treatise on the paradoxes of strategy [129], just at the time the Soviet Union was collapsing and the United States was emerging as the sole superpower. As ever, several writers delved into the classics for insight. Gat sought to place Clausewitz in his proper cultural context [72]; Simpkin explored mobility in war and updated Liddell Hart [178]; and Gray updated Mackinder, at the very moment when the 'heartland' superpower was collapsing [81].

The historical role of war itself, the central *problèmatique* in realist international theory, was challenged by several writers. Mueller and Luard brought together empirical evidence and much argument to support the proposition that people can and do learn, and that the institution of war is in historic decline [150, 151, 127]. Attracting more popular attention, however, was Fukuyama's thesis about the 'end of history' which equated the triumph of liberal democracy with the end of war among its proponents [66, 67, 68]. In rebuttal, Seabury and Codevilla wrote *War, Ends & Means*, which defended the traditional canons about the centrality of war and the utility of military force [173].

The theoretical framework of strategic studies in the 1980s was that of neorealism. This approach led to the security problems of the 'New Europe' becoming a bitter academic battleground, just when it seemed unlikely that it would ever be one for the superpowers. The parsimonious neorealist perspective on European security was prominently championed by Mearsheimer, who foresaw the reemergence of traditional patterns of international rivalry [144]. His challenge prompted a lively debate, as much about international political theory as about developments in the New Europe. Buzan and his collaborators wrote from a sophisticated neorealist perspective [29]. Wide-ranging contributions to the debate were by Van Evera and Hyde-Price, and the collections of McInnes and Pugh [206, 96, 139, 167].

The criticism of 'golden age' strategic studies as ethnocentric engendered several significant attempts to overcome the problem. Gray did not allow his explicit neorealist stance to inhibit his evident concern for cultural variables, as indicated in his bravura *Nuclear Strategy and National Style* [80]. He staunchly defended strategists as 'without apologies, neo-realists' [79]. Nevertheless, the attention given to 'strategic culture' and to the Fukuyama thesis equating liberal democracy and peace [66] indicated that many academic strategists were neorealists by profession rather than conviction. Jacobsen and his numerous supporters constructed a multi-faceted and comparative US–USSR study based on the concept of 'strategic culture' [98]. Notable empirical contributions were MccGwire's seminal studies of the new security thinking of Gorbachev's Kremlin [135, 136], together with the work of Garthoff, Meyer and Snyder [70, 71, 146, 185]. Equally, the contributions of Thomas [195, 196, 198], Azar and Moon [2] and Job [103] were sensitive to the differing security perspectives in those regions still called, somewhat inaccurately, the Third World.

There were other manifestations of increased methodological self-awareness. More writers began to ask questions about truth, validation and values; and words like 'epistemology' and names such as Kant intruded into the discussion. The writing of dead, and living, sociologists started appearing [76, 117, 176, 180]. As a category for understanding world politics, 'society' was coming to be accepted by some as being at least as important as 'state'. Traditional theory was questioned, and not always by radicals. Some well-known 'owls' – a self-congratulatory group which distanced itself from those it considered either 'hawks' or 'doves' – expressed doubts. Nye, for example, criticized the nature of deterrence theory [154], while Jervis pointed out the unusual scope left for ideas in the absence of 'objective answers' to so many strategic questions [102]. Lawrence's *Preparing for Armageddon* was a critique of the modes of Western strategic thinking from a more radical perspective [118]. Williams subtly exposed some of the assumptions and contradictions of neorealist writing about strategy [216].

The language of strategic studies was another area of methodological concern but not one which offered ready solutions. Not only was strategic language given to euphemism, jargon and oxymoron, but the hyper-rationalization of the theory determined that its linguistic building-blocks would be made to fit the needs of the theory. Several critics drew attention to such problems [15, 109, 123]. An additional dimension was the feminist critique of the language of the gendered world of male defence intellectuals [44, 45].

The uncertainties and debates within strategic studies in the second half of the 1980s were not only a response to the dramatic developments in world affairs; they were also related to the crisis of representation which was taking place in the study of international relations as a whole. This was the result of the work of students of critical theory, gender and postmodernism. The strategist's familiar world was not only being revolutionized in practice; it was also fracturing in theory [49, 78, 125]. Little of this touched yet on the writing about the sharp edge of strategy – discussion of hardware and doctrine – but inroads into the core were being attempted from different perspectives by writers such as Cohn [44, 45], Elshtain [55], Klein [111, 112] and Booth [19]. The phrase 'established knowledge' in strategy was becoming an oxymoron.

(b) Theories and concepts

The theories and concepts of the 'golden age' still dominated the strategic studies agenda in the late 1980s, but the tone was different and the perspectives were wider. In particular, the canons of the 'golden age' were scrutinized by the academic exponents of 'new thinking', an approach personified on the world stage by Gorbachev. The 'old thinking' embodied in the Reaganite–Brezhnevite agenda now began to be replaced by an alternative agenda consisting of common security, denuclearization, reasonable sufficiency, a political conception of security, confidence-building measures, unilateralism, crisis prevention, dealignment, demilitarization, non-intervention and non-offensive defence (NOD) [1, 3, 17, 21, 25, 48, 61, 147, 148, 203, 208, 213, 218, 219]. Gates was a persistent critic of the military dimension of these ideas [73]. The balance of new and old thinking at the end of the 1980s was summarized by Booth [18].

As in earlier phases of strategic studies, nuclear deterrence was given considerable attention. Strategists still wrote at length about nuclear deterrence and rationality [221, 222] and about US deterrence policy in particular [11, 77]. Unlike earlier periods, however, the literature on deterrence tended to be apologetic, if not critical. In particular, some writers in the later 1980s attempted to restore practical wisdom into nuclear deterrence theory. They wrote about actually existing deterrence rather than what Kull had called 'hyper-rationalisation' [115], or Herring called nuclear 'strategizing' [93]. Of particular importance was Bundy's argument that nuclear deterrence is 'existential' – an unavoidable fact of life – rather than a deliberate act of policy [26, 27].

The weight of opinion in the nuclear debate moved towards Bundy's position. As Buzan put it, nuclear deterrence of nuclear attack is 'easy' rather than 'hard' [28]; while Jervis, along the same lines, described mutual assured destruction (MAD) as a 'fact of life' not a 'policy' [102]. The ideas of the warfighters of the Reagan years looked increasingly irrelevant, if not bizarre. Discussion about deterrence fell increasingly into the hands of dissidents, but as Kolkowicz's collection shows, these came from across the spectrum of analysts, and could not simply be marginalized and dismissed as 'radicals' [113]. Nye criticized deterrence as a fundamentally 'static' doctrine [154]; Jervis, Lebow and Stein gave empirical and theoretical weight to the old idea that deterrence is a psychological phenomenon and therefore susceptible to human error [101]; Sagan analysed the problems of deterrence in an operationally changing setting [171]; and Gregory warned of the hidden costs of deterrence [83]. In a significant article MccGwire explained with persuasive insight that nuclear deterrence is 'the problem not the solution' [134]. Ideas which in the golden age had been rejected or even ridiculed now came to be treated seriously. Former 'insiders' such as Bundy [26, 27], McNamara [141, 142] and Halperin [89] pressed for minimum nuclear deterrence, while others looked towards security 'beyond nuclearism' [20, 107].

As Cold War rivalries subsided, nuclear anxieties at the turn of the 1980s/90s shifted away from the East–West context and towards the danger of nuclear proliferation elsewhere. This problem had been recognized since the 1960s, but the growth of the literature had always outpaced the rate of actual proliferation. The pattern continued. There were many useful empirical studies which monitored the proliferation of nuclear and other weapons of mass destruction, but little was added to existing theory [126, 152, 164, 169, 179, 187, 188]. Meanwhile, several detailed analyses were published of the nuclear options and rationales of the existing (non-superpower) nuclear powers – the first proliferators [106, 124, 137, 170, 174]. The relatively simple nuclear world of the strategists of the 'golden age' had vanished, and an original book on nuclear fears and strategies in a fractious and proliferating environment remained to be written. Despite the ritualistic endorsements of neorealism from within the strategic profession, Waltz's pro-proliferation neorealist scripture found few disciples [210].

As with nuclear proliferation, there were no significant additions to general arms race theory in the late 1980s. Thee wrote about the irrational momentum of research and development [194] and Jacobsen and his collaborators about the interplay between new weapons and old mindsets [97]. Evangelista effectively discredited those who assumed that US and Soviet weapons' innovation processes were the same [57]. One action-reaction phenomenon did attract considerable attention, however, namely the dialectic of strategic defence versus strategic offence. The Strategic Defense Initiative (SDI) of President Reagan – whose fantastical element was encapsulated in the popular 'Star Wars' tag – would not disappear, although it was increasingly obvious that it would not (could not) be built in its original conception. Nevertheless, it launched a prolonged boost phase of both partisan [36, 163, 200, 205] and sophisticated [24, 99, 188] literature, though no decisive theoretical ideas were added to those earlier debates about ballistic missile defence which had first been heard in the late 1960s.

Preventing the militarization of space was one of the concerns of arms controllers; here again theoretical development was limited. For nearly 30 years arms control had been a concept which had been central to the credo of nuclear stability, but in the Gorbachev era its advocates appeared bewildered. Commentary prevailed over theoretical development [192]. Disillusionment with the formal arms control which had developed in the 1960s and 1970s – focusing on numerical balances – had been growing for some years. Instead, the emphasis was shifting to ideas associated with confidence-building and crisis management [10]. A variety of overviews were written [9, 33, 211] but little original theory. Usefully, O'Neill and Schwarz went back to the beginnings and brought together Bull's influential writings about arms control [158].

Declining confidence in 'golden age' theory was also evident in the work on crisis management. McNamara continued to argue that crisis management was the essence of strategy [141], but now the hubris of the Kennedy crisis managers was called into question: 'from Cuba to Sarajevo' was how Williams aptly described it [217]. It was hardly a coincidence that the Reagan–Brezhnev confrontation gave new life to anxieties about the 'Sarajevo syndrome' which had led to the First World War and to the relevance of political psychology. Lebow incorporated psychological insights into a discussion about miscalculation and ways of improving crisis stability [119, 120]. Jervis, Lebow and Stein demonstrated the importance of domestic pressures and other 'irrational' factors [101]. George brought specialists together to try to draw up 'principles' of crisis management and to bridge the gap between theory and practice [75]. Their verdict was more optimistic than Lebow's and, like much of what was written in the late 1980s, was more readily applicable to the bipolar world which was dissolving than to the more complex reality which was emerging. New studies of the Falklands War, which showed how politico–military crises should not be handled, tended to support Lebow [65]. Betts wrote an important book on the role of nuclear weapons in Cold War crises and on the political significance of nuclear weapons generally [8]. Others, such as Herring, preferred to emphasize the decline of nuclear diplomacy [93].

One effect of the new Cold War was to re-focus attention on the ethical dimension of the nuclear confrontation. Needless to say, anti-nuclear opinion found deterrence ethically wanting, and these arguments continued to be elaborated through the 1980s [59, 110]. The moral complexities of deterrence were well exposed by a number of writers [91, 156, 162]. By the mid-1980s pro-nuclear moralists were retaliating against the counter-value attack they had suffered, and a salvo of books and chapters argued in favour of the 'just deterrent' [50, 60, 108, 153, 160, 220]. The arguments were sophisticated, on a mixture of moral and consequentialist grounds, but they failed to answer the concern of anti-nuclear writers that the 'just deterrent' could justify anything [15].

Speculation about nuclear ethics, deterrence and crises added to the renewed interest in political psychology. Notable books, in addition to that of Jervis et al. [101] were Kull's Minds at War [115] and Lifton and Markusen's The Genocidal Mentality [123]. The Oxford Research Group produced a series of studies which attempted to identify who actually made nuclear decisions and what their assumptions were [56, 90, 140]. The lack of attention which these works received within the mainstream strategic studies' community proved to be a perfect illustration of the behaviour described by Kull, Lifton and Markusen, namely disassociation, psychic numbing, rationalization, disavowal and denial.

Behaviour of a different sort was examined by other students of strategy who began to look seriously at norms rather than 'nukes'. The Gorbachev era saw a growing realization of the contribution of norms in maintaining stability. One version of this was the interest in the alleged relationship between liberal democracy and peace [52, 66, 68]. Another was the burgeoning literature on regime theory which began to have some impact on thinking about security relations. The most weighty volume was George's multi-contributor *US–Soviet Security Cooperation* [74], which successfully integrated theory and case studies.

Interest in regimes converged with the literature on common security and military confidence-building. Security *with* rather than *against* others was now increasingly in vogue in the industrialized world [1, 25, 147, 208, 219]. The 'alternative' ideas of the early 1980s were now slipping into the Western mainstream but not easily. These included Kaldor's designation of the Cold War as an 'imaginary war' – a technique by which the superpowers used 'strategy' as a device to manage and dominate their respective alliances [104]; Sharp's ideas about civilian-based defence [175]; Chomsky's argument about US imperialism deterring democracy [38]; and Gorbachev's goal of security without nuclear weapons [107].

(c) Issues

In addition to theoretical questions, strategists found the 1985–91 period full of pressing policy issues. Strategic studies had always been hounded by events, but in the Gorbachev era the subject could simply not keep up. Strategic studies lost its context; not with the long-feared bang but with a whimper.

The strategic policy issues of the late 1980s demanded greater theoretical speculation than they received. In particular, '1989' remained to be explained. Were these events simply a vindication of tough Western policies? Others argued that the Soviet breakdown had been the result of internal collapse rather than external pressure [88, 136] and that the new agenda included such problems as nationalism, migration, economic instability and lack of political development. This broader agenda was evident in the wide-ranging debate about European security after the Cold War [64, 96, 139, 144, 167, 206].

The participants in the debate about the New Europe generally argued that security and military power could no longer be seen as synonymous. An early signal of this had been Smith and Thompson's *Prospectus for a Habitable Planet* [183], which was an updating of their influential *Protest and Survive*. A special issue of *Survival* on the 'Non-military aspects of security' [190] showed that a broader agenda was on the way to being accepted by the professional establishment [37]. It became increasingly common to place the degradation of nature on the security agenda [30, 166, 195].

The broadening range of issues, together with the ending of the Cold War, naturally led to closer consideration being given to a range of security problems in the Third World [40, 47, 53, 121, 157, 195, 199, 207]. Actual conflicts, notably the wars in the Gulf [39, 193], were examined, and issues of intervention, peacekeeping and conflict resolution rose in importance, though for the moment they were not much embraced by strategists [32, 128, 131, 191]. Renewed attention was given to problems of terrorism and low-intensity warfare [43, 62, 116, 145, 181, 215] and naval power [13, 31,

58, 87, 94, 149, 211]. For the most part, in these areas, authors were simply updating and elaborating their earlier theories. Conventional defence on land attracted renewed interest in reaction to Airland Battle, FOFA and the nuclearmania of the early 1980s [6, 7, 204].

If the mainstream strategic community felt under pressure as the Cold War context evaporated, so did advocates of common security and non-offensive defence, were these ideas conceived for the European context in the Cold War also as time-bound and place-bound as the concepts of high strategic theory? For example, did the collection by Boserup and Neild, *The Foundations of Defensive Defence* [21] represent the end of theorizing about military restructuring on NOD principles, rather than just a stage? And were the ideas about NOD in the 21st century [214] obsolete before they were published?

Beyond the end of strategic studies

The history of strategic studies, as the academic world had come to know the subject, was intimately connected with the nuclear revolution and the Cold War. When Gorbachev rose to power, the old world order still prevailed; by the time he lost power, and the Soviet Union itself had collapsed, the global strategic context had altered dramatically. Such an experience was naturally a severe dislocation for those whose professional lives had been based on trying to explain and understand – and in some cases advocate – the business of nuclear strategy in the Cold War. When the Iron Curtain was finally dismantled it became apparent that it had imprisoned many minds on both sides – and notably students of strategy – into old ways of thinking about the 'games nations play'.

To say that strategic studies is now at an end is merely to draw a line under a particular period of thought. Without doubt, many of the theories, concepts and approaches elaborated in the 49 years since the Second World War will survive. The study of the military dimension of world politics will continue, although subsumed, in all probability, within the broader subfield of 'security studies'. Yet some viewpoints still continue to equate 'security' with 'strategy' [208]. Chipman, on the other hand, argues [37] that strategic studies, after a 40-year narrowing, can now go back to its broader nature; while the prescription is promising, this argument fails to recognize that strategic studies as we now understand it did not exist before the nuclear revolution. Strategic studies should not be mistaken for strategy (or security) either before its birth or after its end. In future, the study of the military dimension of international relations will probably be less like the period of high strategic theory and more like 'war studies' as presaged by McInnes and Sheffield [138].

The arguments over the subject's focus, boundaries, philosophy and definition are set to continue but with a greater methodological self-consciousness, as the study of the military dimension of world politics responds to the far-reaching debates taking place in international political theory [86, 216]. The intellectual uncertainties of strategic studies' late period

– when the breaking of paradigms took place alongside the breaking of military blocs – was underlined by the way self-consciously neorealist analysts embraced cultural, historical and ideological factors. In contrast to these years dominated by neorealist ideology, there will in future be much greater explicit emphasis on area studies, history, agency, language, comparative politics, culture, society and subjectivity. The study of strategy will, intellectually, open up. Equally, a wider agenda of issues will be addressed. Priorities will change from European security and nuclear deterrence between the superpowers to questions of intervention, the dissemination of weapons of mass destruction, conventional warfare, regional alliances and arms control, peacekeeping, disarmament and nuclear deterrence in a South/North context and nuclear ambitions versus nuclear taboos.

A reconceptualized field of 'security studies' will not replace strategic studies; it will be the latter's new intellectual home. Violence, without doubt, will continue to be a pervasive feature of the world scene; what we are now seeing is the replacement of the 'grand narrative' of nuclear theory by a pattern of postmodern violence which is both more localized and not easily definable as 'internal' or 'external'. In the struggle to explain and understand politics on a global scale the systematic study of the military dimension will no longer be the major subfield of the past but will instead constitute a sub-subfield. For the moment at least, to adapt a line of Robert Lowell, strategic studies has talked our extinction to death.

Bibliography

1. Alternative Defence Commission *The Politics of Alternative Defence: a Policy for a Non-nuclear Britain.* London, Paladin, 1987.
2. Azar, E.E. and Moon, C. (eds) *National Security in the Third World: The Management of Internal and External Threats.* Aldershot, Edward Elgar, 1988.
3. Barnaby, F. *The Automated Battlefield.* New York, Free Press, 1986.
4. Baylis, J. *et al. Contemporary Strategy* (2 vols), London, Croom Helm and New York, Holmes & Meier, 1987.
5. Baylis, J. and Garnett, J.C. (eds) *The Makers of Nuclear Strategy.* London, Pinter, 1991.
6. Bellamy, C. *The Future of Land Warfare.* London, Croom Helm and New York, St. Martin's Press, 1987.
7. Bellany, I. and Huxley, T. (eds) *New Conventional Weapons and Western Defence.* London, Cass, 1987.
8. Betts, R.K. *Nuclear Blackmail and Nuclear Balance.* Washington DC, The Brookings Institution, 1987.
9. Blackwill, R.D. and Larrabee, S. *Conventional Arms Control and East–West Security.* Durham, Duke University Press and Oxford, Clarendon Press, 1989.
10. Blechman, B.M. (ed.) *Preventing Nuclear War: A Realistic Approach.* Bloomington and Indianapolis, Indiana University Press, 1985.
11. Bobbit, P. *et al. US Nuclear Strategy: A Reader.* London, Macmillan, 1989.
12. Booth, K. *Strategy and Ethnocentrism.* London, Croom Helm, 1979.
13. Booth, K. *Law, Force and Diplomacy at Sea.* London, George Allen & Unwin and Winchester, Unwin Hyman, 1985.

14. Booth, K. 'New Challenges and Old Mindsets: Ten Rules for Empirical Realists' in C.G. Jacobsen (ed.) *The Uncertain Course: New Weapons, Strategies and Mind-Sets*. Oxford, Oxford University Press, 1987, pp. 39–66.

15. Booth, K. 'Nuclear Deterrence and "World War III": How Will History Judge?' in R. Kolkowicz (ed.) *The Logic of Nuclear Terror*. Boston, Allen and Unwin, 1987, pp. 251–82.

16. Booth, K. 'The Evolution of Strategic Thinking' in J. Baylis *et al.* (eds) *Contemporary Strategy*. Vol. I: *Theories and Concepts*. New York, Holmes & Meier, 1987, pp. 30–70.

17. Booth, K. and Baylis, J. *Britain, NATO and Nuclear Weapons. Alternative Defence versus Alliance Reform*. London, Macmillan, 1989.

18. Booth, K. *New Thinking About Strategy and International Security*. London, HarperCollins, 1991.

19. Booth, K. 'Security and Emancipation'. *Review of International Studies*, vol. 17, no. 3, 1991, pp. 313–26.

20. Booth, K. and Wheeler, N.J. 'Beyond Nuclearism' in R.C. Karp (ed.) *Security Without Nuclear Weapons?* Oxford, Oxford University Press, 1992, pp. 22–55.

21. Boserup, A. and Neild, R. (eds) *The Foundations of Defensive Defence*. London, Macmillan and New York, St. Martin's Press, 1990.

22. Brodie, B. *et al.* *The Absolute Weapon: Atomic Power and World Order*. New York, Harcourt, Brace, 1946.

23. Brodie, B. *War and Politics*. London, Collins and New York, Macmillan, 1973.

24. Bulkeley, R. and Spinardi, G. *Space Weapons. Deterrence or Delusion?* Cambridge, Polity Press and New York, Barnes & Noble Books, 1986.

25. *Bulletin of the Atomic Scientists*, 'A New European Defense'. vol. 44, no. 7, September, 1988. Special issue.

26. Bundy, McG. 'Existential Deterrence and its Consequences' in D. Maclean (ed.) *The Security Gamble: Deterrence Dilemmas in the Nuclear Age*. Totowa, Rowman and Allanheld, pp. 3–13.

27. Bundy, McG. *Danger and Survival: Choices about the Bomb in the First Fifty Years*. New York, Random House, 1990.

28. Buzan, B. *An Introduction to Strategic Studies*. London, Macmillan, 1987 and New York, St. Martin's Press, 1988.

29. Buzan, B. *et al.* *The European Security Order Recast: Scenarios for the Post Cold-War Era*. London, Pinter, 1990.

30. Buzan, B. *People States & Fear. An Agenda For International Security Studies in the Post-Cold War Era. Second Edition*. Boulder, Lynne Rienner, 1991 and London, Harvester Wheatsheaf, 1990.

31. Cable, J. *Navies in Violent Peace*. London, Macmillan, 1989.

32. Calvocoressi, P. *A Time for Peace: Pacifism, Internationalism and Protest Forces in the Reduction of War*. London, Hutchinson, 1987.

33. Carnsale, A. and Haass, R. *Superpower Arms Control: Setting the Record Straight*. Cambridge, MA, Ballinger Publishing Co., 1987.

34. Carter, A. *Success and Failure in Arms Control Negotiations*. Oxford, Oxford University Press, 1989.

35. Ceadel, M. *Thinking About Peace and War*. Oxford, Oxford University Press, 1987.

36. Chalfont, A. *Star Wars: Suicide or Survival?* London, Weidenfeld and Nicolson, 1985.

37. Chipman, J. 'The Future of Strategic Studies'. *Survival*, vol. 34, no. 1, Spring, 1992, pp. 109–31.

38. Chomsky, N. *Deterring Democracy*. London, Verso and New York, Hill & Wang, 1991.
39. Chubin S. and Tripp, C. *Iran and Iraq at War*. London, I.B. Tauris, 1988.
40. Clapham, C. and Philip, G. *The Political Dilemmas of Military Regimes*. London, Croom Helm, 1985.
41. Clark, I. *Waging War: A Philosophical Introduction*. Oxford, Oxford University Press, 1988.
42. Clausewitz, K. Von *On War*, edited and translated by M. Howard and P. Paret. Princeton, Princeton University Press, 1976.
43. Cline, R.S. and Alexander, Y. *Terrorism as State Sponsored Covert Warfare*. Fairfax, Hero, 1986.
44. Cohn, C. 'Sex and Death in the Rational World of Defense Intellectuals'. *Signs*, vol. 12, no. 4, Summer, 1987, pp. 687–718.
45. Cohn, C. 'Slick-ems, Glick-ems, Christmas Trees, and Cookie Cutters: Nuclear Language and How We Learned to Pat the Bomb'. *Bulletin of the Atomic Scientists*, vol. 43, no. 5, 1987, pp. 17–24.
46. Crawford, N.C. 'Once and Future Security Studies'. *Security Studies*, vol. 2, Winter, 1991, pp. 283–316.
47. David, S.R. *Third World Coups d'État and International Security*. Baltimore, Johns Hopkins Press, 1986.
48. Dean, J. *Watershed in Europe: Dismantling the East–West Military Confrontation*. Lexington, Lexington Books, 1987.
49. Der Derian, J. and Shapiro, M.J. (eds) *International/Intertextual Relations. Postmodern Readings of World Politics*. Lexington, Lexington Books, 1990.
50. Dougherty, J.E. *The Bishops and Nuclear Weapons: The Catholic Pastoral Letter on War and Peace*. Hamden, Archon Books, 1984.
51. Douhet, G. *The Command of the Air*. New York, Coward-McCann, 1942.
52. Doyle, M.W. 'Kant, Liberal Legacies and Foreign Affairs'. *Philosophy and Public Affairs*, vol. 12, no. 3, 1983, pp. 205–35.
53. Duner, B. *Military Intervention in Civil Wars: the 1970s*. Aldershot, Gower and New York, St. Martin's Press, 1985.
54. Earle, E.M. (ed.) *Makers of Modern Strategy: Military Thought From Macchiavelli to Hitler*. Princeton, Princeton University Press, 1961.
55. Elshtain, J.B. *Women and War*. Brighton, Harvester, 1987 and New York, Basic Books, 1988.
56. Elworthy, S. *Telling the Truth: Women and Decisions on Nuclear Weapons*. Oxford, Oxford Research Group, 1987.
57. Evangelista, M. *Innovation and the Arms Race: How the United States and Soviet Union Develop New Military Technologies*. Ithaca, Cornell University Press, 1988.
58. Fieldhouse, R. (ed.) *Security at Sea: Naval Forces and Arms Control*. Oxford, Oxford University Press, 1989.
59. Finnis, J., Boyle, J. and Grisez, G. *Nuclear Deterrence, Morality and Realism*. Oxford, Clarendon Press, 1987.
60. Fisher, D. *Morality and the Bomb: An Ethical Assessment of Nuclear Deterrence*. London, Croom Helm, 1985.
61. Forsberg, R. *The Case for a Third-World Nonintervention Regime*. Brookline, IDDS, 1987.
62. Freedman, L. *et al. Terrorism and International Order*. London, Routledge and Kegan Paul, 1986.
63. Freedman, L. *The Evolution of Nuclear Strategy*. second edition, London, Macmillan, 1989.

64. Freedman, L. and Saunders, J. (eds) *Population Change and European Security*. Oxford, Brassey's, 1991.
65. Freedman, L. and Gamba-Stonehouse, V. *Signals of War: The Falklands Conflict of 1982*. London, Faber, 1990 and Princeton, Princeton University Press, 1991.
66. Fukuyama, F. 'The End of History'. *The National Interest*, vol. 16, no. 1, 1989, pp. 3–18.
67. Fukuyama, F. 'Democratization and International Security'. *Adelphi Paper* no. 265, London, IISS, 1992, pp. 14–24.
68. Fukuyama, F. *The End of History and the Last Man*. London, Hamish Hamilton and New York, The Free Press, 1992.
69. Garnett, J.C. (ed.) *Theories of Peace and Security*. London, Macmillan and New York, St. Martin's Press, 1970.
70. Garthoff, R.L. *Detente and Confrontation*. Washington, DC, Brookings, 1985.
71 Garthoff, R.L. *Deterrence and the Revolution in Soviet Military Doctrine*. Washington, DC, Brookings, 1990.
72. Gat, A. *The Origins of Military Thought From the Enlightenment to Clausewitz*. Oxford, Oxford University Press, 1991.
73. Gates, D. *Non-Offensive Defence. An Alternative Strategy for NATO?* London, Macmillan and New York, St. Martin's Press, 1991.
74. George, A.L. *et al. U.S.–Soviet Security Cooperation: Achievements, Failures, Lessons*. New York, Oxford University Press, 1988.
75. George, A.L. (ed.) *Avoiding War. Problems of Crisis Management*. Boulder, and London, Westview Press, 1991.
76. Giddens, A. *The Nation-State and Violence*. Cambridge, Polity Press, 1985 and Berkeley, University of California Press, 1987.
77. Glaser, G. *Analysing Strategic Nuclear Policy*. Washington, DC, Brookings, 1991.
78. Grant, R. and Newland, K. (eds) *Gender and International Relations*. Bloomington and Indianapolis, Indiana University Press and Milton Keynes, Open University Press, 1991.
79. Gray, C.S. *Strategic Studies and Public Policy: The American Experience*. Lexington, University Press of Kentucky, 1982.
80. Gray, C.S. *Nuclear Strategy and National Style*. Lanham, University Press of America, 1986.
81. Gray, C.S. *The Geopolitics of Super Power*. Lexington, University Press of Kentucky, 1988.
82. Green, P. *Deadly Logic: The Theory of Nuclear Deterrence*. Columbus, Columbus University Press, 1966.
83. Gregory, S. *The Hidden Cost of Deterrence: Nuclear Weapons Accidents*. London, Brassey's, 1990.
84. Griffith, S.B. *Sun Tzu: The Art of War*. Oxford, Oxford University Press, 1963.
85. Groom, A.J.R. 'Strategy' in M. Light and A.J.R. Groom (eds) *International Relations. A Handbook of Current Theory*. London, Pinter, 1985, pp. 141–55.
86. Groom, A.J.R. 'Paradigms in conflict: the strategist, the conflict researcher and the peace researcher'. *Review of International Studies*, vol. 14, no. 2, April, 1988, pp. 97–115.
87. Grove, E. *The Future of Sea Power*. Annapolis, Naval Institute Press and London, Routledge, 1990.
88. Halliday, F. 'International Relations: Is There a New Agenda?'. *Millennium*, vol. 20, no. 1, Winter, 1990, pp. 57–72.
89. Halperin, M.H. *Nuclear Fallacy: Dispelling the Myth of Nuclear Strategy*. Cambridge, MA, Ballinger, 1987.

90. Hamwee, J. Miall, H. and Elworthy, S. *Assumptions of British Nuclear Weapons Decision-makers.* Oxford, Oxford Research Group, 1989.
91. Hardin, R. *et al.* (eds) *Nuclear Deterrence: Ethics and Strategy.* Chicago, Chicago University Press, 1985.
92. Herken, G. *Counsels of War.* New York, Oxford University Press, 1987.
93. Herring, E. 'The Decline of Nuclear Diplomacy' in K. Booth (ed.) *New Thinking about Strategy and International Security.* London, HarperCollins, 1991, pp. 90–109.
94. Hill, J.R. *Arms Control at Sea.* London, Routledge, 1988.
95. Holsti, K.J. *The Dividing Discipline: Hegemony and Diversity in International Theory.* Boston, Unwin Hyman, 1987.
96. Hyde-Price, A. *European Security Beyond the Cold War: Four Scenarios for the Year 2010.* London, Sage, 1991.
97. Jacobsen, C.G. (ed.) *The Uncertain Course: New Weapons, Strategies and Mind-Sets.* Oxford, Oxford University Press, 1987.
98. Jacobsen, C.G. (ed.) *Strategic Power: USA/USSR.* London, Macmillan and New York, St. Martin's Press, 1990.
99. Jasani, B. (ed.) *Space Weapons and International Security.* Oxford, Oxford University Press, 1987.
100. Jervis, R. *Perception and Misperception in International Politics.* Princeton, Princeton University Press, 1976.
101. Jervis, R., Lebow, R.N. and Stein, J.G. *Psychology and Deterrence.* Baltimore, Johns Hopkins University Press, 1985.
102. Jervis, R. *The Meaning of the Nuclear Revolution: Statecraft and the Prospect of Armageddon,* Ithaca, Cornell University Press, 1989.
103. Job, B.L. (ed.) *The Insecurity Dilemma: National Security of Third World States.* Boulder and London, Lynne Rienner, 1992.
104. Kaldor, M. *The Imaginary War.* Oxford, Blackwell, 1990.
105. Kaplan, F. *The Wizards of Armageddon.* New York, Simon & Schuster, 1983.
106. Karp, R.C. *Security with Nuclear Weapons?: Different Perspectives on National Security.* Oxford, Oxford University Press, 1991.
107. Karp, R.C. (ed.) *Security Without Nuclear Weapons?* Oxford, Oxford University Press, 1992.
108. Kavka, G. *Moral Paradoxes of Nuclear Deterrence.* Cambridge, Cambridge University Press, 1987.
109. Kennan, G.F. *The Nuclear Delusion: Soviet–American Relations in the Atomic Age.* London, Hamish Hamilton and New York, Pantheon Books, 1984.
110. Kenny, A. *The Logic of Deterrence.* Chicago, University of Chicago Press and London, Firethorn, 1985.
111. Klein, B. 'Hegemony and Strategic Culture'. *Review of International Studies,* vol. 14, no. 2, April, 1988, pp. 133–48.
112. Klein, B. 'How the West was One: Representational Politics of NATO'. *International Studies Quarterly,* vol. 34, no. 3, September, 1990, pp. 311–25.
113. Kolkowicz, R. (ed.) *The Logic of Nuclear Terror.* Boston, Unwin Hyman, 1987.
114. Kolodziej, E.A. 'What is Security and Security Studies?' *Arms Control,* vol. 13, no. 1, April, 1992, pp. 1–31.
115. Kull, S. *Minds at War: Nuclear Reality and the Inner Conflict of Defense Policymakers.* New York, Basic Books, 1990.
116. Laqueur, W. *The Age of Terrorism.* London, Weidenfeld and Nicolson, 1987 and Boston, Little, Brown & Company, 1988.

117. Lawrence, P.K. 'Nuclear Strategy and Political Theory: A Critical Assessment'. *Review of International Studies*, vol. 11, no. 2, April, 1985, pp. 105–21.

118. Lawrence, P.K. *Preparing for Armageddon: A Critique of Western Strategy*. Brighton, Wheatsheaf and New York, St. Martin's Press, 1988.

119. Lebow, R.N. *Between Peace and War: The Nature of International Crisis*. Baltimore, Johns Hopkins University Press, 1981.

120. Lebow, R.N. *Nuclear Crisis Management: a Dangerous Illusion*. Ithaca, Cornell University Press, 1987.

121. Leifer, M. *ASEAN and the Security of South-East Asia*. London, Routledge, 1988.

122. Liddell Hart, B.H. *Strategy: The Indirect Approach*. London, Faber, 1967.

123. Lifton, R.J. and Markusen, E. *The Genocidal Mentality: Nazi Holocaust and Nuclear Threat*. New York, Basic Books, 1990.

124. Lin, C-P. *China's Nuclear Weapons Strategy. Tradition within Evolution*. Lexington, Lexington Books, 1988.

125. Linklater, A. *Beyond Realism and Marxism: Critical Theory and International Relations*. London, Macmillan, 1990.

126. Lomas, P. and Muller, H. *Western Europe and the Future of the Nuclear Non-Proliferation Treaty*. Brussels, Centre for European Policy Studies and the Frankfurt Peace Research Institute, 1989.

127. Luard, E. *War in International Society*. London, I.B. Tauris and New Haven, Yale University Press, 1986.

128. Luard, E. *The Blunted Sword: The Erosion of Military Power In Modern World Politics*. London, I.B. Tauris, 1988.

129. Luttwak, E. *Strategy: The Logic of War and Peace*. Cambridge, MA, Belknap Press, 1987.

130. Machiavelli, *The Prince* in A. Gilbert (ed.) *Machiavelli: The Chief Works and Others*. Durham, Duke University Press, 1965, pp. 5–96.

131. Mackinlay, J. *The Peacekeepers. An Assessment of Peacekeeping Operations at the Arab–Israeli Interface*. London, Unwin Hyman, 1989.

132. Mahan, A.T. *The Influence of Sea Power upon History 1660–1783*. London, Methuen, 1965.

133. Mao Tse-tung, *Basic Tactics*, New York, Praeger, 1966.

134. MccGwire, M. 'Deterrence: the Problem – Not the Solution'. *International Affairs*, vol. 62, no. 1, Winter, 1985–6, pp. 55–70.

135. MccGwire, M.K. *Military Objectives in Soviet Foreign Policy*. Washington, DC, Brookings, 1987.

136. MccGwire, M.K. *Perestroika and Soviet National Security*. Washington, DC, Brookings, 1991.

137. McInnes, C. *Trident: The Only Option?* London, Brassey's, 1986.

138. McInnes, C. and Sheffield, G.D. (eds) *Warfare in the Twentieth Century: Theory and Practice*. London, Unwin Hyman, 1988.

139. McInnes, C. (ed.) *Security and Strategy in the New Europe*. London and New York, Routledge, 1992.

140. McLean, S. (ed.) *How Nuclear Decisions are Made*. London, Macmillan, 1986.

141. McNamara, R.S. *Blundering into Disaster: Surviving the First Century of the Nuclear Age*. London, Bloomsbury and New York, Pantheon, 1987.

142. McNamara, R.S. *Out of the Cold. New Thinking for American Foreign and Defense Policy in the 21st Century*. London, Bloomsbury, 1990 and New York, Simon & Shuster, 1989.

143. Mearsheimer, J.J. *Conventional Deterrence*. Ithaca, Cornell University Press, 1983.

144. Mearsheimer, J.J. 'Back to the Future: Instability in Europe after the Cold War'. *International Security*, vol. 15, no. 1, Summer, 1990, pp. 5–52.
145. Merkl, P.H. (ed.) *Political Violence and Terror: Motifs and Motivations.* Berkeley, Los Angeles and London, University of California Press, 1986.
146. Meyer, S.M. 'The Sources and Prospects of Gorbachev's New Political Thinking on Security'. *International Security*, vol. 13, no. 2, Fall, 1988, pp. 124–63.
147. Moller, B. *Common Security and Nonoffensive Defense: A Neorealist Perspective.* Boulder, Lynne Rienner, 1992.
148. Moller, B. *The Dictionary of Alternative Defence.* London, Adamantine Press, 1992 and Boulder, Lynne Rienner, 1993.
149. Morris, M.A. *Expansion of Third World Navies.* London, Macmillan, 1987 and New York, St. Martin's Press, 1988.
150. Mueller, J. 'The Essential Irrelevance of Nuclear Weapons'. *International Security*, vol. 13, no. 2, Fall, 1988, pp. 55–79.
151. Mueller, J. *Retreat From Doomsday.* New York. Basic Books, 1990.
152. Nolan, Janne, E. *Trappings of Power: Ballistic Missiles in the Third World.* Washington, DC, Brookings, 1992.
153. Nye Jr, J.S. *Nuclear Ethics.* New York, Free Press, 1986.
154. Nye Jr, J.S. 'The Long-term Future of Deterrence' in R. Kolkowicz (ed.) *The Logic of Nuclear Terror.* Boston, Allen & Unwin, 1987, pp. 234–47.
155. Nye Jr, J.S. and Lynn-Jones, S.M. 'International Security Studies'. *International Security*, vol. 12, no. 4, Spring, 1988, pp. 5–27.
156. O'Brien, W.V. and Langan, J. (eds) *The Nuclear Dilemma and the Just War Tradition.* Lexington, Lexington Books, 1986.
157. O'Neill, R. (ed.) *The Conduct of East–West Relations in the 1980s.* Hamden, Shoe String Press and London, Macmillan, 1985.
158. O'Neill, R. and Schwartz, D.N. *Hedley Bull on Arms Control.* London, Macmillan and New York, St. Martin's Press, 1987.
159. Osgood, R.E. and Tucker, R.W. *Force, Order and Justice.* Baltimore, Johns Hopkins Press, 1967.
160. Osgood, R.E. *The Nuclear Dilemmas in American Strategic Thought.* Boulder and London, Westview Press, 1988.
161. Paret, P. (ed.) *Makers of Modern Strategy from Machiavelli to the Nuclear Age.* Princeton, Princeton University Press, 1986.
162. Paskins, B (ed.) *Ethics & European Security.* London, Croom Helm and Westport, Greenwood Publishing Group, 1986.
163. Payne, K.B. *Strategic Defense: 'Star Wars' in perspective.* Lanham, University Press of America, 1986.
164. Pilat, J.F. and Pendley, R.E. (eds) *Beyond 1995: The Future of the NPT Regime.* New York, Plenum Press, 1990.
165. Posen, B.R. *The Sources of Military Doctrine: France, Great Britain, and Germany Between the World Wars.* Ithaca, Cornell University Press, 1984.
166. Prins, G. and Stamp, R. *Top Guns & Toxic Whales: The Environment & Global Security.* London, Earthscan Publications and Post Mills, Chelsea Green Publishing Company, 1991.
167. Pugh, M.C. (ed.) *European Security – Towards 2000.* Manchester, Manchester University Press, 1992.
168. Rapoport, A. *Strategy and Conscience.* New York, Harper & Row, 1965.
169. Reiss, M. *Without the Bomb, The Politics of Nuclear Non-Proliferation.* New York, Columbia University Press, 1989.
170. Roper, J. (ed.) *The Future of British Defence Policy.* Aldershot, Gower, 1985.

171. Sagan, S.D. *Moving Targets: Nuclear Strategy and National Security*. Princeton, Princeton University Press, 1990.
172. Scheer, R. *With Enough Shovels: Reagan, Bush and Nuclear War*. London, Secker and Warburg and New York, Random House, 1983.
173. Seabury, P. and Codevilla, A. *War. Ends & Means*. New York, Basic Books, 1989.
174. Segal, G. *Defending China*. Oxford, Oxford University Press, 1985.
175. Sharp, G. *Making Europe Unconquerable: the Potential of Civilian-Based Deterrence and Defence*. Cambridge, MA, Ballinger Publishing Co. and London, Taylor and Francis, 1985.
176. Shaw, M. *Dialectics of War: an Essay in the Social Theory of Total War and Peace*. London, Pluto, 1988.
177. Sheehan, M.J. *Arms Control: Theory and Practice*. Oxford, Blackwell, 1988.
178. Simpkin, R.E. *Race to the Swift: Thoughts on Twenty-First Century Warfare*. London, Brassey's, 1985.
179. Simpson, J. (ed.) *Nuclear Non-Proliferation: An Agenda for the 1990s*. Cambridge, Cambridge University Press, 1987.
180. Skocpol, T. *States and Social Revolutions: A Comparative Analysis of France, Russia and China*. Cambridge, Cambridge University Press, 1979.
181. *Small Wars and Insurgencies* (1991–) London, Frank Cass, three issues per year.
182. Smith, S. 'Mature Anarchy, Strong States and Security'. *Arms Control*, vol. 12, no. 2, September, 1991, pp. 325–39.
183. Smith, D. and Thompson, E.P. (eds) *Prospectus for a Habitable Planet*. Harmondsworth, Penguin, 1987.
184. Smoke, R. and Kortunov, A. (eds) *Mutual Security: A New Approach to Soviet–American Relations*. London, Macmillan, 1991 and New York, St. Martin's Press, 1990.
185. Snyder, J. *The Ideology of the Offensive: Military Decision Making and the Disaster of 1914*. Ithaca, Cornell University Press, 1984.
186. Snyder, J. 'The Gorbachev Revolution: A Waning of Soviet Expansionism?' *International Security*, vol. 12, no. 3, Winter, 1987/88, pp. 93–131.
187. Spector, L. *Nuclear Ambitions: The Spread of Nuclear Weapons*. Boulder, Westview, 1990.
188. Stares, P.B. *Space Weapons and U.S. Strategy: Origins and Developments*. London, Croom Helm, 1985.
189. Subrahmanyan, K. *Nuclear Proliferation and International Security*. New Delhi, Institute for Defence Studies and Analysis, 1985.
190. *Survival* 'Non-military Aspects of Strategy', vol. 31, no. 6, November/December, 1989. Special Issue.
191. *Survival* 'United Nations Peacekeeping', vol. 32, no. 3, May/June, 1990. Special Issue.
192. *Survival* 'Arms Control and the New Strategic Environment', vol. 32, no. 4, July/August, 1990. Special Issue.
193. *Survival* 'The United States, The Gulf And Europe', vol. 33, no. 1, January/February, 1991. Special Issue.
194. Thee, M. *Military Technology, Military Strategy and the Arms Race*. London, Croom Helm and New York, St. Martin's Press, 1986.
195. Thomas, C. *The Environment in International Relations*. London, Royal Institute of International Affairs, 1992.
196. Thomas, C. *In Search of Security: The Third World in International Relations*. Brighton, Wheatsheaf and Boulder, Lynne Rienner, 1987.

197. Thomas, C. *New States, Sovereignty and Intervention*. Aldershot, Gower, 1985.
198. Thomas, C. and Saravanamuttu, P. (eds) *Conflict and Consensus in South/North Security*. Cambridge, Cambridge University Press, 1989.
199. Thomas, C. and Saravanamuttu, P. (eds) *The State and Instability in the South*. London, Macmillan, 1989.
200. Thompson, E.P. (ed.) *Star Wars: Science-fiction Fantasy, or Serious Probability?* London, Penguin, 1985.
201. Thompson, R. *Defeating Communist Insurgency: Experiences from Malaya and Vietnam*. London, Chatto Windus, 1966.
202. Thucydides, *The Peloponnesian War*. New York, Modern Library, 1951.
203. Tromp, H.W. (ed.) *War in Europe. Nuclear and Conventional Perspectives*. Aldershot, Gower, 1989.
204. Unterseher, L. *The Spider and the Web: the Case for a Pragmatic Defence Alternative*. Bonn, Studiengruppe Alternative Ssicherheitspolitik, 1989.
205. Van Cleave, W.R. *Fortress USSR: The Soviet Strategic Defense Initiative and the US Strategic Defense Response*. Stanford, Hoover Institution Press, 1986.
206. Van Evera, S.W. 'Primed for Peace: Europe after the Cold War'. *International Security*, vol. 15, no. 3, Winter, 1990/91, pp. 7–57.
207. Van Evera, S. 'American Intervention in the Third World: Less Would be Better'. *Security Studies*, vol. 1, no. 1, Autumn, 1991, pp. 1–24.
208. Väyrynen, R. (ed.) *Policies for Common Security*. London, Taylor and Francis, 1985.
209. Walt, S.M. 'The Renaissance of Security Studies'. *International Studies Quarterly*, vol. 35, no. 2, June, 1991, pp. 211–39.
210. Waltz, K.N. 'The Spread of Nuclear Weapons: More May be Better'. *Adelphi Paper*, no. 171, London, IISS, September, 1981.
211. Watkins, J.D. 'The Maritime Strategy'. *US Naval Institute Proceedings*, January, 1986, Special Issue.
212. Warner, E.L. and Ochmanek, D.A. *Next Moves: An Arms Control Agenda for the 1990s*. New York, Council on Foreign Relations, 1989.
213. Weston, B.H. (ed.) *Alternative Security: Living Without Nuclear Deterrence*. Boulder, Westview, 1990.
214. Wiberg, H. and Moller, B. *NOD in the Twenty-First Century*, forthcoming.
215. Wilkinson, P. and Stewart, A.M. (eds) *Contemporary Research on Terrorism*. Aberdeen, Aberdeen University Press, 1987.
216. Williams, M.C. 'Neorealism and the Future of Strategy'. *Review of International Studies*, vol. 19, no. 2, April, 1993, pp. 103–21.
217. Williams, P. 'Crisis Management: from Cuba to Sarajevo' in K. Booth (ed.) *New Thinking about Strategy and International Security*. London, HarperCollins, 1991, pp. 140–62.
218. Windass, S. (ed.) *Avoiding Nuclear War: Common Security as a Strategy for the Defence of the West*. London, Brassey's, 1985.
219. Windass, S. and Grove, E. *The Crucible of Peace: Common Security in Europe*. Oxford, Brassey's 1986.
220. Woolsey, R.J. *Nuclear Arms: Ethics, Strategy, Politics*. San Francisco, Institute for Contemporary Studies, 1984.
221. *World Politics*, 'Rational deterrence theory', vol. 61, no. 2, April, 1989, Special Issue.
222. Zagare, F.C. 'Rationality and Deterrence'. *World Politics*, vol. 62, no. 2, January, 1990, pp. 238–60.

9 Conflict research
Christopher Mitchell

Somebody once wrote that you knew when you had successfully 'arrived' in academia; others adopted your ideas, misunderstood them, presented them as their own and then made extravagant claims for their relevance and effectiveness. Something of the sort has happened to conflict analysis and resolution over the last five or six years, as mainstream scholarly attention has switched from issues of threat manipulation, deterrence, military security and the intellectual problems presented by a loosely bipolar global political system. Suddenly, as previously latent conflicts emerge and escalate into protracted violence in, for example, the former Yugoslavia and the countries of the CIS (joining those already being fought out in Africa, the Middle East and Asia), a range of scholars have discovered that they have 'really' been doing conflict resolution 'all along'. Thus, it is becoming increasingly possible to attend conferences and listen to ex-strategic theorists, military security experts, Sovietologists and area specialists holding forth about the best means of 'resolving' conflicts. (On some such occasions, the means of 'conflict resolution' being advocated involve the sending of a peace enforcement force, the use of economic sanctions, the employment of selective air strikes or the use of 'mediation with muscle'.) A recent puff for the *Journal of Conflict Resolution* announced that it covered the 'key issues in conflict resolution' – nuclear war, defence burdens; foreign policy, technology; disarmament; power behaviour of nations; terrorists and political violence.

The language and concepts of the discipline, if not their exact original meaning, are thus becoming increasingly familiar in the mouths of media pundits, political leaders and policy advisers. In short, the field has 'arrived' at the centre of academic and political attention and at least some of its central ideas, hopefully not too distorted, will affect the way in which people think about the world and its problems, at least for a time.

Amid all this, those working in the field have continued to develop and refine its central concepts and to try to build a coherent body of theories about the causes of various kinds of conflict, the manner in which they emerge and escalate, the factors that maintain and protract them and the various means by which conflicts, at all social levels, might be ameliorated, settled by agreement or finally resolved and the relations between the conflicting parties transformed so that the conflict does not re-emerge, 40 years later, to devastate new generations. In doing this, conflict researchers continue to employ a wide variety of approaches but hold to a common belief that a general understanding (if not a general theory) of all social conflicts is possible. It can be attained by seeking common patterns and processes in conflicts in all social arenas, from the local community to the international system, and transferring findings between different arenas (or levels) to increase understanding of this complex and universal phenomenon.

General surveys and textbooks

The field still lacks a good general textbook that might serve as an introduction to students from other disciplines coming fresh to the field. An up-dated version of Kriesberg's *Social Conflict* [61] might be the best way of filling an obvious gap, but the work remains out of print and virtually unobtainable. An alternative would be to start with Pruitt and Rubin's short introduction [79], easily recognizable as the work of two psychologists or with Suter's little known but very readable work [100] which approaches conflict from an international relations, almost peace research background. Also from Australia is the collection of materials (audio tape as well as texts) produced by Tillett [101], an excellent and eclectic introduction to the field, which is determinedly a-disciplinary and which treats conflict as a universal rather than arena-specific phenomenon.

In more conventional mode, two surveys by Groom [42, 43] and two collections of writings edited by Sandole give a broad overview of the field of conflict research and are useful introductions to the range of conflicts and management or resolution mechanisms currently available as remedies. The older of the Sandole collections [87] is more uneven and fragmentary, in spite of the editors' efforts to integrate the material, but it does give readers an impression of the richness of the field as it was emerging in the mid-1980s. The second collection [88] is both more substantial and more up to date and concentrates upon the relationship between theory and practice – a key issue in a field which began and remains firmly committed to the idea that theory has to be applicable and applied to be of any use at all and that practitioners of conflict resolution should, in Kurt Lewin's words, be 'practical theorists'.

Other recent works deal with conflicts in more narrowly circumscribed arenas, and within more focused theoretical frameworks. The latest edition of Hocker and Wilmott's work on interpersonal conflict [45] has grown into a large and comprehensive text offering many insights into conflicts at levels other than the interpersonal and can be recommended for general readership in the field. In other arenas or at other social levels, a variety of works offer useful overviews, including a large symposium intended for use in law schools [40] but with many useful articles on the wider theme of dispute resolution.

In another vein entirely is Burton's latest four-volume work, in which he sets out in its most coherent and comprehensive form his theory about the relationship between basic human needs and the development of protracted, deep-rooted conflict, together with his views on how such conflicts might best be resolved, as opposed to managed or settled. Two of the books consist of readings selected by Burton and Dukes, one on human needs theories [14] and one on conflict resolution processes [16]. The other two are written by Burton and Dukes [15] and by Burton himself [13] and parallel the readings by dealing with theories of human needs on the one hand and conflict resolution practices on the other. Even if one does not share their enthusiasm for human needs theories, they make more sense than other 'root cause' theories that deal with human aggressiveness, drives for power or struggles between ego and id. The four books present an admirable introduction to the field and a challenge to those who hold differing views about the starting point of deep-rooted and intractable social conflicts. Another approach to this problem of 'intractability' is the set of papers edited by Kriesberg *et al.* [64], a disappointing and rather disjointed collection which never really gets to grips with the nature of intractability, let alone its causes and consequences.

Works on the relationship between power and social conflict continue to proliferate, most particularly in literature that deals with interpersonal conflict and in feminist work that is concerned with gender-based conflict. Most ambitious is Blalock's attempt at a general theory relating power and conflict [9], although Boulding's work on various aspects of power is livelier and more accessible [10]. From a feminist and postmodern viewpoint, the work of Fraser [37] and Brock-Utne [11] is thoughtful and original, while a great deal of attention has been paid by a variety of writers to the slippery issue of 'power imbalance' in conflicts and efforts to resolve them, without any very satisfactory conclusions, theoretical or practical, being reached [18, 97, 98].

For those with a taste for formal analyses, a number of recent works continue the tradition established by Richardson, Rapoport and the late, very much lamented Kenneth Boulding. Isard continues to work on formal analysis of conflict and means for its resolution [48]. In similar formal and eclectic manner, Fraser and Hipel [38] cover the use of a wide variety of formal, analytical tools from stability analysis to hypergames. More single mindedly, Axelrod [2] examines the neglected topic of co-operation through the lens of game theory, coming to the conclusion that some form of 'Do unto others as they do unto you' is the best strategy for eliciting co-operative behaviour.

Ethnicity and ethnic conflicts

While the field of conflict research is more resistant to academic fashion than most – there were *always* protracted and deep-rooted conflicts around to justify study and research – it is not completely immune to trends in the outside world. One trend that has had a significant impact on scholarly work in recent years has been the apparent proliferation of conflicts based upon ethnic identity groups. Earlier analysis tended to treat such conflicts within the conceptual framework of nationalism, state-building and national identity, or in some cases as involving 'cultural sub-nationalism' or 'primordial loyalties'. Now, however, and in response to events in Eastern Europe, South Asia, the Horn of Africa and elsewhere, a large literature is emerging that deals specifically with ethnic divisions and ethnically based conflicts. Among the many works of this genre produced recently, Horowitz's [46] book on divided societies is certainly the most thorough and comprehensive, but Smith's work [92, 93] is full of insights. Others who contribute interesting ideas to the study of this type of protracted conflict deal with the question broadly, as in the case of works by Ryan [85], who examines ethnic conflict from the viewpoint of inter-state relations and Rex [82], who starts from the viewpoint of race relations. A different approach is to take a particular instance of a divided society or an ethnically based conflict and use that as a vehicle for suggesting general lessons about the sources, dynamics and management of this type of dispute. Among this latter work, excellent examples are those on Northern Ireland [21], Sri Lanka [23] and the Middle East [7].

The literature on what might be done to ameliorate, manage or even resolve such conflicts is much less satisfactory, although Nordlinger's old book [75] still remains relevant and useful as does Lijphart's work on consociational democracy [67]. A good collection of essays on the problem of managing conflict in divided societies recently published by Montville [72] offers a wide range of structures and processes for dealing with ethnic divisions so that they do not give rise to conflict or, if they do, so that the conflict can be managed within an accepted, functional framework.

Some recent work on ethnic conflicts also touches upon one of the major debates in the field from the 1980s which involved the extent to which culture affected the causes, nature and playing out of conflicts in different societies; and whether cultural differences were so influential as to vitiate the possibility of any generalizations about conflict, let alone any general theories. The debate remains unresolved, but some interesting literature has emerged which partly arises from older, more specific work on cultural differences in negotiating styles. Cohen [17] offers a recent up-date and the subject is thoroughly discussed in the recent book by Avruch, Black and Scimecca [1].

Psychological aspects of conflict

One somewhat surprising development in recent conflict research has been the renewed interest in the psychological aspects of conflict and the development of several new lines of thought and research under this general heading. Among the latter have been new efforts to move beyond the familiar insights of cognitive psychology (images and perceptions, stereotyping and processes of group identification) towards depth psychology, particularly in considering the nature and possible need for 'an enemy'. Volkan's work [106] is of particular interest in this regard.

Much other research has centred around the psychological aspects of 'reconciliation' and the mutual sense of 'victimization', and these studies appear to have particular relevance both to processes preparing the ground for an agreement to terminate the overt conflict and to those needed subsequently to remove residues of hatred, mistrust and a sense of having been wronged, all of which can remain latent sources of future conflicts and violence if not deliberately tackled as part of a conflict resolution process. In the former case, Saunders' work (now reprinted) on the psychology of the Arab–Israeli dispute is a thoughtful set of reflections by a distinguished practitioner [89]. In the latter, the two-volume collection of papers edited by Volkan, Montville and Julius [107] covers this and an allied range of issues.

Fisher [34], in contrast, takes a more familiar set of ideas but is highly innovative in that he goes beyond the customary survey of the psychological aspects of conflict and examines the psychology of conflict resolution as well as of conflict creation and maintenance. The work is particularly interesting in its examination of some of the more recently developed procedures for helping to resolve conflict and their claims to provide new insights into conflict and means of its resolution. Another good survey along these lines is that of Stroebe et al. [96], while Glad's study [39] of the psychological origins of war is well worth reading. Fortunately for the field, White continues to publish on the same topic, and his most recent two books [108, 109] carry forward his long standing interest in the psychology of the 'Cold War' and its nuclear arsenals.

Quite apart from works which deliberately set out to examine conflicts from a psychological standpoint, a number of recent concepts and theories developed in mainstream social psychology have obvious relevance for conflict and its resolution. Work on entrapment and how it helps to explain the manner in which conflicts are maintained over long periods of time continues (see, for example, articles by Mitchell [70] and by Staw [94] among others), even though it has only occasionally been applied directly to the protraction of conflicts. There has not yet been a worthy successor to Iklé's old book on the ending of wars [47], but Sigal's volume on the ending of the Pacific War in 1945 [91] is a fine case study which adopts a bureaucratic politics model to illuminate why the Japanese leaders continued a struggle they knew to be lost and why the Allies continued to insist on unconditional surrender. By undermining the traditional 'rational actor' explanation as to why decisions were taken to drop atomic bombs on Hiroshima and Nagasaki, the book should put to rest debates on why the Truman Government 'really' used these weapons.

Two other interesting developments involve work undertaken on 'framing' (how people react to the same situation being described – or framed – in different ways) and the critical re-examination of the concept of 'rationality' undertaken by psychologists, philosophers and economists over the last decade. In the former case, work on 'framing' such as that by Nisbett and Ross [74] or Tversky and Kahneman [103] obviously has implications – yet to be fully worked out – for methods of conflict resolution, particularly when one bears in mind the struggle that occurs in many conflicts to determine what the conflict is 'really' about and for ways of creatively describing the conflict in such a way that 'win–win' as opposed to 'lose–lose' or 'win–lose' solutions are possible.

In the latter case, the whole re-examination of the nature of 'rational' choice and how real people (as opposed to 'economic man') actually make decisions might seem somewhat dated, given that Allison's seminal work on decision-making models was published over 20 years ago. However, thinking about decision making in conflict relationships still appears to be dominated by assumptions of 'rational choice' (particularly on the part of the adversary) and of the calculated causing of harm. Anything that shows decision making in protracted conflicts for the non-rational process that it is cannot but help to make analysis of conflict dynamics more real. In this light, work by scholars such as Elster [29, 30] has direct relevance to the field of conflict analysis and should form part of the literature of the field.

Conflict resolution; peace processes

Much conflict research over the last decade has concentrated upon the problems of managing and resolving protracted disputes and dealt anew with familiar topics such as de-escalation, the various stages of negotiation and the role of third parties in reaching agreement. One relatively recent – if seemingly obvious – innovation has been to treat all of these (and other) procedures as part of an overall, interdependent 'peace process', which may eventually arrive at a satisfactory resolution of deep-rooted conflicts and at a transformation of the relationship between adversaries. Kriesberg, in a rich and suggestive work [62] has used such an approach to analyse efforts to resolve the Arab–Israeli conflict in the Middle East and the US–Soviet confrontation, and to explain when and why the process succeeded or faltered.

Another new development in the field has been the scholarly attention paid to the 'pre-negotiation' phase of any conflict-resolution process and the efforts that might be needed to 'get parties to the table' – although, as some scholars such as Lederach [65] have pointed out, the whole idea of face-to-face negotiations at a formal table might – culturally – be a very Western way of dealing with conflicts, inappropriate to conflicting parties from other cultural backgrounds. Be that as it may, work on pre-negotiation phases, tactics and procedures has 'taken off' from Hal Saunders's pioneering article in *Negotiation Journal* [90], and the literature on pre-negotiation has proliferated, with interesting collections edited by Stein [95] and Mitchell and Webb [71], while Kriesberg and Thorson's later collection [63] probably provides the best overview of current thinking on issues of timing and de-escalation. Allied to this interest in the pre-negotiation phase is a continued interest in the question of the timing of de-escalatory moves and the question of how one determines 'the ripe moment' – if such a thing exists. Currently, the core conception in this literature is that of a 'hurting stalemate', first developed by Zartman [111], as a somewhat more subtle concept than the crude 'are both sides suffering enough destruction yet?' interpretation put on it by some. Haass's book on unending conflicts [44] also explores this issue of 'ripeness' in the context of a number of protracted intra-national conflicts and possible US responses to such disputes as Cyprus, South Africa and Northern Ireland.

Work on negotiation and bargaining continues, although this seems to have become less of a central focus for the field than previously. Both Pruitt [77, 78] and Druckman [27, 28] continue to publish prolifically on various aspects of negotiation and pre-negotiation theory, while the pages of *Negotiation Journal* provide regular reports on progress in this part of the field, whether analysis adopts a concession–convergence or a formula–detail approach to the process. Bendahmane and McDonald [5] have gathered together some official and non-official views about the art of the negotiator, while other works in the general area of negotiation theory include works by Jandt [50], Lewicki and Litterer [66] and Mautner-Markhoff [69].

Third-party involvement

If research on negotiation processes seems to have declined in volume recently, that on the activities of third parties has increased tremendously in quantity, if not quality. There remains a strong division in the field between those who hold that powerful, interested and resourceful third parties provide the best hope of a mediated or negotiated resolution and those who argue that such procedures merely arrive at an externally imposed, and hence temporary, settlement, so that the only path towards a sustainable resolution lies through the use of disinterested and facilitative third parties whose role is to assist the adversaries to arrive at their own solution to their conflict. Another interesting debate just starting to 'take off' concerns whether 'impartial' outsiders have a better chance of helping parties towards a solution than 'partial' insiders, who enjoy a relationship with the adversaries and also the latter's confidence.

Whatever the outcome of the scholarly debate, it seems clear that in the outside world the actual means of 'handling' conflict are beginning to range from the use of peace-enforcement troops to the holding of grass-roots workshops and dialogue groups to build bridges between adversaries, so that the literature reflecting that reality is inevitably diverse and somewhat confusing. It seems inevitable that political developments in the late 1980s and early 1990s will revive interest in both the conflict-management roles of international organizations, from the UN to the Red Cross and Crescent, via ECOWAS, the OAS, ASEAN, the Islamic Conference *et al*; and in the problems of using military force to 'keep the peace'. There has been little work on this latter topic in recent years, distinguished exceptions being two general surveys of peacekeeping by Rikye [83] and Wiseman [110]. However, it is clearly the case that the next few years will see a renewal of interest in this form of conflict reduction, hopefully acknowledging that the procedure needs to be accompanied by other processes aimed at finding a solution to the conflict itself, rather than at altering the behaviour of the parties in conflict.

Studies dealing directly with the more conventional forms of international mediation have been numerous in recent years, and much research and thinking about the nature of the mediatory process carried out by third parties with both leverage and with an interest in final outcomes has been undertaken by Touval and Zartman [101]. A more recent work by Princen [76] spans a broader range of mediator types and processes and provides some interesting insights into common strategies employed by those with and without 'leverage' – at least as that is traditionally conceived. Works on individual cases of mediation by third parties 'with leverage' include two interesting studies of peacemaking in Africa, one on Namibia by Jabri [49] and another on the ending of the Rhodesian/Zimbabwean conflict by Davidow [22].

Mitchell and Webb's volume [71] covers a number of different approaches to international mediation, while Moore's text [73] should be of considerable interest to anyone concerned with international mediation, even though his general lessons about successful mediation are mainly derived from conflicts in local and intra-national arenas. Bercovitch's work [8] also covers a broad range of types of mediation and third-party interventions and is a good introduction to the way in which conflict researchers 'cross levels' in their search for generalizations. For anyone interested in how research into mediation processes might be carried out, apart from using traditional historical analysis, Kressel and Pruitt's book [60] is an essential starting place.

Examples abound of recent monographs surveying the efforts of 'unofficial diplomats', of practitioners of 'Track Two' intervention, of 'scholar-practitioners' or of 'mediators without muscle'. The most recent work of Burton, the originator of the problem-solving workshop, is reviewed in two books, one by Azar [3] and one by Azar and Burton [4], while the use of this approach to attempt to repair UK–Argentine relationships post 1982 is available in Little and Mitchell's discussion of 'the aftermath' [68]. Kelman continues to write thoughtfully about the extension of the workshop technique in a series of articles arising from his own work in the Middle East [57, 58, 59], while Keashley and Fisher have extended thinking about the use of the problem-solving workshop by placing it in the context of a sequenced array of approaches to resolving protracted conflict under the title of a 'contingency model' [35, 56].

More broadly, Rothman [84] discusses the use of a variety of informal procedures as contributions to the resolving of deep-rooted conflict, while Diamond and McDonald [25] have extended the existing concept of Track Two unofficial diplomacy to a 'Multi-Track' approach, involving nine 'tracks' or levels at which individuals and groups, from the official to the grass roots, can contribute to a conflict-resolution process.

Another proliferating literature in the general area of works on third-party activity involve 'How to . . .' books, which seek to provide practical guidance about appropriate techniques to aspiring third parties. Burton has contributed to this genre with a sternly exacting list of 'rules' for successfully conducting a problem solving exercise [12], while Susskind and Cruikshank [99] and Katz and Lawyer [55] have provided interesting – and more flexible

– accounts of various ways in which it might be possible to get round deadlocks and move towards agreement. Curle has also contributed to this genre with his own realistic account of what it is like to be 'in the middle' as a Quaker intermediary [19].

The 'Getting to . . .' books grind remorselessly on [33, 104], until one hopes for the final volume on 'Getting to the End'. However, the series is worth reading as an indication of how the focus of interest of the overall field has changed and broadened since the publication of the original Fisher and Ury volume [32].

A more interesting development in the field has been a growing interest in the conception of *conflict transformation,* which has emphasized that the idea of resolution has to encompass a long-term process of reconciliation and healing and – in many cases – a radical change in the relationships between erstwhile adversaries. Again, Curle has contributed thoughtfully to this development [20], while a great deal of the recent work on healing and forgiveness deals, at least partly, with an important aspect of this complex and little studied process [107]. Another interesting collection of papers is that gathered by Väyrynen [105].

Much of the initial work assumes that conflict resolution should aim at something better than a 'cold peace' and tries to deal with the question: 'after the agreement, what?'

Conclusion

In a field as heterogeneous and dynamic as conflict research, a short review can do no more than indicate the main trends within recent literature and highlight some important works on the analysis of protracted conflict and its resolution. Most of the books mentioned above deserve more than a cursory mention, and many in the accompanying bibliography deserve more than a bare bibliographic entry. Hopefully, this chapter will enable interested scholars to gain an outline of the 'terrain' of conflict research in the early 1990s and make an informed entry into this exciting field.

In conclusion, I should also mention a work that seems to me to combine many of the insights of the field from the last 30 years and which should not be left out of any self-respecting review of conflict research. Many years ago, my international law professor told me that the only work one needed to read to understand international conflict was Thucydides *The Peloponnesian War.* At the time I thought he was wrong, and I still do. However, if one really wants to examine a major case study of a protracted, deep-rooted conflict, which illuminates our understanding of the why and how of its emergence, of its escalation and dynamics, of the sources of its intractability and of the shortcomings of the conflict resolution processes utilized by the adversaries, then I would thoroughly recommend Donald Kagan's magnificent, four-volume reworking of Thucydides' study [51, 52, 53, 54]. This *is* a book no conflict researcher should miss.

Bibliography

1. Avruch, Kevin, Black, Peter W. and Scimecca, Joseph A. *Conflict Resolution: Cross Cultural Perspectives*. New York, Greenwood Press, 1991.
2. Axelrod, Robert M. *The Evolution of Cooperation*. New York, Basic Books, 1984.
3. Azar, Edward E. *The Management of Protracted Social Conflict*. Aldershot, Dartmouth Publishing Co., and Brookfield, Gower Publishing Company, 1990.
4. Azar, Edward E. and Burton, John W. (eds) *International Conflict Resolution: Theory and Practice*. Brighton, Wheatsheaf and Boulder, Lynne Rienner, 1986.
5. Bendahmane, D.B. and McDonald, John W. *Perspectives on Negotiation: Four Case Studies and Interpretations*. Washington, DC, Foreign Service Institute, 1986.
6. Bendahmane, D.B. and McDonald, John W. (eds) *Conflict Resolution: Track Two Diplomacy*. Washington, DC, Foreign Service Institute, 1987.
7. Ben-Dor, Gabriel and Dewitt, D.B. (eds) *Conflict Management in the Middle East*. Lexington, Lexington Books, 1987.
8. Bercovitch, Jacob *Social Conflicts and Third Parties: Strategies of Conflict Resolution*. Boulder, Westview Press, 1984.
9. Blalock Jr, Hubert M. *Power and Conflict: Towards a General Theory*. Newbury Park and London, Sage Publications, 1989.
10. Boulding, Kenneth E. *Three Faces of Power*. Newbury Park and London, Sage Publications, 1989.
11. Brock-Utne, Birgitte, *Educating for Peace: A Feminist Perspective*. Oxford and New York, Pergamon Press, 1985.
12. Burton, John W. *Resolving Deep-Rooted Conflict: A Handbook*. Lanham, University Press of America, 1987.
13. Burton, John W. *Conflict: Resolution and Provention*. London, Macmillan, 1990.
14. Burton, John W. (ed.) *Conflict: Human Needs Theory*. London, Macmillan and New York, St. Martin's Press, 1990.
15. Burton, John W. and Dukes, Frank *Conflict: Practices in Management, Settlement and Resolution*. London, Macmillan and New York, St. Martin's Press, 1990.
16. Burton, John W. and Dukes, Frank (eds) *Conflict: Readings in Management and Resolution*. London, Macmillan, 1990.
17. Cohen, Raymond *Negotiating Across Cultures: Communication Obstacles in International Diplomacy*. Washington, DC, United States Institute of Peace Press, 1991.
18. Cormick, Gerald and Patton, Leah K. 'Environmental Mediation: Potentials and Limitations'. *Environmental Comment*, vol. 3, no. 3, May, 1977, pp. 3–24.
19. Curle, Adam, *In the Middle: Non-Official Mediation in Violent Situations*. Leamington Spa and New York, Berg, 1987.
20. Curle, Adam *Tools for Transformation: A Personal Study*. Stroud, Hawthorn Press, 1990.
21. Darby, John *Intimidation and Control of the Conflict in Northern Ireland*. Dublin, Gill and Macmillan and Syracuse, Syracuse University Press, 1986.
22. Davidow, Jeffrey *A Peace in South Africa: The Lancaster House Conference on Rhodesia*. Boulder, Westview Press, 1984.
23. de Silva, Kingsley M. *Managing Ethnic Tensions in Multi-Ethnic Societies*. Lanham, University Press of America, 1986.
24. Deng, Francis and Zartman, I. William (eds) *Conflict Resolution in Africa*. Washington, DC, Brookings Institution, 1991.

25. Diamond, Louise and McDonald, John D. *Multi-Track Diplomacy: A Systems Guide and Analysis*. Grinnell, Iowa Peace Institute, 1991.
26. Doob, Leonard W. *The Pursuit of Peace*. Westport, Greenwood Press, 1981.
27. Druckman, Daniel 'Stages, Turning Points, and Crises: Negotiating Military Base Rights, Spain and the United States'. *Journal of Conflict Resolution*, vol. 30, no. 2, 1986, pp. 327–360.
28. Druckman, Daniel *et al.* 'Value Differences and Conflict Resolution: Facilitation or De-Linking?' *Journal of Conflict Resolution*, vol. 32, no. 3, 1988, pp. 489–510.
29. Elster, Jon *Ulysses and the Sirens: Studies in Rationality and Irrationality*, Revised edition, Cambridge and New York, Cambridge University Press, 1988.
30. Elster, Jon *Sour Grapes: Studies in the Subversion of Rationality*. Cambridge and New York, Cambridge University Press, 1983.
31. Esman, Milton J. and Rabinovich, Itamar *Ethnicity, Pluralism and the State in the Middle East*. Ithaca, Cornell University Press, 1988.
32. Fisher, Roger, Ury, William and Patton, Bruce *Getting to YES: Negotiating Agreement Without Giving In*. Boston, Houghton Mifflin, 1981.
33. Fisher, Roger and Brown, Scott *Getting Together: Building a Relationship that Leads to YES*. Boston, Houghton Mifflin, 1988.
34. Fisher, Ronald J. *The Social Psychology of Inter-group and International Conflict Resolution*. New York, Springer Verlag, 1989.
35. Fisher, Ronald J. and Keashley, Loraleigh 'Third Party Intervention in Intergroup Conflict; Consultation is *Not* Mediation'. *Negotiation Journal*, vol. 4, no. 4, 1988, pp. 381–93.
36. Folberg, Jay and Taylor, Alison *Mediation: A Comprehensive Guide to Resolving Conflicts without Litigation*. San Francisco, Jossey Bass, 1984.
37. Fraser, Nancy *Unruly Practices: Power, Discourse and Gender in Contemporary Social Theory*. Minneapolis, University of Minnesota Press, 1989.
38. Fraser, Niall M. and Hipel, Keith W. *Conflict Analysis: Models and Resolutions*. New York, North-Holland, 1984.
39. Glad, Betty (ed.) *Psychological Dimensions of War*. Newbury Park, Sage Publications, 1990.
40. Goldberg, Stephen B., Green, Eric D. and Sander, Frank E.A. (eds) *Dispute Resolution*. Boston, Little, Brown, 1984.
41. Goldman, R.B. and Wilson, A.J. (eds) *From Independence to Statehood: Managing Ethnic Conflict in Five African and Asian States*. London, Frances Pinter, 1984.
42. Groom, A.J.R. 'Old Way and New Insights: Conflict Resolution in International Conflicts' in E.O. Czempiel *et al.* (eds) *Non-Violence in International Cases*. Vienna, European Co-ordination Centre for Research & Development in Social Sciences, 1990, pp. 11–25.
43. Groom, A.J.R. *Approaches to Conflict and Co-operation in International Relations: Lessons from Theory for Practice*. Canterbury, Kent Papers in Politics and International Relations, Series 2, no. 2, 1993.
44. Haass, Richard N. *Conflicts Unending: The United States and Regional Disputes*. New Haven and London, Yale University Press, 1990.
45. Hocker, Joyce L. and Wilmot, William W. *Interpersonal Conflict*, Third edition, Dubuque, Wm C. Brown Publishers, 1991.
46. Horowitz, Donald L. *Ethnic Groups in Conflict*. Berkeley, University of California Press, 1985.

47. Iklé, Fred C. *Every War Must End*, Revised edition, New York, Columbia University Press, 1991.
48. Isard, Walter *International Conflict and the Science of Peace*. Cambridge, MA, Blackwell, 1992.
49. Jabri, Vivienne *Mediating Conflict: Decision-Making and Western Intervention in Namibia*. Manchester, Manchester University Press, 1990.
50. Jandt, Fred E. *Win–Win Negotiating: Turning Conflict into Agreement*. New York, John Wiley, 1987.
51. Kagan, Donald *The Outbreak of the Peloponnesian War*. Ithaca, Cornell University Press, 1969.
52. Kagan, Donald, *The Archidamian War*. Ithaca, Cornell University Press, 1974.
53. Kagan, Donald *The Peace of Nicias and the Sicilian Expedition*. Ithaca, Cornell University Press, 1981.
54. Kagan, Donald *The Fall of the Athenian Empire*. Ithaca, Cornell University Press, 1987.
55. Katz, Neil M. and Lawyer, J.W. *Communication and Conflict Management Skills*. Dubuque, Kendall/Hunt Publishing Company, 1985.
56. Keashley, Loraleigh and Fisher, Ronald J. 'Towards a Contingency Approach to Third Party Intervention in Regional Conflict: A Cyprus Illustration'. *International Journal*, vol. XLV, no. 2, Spring, 1990, pp. 424–53.
57. Kelman, Herbert C. 'Creating the Conditions for Israeli–Palestine Negotiations'. *Journal of Conflict Resolution*, vol. 26, no. 1, 1982, pp. 39–75.
58. Kelman, Herbert C. 'Overcoming the Psychological Barrier: An Analysis of the Egyptian–Israeli Peace Process'. *Negotiation Journal*, vol. 1, no. 3, 1985, pp. 213–34.
59. Kelman, Herbert C. 'The Political Psychology of the Israeli–Palestine Conflict: How Can We Overcome the Barriers to a Negotiated Solution?' *Political Psychology*, vol. 8, no. 3, 1987, pp. 347–63.
60. Kressel, Kenneth, Pruitt, Dean G. *et al*. *Mediation Research: The Process and Effectiveness of Third Party Intervention*. San Francisco, Jossey Bass, 1989.
61. Kriesberg, Louis, *Social Conflict*, Second edition, Englewood Cliffs, Prentice-Hall, 1982.
62. Kriesberg, Louis, *International Conflict Resolution: The US–USSR and the Middle East Cases*. New Haven and London, Yale University Press, 1992.
63. Kriesberg, Louis and Thorson, Stuart J. *Timing the De-escalation of International Conflicts*. Syracuse, Syracuse University Press, 1991.
64. Kriesberg, Louis, Northrop Terrell A. and Thorson, Stuart J. (eds) *Intractable Conflicts and their Transformation*. Syracuse, Syracuse University Press, 1989.
65. Lederach, John Paul, 'Conflict Transformation in Protracted Internal Conflicts: The Case for a Comprehensive Framework' in K. Rupasinghe (ed.) *Conflict Transformation in Protracted Internal Conflict*. London, Macmillan, 1994.
66. Lewicki, Roy J. and Litterer, Joseph A. *Negotiation: Readings, Exercises, and Cases*. Homewood, Richard D. Irwin, 1985.
67. Lijphart, Arend *Democracy in Plural Societies: A Comparative Exploration*. New Haven and London, Yale University Press, 1977.
68. Little, Walter and Mitchell, Christopher R. (eds) *In the Aftermath: Anglo–Argentine Relations Since the Falklands War*. College Park, University of Maryland Press, 1989.
69. Mautner-Markhof, F. (ed.) *Processes of International Negotiations*. Boulder, Westview Press, 1989.

70. Mitchell, C.R. 'Ending Conflicts and Wars: Judgement, Rationality and Entrapment'. *International Social Science Journal*, vol. XLIII, no. 1, 1991, pp. 35–56.
71. Mitchell, C.R. and Webb, K. (eds) *New Approaches to International Mediation*. New York, Greenwood Press, 1988
72. Montville, Joseph V. (ed.) *Conflict and Peacemaking in Multi-Ethnic Societies*. Lexington, Lexington Books, 1990.
73. Moore, Christopher W. *The Mediation Process: Practical Strategies for Resolving Conflict*. San Francisco, Jossey Bass, 1986.
74. Nisbett, Richard and Ross, Lee *Human Inference: Strategies and Shortcomings of Social Judgement*. Englewood Cliffs, Prentice-Hall, 1980.
75. Nordlinger, E.A. *Conflict Regulation in Divided Societies*. Cambridge, MA, Harvard University Center for International Studies, 1972.
76. Princen, Tom *Intermediaries in International Conflict*. Princeton, Princeton University Press, 1992.
77. Pruitt, Dean G. *et al.* 'Incentives for Co-operation in Integrative Bargaining' in R. Tietz (ed.) *Aspiration Levels in Bargaining and Economic Decision Making*. Berlin, Springer-Verlag, 1983, pp. 22–34.
78. Pruitt, Dean G. and Syna, H. 'Successful Problem Solving' in D. Tjosvold and D.W. Johnson (eds) *Productive Conflict Management: Prospectives for Organizations*. New York, Irvington, 1983.
79. Pruitt, Dean G. and Rubin, Jeffrey Z. *Social Conflict: Escalation, Stalemate and Settlement*. New York, Random House, 1986.
80. Rahim, M.A. (ed.) *Managing Conflict: An Interdisciplinary Approach*. New York, Praeger, 1989.
81. Rapoport, Anatol *The Origins of Violence: Approaches to the Study of Conflict*. New York, Paragon House, 1989.
82. Rex, John and Mason, D. (eds) *Theories of Race and Ethnic Relations*. Cambridge, Cambridge University Press, 1988.
83. Rikhye, Indar Jit *The Theory and Practice of Peacekeeping*. London, Hurst and New York, St. Martin's Press, 1984.
84. Rothman, Jay *From Confrontation to Co-operation: Resolving Ethnic and Regional Conflict*. Newbury Park, Sage Publications, 1992.
85. Rupesinghe, Kumar 'Theories of Conflict Resolution and their Applicability to Protracted Ethnic Conflict'. *Bulletin of Peace Proposals*, vol. 18, no. 4, 1986, pp. 527–39.
86. Ryan, Stephen *Ethnic Conflict and International Relations*. Aldershot and Brookfield, Dartmouth Press, 1990.
87. Sandole, Dennis J.D. and Sandole-Staroste, Ingrid (eds) *Conflict Management and Problem Solving: Interpersonal to International Applications*. New York, New York University Press, 1987.
88. Sandole, Dennis J.D. and van der Merwe, Hugo *Conflict Resolution, Theory and Practice: Integration and Application*. Manchester, Manchester University Press and New York, St. Martin's Press, 1993.
89. Saunders, H.H. *The Other Walls: The Politics of the Arab–Israeli Peace Process*, Revised edition, Princeton, Princeton University Press, 1991.
90. Saunders, H.H. 'We Need a Larger Theory of Negotiation: The Importance of Pre-Negotiation Phases'. *Negotiation Journal*, vol. 1, no. 3, 1985, pp. 249–62.
91. Sigal, Leon V. *Fighting to a Finish: The Politics of War Termination in the United States and Japan 1945*. Ithaca, Cornell University Press, 1988.
92. Smith, Anthony D. *The Ethnic Revival*. Cambridge, Cambridge University Press, 1981.

93. Smith, Anthony D. *The Ethnic Origin of Nations*. Oxford and New York, Basil Blackwell, 1986.

94. Staw, Barry M. 'Knee Deep in the Big Muddy: A Study of Escalating Commitment to a Chosen Course of Action'. *Organizational Behavior and Human Performance*, vol. 16, no. 1, 1976, pp. 27–44.

95. Stein, Janice Gross, (ed.) *Getting to the Table: The Process of International Prenegotiation*. Baltimore, Johns Hopkins University Press, 1989.

96. Stroebe, W. *et al.* (eds) *The Social Psychology of Intergroup Conflict: Theory, Research and Applications*. Berlin and New York, Springer-Verlag, 1988.

97. Stulberg, Joseph B. 'The Theory and Practice of Mediation: A Reply to Professor Susskind'. *Vermont Law Review*, vol. 6, no. 1, 1981, pp. 85–117.

98. Susskind, Lawrence, 'Environmental mediation and the Accountability Problem'. *Vermont Law Review*, vol. 6, no. 1, 1981, pp. 1–47.

99. Susskind, Lawrence and Cruikshank, Jeffrey *Breaking the Impasse: Consensual Approaches to Resolving Public Disputes*. New York, Basic Books, 1987.

100. Suter, Keith *Alternative to War: Conflict Resolution and the Peaceful Settlement of International Disputes*. Sydney, Womens International League for Peace & Freedom, 1986.

101. Tillett, Greg *et al.* *HPP Conflict Resolution XI: Independent Learning Package*. Centre for Evening and External Studies, Macquarie University, New South Wales, 1990.

102. Touval, Saadia and Zartman, I. William (eds) *International Mediation: Theory and Practice*. Boulder, Westview Press, 1985.

103. Tversky, Amos and Kahneman, Daniel *Judgement Under Uncertainty: Heuristics and Biases*. Cambridge and New York, Cambridge University Press, 1982.

104. Ury, William L., Brett, Jeanne M. and Goldberg, Stephen B. *Getting Disputes Resolved: Designing Systems to Cut the Costs of Conflict*. San Francisco, Jossey-Bass, 1988.

105. Väyrynen, Raimo *New Directions in Conflict Theory: Conflict Resolution and Conflict Transformation*. Newbury Park, Sage Publications, 1991.

106. Volkan, Vamik D. *The Need to have Enemies and Allies: From Clinical Practice to International Relationships*. Northvale, Aronson, 1988.

107. Volkan, Vamik D., Montville, Joseph V. and Julius, Demetrios A. (eds) *The Psychodynamics of International Relationships*, 2 vols, Lexington, Lexington Books, 1990.

108. White, Ralph K. *Fearful Warriors: A Psychological Profile of US–Soviet Relations*. New York, Free Press, 1984

109. White, Ralph K. (ed.) *Psychology and the Prevention of Nuclear War*. New York, New York University Press, 1986.

110. Wiseman, H. (ed.) *Peacekeeping: Appraisals and Proposals*. New York, Pergamon Press, 1983.

111. Zartman, I. William *Ripe for Resolution: Conflict and Intervention in Africa*, updated edition, Oxford and New York, Oxford University Press, 1989.

10 Marxism and international relations theory
Hazel Smith*

There is still no significant body of literature which has integrated Marxist insights with the IR literature in English. Attempts to do so, such as Linklater [74] and Rosenberg [100], are exceptional and we are left with isolated contributions in the various sub-fields of IR from scholars who have been influenced, favourably or otherwise, by Marxist theory. The partial and fragmented integration of Marxist theory into the discipline is discussed in useful overviews in Thorndike [113], Gills [37] and MacLean [78]. Thorndike's review remains the most comprehensive and accessible introduction to the interrelationship of Marxist ideas with IR scholarship.

Marxist theory has been considered inadequate or insufficient by mainstream theorists for the task of explaining international relations [123, 125]. Even recently, debates on the contribution of Marxist-related scholarship sometimes verged on the vitriolic [65, 66, 42]. Despite this inhospitable academic climate, however, some important work has been completed and there are hopeful signs that in the post Cold War period, new thinking in IR will have a constructive input from previously marginalized scholarship [8].

The Marxist theoretical heritage

Karl Marx was born in Trier, Germany in 1818 and died in London in 1883. A good introductory selection of his writings, some co-written with Friederich Engels, can be found in McLellan [79]. Marx has been enormously influential in shaping the 20th-century political landscape. From the Mexican revolution of 1911 until the fall of the Berlin Wall in 1989, political debates have revolved around the Communism/Capitalism axis – a move away from the ideological debates of the 19th century which were equally about revolution and counterrevolution but which took place

* Thanks are due to Kevin Magill for comments and advice.

142

between 'Conservativism' – broadly defined to include Whigs and Liberals – and 'Radicalism'.

Marx and Engels are hard to classify in conventional IR theoretical categories. They did not consider inter-state relations as their primary focus of analysis. For them, the distinguishing feature of human society was the capacity for cooperative labour, making labour and production the key analytical notions in the study of social relations. The analytical foci were forces and relations of production, and the normative focus was (arguably) the individual whose human potential would only be realized with the attainment of a universal classless society (ie Communism). Brown [12] has offered an intellectual contextualization of Marxist thought as rooted in cosmopolitan theory.

A glance through *The Communist Manifesto* [81] or *The German Ideology* [82] confounds the often made allegation, most famously by Kubálková and Cruikshank [64], that Marx and Engels were uninterested in international relations. Brown [13] acknowledges the journalistic interest of Marx and Engels in 'foreign affairs', but his otherwise useful critique also judges that they 'produced no "Marxist theory" of the state or international relations'. Similarly Kaldor [55] claims that there exists no specifically Marxist theory of IR because there is no Marxist theory of the state as such. While Marxist theory did not adopt the state as the focal unit of analysis, such work, and *The German Ideology* in particular, develops what can be understood as a notion of man and international relations which insists on placing man, history, the state and relations of production within a 'world-historical' context; an 'international' if not an 'inter-state' perspective is arguably central to the theory of Marx and Engels. As Williams [128] notes, 'Marx's political theory is . . . inherently an international theory'. What Marx and Engels offer is a theory of international relations, the philosophical, methodological and conceptual foundation of which is that of historical materialism. In addition, both Marx, and particularly Engels, concerned themselves with the central problems for international relations – peace and war [31, 103]. Engels' further contribution is to a discussion which moved centre stage in international theorizing in the 1980s [25]: what is the nature of the state and how do the various conceptions of the state affect the way we understand both it and the international system [26, 43, 107]?

No discussion of Marxism and IR would be complete without reference to the third of the trinity of classical historical materialist scholarship. Lenin's work on imperialism [72] took concepts formulated and articulated by Marx and Engels and synthesized them with liberal approaches, particularly those of the radical English Liberal, Hobson [50]. Lenin discussed the integration of industrial and finance capital and what he saw as the consequent division of the world by the Great Powers. For Lenin, imperialism was the monopoly stage of capitalism. This thesis formed the intellectual baseline for subsequent generations of theorists concerned to explore the interrelationship of capital and class on an international scale [10, 28, 94, 124].

Lenin wrote on a range of subjects still exercising international theorists today including the state [69], nationalism [71] and the idea of a 'United

States of Europe' [70]. There have been few studies informed by Marxist scholarship of the latter two areas, although Nairn's study of nationalism [85] and Mandel's analysis of the European Community [80] fill in some of the gaps.

There remains a deep-rooted controversy as to which theorists should be considered as comprising part of the classical Marxist heritage. Apart from Marx, Engels and Lenin, Stalin and Trotsky are suggested as forming an integral part of this tradition based on Stalin's analysis of nationalism [109] and Trotsky's theses about the bureaucratic degeneration of the Soviet Union and the theory of 'permanent revolution' [115, 116].

Marxism and contemporary international theory

An historical materialist basis for theorizing about IR begets a radically different view of the subject from that based on the positivist or idealist traditions with which most non-Marxist 20th-century IR theorists feel comfortable. This may be why contemporary mainstream international theory has only been influenced by scholarship informed by Marxist theory 'at the margins'. Halliday's ideas on state and revolution [43, 47], Rosenberg's scrupulous intellectual and empirical demolition of Political Realism [98, 99, 100], MacLean's methodological and philosophical inquiries [76, 77, 78], Lawson's review of how class conflict affected foreign policy decision making in Imperial Germany [68] and Burnham's inquiry into the Marxist credentials of the neo-Gramscian's discovery of the concept of hegemony [14] are exceptions which prove the rule.

Current work at the 'cutting edge' of scholarship on the changing nature of imperialism can be found in the consistently excellent scholarship found in the journal *Race and Class*. Sivanandan's work is particularly useful in his discussion of imperialism of the late 1980s. He argues that the production of wealth and profit is no longer based on manufacturing but on service industries. There is thus a concomitant shift from employment patterns reflected less on mass concentrations of relatively powerful workers in the metropoles towards a fragmented, decentralized and global working class. From this thesis Sivanandan also charts the demise of the nation state 'as a viable economic unit' [104]. These themes are further pursued as part of a response to self-styled 'new Marxists' who, Sivanandan argues [105], have failed to understand the 'revolution' in the global reorganization of production and who have abandoned a still necessary class analysis for aimless and, by implication, self-indulgent pluralism.

Warren's iconoclastic thesis [124] is interesting in that he utilizes classical Marxism to defend imperialism as the bearer of capitalism to the less developed economies of the world. He argues that the capitalism thus engendered helps to create a working class (as well as some form of economic development), and it is this incipient working class which has the potential to make socialist revolution. Post-war Soviet policy which promoted cooperation with indigenous 'anti-imperialist' nationalist bourgeoisies is viewed by Warren as a distortion of Lenin's theses on 'imperialism' – if politically useful for the Soviet state. Naturally, orthodox Soviet theorists viewed this issue rather differently. 'Socialist internationalism' was and should be based on respect for the principle of self-determination of nations (not the international proletariat). This principle, it was argued, formed the basis for the Soviet state's foreign policy. Soviet scholars further commented that this principle had later been adopted by the international community [58].

The paucity of Marxist scholarship in IR is worth comparing to the tremendous impact which Marxist thought of one form or another has had on international relations in practice. Socialist states, national liberation movements, social democratic parties and governments, liberation theologists, counterrevolutionists and US policymakers – to name but a few – have all been exercised in their foreign policy involvements by influence from, or a reaction to, Marxist thought. Marxist scholarship has, however, made a contribution to the study of the practice of post-war international relations even if these empirical studies have in the main been concentrated in a few specific areas.

Marxist theory and contemporary IR

Marxism, or rather its ideological derivative 'Marxism-Leninism', was the official ideology of one of the two major protagonists in the Cold War. The IR literature thus concerned itself, among other things, with explaining the relationship of Marxist thought to the foreign policy of countries which utilized Marxist-derived approaches to develop ideological perspectives which shaped both domestic and foreign policy [63]. Light's work on Soviet foreign policy [73], Carr on early Bolshevik foreign policy [17] and Yahuda on China [129] consider the foreign policies of these most influential socialist states. Halliday on Yemen [44] and Smith on Sandinista Nicaragua [108] relate to specific instances of small-state revolutionary foreign policy, although the definitive work on the foreign policy of smaller revolutionary states has yet to be written. Hence much of the material for the study of the foreign policy of Marxist-influenced revolutionary or radical states is still mainly available in the form of speeches and writings from the participants themselves. A representative sample might be Guevara [39], Jagan [51], Mugabe [84], Nkrumah [86], and Kim [59].

Marxist-inspired theorizing has been prevalent in the study of US foreign policy and the Cold War. O'Connor's work on US imperialism is worth revisiting here [87]. Halliday [41] moves away from a generalized review of US foreign policy in his pamphlet on the 'Reagan Doctrine' which combines an understanding of the relevance of economics to US military strategy abroad with a specific analysis of the foreign policy of the Reagan administration. But the sharpest (and most entertaining) Marxist critique of US policy abroad can be found in Parenti, whose work on US foreign policy [92] is informed by his studies of the relations of class power within the United States [91, 93]. Scholarship from the former Soviet Union, of course, utilized a particular version of Marxism to analyse US foreign policy: Trofimenko provides a non-propagandistic discussion [114].

The Cold War(s) generated a corpus of historiography and analysis in which Marxist-influenced scholarship considered causes, processes and likely outcomes. 'Radical revisionism' is the term Cox [19] uses to describe the mainly US Marxist-influenced historical scholarship which located a greater share of the blame for the Cold War in US foreign policy – as opposed to Soviet expansionism. The Kolkos [60, 61, 62] provide some of the best examples of this literature, a broad overview of which can be found in Melanson [83]. Halliday's work on the 'second cold war' provides probably the best known of Cold War theories – with his understanding of Cold War as 'inter-systemic conflict' [40, 45, 46, 49]. Halliday's work has been subject to comment from a range of perspectives, from those rooted in Marxist thought [18] to more broad-based radical views [112] and conservative criticisms [66]. He has replied to these criticisms [42, 48].

In this context it should be mentioned that the Cold War literature has also been marked by contributions from a liberal 'peace activist' tradition, ranging from those hostile to those operating within a Marxist tradition. Such scholars have had an impact on the discipline in the engendering and sustaining of serious debate on the Cold War from the perspective of a very broad liberal/left constituency [56, 55, 110, 111].

The major impact of Marxism on the study of international relations, however, has been neither in terms of classical Marxist theoretical investigation, nor in empirical interpretations of contemporary international relations. It has been the contribution of Marxist thought in its widest sense – sometimes termed 'neo-Marxism' – to the developments in international theory which have been identified by Banks and others as 'structuralist' [6, 88]. Another, less studied phenomena, has been the impact of Marxist thought on those scholars concerned with the interrelationship of race, class and international relations.

Neo-Marxism

Neo-Marxist explanations of international politics provide a broad framework of analysis which considers class as a major factor in international relations, economic relationships (although not specifically or only the relations of production) as the key dynamics and international justice and equality (not incidentally the normative focus for Marx) as the most important normative concerns. Neo-Marxist theories borrow concepts developed by Marx, such as 'exploitation' and the notion of an oppressed 'proletariat', to help explain the rise of capitalism. They share the Marxist conviction that domestic and international economic processes are key explanatory features of the international system. These theories also have in common with classical Marxist analysis a tendency to incorporate prescriptive and normative features, concerned with ways to change the world as well as to analyse it.

Yet neo-Marxism differs from the classical approach in that it is much less rigorous in its use of the conceptual and methodological apparatus constructed by Marx, Engels and Lenin. Such theorizing raises questions of epistemological consistency since some theorizing reflects an uneasy mix of ostensibly Marxist concepts within distinctly pluralist intellectual frameworks. Burnham [14] discusses this problem with respect to those who have sought to incorporate Gramscian insights into their explanations of international relations. This mix is, of course, no problem for those like Galtung [32] who make no claim to being part of a Marxist heritage. The ambivalences are more acute for those who have sought consciously to draw upon the Marxist heritage in a selective manner, thus running the risk of denuding the borrowed concepts of the theoretical significance in which they cohere.

Neo-Marxism has penetrated the discipline of IR by way of three major theoretical contributions. The first is the dependency/development studies' literature. The second is the 'world system' approach and the third is the neo-Gramscian insertion into the sub-field of international political economy.

Dependency theories reflect a range of political and theoretical perspectives including economistic Marxism [7], reformism [96], the vision of the world as the structural domination of an exploited periphery subordinated by an exploiting core [30, 33], the emphasis on capitalist development in the South as being characterized by 'dependent development' [15] and theories stressing the mechanisms of core–periphery exploitation based on a dynamic of 'unequal exchange' [23]. The bulk of the literature has centred on the experience of the Latin American countries which, although achieving political independence in the early 19th century, were still poor and economically underdeveloped. However, a discussion of the African continent and its relationship with the industrialized world can be found in Emmanuel [24], Amin [2, 3, 4] and Rodney [97]. Roxborough [101] systematically evaluates the theoretical debates which have riven the dependency literature, while Kay [57] offers a useful review of Latin American dependency theories. Alavi and Shanin [1] provide a representative anthology of some of the theoretical debates.

One influential classical Marxist has dismissed dependency theory outright as 'nationalist mythology' [124], but the main Marxist criticisms of dependency have centred on a quarrel related to conceptual correctness [29]. The concept in question is that of 'capitalism'. Thus, in terms of the Marxist heritage, the major theoretical schism has revolved around historical arguments about the nature of the transition from feudalism to capitalism in Europe. The two camps divide into those who, like Brenner [9] and Laclau [67], view class-based relations of production as the key analytical focus and consider an important characteristic of capitalist development as the drive to ever-increasing productivity and those like Frank [30] and Wallerstein [118, 119] who see the development of an international market as the key determining factor. For Wallerstein and Frank the defining characteristic of capitalist development is the linear and quantitative increase in the surplus of capital produced. This compares with Brenner's understanding of capitalist development as being defined by qualitative changes in production processes and relations.

The relevance for contemporary understandings of the international relations of dependency are examined by Brenner [9] who argues that if capitalist development can simply be understood as one vast expanding and developing market, then the only logical solution to the problem of dependency is autarky – a solution which he argues Frank and Wallerstein do not directly advocate. If on the other hand the key analytical factor in our understanding of capitalist development is that of a set of relations of production whereby landless and propertyless labour (so-called 'free labour') is exploited at work by a property-owning bourgeoisie, then an alternative policy to autarky may become possible. The propertyless can take control of property (the means of production) and thus opt for a socialist alternative which redistributes wealth within a particular nation-state but which does not necessarily entail international isolation from the capitalist world.

Wallerstein's importance in the literature, however, is more for his development and articulation of what has become known as the 'world systems' approach to the study of international relations. Wallerstein's understanding of the 'modern world system' is an evolving, interlocking world capitalist economy which emerged in its discernible modern form in the 16th century. The world system is the world economic system, and it is this which forms the primary level of analysis in Wallerstein's work. He does not use the classical Marxist concept of 'relations of production' to analyse the development of the capitalist system but a much broader interpretation of Marx's understanding of the essence of capitalism [122]. Wallerstein's conception of capitalism is underpinned by the notion of ever-expanding international commerce. In this way for Wallerstein the modern world system, including the former Soviet Union and all the professedly socialist states, should have been characterized as capitalist simply by virtue of the fact that they traded in a world market [117, 118, 119, 120, 121]. His approach has its critics, notably for its teleological methodology [106]. However, the very neatness of Wallerstein's argument, as Brown points out [11], gives it the merit of coherence.

The third group of theories are those which have utilized Cox's work to develop the Gramscian notion of 'hegemony' as a concept to explain how major powers, particularly the United States, maintain their dominance within the international system [20, 33]. Augelli and Murphy [5], and Gill [34] provide a sustained effort to apply the theoretical discussion to actual practice. This group of 'critical' theorists has also attempted to develop a sometimes idiosyncratic view of the Marxist method of historical materialism [20, 21, 22, 35, 36]. Cox has been the real path-breaker, introducing into mainstream IR theory Marxian concepts by way of the work of the Italian Communist scholar, Gramsci [38]. Cox is justly renowned for questioning the prevailing methodological bias of much of international theory.

Race, class and international relations

One group of theorists writing on IR in its broadest sense is that which enters the discourse of international theory with a view of the world which could well be distinguished as a separate paradigm in itself. This is the view of the world which is shaped by the conceptual category of race (not state) and which is utilized in concert with that of class. Besides Rodney [97] and Sivanandan [104, 105], scholarship informed by Marxist-influenced notions of race and class includes Carew [16], Fanon [27], Padmore [89, 90], Williams [126, 127] and many others.

Specific mention should be made of James, who produced a number of seminal studies in the fields of political and social theory. His best known work is still the definitive study of the Haitian revolution [52]. He also predated contemporary postmodernist fascination with sport as politics – the 'sport/war intertext' [102] – in his analysis of the international politics of colonialism in the Caribbean in relationship to the eventually successful campaign to have a Black captain of the West Indies cricket team [53]. James was a political activist as well as a scholar and, as a matter of anecdotal as well as theoretical interest, his conversations with Trotsky on the 'race question' are recorded in collections of his work [54].

As with the revolutionary foreign policies of small states, however, the definitive account of the interplay of Marxist scholarship with race, class and international relations has yet to be written, although Thorndike [113] recognizes the issue as a problem for international theory.

Textbooks and journals

Textbooks reflect the concerns and conventions of any discipline, and IR textbooks are no exception. Thus there are few textbooks in the discipline informed by a Marxist perspective, a partial exception being Pettman [95]. The Little and Smith reader [75] includes a substantial section representative of neo-Marxist approaches. Relevant journals include *Race and Class*, *Radical Philosophy*, *Capital and Class* and *New Left Review* – all published in Britain. In the United States, *Nature, Society and Thought*, published by the Marxist Educational Press based in St. Paul, Minnesota, is a useful source. Worthwhile discussions of contemporary international politics which utilize a Marxist framework of analysis can also be found in the periodical *Analysis* published in Britain and in *Zeta Magazine* published in Boston in the United States.

Bibliography

1. Alavi, Hamza and Shanin, Teodor (eds) *Introduction to the Sociology of "Developing Societies"*. London, Macmillan and New York, Monthly Review Press, 1982.
2. Amin, Samir *Imperialism and Unequal Development*. Hassocks, Harvester Press and New York, Monthly Review Press, 1977.
3. Amin, Samir *Accumulation on a World Scale*, vols 1 and 2, New York, Monthly Review Press, 1974.

4. Amin, Samir *Eurocentrism*. London, Zed Books and New York, Monthly Review Press, 1989.
5. Augelli, Enrico and Murphy, Craig *America's Quest for Supremacy and the Third World: a Gramscian Analysis*. London, Pinter, 1988 and New York, St. Martin's Press, 1989.
6. Banks, Michael 'The Inter-Paradigm Debate' in Margot Light and A.J.R. Groom (eds) *International Relations: A Handbook of Current Theory*. London, Frances Pinter, 1985, pp. 7–26.
7. Baran, Paul A. *The Political Economy of Growth*. Harmondsworth, Penguin, 1973.
8. Bowker, Mike and Brown, Robin (eds) *From Cold War to Collapse: Theory and World Politics in the 1980s*. Cambridge and New York, Cambridge University Press, 1993.
9. Brenner, Robert 'The Origins of Capitalist Development: A Critique of Neo-Smithian Marxism'. *New Left Review*, no. 104, 1977. Abridged edition in Hamza Alavi and Teodor Shanin (eds) *Introduction to the Sociology of "Developing Societies"*. London, Macmillan and New York, Monthly Review Press, 1982, pp. 54–71.
10. Brewer, Anthony *Marxist Theories of Imperialism: A Critical Survey*, second edition, London and New York, Routledge & Kegan Paul, 1990.
11. Brown, Chris 'Development and Dependency' in Margot Light and A.J.R. Groom (eds) *International Relations: A Handbook of Current Theory*. London, Frances Pinter, 1985, pp. 60–73.
12. Brown, Chris *International Relations Theory: New Normative Approaches*. Hemel Hempstead, Harvester Wheatsheaf, 1992 and New York, Columbia University Press, 1993.
13. Brown, Chris, 'Marxism and International Ethics' in Terry Nardin and David R. Mapel (eds) *Traditions of International Ethics*. Cambridge, Cambridge University Press, 1992, pp. 225–49.
14. Burnham, Peter 'Neo-Gramscian Hegemony and the International Order'. *Capital and Class*, Volume 1991–92, Nos 43–47, no. 45, Autumn, 1991, pp. 73–93.
15. Cardoso, Fernando Henrique and Faletto, Enzo *Dependency and Development in Latin America*. Berkeley, University of California Press, 1979.
16. Carew, Jan, R. *Fulcrums of Change*. Trenton, Africa World Press, 1988.
17. Carr, E.H. *The Bolshevik Revolution 1917–1923*, vol. 3. Harmondsworth, Pelican, 1984 and New York, Norton, 1985.
18. Cox, Michael 'The Cold War and Stalinism in the Age of Capitalist Decline'. *Critique*, No. 17, 1986, pp. 17–82.
19. Cox, Michael 'Radical Theory and the New Cold War' in Mike Bowker and Robin Brown (eds) *From Cold War to collapse: theory and world politics in the 1980s*. Cambridge, Cambridge University Press, 1993, pp. 35–58.
20. Cox, Robert W. 'Gramsci, Hegemony and International Relations: An Essay in Method'. *Millennium*, vol. 12, no. 2, Summer, 1983, pp. 162–75.
21. Cox, Robert W. 'Social Forces, States and World Orders: Beyond International Relations Theory' in Robert O. Keohane (ed.) *Neorealism and Its Critics*. New York, Columbia University Press, 1986, pp. 204–54.
22. Cox, Robert W. *Production, Power and World Order: Social Forces in the Making of History*. New York, Columbia University Press, 1987.
23. Emmanuel, Arghiri *Unequal Exchange: A Study of the Imperialism of Trade*. New York, Monthly Review Press, 1972.
24. Emmanuel, Arghiri 'White-Settler Colonialism and the Myth of Investment Capitalism'. *New Left Review*, no. 73, 1972. Abridged version in Hamza Alavi

and Teodor Shanin (eds) *Introduction to the Sociology of "Developing Societies"*. London, Macmillan and New York, Monthly Review Press, 1982, pp. 88–106.

25. Engels, Friederich, *The Origin of the Family, Private Property and the State*. Harmondsworth. Penguin, 1986.

26. Evans, Peter B., Rueschemeyer, Dietrich and Skocpol, Theda (eds) *Bringing the State Back In*. Cambridge and New York, Cambridge University Press, 1985.

27. Fanon, Frantz *The Wretched of the Earth*. Harmondsworth, Penguin, 1985.

28. Fieldhouse, D.K. *The Theory of Capitalist Imperialism*. London, Longmans, 1967.

29. Foster-Carter, A. 'The Modes of Production Controversy'. *New Left Review*, no. 107, 1978, pp. 47–77.

30. Frank, André Gunder *Capitalism and Underdevelopment in Latin America: Historical Studies of Chile and Brazil*, revised edition, Harmondsworth, Penguin, 1971.

31. Gallie, W.B. *Philosophers of Peace and War: Kant, Clausewitz, Marx, Engels and Tolstoy*. Cambridge and New York, Cambridge University Press, 1978.

32. Galtung, Johan 'A Structural Theory of Imperialism'. *Journal of Peace Research*, vol. 13, no. 2, 1971, pp. 81–94. Excerpt in Richard Little and Michael Smith (eds) *Perspectives on World Politics: A Reader*. London and New York, Routledge, 1991, pp. 292–304.

33. Gill, Stephen and Law, David *The Global Political Economy: Perspectives, Problems, and Policies*. London, Harvester and Baltimore, Johns Hopkins University Press, 1988.

34. Gill, Stephen *American Hegemony and the Trilateral Commission*. Cambridge and New York, Cambridge University Press, 1990.

35. Gill, Stephen 'Historical Materialism, Gramsci, and International Political Economy' in Craig N. Murphy and Roger Tooze (eds) *The New International Political Economy*. Boulder, Lynne Rienner, 1991, pp. 51–75.

36. Gill, Stephen (ed.) *Gramsci, Historical Materialism and International Relations*. Cambridge and New York, Cambridge University Press, 1993.

37. Gills, B.K. 'Historical Materialism and International Relations Theory'. *Millennium*, vol. 16, no. 2, Summer, 1987, pp. 265–72.

38. Gramsci, Antonio *Selections from Prison Notebooks*. London, Lawrence and Wishart, 1986.

39. Guevara, Ernesto Che *Che Guevara and the Cuban Revolution: Writings and Speeches of Ernesto Che Guevara*. London, Pathfinder, 1987.

40. Halliday, Fred *The Making of the Second Cold War*, second edition, London, Verso, 1986.

41. Halliday, Fred *Beyond Irangate: The Reagan Doctrine and the Third World*. Amsterdam, Transnational Institute, 1987.

42. Halliday, Fred 'Vigilantism in International Relations: Kubálková, Cruikshank and Marxist theory'. *Review of International Studies*, vol. 13, no. 3, July, 1987, pp. 163–75.

43. Halliday, Fred 'State and Society in International Relations: A Second Agenda'. *Millennium*, vol. 16, no. 2, Summer, 1987, pp. 215–27.

44. Halliday, Fred *Revolution and Foreign Policy: the Case of South Yemen 1967–1987*. Cambridge and New York, Cambridge University Press, 1989.

45. Halliday, Fred *Cold War, Third World: An Essay on Soviet–American Relations*. London, Hutchinson Radius, 1989.

46. Halliday, Fred 'The Ends of Cold War'. *New Left Review*, no. 180, March–April, 1990, pp. 35–50.

47. Halliday, Fred '"The Sixth Great Power": On the Study of Revolution and International Relations'. *Review of International Studies*, vol. 16, no. 3, July, 1990, pp. 207–21.

48. Halliday, Fred 'A Reply to Edward Thompson'. *New Left Review*, no. 182, July/August, 1990, pp. 147–50.

49. Halliday, Fred 'Cold War as Inter-systemic Conflict – Initial Theses' in Mike Bowker and Robin Brown (eds) *From Cold War to Collapse: Theory and World Politics in the 1980s*. Cambridge, Cambridge University Press, 1993, pp. 21–34.

50. Hobson, J.A. *Imperialism: a Study*. Ann Arbor, University of Michigan Press, 1965.

51. Jagan, Cheddi *Forbidden Freedom: The Story of British Guiana*. London, Hansib Publishing, 1991.

52. James, C.L.R. *The Black Jacobins: Toussaint L'Ouverture and the San Domingo Revolution*, second revised edition, New York, Vintage Books, 1963.

53. James, C.L.R. *Beyond a Boundary*. New York, Pantheon, 1984.

54. James, C.L.R. *At the Rendezvous of Victory*. London, Allison & Busby, 1984.

55. Kaldor, Mary *The Imaginary War: Understanding the East–West Conflict*. Oxford and Cambridge, MA, Basil Blackwell, 1990.

56. Kaldor, Mary, Holden, Gerard and Falk, Richard (eds) *The New Detente: Rethinking East–West Relations*. London and New York, Verso and Tokyo, United Nations University, 1989.

57. Kay, Cristóbal *Latin American Theories of Development and Underdevelopment*. London and New York, Routledge, 1989.

58. Kim, Georgi *The Great October Revolution and the Destinies of the Peoples of Asia, Africa and Latin America*. Moscow, Novosti Press Agency, 1987.

59. Kim, Il Sung *Works*. Pyongyang, Foreign Languages Publishing House, various dates.

60. Kolko, G. *The Politics of War: The World and United State Foreign Policy, 1943–1945*. London, Weidenfeld and Nicolson and New York, Random House, 1968.

61. Kolko, G. and Kolko, J. *The Limits of Power: the World and United States Foreign Policy, 1945–1954*. New York, Harper and Row, 1972.

62. Kolko, J. *America and the Crisis of World Capitalism*. Boston, Beacon Press, 1972.

63. Kubálková, V. and Cruikshank, A.A. *Marxism-Leninism and Theory of International Relations*. London and Boston, Routledge & Kegan Paul, 1980.

64. Kubálková, Vendulka and Cruikshank, Albert *Marxism and International Relations*. Oxford and New York, Clarendon, 1985.

65. Kubálková, V. and Cruikshank, A.A. 'The "New Cold War" in "Critical International Relations Studies"'. *Review of International Studies*, vol. 12, no. 3, July, 1986, pp. 163–85.

66. Kubálková, V. and Cruikshank, A.A. 'A Rambo Come to Judgement: Fred Halliday, Marxism and International Relations'. *Review of International Studies*, vol. 15, no. 1, January, 1989, pp. 37–47.

67. Laclau, Ernesto *Politics and Ideology in Marxist Theory: Capitalism, Fascism, Populism*. London, Verso, 1979.

68. Lawson, Fred. H. 'Domestic Conflict and Foreign Policy: the Contribution of Some Undeservedly Neglected Historical Studies'. *Review of International Studies*, vol. 11, no. 4, October, 1985, pp. 275–99.

69. Lenin, V.I. 'The State and Revolution' in V.I. Lenin *Marx, Engels, Marxism*. Moscow, Progress Publishers, 1973, pp. 329–49.

70. Lenin, V.I. 'On the Slogan for a United States of Europe' in V.I. Lenin *Marx, Engels, Marxism.* Moscow, Progress Publishers, 1973, pp. 275–79.
71. Lenin, V.I. 'The Right of Nations to Self-Determination' in V.I. Lenin *Selected Works, Vol. 1.* Moscow, Progress Publishers, 1977, pp. 567–617.
72. Lenin, V.I. *Imperialism, the Highest Stage of Capitalism.* Moscow, Progress Publishers, 1982, pp. 567–617.
73. Light, Margot *The Soviet Theory of International Relations, 1917–1982.* Brighton, Wheatsheaf and New York, St. Martin's Press, 1988.
74. Linklater, Andrew *Beyond Realism and Marxism: Critical Theory and International Relations.* London, Macmillan and New York, St. Martin's Press, 1990.
75. Little, Richard and Smith, Michael (eds) *Perspectives on World Politics: A Reader.* London and New York, Routledge, 1991.
76. MacLean, John 'Marxist Epistemology, Explanations of "Change" and the Study of International Relations' in Barry Buzan and R.J. Barry Jones (eds) *Change and the Study of International Relations: The Evaded Dimension.* London, Pinter, 1981, pp. 46–67.
77. MacLean, John 'Belief Systems and Ideology in International Relations: a Critical Approach' in Richard Little and Steve Smith (eds) *Belief Systems and International Relations.* Oxford and New York, Basil Blackwell, 1988, pp. 57–82.
78. MacLean, John 'Marxism and International Relations: A Strange Case of Mutual Neglect'. *Millennium*, vol. 17, no. 2, Summer, 1988, pp. 295–319.
79. McLellan, David (ed.) *Karl Marx: Selected Writings.* Oxford, Oxford University Press, 1990.
80. Mandel, E. *Europe Versus America? Contradictions of Imperialism.* London, NLB and New York, Monthly Review Press, 1970.
81. Marx, Karl and Engels, Friedrich *The Communist Manifesto.* Oxford, Oxford University Press, 1992.
82. Marx, Karl and Engels, Frederick *The German Ideology.* London, Lawrence & Wishart, 1989.
83. Melanson, Richard, A. *Writing History and Making Policy: The Cold War, Vietnam and Revisionism.* Lanham, University Press of America, 1983.
84. Mugabe, Robert *Our War of Liberation.* Harare, Mambo Press, 1983.
85. Nairn, Tom *The Break-Up of Britain: Crisis and Neo-nationalism.* London, NLB, 1981.
86. Nkrumah, Kwame, *Handbook of Revolutionary Warfare.* London, Panaf Books and New York, International Publishers, 1968.
87. O'Connor, James 'The Meaning of Economic Imperialism' in Richard Little and Michael Smith (eds) *Perspectives on World Politics: A Reader.* London, Routledge, 1991, pp. 277-91.
88. Olson, William C. and Groom, A.J.R. *International Relations Then and Now: Origins and Trends in Interpretation.* London, Routledge, 1992.
89. Padmore, G. *Africa and World Peace.* London, Secker & Warburg, 1937.
90. Padmore, G. *Africa – Britain's Third Empire.* London, Dennis Dobson, 1949.
91. Parenti, Michael *Power and the Powerless.* New York, St. Martin's Press, 1978.
92. Parenti, Michael *The Sword and the Dollar: Imperialism, Revolution, and the Arms Race.* New York, St. Martin's Press, 1989.
93. Parenti, Michael *Inventing Reality: The Politics of the News Media*, second revised edition, New York, St. Martin's Press. 1993.
94. Petras, James *Critical Perspectives on Imperialism and Social Class in the Third World.* New York, Monthly Review Press, 1978.

95. Pettman, Ralph *International Politics: Balance of Power*. Boulder, Lynne Rienner, 1991.

96. Prebisch, R. *The Economic Development of Latin America and its Principal Problems*. New York, United Nations, 1950.

97. Rodney, Walter *How Europe Underdeveloped Africa*, revised edition, London, Bogle-L'Ouverture, 1983 and Washington, DC, Howard University Press, 1981.

98. Rosenberg, Justin 'What's the Matter with Realism?' *Review of International Studies*, vol. 16, no. 4, October, 1990, pp. 285–303.

99. Rosenberg, Justin 'Secret Origins of the State: the Structural Basis of *Raison d'état*'. *Review of International Studies*, vol. 18, no. 2, April, 1992, pp. 131–59.

100. Rosenberg, Justin *The Empire of Civil Society: A Critique of the Realist Theory of International Relations*. London, Verso, 1994.

101. Roxborough, Ian *Theories of Underdevelopment*. London, Macmillan, 1979.

102. Shapiro, Michael J. 'Representing World Politics: The Sport/War Intertext' in James Der Derian and Michael J. Shapiro (eds) *International/Intertextual Relations*. Lexington, Lexington Books, 1989, pp. 69–96.

103. Shaw, Martin (ed.) *War, State and Society*. London, Macmillan and New York, St. Martin's Press, 1984.

104. Sivanandan, A. 'New Circuits of Imperialism'. *Race and Class*, vol. 30, no, 4, April–June, 1989, pp. 1–19.

105. Sivanandan, A. 'All that Melts Into Air is Solid: The Hokum of New Times'. *Race and Class*, vol. 31, no. 3, January–March, 1990, pp. 1–30.

106. Skocpol, Theda 'Wallerstein's World Capitalist System: A Theoretical and Historical Critique'. *American Journal of Sociology*, vol. 82, no. 5, March, 1977, pp. 1075–90.

107. Skocpol, Theda *States and Social Revolutions*. Cambridge and New York, Cambridge University Press, 1985.

108. Smith, Hazel *Nicaragua: Self-determination and Survival*. London and Concord, Pluto, 1993.

109. Stalin, J.V. *Works, Vol. 2, 1907–1913*. Moscow, Foreign Languages Publishing House and London, Lawrence & Wishart, 1953.

110. Thompson, E.P. *et al. Exterminism and Cold War*. London, Verso and NLB, 1982.

111. Thompson, E.P. *Beyond the Cold War: a New Approach to the Arms Race and Nuclear Annihilation*. New York, Pantheon, 1982.

112. Thompson, Edward 'The Ends of Cold War'. *New Left Review*, no. 182, July/August, 1990, pp. 139–46.

113. Thorndike, Tony 'The Revolutionary Approach: the Marxist Perspective' in Trevor Taylor (ed.) *Approaches and Theory in International Relations*. London, Longman, 1978, pp. 54–99.

114. Trofimenko, G.A. *The U.S. Military Doctrine*. Moscow, Progress Publishers, 1986.

115. Trotsky, Leon *The Permanent Revolution*. New York, Pathfinder, 1978.

116. Trotsky, Leon *The Revolution Betrayed: What is the Soviet Union and Where is it Going?* London, Pathfinder, 1987.

117. Wallerstein, Immanuel 'The Rise and Future Demise of the World Capitalist System: Concepts for Comparative Analysis'. *Comparative Studies in Society and History*, vol. 16, no. 4, 1974, pp. 387–415. Excerpt in Richard Little and Michael Smith (eds) *Perspectives on World Politics: A Reader*. London and New York, Routledge, 1991, pp. 305–17.

118. Wallerstein, Immanuel, *Historical Capitalism*. London, Verso, 1983.

119. Wallerstein, Immanuel *The Modern World-System I*. New York, Academic Press, 1974.

120. Wallerstein, Immanuel *The Modern World-System II*. New York, Academic Press, 1980.

121. Wallerstein, Immanuel *The Modern World-System III*. San Diego, Academic Press, 1989.

122. Wallerstein, Immanuel *Unthinking Social Science: The Limits of Nineteenth-Century Paradigms*. Cambridge, Polity Press and Cambridge, MA, Basil Blackwell, 1991.

123. Waltz, Kenneth N. *Man, the State and War*. New York, Columbia University Press, 1959.

124. Warren, Bill *Imperialism: Pioneer of Capitalism*. London, Verso and NLB, 1980.

125. Wight, Martin 'Why is There No International Theory?' in H. Butterfield and M. Wight (eds) *Diplomatic Investigations*. London, George Allen and Unwin, 1966, pp. 17–34.

126. Williams, Eric *From Columbus to Castro: The History of the Caribbean 1492–1969*. London, Andre Deutsch, 1983.

127. Williams, Eric *Capitalism and Slavery*. London, Andre Deutsch, 1964.

128. Williams, Howard *International Relations in Political Theory*. Milton Keynes and Philadelphia, Open University Press, 1992.

129. Yahuda, Michael B. *China's Role in World Affairs*. London, Croom Helm, 1978.

11 International political economy
Richard Higgott*

Introduction

International political economy (IPE) has been a major growth area in the study of IR over the last decade on both sides of the Atlantic and elsewhere. This chapter accounts for the growth and provides a review of the schools of thought and debates within IPE. This is a difficult task since a proliferation of texts and edited collections have attempted to review and illustrate the state of IPE as a scholarly enterprise rather than as practice.

A complete list cannot be provided here. Of the major texts, representative of varying persuasions, Gilpin [26], Gill and Law [23], Strange [63], Spero [59], Isaak [34] are of special importance. The most recent edited collections include Frieden and Lake [19], Crane and Amawi [18], Murphy and Tooze [50] and the outstanding collection of original essays in Stubbs and Underhill [68]. There are also several important series in international political economy. Four are worth noting – the Cornell Series edited by Peter Katzenstein, the Columbia series edited by John Ruggie and Helen Milner, the Macmillan series edited by Tim Shaw and *The International Political Economy Yearbook* produced under the auspices of the International Political Economy Group of the International Studies Association (North America). For many years in the USA, *International Organization* has been the vehicle for the publication of innovative work of a specifically American flavour in international political economy. A new journal, *The Review of International Political Economy*, will be published in the UK in 1994.

This proliferation has led to a range of competitive, or more often semi-competitive, definitions and typologies. Thus, the working assumption of this chapter is that there is no established general explanation of IPE – merely the recognition of IPE as an important series of practices (of considerable historical stature) and a now identifiable 'field of inquiry' [11], 'area of investigation' [71], or 'set of questions' [26] constantly undergoing redefinition and reconceptualization.

* Support of the Hallsworth Fellowship at the University of Manchester in the production of this chapter is gratefully acknowledged.

Contemporary IPE has developed a series of typologies that are variations on a set of themes – realist or mercantilist, liberal or interdependence, Marxist and dependency. The first section of the chapter focuses specifically on the dominant realist and liberal orthodoxies that have developed principally in the United States over the last two decades. It offers only passing reference to the Marxist intellectual tradition in political economy which has not featured prominently in the development of IPE. The second section considers important non-US developments affecting the orthodoxy outlined in the first section. It does so by highlighting the substantive changes taking place in the structure of the global economy, especially processes of globalization (and all that is implied by this often vague and confusing term) and their implications for the study of IPE. It considers the development of a 'counter hegemonic' international political economy throughout the 1980s and early 1990s and broaches some of the substantive issues that are of concern to the contemporary student of IPE. Finally, the chapter considers how IPE might evolve over the short to medium term.

Early IPE

Intellectual development: The evolution of IPE does not presume that a consensus exists on what constitutes international political economy. Rather 'IPE' is a 'hosting metaphor' connoting, first, the exploration of the relationship between power and wealth, and second, the interface of the study of IR and economics. It rejects the dichotomy that has prevailed for much of the 20th century between these scholarly enterprises.

The recent growth of interest in IPE can be dated to the late 1960s and the early 1970s. In a now classic article, Strange noted the mutual neglect of economics and political science as scholarship, with a consequent ignorance of important dimensions of the international policy agenda beyond concerns with security [60]. But contemporary IPE was more than a critique of the limitations of two disciplines [61] or an attempt to combine the dominant traditions in IR and international economics; it was the product of other explicit and non-explicit values. Epistemological differences are important to understanding the development of IPE [72]. Two of the major IPE texts illustrate the point. Gilpin [26] sees the relationship between the state and the market as fundamental to any understanding of the *issues* involved in economic and political change and the ordering of human relationships. For Strange [63], on the other hand, IPE is bounded by a mix of values (security, wealth, freedom and justice) within a market-authority relationship that affects the *structures* of power in the world economy.

Important historical and structural changes also affected the evolution of IPE. It was given a great impetus by the expansion of the world economy during the 'long boom' after the Second World War and especially because international commercial activity, facilitated by the growth of the multi-national enterprise and the growing economic power of Japan and the EC, developed faster than most national economies. This growth and the end of the Bretton Woods' system curtailed the 'golden days' of a Keynesian Liberal

International Economic Order underwritten by US hegemony that had followed the Second World War. Implicit in this process, and the problems that flowed from it, was a recognition that the maintenance of the international economy was now as much a political as a technical question.

Further, if it had been politically expedient in international relations (as both theory and practice) to depoliticize issues of redistribution between rich and poor during the period of decolonization, this was no longer the case by the 1970s. The politicization of the 'development question', especially the structuralist critiques of liberal economics by the UN Economic Commission for Latin America during the 1960s and the subsequent radicalization of the north–south relationship after the first oil shock, gave impetus to the development of IPE (see Cox, [13]).

While some of the earliest forays into IPE came from Latin America and the UK, it was soon captured and developed by American political scientists. Gilpin and Keohane enunciated standard definitions of IPE as 'the reciprocal and dynamic interaction in international relations of the pursuit of wealth and the pursuit of power' [24, p. 43] and 'the intersection of production and exchange on the one hand and power on the other' [38, p. 21]. Keohane and Nye [41, 42] came to the forefront of IPE with their studies of transnational relations and interdependence in world politics. Other definitions of IPE that emerged varied by language rather than substance from these initial definitions.

It was thus no coincidence that the first internationally acclaimed text in IPE, Spero's *Politics of International Economic Relations* [59], focused on (i) OECD interdependence, (ii) East–West independence and (iii) southern dependence on the north. Along with Krasner's realist attempt to understand and defend US hegemony in *Defending the National Interest* [44], the complex interdependence school in its neorealist form dominated the emerging agenda of IPE. Given the numerical preponderance of American scholars, this agenda overshadowed the initial 'southern' debate about the relationship between the haves and have-nots of the global economic order much more in North America than in other parts of the world.

However, interest in the economic dimension of IR was not new. Carr, for example, always recognized the importance of the relationship between economics and international relations. Much of the earlier literature either had a distinctly mercantilist flavour [74] or was concerned with questions of statecraft based on economic capabilities and asymmetries in the relationship between states [57].

But it had become clear by the 1970s that a greater fusion was needed. The initial formulations of Keohane and Nye et al. found little favour with many of their intellectual opponents. From within the realist camp it was suggested variously that they had overestimated both the demise of the state and the importance of 'low' politics [48]. From a 'southern' perspective, the theoretical focus on interdependence marginalized the south's ability to expose the asymmetries of power and wealth identified in theories of dependence [10].

Assumptions: The juxtaposition of power and wealth has been an important dimension of thinking about IR since the emergence of the market economy in the 17th and 18th centuries. It was central to the early political economists, whether they were classical liberals (Smith and Ricardo), classical mercantilists (Hamilton and List) or early Marxists (Lenin and Luxemburg) [18]. Indeed, various schools of contemporary IPE draw much of their intellectual strength from them [31].

But these legacies are of consequence to this chapter only to the extent that they inform the contemporary study of IPE. Specifically, the post-1870 rise of marginalist economics, and the development of marginal calculus as an analytical tool, has been especially influential in the development of IPE. The neo-classical agenda's privileging of questions concerning the logic of human action (more than classical and Marxist questions of production) gave rise to a definition of economics as a theory of choice under constraint. It is the essence of this neo-classical approach – with its emphasis on the individual actor as the agent of choice – that underpins IPE as it has developed in the USA over the last two decades.

Thus in methodological terms, political economy has become the application of economic analysis to the various arenas (domestic and international) of politics. 'Economics is a way of acting, politics is a place to act' [12, p. 31]. In this mode of thinking, economics is not just about market relations or material provisioning but also about calculation using rational choice theory to allocate preferences for welfare maximization in the international economy. Two issues are central to the development of IPE driven by these neo-classical premises: first, the evolution of international public goods, especially the building and maintenance of regimes and institutions to facilitate international economic cooperation, and second, the role of leadership, especially hegemonic leadership by the USA in the post-Second World War era, in the provision of these international public goods. They can be subsumed under the heading hegemonic stability theory (HST).

Hegemonic stability theory: HST asserts that an international economic order is possible thanks to the presence of an hegemonic state that establishes and underwrites public goods of order and openness. As Kindleberger puts it '. . . for the world economy to be stabilized there needs to be a stabilizer – one stabilizer' [43, p. 304]. The reverse side of the thesis is that the absence of a hegemon (as in the inter-war period) creates a vacuum in the management of the existing international economic order. *Pax Britannica* prior to the First World War and *Pax Americana* after the Second World War are held to be exemplar hegemonic orders in which a hegemon '. . . created and enforced the rules of a liberal international economic order' [25, p. 145].

These assumptions about the importance of hegemonic power for stability were shared throughout much of the 1970s and 1980s across the spectrum of North American IPE. The major point of difference was between a realist perspective which expects to see 'self-regarding' action on the part of the hegemon [26, p. 345] and a liberal, 'other-regarding' [43, p. 28] perspective in which the hegemon provides public goods. This divide is repeated in the currently fashionable debate between neorealists and neoliberals on how best to explain international economic cooperation.

For neorealists the pursuit of relative gains [28, 29, 45] is more important than securing absolute gains or improving one's welfare [38, 40, 4]. Consequently, the desire for relative success rather than absolute success is held to inhibit cooperation. Neorealists see states as rational actors exercising clearly defined preferences. While using the same rationalist method, neoliberals assume that states can be indifferent to the gains that others might make, so long as international transactions result in welfare maximization. Further, neorealists and neoliberals ascribe differing levels of importance to the role of institutions in the mitigation of conflict and the development of cooperation in the international political and economic order [49]. In addition, neoliberals have a less deterministic view than realists of anarchy in international relations [75].

But both neorealists and neoliberals place great emphasis on the necessity of hegemony for the provision of international public goods. Hegemonic periods are characterized by freer, more open trading systems and loose centre–periphery relations, and declining hegemony by tighter centre–periphery relations, protectionism and bilateralism [27]. Indeed, it was in the significance attached to US hegemony for the provision of public goods in international economic life that realism and liberalism found common cause in the development of American IPE throughout the 1970s–80s.

Yet these analyses of hegemony were deficient in a number of ways. They did not really explain how hegemonic power promoted international order, and their understanding of power in HST was relational rather than structural. But relational approaches to power analysis – especially the transformation mechanisms for converting brute economic and military might into hegemonic domination – were shown by Strange [62, 63] to be inadequate. Despite its historical-cum-universalist theoretical pretensions, HST was unicentric international economic history. It constructed a view of the USA as possessing, after the Second World War, both the will and the capability to construct a global order both for its own purposes and as a wider contribution to the public good.

More nuanced readings contest this understanding of international order underwritten purely by US power. Ruggie [56] argued that the post-Second World War economic order represented an 'embedded liberal' compromise between US desires for a liberal multilateral system and the more interventionist preferences of its European allies. The compromise allowed for domestic interventionism to ensure political harmony between competing socio-economic sectors in a given community and a limited multilateral liberalism to foster the evolution of the international economic order.

Yet whether one adopts a realist interpretation of hegemonic stability [25, 26], a liberal interpretation [43, 38, 40], a mix of realist and liberal approaches [8], a collective action interpretation [52] or a partial analysis [56, 33], one common element remains: most scholarship in IPE over the last two decades has focused, in one way or another, on the question of US hegemony in the global order.

Central to the methodology of this line of inquiry has been the intellectual hegemony of rationalist theory. Even the most philosophically sensitive mainstream scholars in the USA, while stressing the need to take account of a reflective critique based on an appreciation of human subjectivity [2], insist on the need to stress 'substantive rationality' and to avoid '. . . diversionary philosophical construction' [39, p. 382] Rigour and parsimony in theorizing are, of course, important [54, 58], but assuming the unfailing primacy of rationality in exchange relations denies a role to other significant dimensions. Prisoners' Dilemmas – the essence of rationality driven theory – ignore the possibility that a sense of obligation may in fact exist between parties to a relationship [35]. Shared values or morally constituted norms provide an important complement or counter to rationally bounded activity.

Rationally ordained, egoistic or self-regarding behaviour is a major inducement to international economic cooperation, but it is not the only one [46, 47]. The study of IPE in the 1990s should permit and expect a process of 'contest among subordinate subjects . . . [rather than] some privileged focus and register of unambiguous and universal truth.' [3, p. 265]. No single entity, even a so-called 'hegemonic state', represents the total embodiment at any given time of accepted practices and norms in international relations in an era of globalization.

IPE in an era of globalization

In some ways, there was an evolution of thinking in IPE in the 1980s. The intense debate over the so-called 'end' of American hegemony can be caricatured as a contest between the 'declinists', exemplified in the work of Kennedy [36], and the 'renewalists', exemplified in Nye's tract *Bound to Lead* [51]. Declinists acknowledged that the USA was still the world's major economic power and not destined inevitably to go the way of the UK. Despite slipping behind in some industrial sectors, the US remains strong in all and predominant in most of the sectors of technology characteristic of post-industrial societies. The decline in national indicators of power such as industrial production and exports as shares of world production and world trade respectively have not cost the USA its informal, non-territorial empire based on the components of 'structural power' in the domains of security, production, credit and knowledge [63]. Much more problematic is Nye's assertion [51, p. 188] that it is still also the major source of 'soft power' in world affairs – that is 'cooptive behavioural power' stemming from the strength of American culture, ideology and institutions.

The understanding of hegemony in American IR scholarship (both realist and liberal) is no longer a self-evident way of enframing the study of power in IPE. Alternative theoretical understandings of hegemony are gaining currency. The distinction between subject/object and fact/value that has underwritten the development of 20th-century social science, and which has been at the core of a rationalist ascendency in IPE (especially in the United States), is now contested in the more critical reaches of recent IR theory in the distinction between IPE as problem solving and IPE as critical theory. Processes of globalization mitigate our traditional understanding of the state system since the Treaty of Westphalia. 'Globalization', in particular, is stripping us of our initial understanding of interdependence. Both theoretical turns represent important criticisms and refinements of more orthodox IPE and are prominent in the work of two of the most important non-US scholars at the forefront of innovation in contemporary IPE – Cox and Strange.

IPE–critical theory and problem solving: According to the Canadian scholar Robert Cox, one of the ways in which we can cut into IPE is by differentiating between problem solving and critical theory. Problem-solving approaches, grounded largely in behavioural-cum-positivist political science, underwrite US scholarship in IPE. By contrast, critical theory, operating from a more explicit normative theoretical base 'is a theory of history concerned with change' [14, pp. 208–9]. Where problem-solving approaches focus on actors, especially the state, critical theory focuses more on structures, especially those of global accumulation.

Nowhere are the differences better illustrated than in their competing approaches to the question of power. Problem solving rejects the notion of the fungibility of power across issues areas (energy, finance, trade, security) and has a restricted notion of state dominance. In this definition, hegemony is underwritten by a state's preponderance of 'material' power. Power is also context specific and lacks the historical and structural dimensions of a critical theory. Critical theory, on the other hand, sees hegemony emerge from the 'configuration of material power, the prevalent collective image of world order. . .and a set of institutions' [17, p. 223, 15, 21, 22]. Order is consensual in a Gramscian sense. State power is not the only source of power and, most importantly, material preponderance is not, on its own, the sufficient prerequisite for hegemony.

The importance of Cox's work is to be found in the difference between his understanding of what constitutes knowledge in IPE and that which is to be found in the mainstream. Cox, like Polanyi and unlike the mainstream, sees markets as socio-political constructs rather than simply rational interactions between economic agents [53, 73]. Similarly, his reflectivist and historical methodologies (stressing the relationship of subject and object) produce an understanding of the global political economy different from that provided by a rationalist methodology (stressing the separation of subject and object). From this position, IPE is about the interaction of a transnational market economy with a competitive system of states and non-state actors across the domestic and international economic space. Earlier approaches to IPE, which merely *juxtaposed* states and markets, failed to capture the full complexity of the global political economy in the latter part of the 20th century.

Cox's conception of hegemony – derived from Gramsci – links ideas to the material world and thus offers a more complicated understanding of hegemony than emanates from HST. Notably, it renders problematic some of the easier assertions about the relationship between US material preponderance and Nye's 'soft power' [51]. Thus the end of the Cold War and the 'triumph of the market' does not necessarily represent the hegemony, or universalization, of American 'soft power'; nor does it imply uniformity of thinking about how best to maximize efficient production and distribution.

Rather, it suggests the evolution of a battle of ideas between competing understandings of capitalism.

Globalization: The rapid globalization of the international economy (especially in the areas of production and finance) and the changing nature of the inter-state system in a post-hegemonic era contribute to the emergence of the *Global* (as opposed to International) Political Economy. In short, this is 'an economic space transcending all country borders, which co-exists still with an international economy based on transactions across country borders and which is regulated by inter-state agreements and practices' [17, p. 260; 23].

The recognition of a Global Political Economy (GPE) is the latest stage in the study of IPE. The first stage saw scholars talk about the Politics of International Economic Relations (PIER), an exchange model epitomized in the texts of Spero [59] and Blake and Walters [8] and in later theories of interdependence in which power was relational and non-fungible, and international linkages between national economies were state-centric. Later scholars, especially outside of the USA, began to talk about an IPE in which relational power (the language of a realist discourse in IR) was subsumed (not supplanted) in the wider context of our understanding of the nature of structural power.

By contrast, GPE does not identify just two spheres of influence – the domestic and the international – with the state as both a territorial and intellectual barrier between them. Rather, it identifies three different levels of economic space (supra-regional, national and sub-regional), and at least three different levels of social organization (social forces, states and national societies, global society). Cox depicts this as a 'multi-level world that challenges the old Westphalian assumption that a state is a state is a state' [17, p. 263, 77]. In this third stage of intellectual understanding, the global economy is gaining strength in its relationship with the other institutions and actors in the international economic order. This has major implications for students and practitioners of IPE.

Thus the central policy question of contemporary IPE revolves around the politics of adjustment, that is, the manner in which governments, irrespective of the power of a given state, can, or cannot, maintain a greater or lesser semblance of authority over their policy-making process in the face of globalization. Neither the strong nor the weak are immune to the effects of globalization.

The declining autonomy of many governments over the policy process has not been due to other states but to a world market economy under less political control than national economies have been in the past [64, 65]. States still have important assets for controlling territory that define the boundaries of a national market. What they cannot control, however, is globalized production for world markets. At the very least, globalization challenges conventional notions of state identity [55]. In this context states can no longer determine, they can only bargain. Thus they become more like firms. But firms are becoming much more important in the inter-relationship between states and markets in a way that was not the case even in the recent past. Firms are now central to alliances that governments make in their attempts to maximize national welfare at the same time as they may also be in competition or conflict with governments.

As globalization proceeds, ownership matters less for production purposes but more for political purposes. Globalization, in contrast to some earlier understandings of interdependence, contains no necessary notion of enhanced inter-state cooperation. Indeed, it exposes many limitations in the structures of international economic governance. Faced with a declining autonomy over their economic policy agenda, states grapple to claw back control. This in part explains the declining support for multilateralism and the increased support for bilateralism and regionalism that has accompanied globalization.

The globalization of production processes and financial interactions, and the manner in which they constrain policy choice, have made IPE scholarship more salient – albeit in different ways for different scholars. For some, especially liberal economists, globalization represents a welcome constraint on state power. For older-style realists and scholars of a more statist persuasion, however, it is an unfortunate undermining of the sovereignty central to the state system. For Cox [17, p. 261) it consolidates the emergence of a 'the transnational managerial class' or, for Strange [65, p. 260], 'an international business civilisation'.

A changing agenda in IPE: Processes of globalization and different understandings of the question of hegemony in the international order call forth a new research agenda in IPE for the next decade. Several dimensions of such an agenda are identified briefly below.

There is a need to address the 'New Diplomacy' identified by Strange and Stopford [67]. Triangular in form, this diplomacy entails commonly understood state-to-state exchanges and firm-to-firm exchanges but also state-to-firm negotiation and bargaining, of both intra- and inter-state varieties. This represents a double power shift: from the 'public to the private' and from 'authority to the market'. This new diplomacy, in which competition for world market share is the prize [65], has implications for practice and for IPE as scholarship. Governments in the 1990s need to know as much about the corporate histories of their major trading and investing partners in the private sphere as they traditionally tried to know about the diplomatic histories and practices of their partners and adversaries in the inter-state system [62].

Moreover, the agenda needs to focus on the changing positions of the principal actors in the international political economy in a post-hegemonic era. There are two implications. At the more theoretical level, IPE will need to focus on the competing approaches to the organization of production and exchange now consolidating in the global economy. In more populist language, we must consider the clash of alternative capitalisms. A range of simple taxonomies already exists. For example Cox [16] sees a struggle between 'hyper-liberalism' and 'state capitalism'; Albert [1] envisages a Rhine versus a neo-American model. Garten [20], extending the competition to the Asia Pacific, contrasts the American liberal market model with the social market-economy model of Germany and the developmental state approach he thinks he identifies in Japan (see also 69]. These analyses are rudimentary and, with the exception of Cox, offer little insight into the potential nature of change in these systems over time, unless it is to exhibit what we might call 'blocism' – the notion that the world is drifting ever more strongly towards three vertical trade blocs focused on the dominant regional actors.

This is too simple. The evolution of hemispheric spheres of influence is a significant international phenomenon, albeit overstated in a number of ways, especially in the Asia-Pacific Region [32]. Alternative visions – for example, a new medievalism, with fragmented and overlapping political structures and permeated sovereignties existing at the local, sub-national and supra-national levels – are not impossible. A research agenda in IPE for the end of the 20th century needs to address these general theoretical questions in a more detailed manner.

More empirical research into the clash of capitalisms in a post-hegemonic era will, inevitably, focus on the durability and nature of the evolution of the institutions of the global economic order. The degree to which the embedded liberal compromise survives the attacks made on it by the new mercantilism – that body of practices such as voluntary export restraints, orderly marketing arrangements, managed trade, aggressive unilateralism, geographically discriminatory arrangements, strategic trade policy – will be a key issue [5, 6, 7]. Given that this agenda will be set by G-7 and OECD states, it is unlikely that questions of a redistributive nature emanating from southern or dependency perspectives will gain much purchase on the broader agenda. Indeed, a characteristic of contemporary IPE is the manner in which it is becoming 'de-regionalized'. Third World conditions are now to be found in North America and Europe, and First World conditions are to be found in Africa, Asia, Latin America.

Lest it be thought that IPE will remain dominated by 'trade' questions, we should also note the manner in which international finance has become much more salient in an era of globalization. Indeed, earlier notions of finance 'as the servant' of the international economy need to be adjusted [30], since the dynamics and influence of foreign direct investment in the global economy will be a major item on any future research agenda of IPE. The IPE agenda has broadened, and it is related to the security agenda and the environmental agenda. Important changes to IPE will also be brought about by the gendering of research [70, 76 and see chapter 3]. Interdisciplinary work across these frontiers will become increasingly salient in years to come.

Conclusion

The central importance of IPE as a field of inquiry over recent decades has been its role in highlighting the disjuncture between the consolidating global nature of the organization of the world economy and the continuing centrality of the territorial state as the principal unit of political organization. This is a tension that is unlikely to be resolved. Early understandings about the nature of hegemony are no longer held with such force. There are few signs, however, that the dominance of a positivist–empiricist methodology – underwritten by a neo-classical approach to rational calculation in which states are the principal utility maximizer – has suffered much erosion as the privileged methodology.

IPE is not, however, simply American scholarship. The rise of other actors (state and non-state) to prominence in the global economy in a post-hegemonic era has produced alternatives to American intellectual hegemony. It has had some impact on scholarship in the USA. More specifically, it offers alternative sets of tools with which to consider the changes that have come about in the practice of international economic relations as a fundamental, indeed inseparable, dimension of IR. Whatever its limitations, the development of IPE has rendered redundant the distinctions between the 'domestic' and the 'international' and the 'economic' and the 'political' which characterized much post-war IR scholarship.

Bibliography

1. Albert, M. *Capitalism against Capitalism*. London, Whurr, 1993.
2. Ashley, R.K. 'The Poverty of Neo-Realism'. *International Organization*, vol. 38, no. 2, 1984, pp. 225–86.
3. Ashley, R.K. 'Imposing International Purpose: Notes on a Problematic of Governance' in E.O. Czempial and J.N. Rosenau (eds) *Global Changes and Theoretical Challenges: Approaches to World Politics for the 1990s*. Lexington, Lexington Books, 1989, pp. 251–90.
4. Axelrod, R. and Keohane, R.O. 'Achieving Cooperation under Anarchy: Strategies and Institutions' in Kenneth Oye (ed.) *Cooperation Under Anarchy*. Princeton, Princeton University Press, 1985, pp. 226–54.
5. Bhagwati, J. *Protectionism*. Cambridge, MA and London, MIT Press, 1988.
6. Bhagwati, J. *The World Trading System at Risk*. Princeton, Princeton University Press, 1991.
7. Bhagwati, J. and Patrick, H. (eds) *Aggressive Unilateralism: America's 301 Trade Policy and the World Trading System*. Ann Arbor, Michigan University Press, 1990 and London, Harvester Wheatsheaf, 1991.
8. Blake, D.H. and Walters, R.S. *The Politics of Global Economic Relations*. Englewood Cliffs, Prentice Hall, 1987 and London, International Paperback Editions, 1991.
9. Calleo, D. *Beyond American Hegemony: The Future of the Western Alliance*. New York, Basic Books, 1989 and Brighton, Wheatsheaf, 1987.
10. Caporaso, J. 'Introduction to the Special Issue on Dependence and Dependency in the Global System'. *International Organization*, vol. 32, no. 1, 1978, pp. 1–12.
11. Caporaso, J. 'International Political Economy: Fad or Field'. *International Studies Notes*, vol. 31, no. 1, 1987, pp. 1–9.
12. Caporaso, J. and Levine, D. *Theories of Political Economy*. New York, Cambridge University Press, 1992.
13. Cox, R. 'Ideologies and the New International Economic Order'. *International Organization*, vol. 33, no. 2, 1979, pp. 275–302.
14. Cox, R. 'Social Forces, States and World Orders: Beyond International Relations Theory' in Robert O. Keohane (ed.) *Neo-Realism and its Critics*. New York, Columbia University Press, 1986, pp. 204–54.

15. Cox, R. *Production, Power and World Order: Social Forces in the Making of History*. New York, Columbia University Press, 1987.
16. Cox, R. 'The Global Political Economy and Social Choice' in D. Drache and M.S. Gertler (eds) *The New Era of Global Competition: state policy and market power*. Montreal and London, McGill–Queen's University Press, 1991, pp. 335–50.
17. Cox, R. 'Structural Issues of Global Governance: Implications for Europe' in S. Gill (ed.) *Gramsci, Historical Materialism and International Relations*. Cambridge, Cambridge University Press, 1993, pp. 259–89.
18. Crane, G.T. and Amawi, A.M. (eds) *The Theoretical Evolution of International Political Economy: a reader*. New York, Oxford University Press, 1991.
19. Frieden, J. and Lake, D. (eds) *International Political Economy: Perspectives on Global Power and Wealth*. New York, St. Martin's Press, 1990 and London, Unwin Hyman, 1991.
20. Garten, J. *A Cold Peace: America, Japan, Germany and the Struggle for Supremacy*. New York, Random House, 1993.
21. Gill, S. *American Hegemony and the Trilateral Commission*. Cambridge, Cambridge University Press, 1992.
22. Gill, S. (ed.) *Gramsci, Historical Materialism and International Relations*. Cambridge and New York, Cambridge University Press, 1993.
23. Gill, S. and Law, D. *The Global Political Economy: Perspectives, Problems and Policies*. Baltimore, Johns Hopkins University Press and London, Harvester, 1988.
24. Gilpin, R. *US Power and the Multinational Corporation*. New York, Basic Books, 1975.
25. Gilpin, R. *War and Change in World Politics*. New York, Cambridge University Press, 1983.
26. Gilpin, R. *The Political Economy of International Relations*. Princeton, Princeton University Press, 1987.
27. Goldstein, J. *Long Cycles: Prosperity and War in the Modern Age*. New Haven and London, Yale University Press, 1988.
28. Grieco. J. 'Anarchy and the Limits of Cooperation: A Realist Critique of the Newest Liberal Institutionalism'. *International Organization*, vol. 42, no. 3, 1988, pp. 485–508.
29. Grieco. J. *Cooperation Among Nations: Europe, America and Non-Tariff Barriers to Trade*. Ithaca, Cornell University Press, 1990.
30. Helleiner, E. 'When Finance was the Servant: International Capital Movements in the Bretton Woods Order' in Philip Cerny (ed.) *Finance and World Politics: Markets, Regimes and States in a Post-Hegemonic Era*. London, Edward Elgar, 1993, pp. 20–51.
31. Higgott, R.A. *Political Development Theory: the Contemporary Debate*. London, Routledge, 1988 and 1990.
32. Higgott, R.A. 'Economic Cooperation: Theoretical Opportunities and Practical Constraints'. *The Pacific Review*, vol. 6, no. 2, 1993, pp. 103–17.
33. Ikenberry, J. 'Rethinking the Origins of American Hegemony'. *Political Science Quarterly*, vol. 104, no. 3, 1989, pp. 375–400.
34. Isaak, R.A. *International Political Economy: Managing World Change*. Englewood Cliffs, Prentice-Hall, 1990.
35. Jervis, R. 'Realism, Game Theory and Cooperation'. *World Politics*, vol. 40, no. 3, 1988, pp. 317–49.
36. Kennedy, P. *The Rise and Fall of the Great Powers*. New York, Random House and London, Fontana, 1989.

37. Keohane, R.O. 'The Theory of Hegemonic Stability and Changes in International Economic Regimes, 1967–77' in O.E. Holsti, R.M. Siverson and A.L. George (eds) *Change in the International System*. Boulder, Westview, 1980, pp. 131–62.
38. Keohane, R.O. *After Hegemony: Cooperation and Discord in the World Political Economy*. Princeton, Princeton University Press, 1984.
39. Keohane, R.O. 'International Institutions: Two Approaches'. *International Studies Quarterly*, vol. 32, no. 4, 1988, pp. 379–96.
40. Keohane, R.O. and Owen, R. *International Institutions and State Power: Essays in International Relations Theory*. Boulder, Westview Press, 1989.
41. Keohane, R.O. and Nye, J. (eds) *Transnational Relations and World Politics*. Cambridge, MA and London, Harvard University Press, 1972.
42. Keohane, R.O. and Nye, J. *Power and Interdependence*. Boston, Little, Brown, 1977 and Glenview, Scott, Foresman, 1989.
43. Kindleberger, C. *The World in Depression, 1929–39*. Berkeley, University of California Press, 1986.
44. Krasner, S. *Defending the National Interest: Raw Materials Investments and US Foreign Policy*. Princeton, Princeton University Press, 1978.
45. Krasner, S. 'Global Communication and National Power: Life on the Pareto Frontier'. *World Politics*, vol. 43, no. 3, 1991, pp. 336–66.
46. Kratochwil, F. *Rules, Norms and Decisions: On the Conditions of Practical and Legal Reasoning in International Relations and Domestic Affairs*. Cambridge, Cambridge University Press, 1989.
47. Lumsdaine, D.H. *Moral Vision in International Politics: The Foreign Aid Regime, 1949–89*. Princeton, Princeton University Press, 1993.
48. Miller, J.D.B. *The World of States: Connected Essays*. London, Croom Helm and New York, St. Martin's Press, 1981.
49. Milner, H. 'International Theories of Cooperation Among Nations: Strengths and Weaknesses'. *World Politics*, vol. 44, no. 3, 1992, pp. 466–94.
50. Murphy, C. and Tooze, R. (eds) *The New International Political Economy*. Boulder, Lynne Rienner, 1991.
51. Nye, J. *Bound to Lead: The Changing Nature of American Power*. New York, Basic Books, 1990.
52. Olson, M. *The Rise and Decline of Nations: Economic Growth, Stagflation and Social Rigidities*. New Haven and London, Yale University Press, 1982.
53. Polanyi, K. *The Great Transformation*. Boston, Beacon Press, 1975.
54. Powell, R. 'Absolute and Relative Gains in International Relations Theory'. *American Political Science Review*, vol. 85, no. 4, 1991, pp. 1303–20.
55. Reich, R.B. *The Work of Nations, Preparing Ourselves for 21st Century Capitalism*. New York, Simon and Schuster, 1993.
56. Ruggie, J.G. 'International Regimes, Transactions and Change: Embedded Liberalism in the Postwar Economic Order'. *International Organization*, vol. 36, no. 2, 1982, pp. 379–415.
57. Servan-Schreiber, J-J. *The American Challenge (Le Défi Americain)*. Translation from French by Ronald Steel, New York, Athenum, 1979. French edition, Paris, Denoel, 1967.
58. Snidal, D. 'Relative Gains and Patterns of International Cooperation'. *American Political Science Review*, vol. 85, no. 3, 1991, pp. 701–26.
59. Spero, J. *The Politics of International Economic Relations*. London, Allen and Unwin and New York, St. Martin's Press, 1990.
60. Strange, S. 'International Economics and International Relations: A Case of Mutual Neglect'. *International Affairs*, vol. 46, no. 2, 1970, pp. 304–15.

61. Strange, S. 'International Political Economy: The Story So Far and the Way Ahead' in W. Ladd Hollist and F. La Mond Tullis (eds) *International Political Economy, Yearbook*, vol. 1. Boulder, Westview Press and London, Pinter, 1985, pp. 13–25.
62. Strange, S. 'The Persistent Myth of Lost Hegemony'. *International Organization*, vol. 41, no. 4, 1987, pp. 551–74.
63. Strange, S. *States and Markets: An Introduction to International Political Economy*. London, Frances Pinter, 1988.
64. Strange, S. 'An Eclectic Approach' in Craig Murphy and Roger Tooze (eds) *The New International Political Economy*. Boulder, Lynne Reinner and London, Macmillan, 1991, pp. 33–49.
65. Strange, S. 'The Name of the Game' in N.X. Rizopoulos (ed.) *Sea-Changes: American Foreign Policy in a World Transformed*. New York and London, Council on Foreign Relations, 1990, pp. 238–73.
66. Strange, S. 'States, Firms and Diplomacy'. *International Affairs*, vol. 68, no. 1, 1992, pp. 1–15.
67. Strange, S. and Stopford, J. *Rival States, Rival Firms: Competition for World Market Shares*. Cambridge, Cambridge University Press, 1991.
68. Stubbs, R. and Underhill, G. (eds) *Political Economy and the Changing Global Order*. London, Macmillan, 1994.
69. Thurow, L. *Head to Head: The Coming Economic Battle Among Japan, Europe and America*. London and New York, Nicholas Brealey, 1992.
70. Tickner, J. Ann. *Gender in International Relations: Feminist Perspectives on Achieving Global Security*. New York, Columbia University Press, 1992.
71. Tooze, R. 'Perspectives and Theory: a Consumers Guide' in Susan Strange (ed.) *Paths to International Political Economy*. London, Allen and Unwin, 1984, pp. 1–22.
72. Tooze, R. 'The Unwritten Preface: IPE and Epistemology'. *Millennium*, vol. 17, no. 2, 1988, pp. 285–93.
73. Underhill, G. 'Conceptualising the Changing Global Order' in Richard Stubbs and Geoffrey Underhill (eds) *Political Economy and the Changing Global Order*. London, Macmillan, 1994.
74. Viner, J. 'Power versus Plenty as Objectives of Foreign Policy in the 17th and 18th Centuries'. *World Politics*, vol. 1, no. 1, 1949, pp. 1–29.
75. Wendt, A. 'Anarchy is What States Make of It: the social construction of power politics'. *International Organization*, vol. 46, no. 2, 1992, pp. 391–425.
76. Whitworth, S. 'Theory as Exclusion: Gender and International Political Economy' in Richard Stubbs and Geoffrey Underhill (eds) *Political Economy and the Changing Global Order*. London, Macmillan, 1994.
77. Zacher, M. 'The Decaying Pillars of the Westphalian Temple: Implications for International Order and Governance' in James Rosenau and Ernst-Otto Czempiel (eds) *Governance without Government: Order and Change in World Politics*. Cambridge and New York, Cambridge University Press, 1992, pp. 58–101.

12 Political geography and geopolitics
Geoffrey Parker

Geography is the holistic study of the phenomena of the surface of the earth, and a modern working definition of political geography is that it is the study of the state as a spatial or terrestrial phenomenon. Geopolitics, on the other hand, is the spatial study of the relationships among states and the implications of these relationships for the morphology of the political map as a whole. The two are of necessity closely bound together since a full understanding of the relationships among any phenomena presupposes some knowledge of the nature of those phenomena themselves. Viewed from this wider perspective geopolitics may thus be deemed to include political geography and the adjective 'geopolitical' may be used to describe them both [40].

The two subdisciplines are products of the closing years of the 19th century when their potential subject matter was for the first time revealed in something approaching its entirety. By then, as Lord Bryce [5, p. 8] put it, the features of the earth had 'passed from the chaos of conjecture to the cosmos of science', something which he considered to be 'an especially great and fateful event'.

The acknowledged father of modern political geography was the German geographer Friedrich Ratzel. In his book *Politische Geographie* [48] he defined the subject as being the study of the state as a 'space organism'. He identified *Raum* (space) and *Lage* (position) as the two principal determinants of the fortunes of states. Each state had its own particular needs arising from the physical conditions of its existence, but adequate *Lebensraum*, living space for its people, was always a fundamental requirement. *Lebensraum*, and the physical and human resources arising from its possession, was seen as being particularly important for the success of those dynamic states which had the potential to become great world powers. Its acquisition necessitated territorial expansion even if the result of this expansion was war. The relationships among states and the implications of these relationships for the international scene as a whole were, to Ratzel, an integral part of the field of study.

The term geopolitics (*Geopolitik*) was coined by the Swedish political scientist Rudolf Kjellén at the University of Gothenburg at about the same time as Ratzel was engaged in defining political geography in Berlin [19]. Kjellén was strongly influenced by Ratzel, and he defined his new subject as 'the science which conceives of the state as a geographical organism or as a phenomenon in space' [22, p. 24]. From this perspective he assessed the influence of geographical factors on the state and its power, and conclusions were drawn regarding the most effective policies to ensure its security and successful development. To Kjellén, the state organism was engaged in a perpetual struggle for life and space, and only the fittest and most adaptable could be expected to survive and prosper. Territory was considered to be one of the most fundamental factors in state power; thus an understanding of the significance of territory was of vital importance to any assessment of the best interests of the state. The 'organic' nature of the state which is very apparent in the ideas of both Ratzel and Kjellén was in keeping with the Darwinism of the time, and it was also to have a strong influence on subsequent developments, particularly in geopolitics.

Political geography and geopolitics are thus very closely related to one another in both their origins and in their subject matter. At first their objectives were also virtually indistinguishable, the one approaching them broadly from the direction of geography and the other broadly from the direction of political science. However, after the First World War the two came to diverge markedly on the whole question of their relationship to the state and to power politics. While political geographers generally preferred to distance their subject from actual policy making, insisting on the essentially academic character of their research, geopoliticians were not inhibited by such considerations, and they put geopolitics firmly at the service of the state. This difference of outlook was most evident in Germany as a result of the close involvement of German *Geopolitik* first with the Nazi party and, after 1933, with the policies pursued by the Third Reich. Following Germany's defeat in the First World War, Ratzel's ideas had been taken up by a group of German geographers who proceeded to use them as the basis for a systematic plan not only for the recovery of Germany but for the country's return to great power status [24]. Their underlying contention was that while political geography was concerned with the spatial conditions of the state, geopolitics was concerned with its spatial requirements. The whole Nazi strategy for German domination in Europe was influenced by the ideas formulated by these geopoliticians [39]. The leading protagonist of this very purposeful and policy-oriented study was Karl Haushofer of Munich and, through his books and in the pages of *Zeitschrift für Geopolitik* which he edited, he and his colleagues outlined a strategy for the rise of the new Germany. Haushofer asserted that since Germany was a relatively small and densely populated country, the acquisition of *Lebensraum* was an essential prerequisite for the development of its power [12]. Germany had to take into account the realities of its geopolitical situation, and its power had to be firmly based on a strong and supportive *Mitteleuropa*. The importance to Germany of this geopolitical region in the heart of Europe had been stressed by earlier German geographers like Partsch [43], and to the geopoliticians, Haushofer [20] and Korinman [24], it was the launching pad for German world power.

These practitioners of *Geopolitik* were strongly criticized by political geographers, particularly in France and the Anglo-Saxon countries, for having allowed the subject to be used in this manner. As a result, in the aftermath of the Second World War geopolitics became thoroughly discredited, both in Germany and elsewhere, and for a generation it came to be regarded with considerable suspicion. Unfortunately, this attitude also cast a long shadow over the wider field, and the whole interface of geography and politics became a rather neglected area during the post-war years.

In France political geography had originated largely as a response to Ratzel's *Politische Geographie* [55], and much French geopolitical writing, notably *Le Sol et l'Etat* by Vallaux [54], was highly Ratzelian in its tone. However, the rise of German *Geopolitik* produced a very adverse reaction in France, and the new departure was roundly condemned as being 'pseudo-geography', the purpose of which was to provide 'so-called scientific arguments for a renewal of pan-Germanism' [1]. To Goblet [18], it was nothing more than 'political alchemy' and 'metaphysics', and he scornfully contrasted '*géographie politique*' with '*Geopolitik spagyrique*'. The French political geographers were alerted to the considerable dangers arising from a powerful Germany pursuing a policy of national aggrandisement, but they were also well aware that France possessed neither the human nor the physical resources to provide an adequate counterweight to it. This awareness underlay the direction taken by French political geography during the inter-war years. Demangeon [10] and others embarked upon a political geography based on co-operation rather than confrontation. Such co-operation entailed a coming together (*groupement*) based on the common European civilization rather than a separation based on divisive nationalism. The whole idea was deeply rooted in the French school of human geography, founded by Vidal de la Blache, which opposed the determinism of Darwinian environmental controls with human free will and opportunity. *Geopolitik*, the 'bronze laws' of which were seen to be leading inevitably towards conflict and destruction, was thus countered not by a French version of the same thing but by the totally different vision of *l'esprit vidalienne* [39].

While the central concern of the French and German political geographers was with the problems of Europe, it was in the two principal Anglo-Saxon countries that the first geopolitical world views were formulated. In the later 19th century Mahan, the American naval strategist, put forward the idea of the global dichotomy of land and sea power and laid stress on the importance of the latter for the security of the world's great maritime states [31]. This theme was soon taken up in Britain by Mackinder who went further than Mahan by proposing an interpretation of world history based on geopolitical thinking. His central contention was that the underlying theme running through world history was the conflict between land power and sea power [29]. The ultimate centre of land power, the world's greatest stronghold, lay in the heart of Asia. Mackinder first called this vast land-locked region 'the Pivot of World History', but he subsequently enlarged it to give it limited access to the sea and renamed it the 'Heartland' [30]. With its enormous economic potential and its virtual inaccessibility to sea power, this region, said Mackinder, would eventually nurture a power capable of dominating the whole world. It was up to the maritime states, led by the British Empire, to ensure that this nightmare scenario was never allowed to become a reality. Other political geographers, including Haushofer, subsequently produced various versions of the Heartland theory and adapted them to their own particular *Weltanschauungen*. During the Second World War an alternative world view was proposed by Spykman. He contended that the real centres of world power lay not in the centre but in a great belt around the periphery of Eurasia [50]. He referred to it as the 'Rimland' and maintained that because of its immense human and physical resources, it was in the interest of both the maritime and the continental states to gain possession of it. In the aftermath of the Second World War, other British and American political geographers examined the new international situation created by the allied victory, and a number of them came up with revised versions of the Heartland theory to explain it [2]. During the Cold War, Mackinder's theory itself was used to provide a geopolitical underpinning for the global ideological confrontation and the policy of containment [56].

In the late 1970s political geography and geopolitics were reassessed by a new generation of geographers. While the misdeeds of the old *Geopolitik* were plain for all to see, doubts were also expressed as to the extent to which political geography itself had always been as fully objective as political geographers had contended. In France, Lacoste asserted in *Hérodote* [26] that geography had in the past been far too much at the service of the state for such purposes as political domination and warmaking. Likewise Nicolas, using the evocative symbolism of the Second Horseman of the Apocalypse, contended that even the most renowned and venerated of political geographers had 'attempted to vindicate war through teaching the love of Mother Earth' which was most powerfully and emotionally expressed in the love of the Mother Country [33].

The new geopolitics thus arose phoenix-like from the ashes of its predecessor and, as with the phoenix, its rise was more rebirth than innovation. In any case, it was not so much the subject itself which had been the object of disquiet as the uses to which it had been put. The re-evaluation of its basic methodology resulted in a fresh perception of its possibilities for shedding new light on the contemporary world scene and illuminating its darker recesses. Not only is the new geopolitics, unlike its predecessor, largely divorced from direct involvement with state power politics but its practitioners have been highly critical of the role played by states in addressing the great issues confronting the world as the Cold War drew towards its close. These issues have included poverty, underdevelopment, environmental pollution, ecological deterioration, resource management and, of course, the persistence of war as the ultimate instrument of state policy. In France the lead in the new geopolitics was taken by the journal *Hérodote* edited by Lacoste. Subtitled *revue de géographie et de géopolitique*, a wide range of subjects from the history of geopolitical ideas to the role of the superpowers and the perennial question of Germany have been discussed in its columns. In Britain and the United States the new political geography and geopolitics had its roots in both humanistic geography [28] and radical geography [44]. Contemporary issues are dealt with in the journal *Political*

Geography, and, as in France, there has been a critical re-evaluation of the established figures of the past. There has also been a renewed interest in the role of anarchist and 'outsider' geographers such as Kropotkin and Reclus.

The new geopolitics has also made a considerable impact outside Europe and North America, and, since the 1980s, much interest has been shown in it in the two most populous countries in the world, India and China. The most significant development in India has been the establishment of the Centre for the Study of Geopolitics at the University of Chandigarh. This Centre has a particular interest in the application of geopolitical methodology to the issues confronting the Afro–Asian countries and to Southern Asia and the Indian Ocean in particular. Indian political geographers have also shown considerable interest in Antarctica, both in the context of the wider Indian Ocean sphere and as an area in which new systems of international co-operation have been pioneered. In the former Soviet Union geopolitics was understood to mean the old *Geopolitik*, and there appeared to be little understanding among Soviet geographers of the immense changes which had been taking place in the subject in the West. In the *Great Soviet Encylopaedia*, geopolitics was condemned as being 'a bourgeois reactionary concept that employs misinterpreted data of physical and economic geography to substantiate and propagandize the aggressive policies of imperialist states'. Stripped of its ideological trappings, this diatribe echoes the condemnation of German *Geopolitik* which had been made by French geographers some 50 years earlier. It reveals that the ideologically constrained Soviet geographical establishment was trapped in a kind of time warp with little awareness of developments elsewhere. However, since the demise of the Soviet Union, young Russian geographers have been taking a new interest in geopolitics and political geography. Finally, in the countries of Latin America the old *Geopolitik* flourished throughout the years of the Cold War and was often influential at the level of policy-making. General Pinochet, the President of Chile, wrote a book on the subject which was widely circulated. There are now distinct signs that the new geopolitics is making an impact, particularly in Brazil and Argentina, but the division between old and new remains firm and frequently confrontational.

Despite their profound differences, the old and the new geopolitics do share two very important characteristics. First, their basic methodology consists of the examination of states as the building blocks of the world's political space, and, second, they are both concerned with the use of geopolitical methods in the resolution of problems. The role of the geographer, said Lacoste [26, p. 2], is 'to use spatial understanding so as to be able to act more effectively'. In this respect the fundamental difference between the old and the new is that while the old geopolitics was concerned primarily with the nation state and the promotion of its interests, the attention of the new geopolitics is directed towards those issues which are of wider concern to humanity as a whole. While the old geopolitics thus focused on the segments which made up the global totality, the new geopolitics focuses on the totality itself. Its starting point, however, is with the nation states which still remain the most significant component parts of the world's geopolitical space.

The understanding of the state as a territorial phenomenon necessitates the examination of such features of its political space as frontiers, resources, population and communications, together with less tangible but still readily identifiable ethnic and cultural elements. These latter are of the greatest significance since they underwrite the very existence of the nation state and have been regularly used as justifications for the policies which it has pursued. Only by understanding the nature of individual states can geopolitical analysis go on to grapple with the complexities of their inter-relationships.

The two most clearly perceptible levels of geopolitical reality are thus seen to be the nation state and the global totality, and explanatory models and theories have been produced for both. Morphological models of the state have been constructed using such characteristics as core regions, frontiers, axes of communication, internal spatial structures and cultural attributes [16]. Such models have been the basis for theorization both on the morphology of the state and the spatial processes connected with it. The link between form and process goes back to Ratzel, but it has been developed and refined by modern political geographers who have also sought to fit the state into a wider framework of analysis [32].

At the other end of the scale from the state is the global totality. That this 'cosmos', as Bryce called it, constitutes a functioning unit has been implicit in geopolitical world views since Mackinder. In modern terminology this 'cosmos' is referred to as the 'world system' and, particularly since the end of the Cold War, the 'world order'. Two interrelated world views have been particularly influential in contemporary geopolitical thought, and both are grounded in the concept of a world divided between haves and have nots. The rough grouping of these two sets of states into hemispheres has given rise to the concept of 'North' and 'South'. Although this terminology was made familiar by the Brandt Report [3], it had already been implicit in the work of the geographer Fairgrieve [14] in the early years of the present century. This links in with the question of the geography of economic development which has as its central thesis the concept of a world centre and a world periphery. While owing much to the work of Wallerstein and Modelski, the 'world-systems approach' has been given a specifically geopolitical context by Taylor [52].

Other political geographers have seen the world system in terms of those networks of financial control which have been instrumental in the entrenchment of Western dominance over the rest of the world [47]. While such contemporary world views are in many ways very different from those of the past, they do share certain common features. First, both describe scenarios which, because of the tremendous inequalities in the distribution of wealth and resources, are unstable and potentially confrontational. Second, the model of a world centre and a world periphery has links with past binary views which have been based on value judgements regarding the international actors. There has been, implicitly if not always explicitly, a world divided into a good and a bad; a light and darkness; an inside and an outside; an 'us' (the Nation, the West) and a 'them' (the East, the South). Even though this in itself gives little cause for optimism about the nature of the post-Cold War 'order', a global framework of analysis, based on a realistic appraisal of the situation, is of particular value for placing contemporary problems in their wider context.

Between the two levels of the state and the global totality there exists another level which consists of groups or clusters of states located within particular geographical areas. Although less clear cut as geopolitical identities than the states themselves, regional clusters of this sort possess certain common features and interests arising from proximity. They may also possess certain overall geographical characteristics, both physical and human, which can constitute a basis for the creation of transnational structures. Such clusters vary considerably in the degree to which any real geopolitical identities have emerged within them, but when they do occur such identities appear to replicate many of the spatial characteristics of the nation state at a transnational level.

The European Union constitutes the most significant example of this type of development and key features such as the existence of a transnational core and periphery can now be clearly identified. The transnational 'Heavy Industrial Triangle' in north-west Europe possesses a number of the characteristics of a core region, and its existence certainly played an important part in the transformation of the ideas on co-operation which turned the European Coal and Steel Community into geographical reality [37]. The subsequent analysis of the spatial characteristics of the European Community revealed the existence of a central axis of communication stretching from the North Sea to the Mediterranean. The name 'Lotharingian axis' given to this suggests a move away from the nation state and towards larger political formations the nature and origins of which are deeply embedded in the geography and history of the continent [11]. The allied concept of the 'Golden Triangle' [58, 34] sought to link Britain with the continental core region and to demonstrate the essential unity of the south-east of England and the adjacent parts of north-west Europe. This extension of the core into Britain then formed part of the wider view of the European Community as an emerging geopolitical reality [38].

During the 1990s these and similar ideas have had to be reviewed in the light of the tremendous changes which have taken place in eastern and central Europe. The wider concept of a 'common European home', to include Russia and those republics of the former Soviet Union located to the west of the Urals, is being discussed seriously, together with its implications for the European Union and other established European organizations. The possibility of radical modifications to the Union and even of the emergence of new geopolitical groupings is no longer excluded [9]. Just before the end of the Cold War, Cohen [7] predicted the development of 'gateways' linking those regions which had been for so long locked in confrontation. Increased contacts on either side of the Iron Curtain also suggested the possibility of the emergence of an 'economic *Mitteleuropa*' in the centre of the continent [38]. With the end of the Cold War, the implications of the possible re-emergence of *Mitteleuropa* as a centre of power have given cause for considerable concern, particularly in France, and they have been discussed in *Hérodote* and other journals. The term *l'Europe médiane* was coined in preference to *l'Europe centrale* (*Mitteleuropa*) to denote the emergence of a region which, while it possessed a distinct geographical identity, did not itself constitute a new centre of power [27, 25].

Finally, there is the existence of sub-state features, in particular minority languages and local cultures. When they have been strong enough these have constituted the basis for the creation of geopolitical identities within states, and collectively they may constitute a distinct geopolitical level below that of the state itself [23]. The issues raised by the existence of such minority groups has become a major concern of political geographers [57]. Fouéré [15] went so far as to assert that the *'Europe des états'* would eventually be forced to give place to the *'Europe des nations'*. Distinct signs of a move from states to nations have been present in Europe and elsewhere during the 1990s, and many sub-state groups have themselves successfully aspired to statehood. This development has important implications for the relationship of the principal geopolitical levels as well as for the future of the world political map as a whole.

This leads on to the relationship between the state as a spatial entity and its behaviour in the international arena. One aspect of this is the state's perception of its own optimum territory and the linked concept of natural frontiers. While the idea of there actually being 'natural' frontiers in some objectively definable sense has long been dismissed by political geographers, the state's perception of its own 'natural' frontiers is an entirely different matter [46]. A state's whole pattern of behaviour and reactions to international events are strongly influenced by such perceptions. There is also a relationship between particular types of state behaviour and the presence of particular spatial characteristics. The central importance of the relationship between the state and the territory which it occupies has, of course, been the basic proposition of political geography and geopolitics since Ratzel. However, it is possible to be far more precise about the interrelationships of *Raum* and *Lage* when these are seen as part of a wider spatial continuum. For example, it can be demonstrated that very aggressive states, identified as being those which have displayed a singular propensity towards territorial expansion, possess certain clearly identifiable geopolitical characteristics. These include the peripheral location of the original core region; an early propensity towards territorial expansion outside the area of the parent culture; the creation of an external core within the conquered territory; expansion back into the territory of the parent culture culminating in an assault on its macrocore region and, finally, a bid to achieve domination over the whole of the territory of the parent culture up to its 'natural' frontiers as proclaimed by the expansionist state itself [41].

It can also be shown that spatial characteristics may be used in the explanation of the patterns of behaviour prevalent in particular geographical regions. The examination of those regions which have been characterized by persistent conflict and instability is likely to reveal a particular set of transnational geopolitical characteristics [6, 8], while those which have displayed a greater propensity for co-operative behaviour, although they may possess some of the same characteristics, are likely also to possess a number of different ones [42]. The link between patterns of behaviour and spatial structure now constitutes an important area of contemporary geopolitical interest.

Since Ge was the Greek Goddess of the Earth, 'geo' in geopolitics can refer both to the study of the influence of geographical factors on political action and to the study of the Earth as a political whole. Ratzel and Kjellén emphasized the former but today it is the latter which is central to contemporary concerns. Since the 1970s geopolitics has been pervaded by a sense of global wholeness, and this relates to a striving towards the attainment of nonconflictual solutions to the problems facing mankind. As O'Loughlin and Heske [36] put it, this represents the conversion of geopolitics from a subject of war into a subject of peace. Glassner [16] has also stressed the important place of the 'geography of peace' in contemporary geopolitical concerns.

The aspiration towards global wholeness has inevitably linked contemporary geopolitical thinking to wider environmental questions. Brunn and Mingst observed that geopolitical writers were widening their interests 'beyond the unidimensional theme of geopolitics towards the multidimensional theme of environmental theories or an ecological perspective' [4, p. 63]. The whole question of the management of the planet was examined by the Sprouts and they encouraged the concept of the total environment as an interacting system within which political action was both possible and necessary [49]. The most important link between geopolitics and environmental concerns in the later stages of the Cold War lay in the implications of the possible use of nuclear weapons for the global environment [45]. Particularly disturbing were the predictions of the catastrophic effects on world climate and the virtually irreversible 'nuclear winter' which could result from a nuclear exchange [13]. Wider questions including population pressures, the planetary capacity for food production, energy supplies and finite natural resources were addressed in *A World in Crisis?* [21]. The relationships of the separate branches of geography were examined, and the necessity for their closer convergence was stressed. In this connection Taylor [52] employed the world-systems analysis of Wallerstein in advocating the development of an all-embracing 'historical social science'. In the context of political action the study of Antarctica from a geopolitical perspective is very significant both because of the continent's importance in the global climatic system and as one of the few places where international co-operation has become a reality [16].

In *The March of Folly* [53], Tuchman dwelt on the past pursuit of illusory grandeur and the attempts to hold on to power which have been so much a part of it. She called this 'Humpty Dumpty Folly', since it is as futile an endeavour as the attempt to reconstruct a broken egg. It is a fundamental contention of geographers that the understanding of geographical reality is the greatest deterrent to such folly. In *Democratic Ideals and Reality* [30], Mackinder asserted the importance of an understanding of geography as a prerequisite to putting ideals into practice. Without such understanding, he maintained, all ideals, however worthy they may seem, are doomed to irrelevance and failure. It is this emphasis on the nature of terrestrial reality which is the particular hallmark of political geography and geopolitics. It constitutes the foundation of their unique contribution to the understanding of the international scene.

Nearly a century after Lord Bryce's Romanes lecture the reluctant recognition that the home of mankind is in physical terms one and indivisible has been accompanied by the search for ways of also making it a geopolitical unity.

Bibliography

1. Ancel, J. *Géopolitique*. Paris, Delagrave, 1936.
2. Blij, H.J. de *Systematic Political Geography*, second edition, New York, John Wiley, 1973.
3. Brandt, W. (Chairman) *North–South: A Programme for Survival*. Report of Independent Commission on International Development Issues. London, Pan and Cambridge, MA, MIT Press, 1980.
4. Brunn, S.D. and Mingst, K.A. 'Geopolitics' in M. Pacione (ed.) *Progress in Political Geography*. London, Croom Helm, 1985, pp. 41–76.
5. Bryce, J. *The Relations of the Advanced and the Backward Races of Mankind*. Romanes Lecture, Clarendon, Oxford, 1902.
6. Cohen, S.B. *Geography and Politics in a World Divided*, second edition, New York, Oxford University Press, 1973.
7. Cohen, S.B. 'The Emerging World Map of Peace' in N. Kliot and S. Waterman (eds) *The Political Geography of Conflict and Peace*. London, Belhaven Press, 1991, pp. 18–36.
8. Cohen S.B. *Geopolitics and the Shaping of a New Middle Eastern Region*. Ellen Churchill Semple Lecture, Worcester, Clark University, 1991.
9. Dawson, A.H. *A Geography of European Integration*. London and New York, Belhaven Press, 1993.
10. Demangeon, A. *Le Déclin de l'Europe*. Paris, Payot, 1920.
11. Despicht, N.S. *The Common Transport Policy of the European Communities*. London, PEP, 1969.
12. Dickinson, R.E. *The German Lebensraum*. Harmondsworth, Penguin Books, 1943.
13. Elsom, D. 'Climatological Effects of a Nuclear Exchange: a Review' in D. Pepper and A. Jenkins (eds) *The Geography of Peace and War*. Oxford and New York, Blackwell, 1985, pp. 126–47.
14. Fairgrieve, J. *Geography and World Power*. London, University of London Press, 1932.
15. Fouéré, Y. *Towards a Federal Europe: Nations or States?* Swansea, Christopher Davies, 1980.
16. Glassner, M.I. *Political Geography*. New York, John Wiley, 1993.
17. Glassner. M.I. and Blij H.J. de *Systematic Political Geography*, fourth edition, New York, John Wiley, 1989.
18. Goblet, Y.M. *The Twilight of Treaties*. London, Bell, 1936.
19. Haggman, B. *Rudolf Kjellén: Founder of Geopolitics*. Helsingborg, Center for Research on Geopolitics, 1988.
20. Haushofer, K. *Jenseits der Grossmächte*. Leipzig, Teubner, 1932.
21. Johnson, R.J. and Taylor P.J. (eds) *A World in Crisis?: Geographical Perspectives*, second edition, Oxford, Blackwell, 1989.
22. Kjellén, R. *Der Staat als Lebensform*. Leipzig, Hirzel, 1917.

23. Kohr, L. *The Breakdown of Nations*. London, Routledge & Kegan Paul, 1957 and 1986.
24. Korinman, M. *Quand l'Allemagne pensait le monde. Grandeur et décadence d'une géopolitique*. Paris, Fayard, 1990.
25. Korinman, M. 'Naissance et renaissance d'un projet géopolitique'. *Hérodote*, 56, 1990.
26. Lacoste, Y. Editorial. *Hérodote*, 1, 1976.
27. Lacoste, Y. 'Editorial: Europe médiane?' *Hérodote*, 56, 1990.
28. Ley, D. and Samuels M.S. (eds) *Humanistic Geography*. London, Croom Helm and Chicago, Maaroufa Press, 1978.
29. Mackinder, H.J. 'The Geographical Pivot of History'. *Geographical Journal*, vol. 23, no. 4, 1904, pp. 421–44.
30. Mackinder, H.J. *Democratic Ideals and Reality: A Study in the Politics of Reconstruction*. London, Constable, 1919.
31. Mahan, A.T. *The Influence of Sea Power on History, 1660–1783*. London, Samson Low, 1889.
32. Muir, R. *Modern Political Geography*, second edition, London, Macmillan, 1981.
33. Nicolas G. and Guanzini C. 'Ancient History for the Future: the Political Role of Geography'. Video English Version G. and E.B. Parker. University of Lausanne, Eratosthéne, 1993.
34. Odell, P. 'London and the Golden Triangle'. *New Society*, vol. 15, no. 398, 1970, pp. 821–23.
35. O'Loughlin, J. (ed.) *Dictionary of Geopolitics*. Westport, Greenwood Press, 1994.
36. O'Loughlin, J. and Heske H. 'From "Geopolitik" to "Geopolitique": Converting a Discipline for War to a Discipline for Peace' in N. Kliot and S. Waterman (eds) *The Political Geography of Conflict and Peace*. London, Pinter, 1991, pp. 37–59.
37. Parker, G. *The Logic of Unity: A Geography of the European Economic Community*, third edition, London, Longman, 1981.
38. Parker, G. *A Political Geography of Community Europe*. London, Butterworths, 1983.
39. Parker, G. *Western Geopolitical Thought in the Twentieth Century*. London, Croom Helm, 1985.
40. Parker, G. 'Geopolitics' in V. Bogdanor (ed.) *The Blackwell Encyclopaedia of Political Institutions*. Oxford, Blackwell, 1987, pp. 254–5.
41. Parker, G. *The Geopolitics of Domination: Territorial Supremacy in Europe and the Mediterranean from the Ottoman Empire to the Soviet Union*. London and New York, Routledge, 1988.
42. Parker, G. 'The Geopolitics of Dominance and International Cooperation' in N. Kliot and S. Waterman (eds) *The Political Geography of Conflict and Peace*. London, Belhaven Press, 1991, pp. 60–6.
43. Partsch, J. *Central Europe*. London, Heinemann, 1903.
44. Peet, R. (ed.) *Radical Geography: Alternative Viewpoints on Contemporary Social Issues*. London, Methuen and Chicago, Maaroufa Press, 1977.
45. Pepper, D. and Jenkins, A. (eds) *The Geography of Peace and War*. Oxford and New York, Blackwell, 1985.
46. Prescott, J.R.V. and Jenkins, A. *The Geography of Frontiers and Boundaries*. London, Hutchinson University Library, 1965.
47. Raffestin, C. *Pour une géographie du pouvoir*. Paris, Librairie Technique, 1980.
48. Ratzel, F. *Politische Geographie*. Munich, Oldenburg, 1897.

49. Sprout, H.H. and Sprout, M. *Toward a Politics of the Planet Earth*. New York, Van Nostrand Reinhold, 1971.
50. Spykman, N.J. *The Geography of Peace*. New York, Harcourt Brace, 1944.
51. Taylor, P.J. 'The World-Systems Project' in R.J. Johnson and P.J. Taylor (eds) *A World in Crisis?* Oxford and New York, Blackwell, 1985, pp. 269–91.
52. Taylor, P.J. *Political Geography: World-Economy, Nation-State and Locality*, second edition, London, Longman and New York, John Wiley, 1989.
53. Tuchman, B. *The March of Folly: From Troy to Vietnam*. London, Michael Joseph, 1984 and New York, Ballantine Books, 1985.
54. Vallaux, C. *Le Sol et l'Etat*. Paris, Doin, 1911.
55. Vidal de la Blache, P. 'La Géographie politique à propos des écrits de Mr Frédéric Ratzel'. *Annales de Géographie* VII, 1898, pp. 79–111.
56. Walters, R.E. *The Nuclear Trap*. Harmondsworth and Baltimore, Penguin Books, 1974.
57. Williams, C.H. 'Minority Groups in the Modern State' in M. Pacione (ed.) *Progress in Political Geography*. London, Croom Helm, 1985, pp. 111–51.
58. Wise, M.J. 'The Common Market and the Changing Geography of Europe'. *Geography*, vol. XLVIII, no. 219, 1963, pp. 129–38.

13 Nationalism in the study of international relations*

James Mayall

It is often said that the academic discipline of international relations (IR) is misnamed, since what is studied is not the relations of nations but of states. This view helps to explain why, in the vast literature on nationalism, so few books are written by students of IR, and conversely why, in the IR literature, nationalism receives only scant attention. However, this explanation ignores the fact that the academic study of the subject, which was later taken over by historians and sociologists, began with the Chatham House Study Group, chaired by E.H. Carr, on the international problems posed by nationalism during the inter-war period [14]. Second, and more importantly, it ignores the extent to which the modern international system rests on the principle of popular sovereignty. In practice it is impossible to define this principle without describing the people, i.e. the nation, which allegedly possess it.

There is a deeper reason why nationalism is problematic for the student of IR. The focus of the subject is on consequences not causes; on the results of wars and the making of peace; on the impact of one country's policies on other countries; on the role of perception in foreign policy; and on the attempt to reconcile the world of contingent events with a legal order. Relations can only be studied if we assume that the identity of the parties, whether individual statesmen, governments or national communities, are held constant, or at least as nearly so as possible. In these post-modern days, we all know that identities, even our own, cannot be taken for granted. And since, at some level, national identities are often the product of international events, it may be plausibly argued that their origins and creation are too central to our concerns to be left safely to the historians and social theorists. On this view, to separate cause and consequence is mere sophistry.

It is a powerful argument. Certainly no student of the subject should ignore altogether recent debates about the causes of nationalism, since inevitably these influence the analysis of its impact on international politics.

---

* The author would like to express his gratitude to Rick Fawn, whose ideas and leg work contributed greatly to this chapter.

Seton-Watson's historical survey remains an essential reference work [100]. The best general overview of theories of nationalism and of the problems of definition is by Smith [102]. The two most influential versions of the argument that nationalism is a byproduct of modernization, by Kedourie [60, 61] and Gellner [33, 34], are best studied at source, as is the more recent theoretical tendency, best exemplified in the work of Anderson [2] and Hobsbawm [49, 50].

Apart from their intrinsic interest, these accounts are important because they offer alternative perspectives on contemporary international problems. Kedourie regarded nationalism as a baleful product of the European romantic movement and, as such, responsible for many of the worst excesses of the 20th century and the current disorder in the international system. By contrast Gellner sees it as a necessary, albeit often disagreeable, accompaniment of the transition from agrarian to industrial society. While he entertains the possibility of a satisfied world order in which affluence will gradually soften nationalist sentiment, there is, meanwhile, no escape from the struggle of cultures to obtain their own states. But if, *pace* Anderson and Hobsbawm, the nation is ultimately a work of fiction, then in principle it could be transcended or at least reinvented with different characteristics from those with which we are currently familiar.

Once it is conceded that the nation is not natural, that there was a time when political communities were organized on different principles, the question of origins becomes of compelling interest. We are led to ask what had to happen, either in terms of moral or material development, before the idea of popular sovereignty and independence, the twin supports of nationalist doctrine, could take hold of the modern mind. The answers provided by the historians of ideas and historical sociologists are suggestive, but they cannot resolve the question. There is something to be said, therefore, if only to reduce the subject to manageable proportions, for maintaining the traditional division of labour, that is to leave to the historians and sociologists the question of causes and to concern ourselves primarily with the consequences of nationalism and its role in contemporary international politics. This is the strategy adopted in the remainder of this chapter.

Nationalism and the international system

The age of nationalism is usually dated from the American and French revolutions at the end of the 18th century. By this time the European states-system that had emerged from the wars of religion had lasted for 140 years. It was a system of sovereign princes whose rivalries were kept in check, legally, by the principle of *cuius regio eius religio* (whosoever's territory, his religion), and politically, by the balance of power. The system was weakened but not destroyed by the revolutions and was restored after the defeat of Napoleon in 1815. It was not until 1918 that the nationalists inherited the states-system, which for the first time became truly international. The first questions to ask are how nationalism has influenced the evolution of the international system in the 20th century, and, conversely, how nationalist doctrine and practice were influenced by the system of inter-state relations established under the *ancien régime*.

Answers to these questions emerged only slowly. This was partly because of an idealist fallacy that held that national self-determination (see below) would lead to a genuine internationalism. The thought that nationalism was as likely to lead to chauvinism or xenophobia as to a universalist commitment to liberty was seldom entertained by liberals. As Isaiah Berlin has pointed out [6, 7], optimism frequently shielded them from the recognition of harsher realities. Even realists, like Carr [15], regarded the nation as a way-station *en route* to some new, unspecified form of political organization, better suited to the scale and dynamism of the industrial world economy. Meanwhile, most realists concentrated on structures of power rather than on powerful identities or the aspirations of those who aspired to power: in other words they either ignored nationalism or took it for granted. The truth was that both liberals and realists were heirs to the European Enlightenment, equally committed to the concept of universal rationality. In Dunn's graphic phrase, there is no escape: nationalism is the shame of the 20th century [26].

The first sustained attempt to consider the impact of nationalism on the international system was by Hinsley [48]. He placed two extended essays side by side, one on the international system which covered some of the same ground as his earlier full length study, *Power and the Pursuit of Peace* [47], and the other on the rise and political impact of nationalism. In an essay published in *The Community of States* [87], Porter argued that the rise of nationalism had severely undermined the sense of community which had helped to civilize inter-state relations prior to the First World War. Mayall [69] concluded that while nationalism was the dominant political ideology of the 20th century without whose support neither liberalism nor Marxism have been able to flourish, success was purchased at the price of major concessions to the existing states-system.

Sovereignty and national self-determination

The reason for these concessions was simply that nationalists aspired to power and once in control of the state were as reluctant to see their sovereignty diluted as their dynastic predecessors. The right of national self-determination was claimed in order to establish an independent state, not to surrender power to an international authority. Sovereignty is a claim not a fact. In practice, as James argues [57], sovereign statehood is invariably qualified by the realities of power politics and economic interdependence, but it remains the central organizing principle of international society.

The main difference between the worlds of dynastic and popular sovereignty is that the latter replaces *cuius regio eius religio* with its secular equivalent, non-interference in the internal affairs of other states. The process by which this transformation was accomplished has been analysed by several authors. The best is Cobban's inter-war study of national self-determination, which was revised in the 1960s to take account of European decolonization

[19, 20]. Emerson's study [28] of this latter subject is also still worth reading. The historical genesis of the idea of self-determination and its contemporary ramifications is a recurrent theme in the collection of essays edited by Best [8] to coincide with the bicentenary of the French Revolution.

The right of national self-determination was originally asserted to encourage the development of democratic institutions. The reasons for holding that democracy required a national state were spelt out by John Stuart Mill in Chapter XVI of *Representative Government* [77]. The contemporary relevance of his central argument – that democracy is likely to be subverted by the stronger group in a multinational society – has become all too clear since the end of the Cold War (see below) and has recently been powerfully restated by the Georgian scholar, Nodia [83]. However, while Mill has had his intellectual heirs among modern students of nationalism such as Ronen [95] and Beran [4, 5], for most of the present century the undoubted political success of the principle – in 1945 it was entrenched as an inalienable human right in the Charter of the United Nations – has been accompanied by academic scepticism. Professional indifference was hardly surprising: few UN member-states were either democracies or nations.

Furthermore, the problem of entrenching national self-determination as the legal basis of international society is that many existing states are not merely socially heterogeneous but also deeply divided internally along ethnic or religious lines. There is thus a potential conflict between the requirements of justice, represented by the right to self-determination, and of order, represented by the priority given to state sovereignty in the UN Charter. This conflict was resolved in practice by equating self-determination with European decolonization. Since few successor states to the European empires had governments whose legitimacy was not open to serious internal challenge, they were heavily dependent on international society – and the United Nations in particular – to underwrite their sovereignty by supporting their nation-building efforts with financial aid and technical assistance.

For the first time in modern history the survival of states, at least as legal entities, depended on the possession of juridical rather than empirical sovereignty. Jackson's writings, first in a series of articles written in collaboration with Rosberg [55] and subsequently on his own account [56] explore this major, and paradoxical, extension of the role and functions of international society.

Economic nationalism

Another extension of traditional international society after 1945 was the creation of an institutional structure – the IMF, IBRD, and GATT – to manage the liberal world economy. This innovation was a direct consequence of the widespread belief that competitive economic nationalism during the 1930s had not only prolonged the Great Depression but, by poisoning the political atmosphere, had also contributed to the drift to war [69, 70, 71].

Economic nationalism has been largely ignored in the literatures of nationalism and political economy. In the former case this is probably because most students of nationalism are more interested in the phenomenon itself than in nationalist policies, many of which were taken over from the pre-nationalist mercantilist era. In the latter case the intellectual hegemony of neo-classicism left little scope for the serious study of nationalism, although two of the most prominent modern economists – Keynes [62] and Viner [112] – gave the subject serious attention. Keynes's purpose was to devise realistic policies for combating mass unemployment, while Viner, writing in the first number of *World Politics*, was concerned more generally to combat the liberal tendency to de-politicize economics.

Except in the area of development studies, liberal economists tended to dismiss economic nationalism as a form of irrationalism. Heilperin [43] is typical of the genre. Perhaps the chief value of this interesting book, sadly now long out of print, is the extensive extracts it provides of Fichte's *Closed Commercial State* [29]. Significantly, Fichte's book, one of the classics of nationalist literature, has never been translated into English. In a world dominated by liberal thinking it is not difficult to understand why: it sets out a blueprint for a totally self-sufficient state, once it has expanded by military means to its natural frontiers.

The one area in which mainstream liberal economic thought gave ground to economic nationalism was in relation to development. The concept of 'infant-industry' protection had been developed by List [67] and others from an explicitly national perspective. They rightly perceived the contemporary international system to be composed of nation-states intent on improving their competitive position within an increasingly global market. But the idea was absorbed by liberal thinkers who ignored, or took for granted, the national objective behind such policies and concentrated on the technical problem of how industrial late-comers could develop a comparative advantage. Their answer was that they were to be allowed to defer their commitment to free trade until their industries were sufficiently mature to compete on level terms with those of the stronger nations.

The idea that the weak needed a special regime to enable them to 'catch-up' with the strong was generalized after the Second World War. In effect a two-tier international society was set up, at least so far as its economic arrangements were concerned. Among the non-communist industrial states, at least in theory, policy was meant to be governed by commercial rather than national criteria, whereas economic nationalism was regarded as both natural and desirable for developing countries. With two notable exceptions [13, 98], these themes have still not been treated adequately in the literature on nationalism, although they have been discussed extensively by development economists.

Secession and irredentism

Between 1945 and 1989 the accommodation of nationalism within the international system survived most of the tests with which it was confronted: indeed, only the forced secession of Bangladesh in 1971 and the peaceful secession of Singapore from the recently formed Malaysian Federation in 1963 broke the pattern. The truth was that the self-interest of all existing states – and most particularly the new ones – in the territorial status quo was powerfully reinforced by the Cold War stalemate. This successfully secured the political map of Europe against revisions on both sides of the ideological divide, although territorial stability did not imply universal consent to the conventional interpretation of national self-determination.

The Cold War calm was broken by periodic civil wars in Asia and Africa and many more low-level secessionist or irredentist insurgencies. Such conflicts raised legal questions about the meaning of self-determination; empirical questions about the circumstances under which secessionist and irredentist movements were most likely to arise; and normative questions about the desirability of creating a legitimate right of secession and the criteria for recognition.

Attempts to answer these questions fall into two categories, although there is considerable overlap between the two: works which address secession and irredentism at the level of general theory and those which are concerned with particular conflicts. In the former category, Buchheit's study of secession [12] is the fullest legal treatment of the subject, while Horowitz [52] provides a comprehensive assessment of the empirical circumstances underlying territorial challenges to the state-system. Also worth consulting are Heraclides [44, 45], Chazan [16], the special issue of *The International Journal of Comparative Sociology* devoted to nationalism [54] and two as yet unpublished doctoral dissertations by Baktus [3] and Von Hippel [113].

The break-up of the Soviet Union finally attracted the interest of moral philosophers to the issue of secession. Buchanan's study [11] attempts to advance a theory of the conditions in which secession is morally desirable by reference to the US Civil War, Bangladesh, Katanga, Biafra, the Baltic Republics, South Africa and Quebec. Whether it will be able to overcome some formidable theoretical as well as practical objections [74] remains to be seen.

It is impossible in the space of a short chapter to do justice to the second category, that is works on particular nationalist or separatist conflicts. However, while ethnic or religious conflict is a feature of many societies, in only relatively few of them have these conflicts assumed a deep structural character with an impact on international relations as well as on domestic politics (see [9] for a comprehensive handbook on current border disputes between states).

There have been several attempts to demonstrate that secessionism is a function of poverty or uneven development (see, in particular, [80, 42, 107]), but in fact these 'indigestible' minorities crop up in all parts of the world, under very different political, economic and ideological circumstances. There is no simple economic correlation and therefore no sensible alternative to engaging with the extensive empirical literature that has grown up around each of these disputes.

In Africa, irredentism and secession are deeply rooted in Morocco, [58, 75, 91, 114, 116] and the Horn of Africa [17, 18, 39, 64, 65, 66, 68, 75, 109]; in south Asia in Kashmir, the Punjab and Sri Lanka [23, 30, 37, 38, 41, 59,

99]; in the Middle East among the Kurds and Palestinians [27, 63, 81, 88]; in North America in Quebec [22, 51, 92]. In Western Europe there are some residual irredentist conflicts, in Ireland over Ulster [84, 85, 86]; and in Spain over Gibraltar [113], although secessionism has not been a major problem since 1945. On the other hand, the idea of a post-nationalist, or at any rate a post-ethnic politics, has not taken root. Indeed, throughout the 1980s there was an ethnic revival in the West [1, 106, 110]. How far this process will go, and what kind of limits it will set, for example on European integration, remain to be seen.

Until the late 1980s it was widely assumed that, however undesirable in other respects, the spread of Soviet power after 1945 had finally stabilized political boundaries in the volatile regions of Eastern Europe and the former Tsarist empire. With the breakup of Yugoslavia and the Soviet Union itself, the peaceful separation of the Czech and Slovak republics, and the reawakening of minority anxieties throughout the region, it has become increasingly clear that the assumption of long-run political stability was mistaken.

The resurgence of nationalism after the Cold War

In the beginning was the deed, not the word. If it is true that reflection and rationalization arise as a result of a desire to impose order on experience, it is not surprising that the violent and largely unexpected resurgence of militant nationalism after the Cold War has not yet given rise to any major theoretical reappraisal. Moynihan's *Pandemonium* [79] is one of the few attempts to draw general conclusions from recent developments by one of the few who did foresee the collapse of communism. As he rightly points out, it is difficult to exaggerate the importance of this development for the future of international relations. At one stroke it swept away the Cold War itself, the confidence that the conventional interpretation of national self-determination had settled the problem of state creation once and for all and the belief that it was possible to manage a successful industrial economy by means of central planning.

The collapse of communism was bound to lead to a resurgence of nationalism for two reasons. First, although liberal capitalism was left alone on the field of battle after the Cold War, it was not immediately in a position to fill the ideological vacuum in post-communist states. Second, the Soviet Union and the Yugoslav Federation had both been organized along national lines. When they disintegrated, it was into their constituent parts.

The nationality policies of the two states during the communist era are authoritatively discussed by Connor [21], Ramet [89, 90], and Schöpflin [96, 97]. The subsequent eruption of nationalist demands and the bloody conflicts and civil wars to which they gave rise have already been the subject of a number of excellent eye-witness accounts. The study of these conflicts and their potential international implications is also fast becoming a growth industry among academics. Glenny's work on the former Yugoslavia [35] stands out as a fine example of direct observation combined with deep historical knowledge and balanced analysis. The volume edited by Bremmer and Taras [10] is a good introduction to recent scholarly work on the Soviet successor states.

The shocks caused to the international system by the new nationalism are only just beginning to be understood and analysed. The end of the Cold War allowed the superpowers to cooperate in 'closing down' a number of regional conflicts, for example, in southern Africa, Ethiopia and Central America. In 1991 there was an even more dramatic demonstration of the new consensus when the Iraqi invasion of Kuwait was repelled under UN auspices during Operation Desert Storm. In its wake there were repeated demands for humanitarian intervention, the international protection of minority rights and peace enforcement. The optimism was short-lived, partly because the UN system was ill-equipped to deal with the problems posed by ethnic conflict. Simultaneously, the major powers were becoming more conscious of the potential threat to themselves posed by large-scale refugee and population movements and consequently more restrictive in their immigration policies. The debate on these questions is best followed in the journals (see, for example, [36, 46, 72, 73, 93, 94]).

A final question concerns the future of nationalism in an increasingly global international environment. Once again, the end of the Cold War shattered many of the assumptions on which the debate had previously been conducted. The previous focus had been on the European Community, and in particular on the question of creating a European political identity to replace the national identities of the member states. The flavour of the debate – and not all authors were in favour of this development or believed it to be feasible – can be gathered from Deutsch [25], Galtung [31], Smith [103, 104, 105], Tomlinson [111] and the special number of *Millennium* [78], on 're-imagining the nation'. The proliferation of ethno–nationalist conflicts since 1989 has not only reopened the question of the strategic rationale for European integration but has refocused the debate on other issues, for example, democratization [24, 83]; the links between religion and nationalism [32, 89]; and the possibility of globalization being accompanied by increased ethnic and national fragmentation rather than integration. Huntington [53] has gone so far as to argue that the ideological divide will be replaced by a clash of civilizations in which nationalism will be subsumed. It is too early to pronounce confidently on the new agenda.

Bibliography

1. Allardt, E. *Implications of the Ethnic Revival in Modern, Industrialised Societies: A Comparative Study of the Linguistic Minorities in Western Europe.* Helsinki, Commentationes Scientiarum Socialium, 1979.
2. Anderson, B. *Imagined Communities: Reflections on the Origin and Spread of Nationalism,* second edition. London, Verso Press and New York, Routledge, 1992.
3. Baktus, V. *Secession: An Analytical Framework Concerning the Decision to Secede.* Unpublished D.Phil. thesis, Oxford University, 1992.

4. Beran, H. *The Consent Theory of Political Obligation*. London and New York, Croom Helm, 1987.
5. Beran, H. 'A Liberal Theory of Secession'. *Political Studies*, vol. XXXII, no. 1, 1984, pp. 21–31.
6. Berlin, I. 'Nationalism, Past Neglect and Present Power' in H. Hardy (ed.) *Against the Current: Essays in the History of Ideas*. London, Hogarth Press, 1979, pp. 333–55.
7. Berlin, I. 'The Bent Twig: On the Rise of Nationalism' in *The Crooked Timber of Humanity: Chapters in the History of Ideas*. London, John Murray, 1990, pp. 238–61.
8. Best, G. (ed.) *The Permanent Revolution: The French Revolution and its Legacy, 1789–1989*. London, Fontana, 1988.
9. *Border and Territorial Disputes*, third edition. Harlow, Longman Current Affairs, 1992.
10. Bremmer, I. and Taras R. (eds) *Nations and Politics in the Soviet Successor States*. Cambridge, Cambridge University Press, 1993.
11. Buchanan, A. *Secession: The Morality of Political Divorce from Fort Sumter to Lithuania and Quebec*. Boulder, San Francisco and London, Westview Press, 1991.
12. Buchheit, L.C. *Secession: The Legitimacy of Self-Determination*. New Haven, Yale University Press, 1978.
13. Burnell, P. *Economic Nationalism in the Third World*. Brighton, Wheatsheaf and Boulder, Westview Press, 1986.
14. Carr, E.H. (ed.) *Nationalism, A Report by a Study Group of Members of the Royal Institute of International Affairs*. London, Oxford University Press for the RIIA, 1939.
15. Carr, E.H. *Nationalism and After*. London, Macmillan, 1945, reprinted 1968.
16. Chazan, N. (ed.) *Irredentism and International Politics*. London, Adamantine Press and Boulder, Lynne Rienner, 1992.
17. Clapham, C. *Transformation and Continuity in Revolutionary Ethiopia*. Cambridge, Cambridge University Press, 1988.
18. Cliffe, L. 'Forging a Nation: The Eritrean Experience'. *Third World Quarterly*, vol. 11, no. 4, 1989, pp. 131–47.
19. Cobban, A. *National Self-Determination*. London, Oxford University Press for the RIIA, 1945.
20. Cobban, A. *The Nation State and National Self-Determination*. London, Collins and New York, Crowell, 1944.
21. Connor, W. *The National Question in Marxist-Leninist Theory and Strategy*. Princeton, Princeton University Press, 1984.
22. Cook, R. *Canada, Quebec and the Uses of Nationalism*. Toronto, McClelland and Stewart, 1986.
23. de Silva, K.M. *A History of Sri Lanka*. London, C. Hurst & Co and Berkeley, University of California Press, 1981.
24. de Nevers, R. 'Democratisation and Ethnic Conflict'. *Survival*, vol. 35, no. 2, Summer, 1993, pp. 31–48.
25. Deutsch, K.W. *Nationalism and its Alternatives*. New York, Knopf, 1969.
26. Dunn, J. *Western Political Theory in the Face of the Future*. Cambridge, Cambridge University Press, 1979.
27. Edmonds, C.J. 'Kurdish Nationalism'. *Journal of Contemporary History*, vol. 6, no. 1, 1971, pp. 87–107.
28. Emerson, R. *From Empire to Nation: The Rise to Self-Assertion of Asian and African Peoples*. Cambridge, MA, Harvard University Press, 1962.

29. Fichte, J.G. *The Closed Commercial State (Der Geschlossen Handelsstaat)*, Tubigen 1800, republished by the Gustav Fischer Verlag in Jena, 1920.
30. Fox, R.G. *Lions of the Punjab: The Sikhs and British India's Culture in the Making*. Berkeley, Los Angeles and London, University of California Press, 1985.
31. Galtung, J. *The European Community: A Superpower in the Making*. London, George Allen & Unwin and Oslo, Universitetforlaget, 1973.
32. Ganguly, S. 'Ethno-Religious Conflict in South Asia'. *Survival*, vol. 35, no. 2, Summer, 1993, pp. 88–109.
33. Gellner, E. *Thought and Change*. London, Weidenfeld & Nicolson, 1964 and Chicago, University of Chicago Press, 1965.
34. Gellner, E. *Nations and Nationalism*. Oxford, Blackwell and Ithaca, Cornell University Press, 1983.
35. Glenny, M. *The Fall of Yugoslavia: The Third Balkan War*. London, Penguin, 1992.
36. Goulding, M. 'The Evolution of United Nations Peacekeeping'. *International Affairs*, vol. 69, no. 3, July, 1993, pp. 451–64.
37. Gupta A. 'Paradise Lost: The Fall of Sri Lanka' in J. Mayall and A. Payne (eds) *The Fallacies of Hope: The Post Colonial Record of the Commonwealth Third World*. Manchester, Manchester University Press, 1991, pp. 44–56.
38. Gupta S. *Kashmir: A Study in India–Pakistan Relations*. Bombay and London, Asia Publishing House, 1967.
39. Halliday, F. and Molyneux, M. *The Ethiopian Revolution*. London, Verso and New Left Books, 1981.
40. Halpern, B. *The Idea of a Jewish State*. Cambridge, MA, Harvard University Press, 1961.
41. Harrison, S. *India: The Most Dangerous Decades*. Princeton, Princeton University Press, 1960.
42. Hechter, M. *Internal Colonialism: The Celtic Fringe in British National Development, 1536–1966*. London, Routledge and Kegan Paul, 1975.
43. Heilperin, M.A. *Studies in Economic Nationalism*. Geneva, Librarie E. Droz and Paris, Librarie Minard, 1960.
44. Heraclides, A. *The Self-Determination of Minorities in International Politics*. London, F. Cass, 1991.
45. Heraclides, A. 'Secessionist Minorities and External Involvement'. *International Organisation*, vol. 44, no. 3, 1990, pp. 341–78.
46. Higgins, R. 'The New United Nations and former Yugoslavia'. *International Affairs*, vol. 69, no. 3, July, 1993, pp. 465–83.
47. Hinsley. F.H. *Power and the Pursuit of Peace: Theory and Practice in the History of Relations Between States*. London, Cambridge University Press, 1963.
48. Hinsley, F.H. *Nationalism and the International System*. London, Hodder & Stoughton and Dobbs Ferry, Oceana Publications, 1973.
49. Hobsbawm, E. *Nations and Nationalism Since 1780: Programme, Myth, Reality*. Cambridge, Cambridge University Press, 1990.
50. Hobsbawm, E. and Ranger, T. (eds) *The Invention of Tradition*. Cambridge, Cambridge University Press, 1983.
51. Holloway, S.K. 'Canada Without Quebec'. *Orbis*, vol. 36, no. 4, 1992, pp. 531–43.
52. Horowitz, D. *Ethnic Groups in Conflict*. Berkeley, University of California Press, 1985.
53. Huntington, S. 'The Clash of Civilisations?'. *Foreign Affairs*, vol. 72, no. 3, 1993, pp. 22–49.
54. *International Journal of Comparative Sociology*, vol. XXXIII, nos 1–2, 1992.

55. Jackson, R.H. and Rosberg, C.G. 'Why Africa's Weak States Persist: The Empirical and the Juridical in Statehood'. *World Politics*, vol. XXXV, no. 1, 1982, pp. 1–24.
56. Jackson, R.H. *Quasi-States: Sovereignty, International Relations and the Third World*. Cambridge, Cambridge University Press, 1990.
57. James, A. *Sovereign Statehood: The Basis of International Society*. London and Boston, Allen & Unwin, 1986.
58. Joffe, G. (ed.) *North Africa: Nation, State and Region*. London and New York, Routledge, 1993.
59. Kapoor, R. *Sikh Separatism: The Politics of Faith*. London and Boston, Allen & Unwin, 1986.
60. Kedourie, E. *Nationalism*. London, Hutchinson, 1960; fourth edition Oxford and New York, Blackwell, 1993.
61. Kedourie, E. (ed.) *Nationalism in Asia and Africa*. London, Weidenfeld & Nicolson, 1971.
62. Keynes, J.M. 'National Self-Sufficiency'. *Yale Review*, vol. 22, 1933, pp. 755–69.
63. Krayenbroek, P.G. and Sperl, S. (eds) *The Kurds: A Contemporary Overview*. London and New York, Routledge, 1991.
64. Lewis, I.M. *A Modern History of Somalia: Nation and State in the Horn of Africa*, revised edition. Boulder, Westview Press, 1988.
65. Lewis, I.M. 'The Ogaden and the Fragility of Somali Segmentary Nationalism'. *African Affairs*, vol. 88, no. 353, 1989, pp. 573–9.
66. Lewis, I.M. (ed.) *Nationalism and Self-Determination in the Horn of Africa*. London, Ithaca Press, 1983.
67. List, F. *The National System of Political Economy*. (1840), translated by Samson S. Lloyd, London, Longmans, Green & Co., 1904.
68. Markakis, J. 'Nationalities and the State in Ethiopia'. *Third World Quarterly*, vol. 11, no. 4, 1989, pp. 118–130.
69. Mayall, J. *Nationalism and International Society*. Cambridge, Cambridge University Press, 1990.
70. Mayall, J. 'The Liberal Economy' in J. Mayall (ed.) *The Community of States*. London and Boston, George Allen & Unwin, 1982, pp. 96–111.
71. Mayall, J. 'Reflections on the "New" Economic Nationalism'. *Review of International Studies*, vol. 10, no. 4, 1984, pp. 313–21.
72. Mayall, J. 'Non-intervention, self-determination and the "new world order"'. *International Affairs*, vol. 67, no. 3, July, 1991, pp. 421–29.
73. Mayall, J. 'Nationalism and international security after the Cold War'. *Survival*, vol. 34, no. 1, Spring, 1992, pp. 19–35.
74. Mayall, J. 'Self-determination Reconsidered: Should There Be a Right to Secede?'. *The Oxford International Review*, vol. 4, no. 1, Winter, 1993, pp. 4–6.
75. Mayall, J. and Simpson, M. 'Ethnicity is Not Enough: Reflections on Protracted Secessionism in the Third World'. *International Journal of Comparative Sociology*, vol. XXXIII, nos 1–2, 1992, pp. 5–25.
76. Meric, E. 'Le conflit Algero–Marocain'. *Revue Française de Sciences Politiques*, vol. 15, no. 4, 1965.
77. Mill, J.S. *Representative Government*, chapter 16, numerous editions.
78. *Millennium*, vol. 20, no. 3, Winter, 1991, 'Reimagining the Nation'.
79. Moynihan, D. *Pandemonium: Ethnicity in International Politics*. Oxford and New York, Oxford University Press, 1993.
80. Nairn, T. *The Breakup of Britain: Crisis and Neo-nationalism*. London, New Left Books, 1977.

81. Nassar, J.R. and Heacock, R. (eds) *Intifada: Palestine at the Crossroads*. New York, Praeger Publishers, 1990.
82. Neuberger, B. *National Self-Determination in Post-Colonial Africa*. Boulder, Lynne Rienner, 1986.
83. Nodia, G. 'Nationalism and Democracy'. *Journal of Democracy*, vol. 3, no. 4, 1992, pp. 3–22.
84. O'Brien, C.C. *God-land: Reflections on Religion and Nationalism*. Cambridge, MA, Harvard University Press, 1988.
85. O'Leary, B. and McGarry, J. (eds) *The Future of Northern Ireland*. Oxford, Clarendon Press and New York, Oxford University Press, 1990.
86. O'Leary, B. and McGarry, J. *The Politics of Antagonism: Understanding Northern Ireland*. London and Atlantic Highlands, Athlone Press, 1993.
87. Porter, B. 'Nationalism' in James Mayall (ed.) *The Community of States*. London and Boston, Allen & Unwin, 1982, pp. 49–60.
88. Quandt, W.B., Jabber, F. and Lesch, M.A. (eds) *The Politics of Palestinian Nationalism*. Berkeley, University of California Press, 1973.
89. Ramet, P. (ed.) *Religion and Nationalism in Soviet and East European Politics*, second edition. Durham and London, Duke University Press, 1989.
90. Ramet, P. *Nationalism and Federalism in Yugoslavia, 1962–91*, second edition. Bloomington and Indianapolis, Indiana University Press, 1992.
91. Raynor, A.S. 'Morocco's International Boundaries: A Factual Background'. *Journal of Modern African Studies*, vol. 1, no. 3, 1963.
92. Richler, M. *Oh Canada! Oh Quebec! A Requiem for a Divided Country*. New York, Knopf and Toronto, Penguin, 1992.
93. Roberts, A. 'Humanitarian War: Military Intervention and Human Rights'. *International Affairs*, vol. 69, no. 3, July, 1993, pp. 429–49.
94. Roberts, A. 'The United Nations and International Security'. *Survival*, vol. 35, no. 2, Summer, 1993, pp. 3–30.
95. Ronen, D. *The Quest for Self-Determination*. New Haven and London, Yale University Press, 1979.
96. Schöpflin, G. 'National Identity in the Soviet Union and East Central Europe'. *Ethnic and Racial Studies*, vol. 14, no. 1, January, 1991, pp. 3–14.
97. Schöpflin, G. 'Nationality in the Fabric of Yugoslav Politics'. *Survey*, vol. 25, no. 3, 1980, pp. 1–19.
98. Seers, D. *The Political Economy of Nationalism*. Oxford and New York, Oxford University Press, 1983.
99. Seevaratnam, N. (ed.) *The Tamil National Question and the Indo–Sri Lanka Accord*. Delhi, Konark Publishers, 1989.
100. Seton-Watson, H. *Nations and States: An Enquiry into the Origins of Nations and the Politics of Nationalism*. London, Methuen and Boulder, Westview Press, 1977.
101. Singh, K. *A History of the Sikhs*. Delhi, Oxford University Press, 1977.
102. Smith, A.D. *Theories of Nationalism*, second edition. London, Duckworth and New York, Holmes & Meier, 1983.
103. Smith, A.D. 'Towards a Global Culture?' *Theory, Culture and Society*, vol. 7, nos 2–3, 1990, pp. 171–91.
104. Smith, A.D. 'National Identity and the Idea of European Unity'. *International Affairs*, vol. 68, no. 1, 1992, pp. 55–76.
105. Smith, A.D. 'The Supersession of Nationalism?' *International Journal of Comparative Sociology*, vol. 31, nos 1–2, 1990, pp. 1–31.
106. Smith, A.D. *The Ethnic Revival*. Cambridge, Cambridge University Press, 1981.

107. Stone, J. (ed.) *Ethnic and Racial Studies*, 2, Special Issue on Internal Colonialism, 1979.
108. *Third World Quarterly*, vol. 11, no. 4, 1989.
109. Tiruneh, A. *Ethiopian Revolution 1974–1987*. Cambridge, Cambridge University Press, 1993.
110. Tiryakian, E.A. and Rogowski, R. (eds) *New Nationalisms in the Developed West*. Boston, Allen & Unwin, 1985.
111. Tomlinson, J. *Cultural Imperialism: A Critical Introduction*. London, Pinter Publishers and Baltimore, Johns Hopkins University Press, 1991.
112. Viner, J. 'Power Versus Plenty as Objectives of Foreign Policy in the Seventeenth and Eighteenth Centuries'. *World Politics*, vol. 1, no 1, 1948, pp. 1–29.
113. Von Hippel, K. *The Intractability of Irredentist Disputes with Reference to Gibraltar, Ceuta and Melilla and Western Sahara*. Unpublished Ph.D. thesis, University of London, 1993.
114. Wild, P.B. 'The Organisation of African Unity and the Algerian–Moroccan Border'. *International Organization*, vol. 20, no. 1, 1966, pp. 18–36.
115. Williams, C.H. (ed.) *National Separatism*. Cardiff, University of Wales Press, 1982.
116. Zartman, I.W. (ed.) *The Political Economy of Morocco*. New York, Praeger, 1987.

Part 3
Methods of analysis

14 The epistemology of international relations

Michael Nicholson and Peter Bennett

Most scholars in a discipline concern themselves with its substantive issues. IR scholars are concerned with what causes war and what promotes peace. They also consider different general approaches and debate schools of thought and problems such as dependency and imperialism. Some analyse the Cold War or the relationship between arms races and wars. Others investigate more particular issues such as the history of the League of Nations. However, a few scholars go behind the substantive concerns of the discipline and concern themselves with its underlying presuppositions. They ask such questions as: 'what does it mean to give an explanation in IR?' 'What does such an explanation consist of, or what ought it to consist of?' 'What is a theory in IR?' The analysis of such fundamental concepts in the natural sciences is commonly known as the philosophy of science. Analogously we are dealing here with the philosophy of IR, which is itself a part of the philosophy of the social sciences. Sometimes the word 'methodology' is used to cover the problems raised in an analysis of how the discipline is done, and this is the term we shall adopt here. Not all philosophical problems which enter into IR are subsumed under this heading – conspicuously, for example, ethical questions are omitted. In this chapter we shall be concerned with the nature of knowledge in IR, that is, with a general analysis of the grounds for believing the various propositions within it.

Like so much else in the field, the issues involved are often very contentious. It is particularly important for a social scientist, especially in IR, to be conscious of the issues because the controversies have direct practical application in the discipline. The battle between the 'behaviouralists' (for example Deutsch, Singer, Boulding), who basically believe that a form of scientific method can be applied to IR, and the 'traditionalists' (for example Morgenthau, Carr, Bull) is essentially an argument about the philosophy of the social sciences. But to discuss the methodology of IR we need to begin by going to more basic questions of methodology in the social sciences and even further back to the methodology of the natural sciences. Unfortunately that area is contentious also, and some of the basic disputes stem from that fact. It is appropriate, therefore, to start with the natural sciences.

The philosophy of science

A good, basic introduction to the philosophy of the natural sciences is by Chalmers [16]. Later, Chalmers [17] felt that he had been somewhat negative about classical scientific method. The natural sciences have been regarded traditionally as the epitome of rationality, and writers in the empiricist and positivist traditions exemplify this view. Braithwaite [11] presents a good, though at times complex, account in this tradition. In *The Logic of Scientific Discovery*, Popper [84] affirms strongly that the development of science is a rational process. His essays *Conjectures and Refutations* [83] are more accessible. A simple account of Popper's ideas is given in Bryan Magee's *Popper* [67]. The view that scientific endeavour is not all rational is put with various degrees of moderation. Quine [86] has long argued that the criteria for scientific truth are difficult to apply strictly and that the relationship between theory and fact is necessarily often tenuous. His views are sympathetically discussed in Gochet [35]. In an elegant book, Hanson [41] argues a different case but again one which leaves some role for subjectivity. The extreme is Feyerabend – in particular and lucidly in *Against Method* [25] – who argues that scientific method is irretrievably subjective and, as far as belief is concerned, that there are no privileged grounds for belief. His phrase, 'anything goes', bluntly summarizes his attitude. His collected papers on *Problems of Empiricism* [27] argue the view at a more technical level. There are many, many accounts of the philosophy of science. Harré's lucid works [44, 45] are helpful and Van Fraassen [109] is illuminating but not easy.

The battle between the rationalists and the non-rationalists peaked in a classic controversy between Lakatos [61] for the rationalists and Kuhn [60] for the non-rationalists. Lakatos's classic paper appears in a collection of essays [62], in which the paper by Masterman [68] is well worth reading. Many of the leading protagonists are represented in this collection including Popper, Kuhn and Feyerabend. The concept of a paradigm, introduced into this discussion by Kuhn, was as warmly received in the social sciences as the natural. Though ill-defined, it refers to the general principles on which the practitioners of a discipline operate – what it means, for example, to do physics or biology. From time to time there are periods of great disruption in a discipline, such as when people began to doubt that the earth was the centre of the universe which put in doubt the whole nature of what it meant to do astronomy. Kuhn argues that at such times, when the accepted way of doing 'normal science' is replaced by another, the jump from one paradigm to another is not strictly rational. The two paradigms are incommensurable, in the sense that neither can be judged by the criteria appropriate to the other. Kuhn himself draws back from describing the choice between paradigms as 'irrational', but his work is often interpreted in that radical way. Lakatos responded to the challenge to rationality with his 'Methodology of Scientific Research Programmes' [61], arguing that the development of sciences and the replacement of one theory by another is essentially a rational process. Inspiration and intuition might play a part in the psychological processes involved in developing a theory, but the ultimate justification of the arguments is rational and can be reconstructed rationally. Since much of this debate is conducted in terms of the natural sciences, it is sometimes heavy going.

The philosophy of the social sciences

The central question in the philosophy of the social sciences is whether the behaviour of human beings can be explained in similar ways to natural (that is, inanimate) behaviour. The problem is that human beings – unlike the objects of physics – interpret their own behaviour, and it is the interpretation which normally makes it interesting. Thus, the concept of an international conference involves not merely a group of people clustered together but an understanding of why they are clustered together, couched in terms which they themselves would recognize. It differs, therefore, from the concept of a forest which can be analysed purely in causal terms and without worrying about the perceptions of the trees. Some of the concepts of IR (including the concept of 'nation') are often defined primarily in terms of the interpretations of the actors. Nevertheless, some scholars argue that this need not alter the fundamental mode of explanation. According to this school, social behaviour can be explained in terms of causal laws, and explanation is used here in a fairly conventional sense. Roughly speaking the behaviouralists (not 'behaviourist' which is something rather different) in political science and IR adopt this point of view. Hempel [47] gives a vigorous and classic statement of this position. Though the argument is stated in terms of historical explanation, it is interpreted readily in terms of all social explanation. Friedman [29] also argues an extreme version of the case in terms of economics but with obvious extensions to IR. A more moderate statement of the position is by Blaug [9].

The classic statement of the opposing point of view is by Winch in the *Idea of a Social Science* [115]. Following Wittgenstein (in the later philosophy of his *Philosophical Investigations* [116]), Winch argues that the idea of a scientific explanation of social behaviour is misconceived from the very start: we have to understand behaviour in terms in which the actors themselves understand it. The debate between explanation and understanding is central in the social sciences. Other followers of the latter school are Taylor [104] and Von Wright [112]. The case is stated simply in Trigg [107], who gives a good introduction to the general argument. Ryan [96] and Rudner [92] provide two good general introductions to the philosophy of the social sciences. Many postmodernists tend to sympathize with ideas similar to those of Winch.

It is interesting but not surprising to find that historians are involved in the same debate. Since history and historical modes of explanation are so important in IR, a brief mention of the issues raised in the historians' debate is useful. Hempel [47] states the case for scientific explanation, while the classical statement of the contrary view is by Collingwood [20]. Gardiner [31] maintains that the general scientific model, the so-called 'covering law' model of explanation, is appropriate in history and argues that it is widely, if unconsciously, used by historians. Dray [24] puts the counter argument. A collection of essays edited by Gardiner [32] surveys the controversies. Popper, notably in *The Poverty of Historicism* [85], attacks the big system builders in history (such as Marx) who seek to predict grand patterns rather than offering more limited explanations. A recent contribution to the general debate which concentrates on the problems of counter-factuals (that is, questions involving 'what would have happened if . . .') is Hawthorn's *Plausible Worlds* [46], which is an interesting discussion for anyone involved in the analysis of any sort of social behaviour.

The philosophy of international relations

The debate about knowledge in IR is similar to the debate in the other social sciences. Hollis and Smith's excellent *Explanation and Understanding in International Relations* [52] is strongly recommended as a clear account of the central features of the debates. Nicholson [77] defends the explanatory mode and later [78] discusses some of the issues further. The most sophisticated statements of the opposing tradition are by Reynolds. In his first book [88] he discusses the problems of explanation in terms of the Cold War. In a later book [89] he discusses explanation in the context of different interpretations of imperialism, while more recently [91] he returns to the Cold War and deals with a number of other issues. Bull [15] made a robust, amusing and often quoted attack on social scientists in a collection of essays edited by Knorr and Rosenau [59] which contains the less frequently cited but damaging rebuttal by Singer.

The debate about the nature of knowledge in IR is often confused with debates about method, in particular the use of quantitative methods. While in general the use of quantitative methods goes with a behaviouralist epistemology, one could accept causal explanations and still be sceptical of the widespread use of statistics in IR. Two different attitudes are expressed by Young [117] and Russett [95] about the use to which quantitative methods should be put. A number of large quantitative studies are conveniently summarized with a commentary in Cioffi-Revilla [19]. One of the best known quantitative studies is the Correlates of War (COW) project which is helpfully analysed in Vasquez [110]. Singer and Diehl [102] edit a useful evaluation of the studies which have come out of COW, and James [in 40] and Midlarsky [73] also give useful surveys. A full discussion of quantitative studies would involve a long bibliographical essay of its own.

The field of epistemology in IR has not altered a great deal recently, and when comparing this survey with other papers in the volume, there are relatively few references from the last five years. This is perhaps to be expected in a purely conceptual field unless there has been some outstanding advance which spawns controversy. The postmodernists (see Chapter 4) have provided the biggest recent challenge to conventional methodologies, but since they refute the usefulness of methodologies, they offer a purely negative criticism. The postmodernist position on methodology is discussed critically by Vasquez [111]. The difficulties postmodernists raise for the behaviouralists were discussed long ago by Winch [115].

Bibliography

1. Almond. G. and Genco. S.J. 'Clouds, Clocks and the Study of Politics'. *World Politics*, vol. XXIX, no. 4, 1977, pp. 489–522.
2. Anderson, R.J., Hughes, J.A. and Sharrock W.W. *Philosophy and the Human Sciences*. London, Croom Helm, 1986.
3. Andreski, S. *Social Science as Sorcery*. London, Deutsch, 1972.
4. Archibald, G.C. 'Refutation or Comparison'. *British Journal For Philosophy of Science*, vol. XVII, no. 4, 1966, pp. 279–96.
5. Ayer, A.J. *Language, Truth and Logic*. Harmondsworth, Penguin, 1990.
6. Ayer, A.J. 'Man as a Subject for Science' in P. Laslett and W.G. Runciman (eds) *Philosophy, Politics and Society*, third series, Oxford, Basil Blackwell, 1967 and New York, Barnes & Noble Books, 1972, pp. 6–24.
7. Ayer, A.J. *The Problem of Knowledge*. Harmondsworth, Penguin, 1990.
8. Blaug, M. 'Kuhn versus Lakatos, or Paradigms versus Research Programmes in the History of Economics'. *History of Political Economy*, vol. 7, no. 4, 1975, pp. 399–433.
9. Blaug, M. *The Methodology of Economics or How Economists Explain*. Cambridge, Cambridge University Press, 1993.
10. Booth, Ken and Smith, Steve *International Political Theory Today*. Cambridge, Polity Press (forthcoming).
11. Braithwaite, R.B. *Scientific Explanation*. Cambridge and New York, Cambridge University Press, 1953.
12. Brodbeck, M. (ed.) *Readings in the Philosophy of the Social Sciences*. New York, Macmillan and London, Collier-Macmillan, 1968.
13. Brown, R. *Explanation in Social Science*. London, Routledge & Kegan Paul, 1963.
14. Bueno de Mesquita, Bruce, Krasner, Stephen J. and Jervis, Robert 'Symposium: Methodological Foundations of the Study of International Conflict'. *International Studies Quarterly*, vol. 29, no. 2, June, 1985, pp. 119–54.
15. Bull, Hedley 'International Theory: The Case for the Classical Approach' in K. Knorr and J.N. Rosenau (eds) *Contending Approaches to International Politics*. Princeton, Princeton University Press, 1969, pp. 20–38.
16. Chalmers, A.F. *What Is This Thing Called Science?* Milton Keynes, Open University Press, second edition, 1982.
17. Chalmers, A.F. *Science and its Fabrication*. Milton Keynes, Open University Press and Minneapolis, University of Minnesota Press, 1990.
18. Charlesworth, J.C. (ed.) *The Limits of Behavioralism in Political Science*. Philadelphia, American Academy of Political and Social Science, 1962.

19. Cioffi-Revilla, Claudio, *The Scientific Measurement of International Conflict: A Handbook of Datasets on Crises and Wars, 1495–1988*. Boulder and London, Lynne Rienner, 1990.
20. Collingwood, R.G. (edited by R.V.D. Dussen) *The Idea of History*. Oxford, Clarendon Press, 1993.
21. Cyert, R.M. and Grunberg, E. 'Assumption, Prediction and Explanation in Economics' in R.M. Cyert and J.G. March (eds) *A Behavioral Theory of the Firm*. Englewood Cliffs and London, Prentice Hall, 1964, pp. 298–311.
22. Deutsch, K.W. 'On Political Theory and Political Action'. *American Political Science Review*, vol. LXV, no. 1, 1971, pp. 11–27.
23. Doyal, L, and Harris, R, *Empiricism, Explanation and Rationality*. London, Routledge & Kegan Paul, 1986.
24. Dray, W.H. *Laws and Explanations in History*. London and Westport, Greenwood Publishing Co., 1979.
25. Feyerabend, Paul K. *Against Method: Outline of an Anarchistic Theory of Knowledge*. London and New York, Verso, 1993.
26. Feyerabend, Paul K. *Realism, Rationalism and Scientific Method*. Series: Philosophical Papers. vol. 1, Cambridge, Cambridge University Press, 1981.
27. Feyerabend, Paul K. *Problems of Empiricism*. Series: Philosophical Papers. vol. 2, Cambridge, Cambridge University Press, 1981.
28. Frank, P.G. (ed.) *The Validation of Scientific Theories*. New York, Collier Books, 1961.
29. Friedman, M. *Essays in Positive Economics*. Chicago, Chicago University Press, 1966.
30. Gallie, W.B. *Philosophy and the Historical Understanding*. London, Chatto & Windus, 1964.
31. Gardiner, P.L. *The Nature of Historical Explanation*. London, Oxford University Press, 1965.
32. Gardiner, P.L. (ed.) *The Philosophy of History*. London and New York, Oxford University Press, 1974.
33. Giddens, A. *New Rules of Sociological Method*. Cambridge, Polity Press and Stanford, Stanford University Press, 1993.
34. Giddens, A. *Positivism and Sociology*. London, Heinemann, 1974.
35. Gochet, Paul, *Ascent to Truth: A Critical Examination of Quine's Philosophy* Munich, Philosophia Verlag, 1986.
36. Goldmannn, L. *The Human Sciences and Philosophy* (translated by H.V. White and R. Anchor). London, Jonathan Cape, 1969.
37. Goodman, N. *Fact, Fiction and Forecast*. Cambridge, MA and London, Harvard University Press, 1983.
38. Gregor, A.J. *An Introduction to Metapolitics*. New York, Free Press, 1971.
39. Gunnell, H.G. *et al.* 'Symposium on Scientific Explanation in Political Science'. *American Political Science Review*, vol. LXIII, no. 4, 1969, pp. 1233–62.
40. Haglund, David and Hawes, Michael (eds) *World Politics: Power, Interdependence and Dependence*. Toronto, Harcourt Brace Jovanovich, 1990.
41. Hanson, Norwood Russell, *Patterns of Discovery: An Inquiry into the Conceptual Foundations of Science*. Cambridge, Cambridge University Press, 1958.
42. Hanson, Norwood Russell, *Observations and Explanation: A Guide to Philosophy of Science*. New York, Harper & Row, 1971 and London, Allen & Unwin, 1972.
43. Hargreaves-Heap, S. *Rationality in Economics*. Oxford, Basil Blackwell Ltd., 1989.

44. Harré, R. *The Philosophies of Science: An Introductory Survey*. London, Oxford University Press, 1972.
45. Harré, R. and Secord, P.F. *The Explanation of Social Behaviour*. Oxford, Basil Blackwell, 1972 and Totowa, Littlefield, Adams & Co., 1979.
46. Hawthorn, G. *Plausible Worlds*. Cambridge, Cambridge University Press 1991.
47. Hempel, C.G. *Aspects of Concept Formation in Empirical Science*. International Encyclopaedia of Unified Science, Chicago, University of Chicago Press, 1967.
48. Hempel, C.G. *Philosophy of Natural Science* (Foundations of Philosophy Series). Englewood Cliffs and Hemel Hempstead, Prentice Hall, 1966.
49. Hempel, C.G. (ed.) *Aspects of Scientific Explanation and Other Essays*. London, Collier-Macmillan, 1965 and New York, Free Press, 1970.
50. Hindess, B. *Philosophy and Methodology in the Social Sciences*. London, Hassocks Harvester Press, 1977.
51. Hirschman, A.O. 'The Search for Paradigms as a Hindrance to Understanding'. *World Politics*, vol. XXII, no. 3, 1970, pp. 329–43.
52. Hollis, M. and Smith, S. *Explaining and Understanding in International Relations*. Oxford, Clarendon Press, 1991.
53. Homans, G.C. *The Nature of Social Science*. New York, Harcourt & Brace, 1967.
54. Hudson, L. *The Cult of the Fact*. London, Jonathan Cape, 1972.
55. Ions, Edmund *Against Behaviouralism: A Critique of Behavioural Science*. Oxford, Basil Blackwell 1977
56. James, Patrick 'The Causes of War' in David Haglund and Michael Hawes (eds) *World Politics: Power, Interdependence and Dependence*. Toronto, Harcourt Brace Jovanovich, 1990.
57. Kalleberg, A.L. 'Concept Formation in Normative and Empirical Studies: Toward Reconciliation in Political Theory'. *American Political Science Review*, vol. LXIII, no. 1 1969, pp. 26–39.
58. King, Gary *Unifying Political Methodology: the Likelihood Theory of Statistical Inference*. Cambridge, Cambridge University Press, 1989.
59. Knorr, K. and Rosenau J.N. (eds) *Contending Approaches to International Politics*. Princeton, Princeton University Press, 1969.
60. Kuhn, T.S. *The Structure of Scientific Revolutions*. (International Encyclopaedia of Unified Science). Chicago and London, University of Chicago Press, 1970.
61. Lakatos, I. 'Falsification and the Methodology of Scientific Research Programmes' in I. Lakatos and A. Musgrave (eds) *Criticism and the Growth of Knowledge: Proceedings of the International Colloquium in the Philosophy of Science* (International Colloquium in the Philosophy of Science 1965). Cambridge and New York, Cambridge University Press, 1970, pp. 91–195.
62. Lakatos, I. and Musgrave, A. *Criticism and the Growth of Knowledge: Proceedings of the International Colloquium in the Philosophy of Science* (International Colloquium in the Philosophy of Science 1965). Cambridge and New York, Cambridge University Press, 1970.
63. Latsis, S. (ed.) *Method and Appraisal in Economics*. Cambridge and New York, Cambridge University Press, 1976.
64. Lessnoff, M. *The Structure of Social Science: A Philosophical Introduction*. London, Allen & Unwin, 1974.
65. Louch, A.R. *Explanation and Human Action*. Oxford, Basil Blackwell, 1966.
66. Macrae, D. *The Social Function of Social Science*. New Haven and London, Yale University Press, 1981.
67. Magee, B. *Popper*. London, Woburn Press, 1982.

68. Masterman, M. 'The Nature of a Paradigm' in I. Lakatos and A. Musgrave (eds) *Criticism and the Growth of Knowledge: Proceedings of the International Colloquium in the Philosophy of Science* (International Colloquium in the Philosophy of Science 1965). Cambridge and New York, Cambridge University Press, 1970, pp. 59–89.

69. Most, Benjamin A. and Starr, Harvey, *Inquiry, Logic and International Politics.* Columbia, University of South Carolina Press, 1989.

70. Meehan, E.J. *Explanation in Social Science.* Homewood and London, Dorsey Press, 1968.

71. Meehan, E.J. *The Theory and Method of Political Analysis.* Homewood, Dorsey Press, 1966.

72. Meehan, E.J. *Value Judgements and Social Science: Explanation in Social Science.* Homewood, Dorsey Press, 1969.

73. Midlarsky, Manus (ed.) *Handbook of War Studies,* Boston and London, Unwin Hyman, 1989.

74. Miller, F. *et al.* 'Positivism, Historicism and Political Inquiry'. *American Political Science Review,* vol. LXVI, no. 3, 1972, pp. 796–873.

75. Myrdal, G. *Objectivity in Social Research.* London, Duckworth, 1970 and Middletown, Wesleyan University Press, 1983.

76. Nagel, E. *The Structure of Science: Problems in the Logic of Scientific Explanation.* London, Routledge & Kegan Paul, 1961 and Indianapolis, Hackett, 1979.

77. Nicholson, Michael *The Scientific Analysis of Social Behaviour: A Defence of Empiricism in Social Science.* London, Frances Pinter and New York, St. Martin's Press, 1983.

78. Nicholson, Michael *Rationality and the Analysis of International Conflict.* Cambridge, Cambridge University Press, 1992.

79. Nidditch, P.H. (ed.) *The Philosophy of Science.* London and New York, Oxford University Press, 1968.

80. Novak, G. *An Introduction to the Logic of Marxism.* New York and London, Pathfinder Press, 1969.

81. Phillips, W.R. 'Where Have All the Theories Gone?', *World Politics,* vol. XXVI, no. 2, 1974, pp. 155–88.

82. Platt, D.C.M. *Mickey Mouse Numbers in World History.* London, Macmillan, 1989.

83. Popper, K.R. *Conjectures and Refutations: The Growth of Scientific Knowledge.* New York, Harper & Collins, 1968 and London, Routledge, 1989.

84. Popper, K.R. *The Logic of Scientific Discovery.* New York, Harper & Collins, 1959 and London, Routledge, 1992.

85. Popper, K.R. *The Poverty of Historicism.* London, Routledge & Kegan Paul, 1960 and New York, Harper Collins, 1964.

86. Quine, W.R.O. *Pursuit of Truth.* Cambridge, MA, Harvard University Press, 1990.

87. Ravetz, J.R. *Scientific Knowledge and its Social Problems.* Harmondsworth, Penguin University Books, 1973 and New York, Galaxy, 1983.

88. Reynolds, C. *Theory and Explanation in International Politics.* London, Martin Robertson, 1973.

89. Reynolds, C. *Modes of Imperialism.* Oxford, Martin Robertson, 1981.

90. Reynolds, C. *The Politics of War: A Study of the Rationality of Violence in Inter-State Relations.* Hemel Hempstead, Harvester Wheatsheaf, 1989.

91. Reynolds, C. *The World of States: An Introduction to Explanation and Theory.* Aldershot, Edward Elgar, 1992.

92. Rudner, R. *The Philosophy of Social Science* (Foundations of Philosophy Series). Englewood Cliffs and Hemel Hempstead, Prentice Hall, 1966.
93. Runciman, W.G. *Social Science and Political Theory*. Cambridge and New York, Cambridge University Press, 1963.
94. Russell, B. *Human Knowledge: Its Scope and Limits*. London, Allen & Unwin, 1948 and New York, Simon & Schuster, 1962.
95. Russett, B.M. 'The Young Science of International Politics'. *World Politics*, vol. XXII, no. 1, 1969, pp. 87–94.
96. Ryan, A.P. *The Philosophy of the Social Sciences*. London, Macmillan, 1970.
97. Ryan, A.P. (ed.) *The Philosophy of Social Explanation*. London and New York, Oxford University Press, 1973.
98. Searle, J. 'The Reith Lectures'. *The Listener*, 8 Nov.–13 Dec. 1984.
99. Shapiro, M.J. *Language and Political Understanding: The Politics of Discursive Practices*. New Haven and London, Yale University Press, 1981.
100. Simon, H.A. 'The Architecture of Complexity'. *Proceedings of the American Philosophical Society*, Philadelphia, 1960.
101. Singer, J. David and Diehl, Paul, *Models Methods and Progress in World Politics*. Beverly Hills, Sage, 1990.
102. Singer, J. David and Diehl, Paul F. (eds) *Measuring the Correlates of War*. Ann Arbor, University of Michigan Press, 1990.
103. Spegele, R.D. 'Deconstructing Methodological Falsification in International Relations'. *American Political Science Review*, vol. LXXIV, no. 1, 1980, pp. 104–22.
104. Taylor, C. *The Explanation of Behaviour*. Atlantic Highlands, Humanities Press, 1964 and London, Routledge & Kegan Paul, 1980.
105. Todd, W. *History as an Applied Science*. Detroit, Wayne State University Press, 1972.
106. Toulmin, S. *Philosophy of Science*. London, Hutchinson, 1953.
107. Trigg, R. *Understanding Social Science: A Philosophical Introduction to the Social Sciences*. London, Oxford University Press, 1985.
108. Van Dyke, V. *Political Science: A Philosophical Analysis*. Stanford, Stanford University Press, 1960.
109. Van Fraassen, Bas C. *The Scientific Image*. Oxford, Clarendon Press, 1980.
110. Vasquez, John A. 'The Steps to War: Toward a Scientific Explanation of Correlates of War Findings'. *World Politics*, vol. 40, no. 1, 1987, pp. 108–45.
111. Vasquez, John A. 'The Post-Positivist Debate: Reconstructing Scientific Inquiry and IR Theory After Enlightenment's Fall' in Ken Booth and Steve Smith (eds) *International Political Theory Today*. Cambridge, Polity Press, forthcoming.
112. Von Wright, G. *Explanation and Understanding*. Ithaca, Cornell University Press, 1971.
113. Walsh, W.H. *An Introduction to Philosophy of History*. London, Thoemmes Press, 1992.
114. Weber, M. *The Methodology of the Social Sciences*. New York, Free Press, 1969.
115. Winch, P. *The Idea of a Social Science*. London, Routledge & Kegan Paul and Atlantic Highlands, Humanities Press, 1990.
116. Wittgenstein, Ludwig. *Philosophical Investigations*, second edition, Oxford, Blackwell, 1963.
117. Young. O.R. 'Professor Russett: Industrious Tailor to a Naked Emperor'. *World Politics*. vol. XXI, no. 3, 1969. pp. 486–511.

15 Formal methods of analysis in IR

Peter Bennett and Michael Nicholson

By 'formal methods' we mean the use of logic and mathematics to build models of international systems or situations. A model is intended as a simplified analogue of 'real life': its deductive structure helps one to explore the consequences of alternative assumptions. This contrasts, for example, with the use of statistical methods solely to summarize empirical data. One can 'experiment with the model' (by changing the assumptions) when it would be quite impossible – or too dangerous – to experiment with the real world. Five strands of work are discussed here: Richardson's arms race model, that of Lanchester on battles, Decision Theory, Game Theory and its extensions, and Artificial Intelligence. This list does not exhaust the possible uses of formal methods: for example, it omits both Catastrophe Theory and Chaos Theory [54]. For those seeking further general reading, a very useful review of formal models and their applications is provided by Intriligator [33], and various recent contributions appear in volumes edited by Luterbacher and Ward [38], Bennett [6] and Zagare [76]. Perusal of the *Journal of Conflict Resolution* and *Journal of Peace Research* should also pay dividends. Some of the literature is quite technical (in a mathematical sense): most collections of papers contain a mix of the abstruse and the more accessible. By concentrating on the latter, it is generally possible to grasp the essentials and to make a judgement of what each approach has to offer.

Richardson's model of arms races [49], originally developed just after the First World War (though then largely ignored), was the first formal model developed in International Relations (IR). It is still the only one to have originated within the field. In its simplest form, it postulates that a state's spending on armaments increases or decreases according to its rival's spending, but this process is damped by the cost of its own arms. In the model, spending is represented by a pair of differential equations. Analysing these shows that some cases allow a stable equilibrium, in which spending tends to revert to a fixed level, while other cases are unstable, leading either to an unrestrained arms race or to complete disarmament. Outlines of the model are given by Rapoport [45, 46], Nicholson [41] and Wilkinson [72]. Richardson's model has had a tremendous impact on peace and conflict research, though arguably not as much as those derived from decision theory and game theory. Some subsequent work has tried to test the model [62] and some to develop it, for example to deal with races among several states [39, 58]. Other work on 'hostility spirals' stems directly from Richardson's model. However its explanatory power seems not to have matched its formal elegance.

Another noteworthy strand of work is derived from Lanchester's analysis of exchange of fire in battle. Though more to do with military operational research than IR proper, it has some more general relevance. Starting, like Richardson, from a very simple model, Lanchester showed that (other things being equal) the fighting effectiveness of a force would be proportional to the square of the numbers engaged [36]. Units outnumbered two-to-one thus need to be four times as efficient to compensate, a result supporting the military principle of concentrating one's forces. In real life, of course, other things are not equal. Much work has therefore gone into trying to include the effects of terrain, morale, different types of weapon and so on. As with all models, the more that is included, the more complex the model becomes and the more (often dubious) assumptions are needed. Although military analysis lies outside the scope of this book, it is worth noting the general principle that successful models depend on felicitous simplification. It is also noteworthy that much conventional military planning (on all sides) makes use of highly developed versions of Lanchester's model. It has thus been a factor in shaping (conventional) arms races and has also had some influence on arms control policy. Conversely, proponents of 'non-offensive' defence such as Neild have argued that new technologies allow Lanchester's Square Law to be circumvented by dispersed defence [40]. Although in Europe the argument has been somewhat overtaken by events *pro tem*, it will remain relevant whenever and wherever conventional wars are considered possible.

Neither of the above approaches focuses on deliberate choices made by the parties involved. Indeed, Richardson described his model as 'what would happen if people did not stop to think' [49]. The following models are concerned with people who *do* stop to think: decision-makers who are weighing up the possible consequences of alternative actions and policies. In IR these are sometimes termed 'rational actor' models. However, this label can make the approaches seem more restrictive than they really are. As will be seen, these models can be developed to take account of multiple objectives or differences in perception. Nor need the actors be self-interested in any material sense: their aims may be altruistic or indeed vindictive. As noted below, at least one approach seeks explicitly to account for strategic effects and origins of emotions. All that is necessary is that, whatever the actors' motivations are, they can be expressed in terms of preferences for different possible outcomes. Theories based on preferences can nevertheless be criticized for over-concentrating on actors' wants or interests, at the expense of attention to needs (for example Burton [14], see Chapter 5 for further discussion and references).

The earliest and simplest formal models of choice are provided by Decision

Theory. This seeks to analyse choices available to an actor who is unsure about the consequences of each possible option. Sometimes the uncertainty can be expressed by a probability – as with Robert Kennedy's famous calculation in the Cuban Missile Crisis that there was a one-in-four chance of nuclear war. The model also demands that the actor should be able to measure the desirability or undesirability (the 'utility') of each possible outcome. One can then work out the expected utility of each available option, by multiplying the utilities of the possible outcomes by their probabilities once that option is chosen. One criterion of 'rational' choice is then to choose the option with the greatest expected utility. In this way, one may seek an optimal balance between potential risks and benefits. The most notable recent work in this vein in IR is that of Bueno de Mesquita [13], on the decision to go to war as a choice maximizing an individual leader's expected utility.

There is much more to Decision Theory, however, than the formula of maximizing expected utility. There are other defensible decision criteria, some of which do not require the probabilities of events to be known. The measurement both of utilities and – if they are to be used – of probabilities raises a host of practical issues. It is widely recognized that an outcome's attractiveness will seldom depend on just one factor (not even – *pace* 'rational economic man' – profit). Usually different outcomes will be better for different reasons. To model how different advantages are weighed up against each other, several forms of multiple criteria analysis have grown up. These either use more complex (multi-attribute) notions of utility or provide other ways of prioritizing competing objectives. Belton [4] provides an overview and Saaty [51, 53] provides applications to IR examples. Such approaches are now quite widely used as aids to decision-making, often using computer software to explore rapidly the consequences of different sets of priorities. They can also be used in negotiations to help to find acceptable trade-offs between different parties' objectives. Another important idea is Simon's bounded rationality [60]. According to this, decision-makers often 'satisfice': rather than explore all alternatives to find the best, they look only until they find something good enough. Modifying Decision Theory in this way may provide a bridge to models invoking bureaucratic politics and the like [19].

Decision Theory has also proved a fruitful starting-point for research on the psychology of choice, particularly on perceptions of probabilities and on attitudes to risk. Wright [75] provides an accessible introduction. Some common biases in estimating probabilities are now well documented for events that are well defined and repeatable. For singular events such as an outbreak of war, the issue remains of how probabilities can sensibly be defined [34, 2]. Clearly people's willingness to take risks varies a good deal and is influenced by many factors. A seminal paper by Tversky and Kahnemann [68] suggests *inter alia* that we often 'play safe' in situations of potential reward but choose high-risk options in situations of threat. In other words, we may be prepared to settle for moderate gain but risk disaster rather than accept moderate loss. Quattrone and Tversky [44] suggest that this may throw light on leaders' willingness to risk war when they believe security is at stake. Other work has indicated that groups tend to make riskier decisions than individuals. Many specific findings remain controversial, but they provide relevant food for thought in an IR context. The volume edited by French provides a good general introduction to Decision Analysis [23].

Despite these developments, Decision Theory still deals only with a single decision-maker or a group already engaged in collective decision. Much of IR, however, concerns the interplay between decisions made separately, by independent actors, but which have an impact on each other. This is the natural territory of Game Theory and its derivatives.

The Theory of Games was developed from early work on Decision Theory, the aim being to extend the analysis to situations involving two or more parties. Von Neumann and Morgenstern provided its first systematic exposition [70]. One reason why the approach has always been controversial is its unfortunate terminology. Although the theory suggests structural analogies between serious issues – in economics, IR and elsewhere – and games in the everyday sense, no sense of trivialization is intended. Rather, the suggestion is to analyse situations in terms of who are the interested parties (players), the actions each can choose to take (strategies), the outcomes that can result from each possible combination of choices and each player's aims – expressed either by measuring each outcome's utility for that player or simply by putting the outcomes in an order of preference. One can then analyse the model to draw conclusions about the players' choices. In some games, called 'zero-sum', one player's gain must necessarily be another's loss. Many parlour games are like this, but fortunately few real-life conflicts (at least, outside the world of military tactics) have this win/lose structure. More usually, the parties' aims are in partial conflict. So the model serves to throw light on the implicit or explicit negotiation and bargaining, and the pattern of threats and promises, liable to ensue.

Originally the aim was to develop a normative theory showing how rational decision-makers should behave, and such a theory proved to be possible for zero-sum games with just two players. However, other cases are much more resistant to neat solutions. Much work has been gone into defining and refining solutions to bargaining problems and on the formation of coalitions. Shubik [59] and Thomas [67] both provide good summaries of most technical developments. Earlier classics include Luce and Raiffa [37]. But for many, the value of game models lay largely in structuring problems of choice and eliciting the paradoxes and dilemmas inherent in trying to behave 'rationally' in situations of partial conflict. Early work, such as that of Rapoport [46], had a major influence on the developing study of international conflict and cooperation as did Schelling's study of deterrence and its problems [55]. Though some of their examples have dated, both still provide very good introductions to the relevant concepts.

By the 1970s, Game Theory had fallen out of favour in many areas of IR. The models had been criticized as being both over-simplified and harmful (see for example Green [26]), and the criticisms seemed to stick, perhaps in reaction to some very optimistic earlier claims (though Rapoport was always careful not to claim too much). To many, the theory became associated with crude international realism and rather hawkish versions of deterrence theory. Nevertheless important theoretical advances continued. Harsanyi [27] and others developed analyses of games with incomplete information in which players are uncertain about each other's aims. Howard concentrated on the paradoxes of rationality exposed by Game Theory, and his Metagame Analysis provided a (controversial) means of resolving some of them [28].

A more recent revival of interest, however, has been prompted by works applying game-theoretic ideas in an accessible form. Axelrod's book on the evolution of cooperation – building on the earlier work of Rapoport *et al.* to weave together diverse applications of a simple model – was particularly well received [3]. Other writers, such as Brams [10, 11, 12] combine attention to theory with thought-provoking analyses of issues in IR. At the same time, new forms of analysis overcome many of the restrictive assumptions inherent in earlier models. For example, Howard's work on metagames has been developed to provide both a practical methodology for helping decision-makers and also encompasses a theory of emotions and preference change [29, 30]. Taylor [66] and Snidal [63] discuss the possibility of co-operation among players who value not only their own direct payoff but also the difference between their payoffs and those of their rivals. Following Harsanyi's pioneering work, games with incomplete information have gained much attention, as has the dynamics of strategy implementation.

Much current theoretical work emphasises various forms of dynamic analysis. Within a given game, analysis concentrates on strategies that can be updated as the game unfolds, rather than being chosen once-and-for-all. Multi-stage models go further by considering series of linked games, the outcome at each stage determining which game is to be played next. Such tools have been used to re-examine 'classic' issues such as deterrence and escalation [38], albeit at a rather abstract level so far. A critical discussion of much of this recent work is given by Varoufakis [69].

Hypergame analysis [5, 6, 8] starts from the supposition that the parties to a conflict may perceive it in quite different terms. Its basic model is thus not a single game seen by all the parties but a set of subjective games, each expressing one party's view of the situation. One current attempt to pull together the various developments just discussed involves replacing the game metaphor with that of an unfolding drama [31].

Despite these advances, some limitations and problems persist. Even given assumptions more definite than are often warranted in practice, many models are only weak predictors of the outcome to be expected. They may be rather better predictors of players' tactical behaviour but frequently leave open the question of whose tactics are likely to succeed. As with other methods, the use of *post hoc* and/or very general case studies can suggest that assumptions have been pulled out of the air to 'prove' preordained conclusions. Reynolds' attack on one recent offering [48] provides an important warning, as does Schrodt's more measured critique [56]. Another perennial problem is deciding the appropriate level at which to define the relevant 'players'. Most models, echoing Snyder and Diesing's phrase [64], have taken IR to be about 'conflict among nations'. Yet there is no reason why the actors need be nations. They can equally well be individuals, political parties, governments, commercial firms, NGOs, churches and so on. The inadequacy of treating any but individuals as unitary actors suggests the need for multi-level models, in which all collective actors (for example governments) are subject to internal games (between ministries, key individuals and the like). But while it is easy enough to suggest that 'every player is a game', it is much more difficult actually to build and analyse multi-level models. A partial solution is to preface formal analysis with more descriptive problem-structuring, showing the linkage of issues at different levels [50, 8].

Our fifth and last approach makes use of Artificial Intelligence (AI) methods. They originate with attempts to build computer systems that simulate human reasoning, made in order to extend the capabilities of computers and the understanding of human intelligence. (It is now acknowledged that these two aims are distinct.) AI has a voluminous literature of its own, and philosophical and moral arguments abound (for example as to what is meant by 'thinking' and whether it is justifiable to blur the distinction between the mechanical and the sentient). Profound but readable introductions can be found in Weizenbaum [73] and Winograd and Flores [74]. One use of AI is in driving systems in which the computer stores and makes use of human knowledge already available on a particular topic. In the more sophisticated systems, this knowledge base is updated so that the computer 'learns' from experience. Such expert systems are demonstrably able to analyse a wide range of problems well beyond the capabilities of any analysis employing only blind deductive logic. They can play chess successfully and provide valuable medical diagnosis, legal advice and fault diagnosis for machinery. However, these are fields in which there is already an established and clearly structured body of expertise on which to draw. This is not evidently the case in most areas of IR, except perhaps international law. Nevertheless, AI methods are increasingly likely to have an impact.

One early AI undertaking was to build systems to mimic the behaviour of specific political figures. By having the machine follow an operational code based on observations of past behaviour, it proved surprisingly easy to mimic behaviour and hence to predict the real politician's response to new situations (George, [24]). Admittedly some targets, such as Barry Goldwater, may have been more predictable than most. More recent applications to IR are discussed by Sylvan and Chan [65] and in the volume edited by Cimbala [17]. Probably the most promising approach uses the idea of 'pattern-matching' [56, 57] which argues, plausibly enough, that humans do not analyse each new situation from scratch but make use of precedents and analogies from past experience. In other words, we try to match the present with some past pattern. Several AI procedures exist for detecting patterns within large volumes of data – and IR is rich in raw data. Using these may thus be an effective way of understanding events themselves and how decision-makers construe and respond to them. Schrodt argues the case persuasively, while being careful not to overstate what has been achieved so far.

An objection to reliance on pattern-matching is that making decisions on the basis of precedent, while undoubtedly common, can be dysfunctional.

Failures are often caused by inappropriate application of past experience. To distinguish helpful from unhelpful analogies, one may need to model the reasons behind observed patterns of behaviour – a path which perhaps leads back towards some sort of rational actor model. Indeed, there are strong general arguments for trying to combine elements of both approaches. The models derived from Game Theory are attractive in treating decision-makers as fully fledged, reasoning beings. However, the theory has little empirical content of its own, and models often make little use of what is known about the specific actors appearing in them or of results from other forms of conflict analysis. One way forward may thus be to use game-based models as structures within which substantive knowledge can be embedded and used, rather than as purely formal systems [7].

To conclude, this is an area in which promising prospects have again appeared. However, it is important to maintain a sense of caution and especially to avoid mistaking any model, however good, for a complete description of reality. This may spare us another cycle of wild over-optimism and subsequent disappointment.

Bibliography

1. Anderson, Paul and Thorson, Stuart 'Artificial Intelligence Based Simulations of Foreign Policy Decision Making'. *Behavioral Science*, vol. 27, 1982, pp. 176–93.
2. Avenhaus R., Brams, S.J., Fichtner, J. and Kilgour, D.M. 'The Probability of Nuclear War'. *Journal of Peace Research*, vol. 26, no. 1, 1989, pp. 91–9.
3. Axelrod, Robert *The Evolution of Cooperation.* New York, Basic Books, 1984.
4. Belton, Val 'Practically the Only Way to Choose' in L.C. Hendry and R.W. Engelese (eds) *OR Tutorial Papers 1990.* Birmingham, Operational Research Society, 1990.
5. Bennett, Peter G. 'Toward a Theory of Hypergames'. *Omega*, vol. 5, no. 6, 1977, 749–51.
6. Bennett, Peter G. (ed.) *Analysing Conflict and its Resolution: Some Mathematical Contributions.* Oxford and New York, Oxford University Press, 1987.
7. Bennett, Peter 'Modelling Complex Conflicts: Formalism or Expertise?' *Review of International Studies*, vol. 17, no. 4, 1991, pp. 349–64.
8. Bennett, Peter, Tait, Andrew and Macderagh, Kieran 'INTERACT: Developing Software for Interactive Decisions'. *Group Decision and Negotiation*, vol. 3, forthcoming, 1994.
9. Boulding, Kenneth *Conflict and Defense: a General Theory.* New York and London, University Press of America, 1988.
10. Brams, Steven J. *Superpower Games: Applying Game Theory to Superpower Conflict.* New Haven, Yale University Press, 1985.
11. Brams, Steven J. and Kilgour, Marc D. *Game Theory and National Security.* Oxford and New York, Basil Blackwell, 1988.
12. Brams, Steven J. *Negotiation Games: Applying Game Theory to Bargaining and Arbitration.* London and New York, Routledge, 1990.
13. Bueno de Mequita, B. *The War Trap.* New Haven, Yale University Press, 1981.
14. Burton, John *Resolving Deep-Rooted Conflicts.* Lanham, University Press of America, 1987.

15. Cioffi-Revilla, Claudio 'A Probability Model of Credibility: Analyzing Strategic Deterrent Systems'. *Journal of Conflict Resolution*, vol. 27, no. 1, 1983, 73–108.
16. Cioffi-Revilla, Claudio *The Scientific Measurement of International Conflict: Handbook of Datasets on Crises and Wars 1495–1988*. Boulder and London, Lynne Rienner, 1990.
17. Cimbala, S.J. (ed.) *Artificial Intelligence and National Security*. Lexington, Lexington Books, 1987.
18. Diehl, Paul F. 'Arms Races and Escalation: a Closer Look'. *Journal of Peace Research*, vol. 20, no. 3, 1983, pp. 205–12.
19. Faber, Jan 'On Bounded Rationality and the Framing of Decisions in International Relations: Towards a Dynamic Network Model of World Politics'. *Journal of Peace Research*, vol. 27, no. 3, 1990, pp. 307–19.
20. Fiorina, M. 'Formal Models in Political Science'. *American Journal of Political Science*, vol. 19, 1975, pp. 133–59.
21. Forward, Nigel *The Field of Nations: An Account of Some New Approaches to International Relations*. London, Macmillan, 1971.
22. Fraser, Niall M. and Hipel, Keith W. *Conflict Analysis: Models and Resolutions*. New York, North-Holland, 1984.
23. French, Simon (ed.) *Readings in Decision Analysis*. Rockville, Chapman & Hall, 1989.
24. George, A.L. 'The Operational Code; a Neglected Approach to the Study of International Political Leaders and Decision-Making'. *International Studies Quarterly*, vol. 13, no. 2, 1969, pp. 190–222.
25. Gillespie, John V. and Zinnes, Dina A. 'Progressions in Mathematical Models of International Relations'. *Synthese*, vol. 31, no. 2, 1975, pp. 289–321.
26. Green, P. *Deadly Logic: The Theory of Nuclear Deterrence*. Columbus, Ohio State University Press, 1966.
27. Harsanyi, John C. 'Games with Incomplete Information Played by "Bayesian" Players, I–III'. *Management Science*, vol. 14, no. 3, 1967, pp. 159–82.
28. Howard, Nigel *Paradoxes of Rationality: Theory of Metagames and Political Behavior*. Cambridge, MA and London, MIT Press, 1971.
29. Howard, Nigel 'The Present and Future of Metagame Analysis'. *European Journal of Operational Research*, vol. 32, no. 1, 1987, pp. 1–25.
30. Howard, Nigel 'The Manager as Politician and General: the Metagame approach to analysing cooperation and conflict' in Jonathan Rosenhead (ed.) *Rational Analysis for a Problematic World*. New York, Wiley, 1989, pp. 239–62.
31. Howard, Nigel, Bennett, P.G., Bradley, M. and Bryant J. 'Manifesto for a Theory of Drama and Irrational Choice'. *Journal of the Operational Research Society* (viewpoints), vol. 44, no. 1, 1993, pp. 99–103.
32. Intriligator, Michael D. 'Formal Models of the Arms Race'. *Journal of Peace Science*, vol. 2, no. 1, 1976, pp. 77–88.
33. Intriligator, Michael D. 'Conflict Theory Research: Analytical Approaches and Areas of Application'. *Journal of Conflict Resolution*, vol. 26, no. 2, 1982, pp. 307–27.
34. Intriligator, Michael D. and Brito, D.L. 'Nuclear Proliferation and the Probability of Nuclear War'. *Public Choice*, vol. 37, 1981, pp. 41–59.
35. Jervis, Robert 'Realism, Game Theory, and Cooperation'. *World Politics*, vol. 40, no. 3, 1988, pp. 317–49.
36. Lanchester, F.W. *Aircraft in Warfare: the Dawn of the Fourth Arm*. London, Constable, 1916.
37. Luce, Duncan and Raiffa, Howard *Games and Decisions: Introduction and Critical Survey*. New York, John Wiley, 1957.

38. Luterbacher, Urs and Ward, Michael D. (eds) *Dynamic Models of International Conflict*. Boulder, Lynne Rienner, 1985.
39. Meyer, Stephen M. *Nuclear Proliferation: Models of Behavior, Choice and Decision*. Chicago, University of Chicago Press, 1984.
40. Neild, Robert R. 'Accuracy and Lanchester's Law: a Case for Dispersed Defence?' in Peter G. Bennett (ed.) *Analysing Conflict and its Resolution: Some Mathematical Contributions*. Oxford and New York, Oxford University Press, 1987, pp. 235–51.
41. Nicholson, Michael *Formal Theories in International Relations*. Cambridge and New York, Cambridge University Press, 1989.
42. Nicholson, Michael *Rationality and the Analysis of International Conflict*. Cambridge and New York, Cambridge, Cambridge University Press, 1992.
43. Ordeshook, P.C. *Game Theory and Political Theory: An Introduction*. Cambridge and New York, Cambridge University Press, 1986.
44. Quattrone, George and Tversky, Amos 'Contrasting Rational and Psychological Analyses of Political Choice'. *American Political Science Review*, vol. 82, no. 3, 1988, pp. 719–36.
45. Rapoport, Anatol 'Lewis Fry Richardson's Mathematical Theory of War'. *Journal of Conflict Resolution*, vol. 1, no. 3, 1957, pp. 249–99.
46. Rapoport, Anatol *Fights, Games and Debates*. Ann Arbor, University of Michigan Press, 1960.
47. Rapoport, Anatol and Chammah, A.M. *Prisoner's Dilemma: A Study of Conflict and Cooperation*. Ann Arbor, University of Michigan Press, 1965.
48. Reynolds, C. 'Deterrence'. *Review of International Studies*, vol. 15, no. 1, 1989, pp. 67–74.
49. Richardson, Lewis Fry 'Generalised Foreign Politics: A Study in Group Psychology' in Oliver M. Ashford, H. Charnock *et al.* (eds) *Collected Papers of Lewis Fry Richardson, Volume 2: Quantitative psychology and studies of conflict*. Cambridge, Cambridge University Press, 1993, pp. 261–350.
50. Rosenhead, Jonathan (ed.) *Rational Analysis for a Problematic World*. New York, John Wiley, 1989.
51. Saaty, Thomas L. *Mathematical Models of Arms Control and Disarmament*. New York, Wiley, 1968.
52. Saaty, Thomas L. *The Analytic Hierarchy Process*, London and New York, McGraw-Hill, 1980.
53. Saaty, Thomas L. 'Conflict Resolution and the Falklands Islands Invasions'. *Interfaces*, vol. 13, no. 6, December, 1983, pp. 68–83.
54. Saperstein, A.M. 'Chaos – a Model for the Outbreak of War'. *Nature*, no. 309, 1984, pp. 303–5.
55. Schelling, Thomas C. *The Strategy of Conflict*. Cambridge, MA, Harvard University Press, 1960.
56. Schrodt, Philip A. 'Adaptive Precedent-Based Logic and Rational Choice; a Comparison of Two Approaches to the Modelling of International Behavior' in Urs Luterbacher and Michael D. Ward (eds) *Dynamic Models of International Conflict*. Boulder, Lynne Rienner, 1985, pp. 373–400.
57. Schrodt, Philip A. 'Pattern Matching, Set Prediction, and Foreign Policy Analysis' in S.J. Cimbala (ed.) *Artificial Intelligence and National Security*. Lexington, Lexington Books, 1987, pp. 89–107.
58. Schrodt, Philip A. *Preserving Arms Distributions in a Multi-Polar World: A Mathematical Study*. Denver, University of Denver, Monograph Series in World Affairs, 1981.

59. Shubik, Martin *Game Theory and the Social Sciences: Concepts and Solutions.* Cambridge, MIT Press, 1982.
60. Simon, Herbert A. *Reason in Human Affairs.* Oxford, Basil Blackwell and Stanford, Stanford University Press, 1983.
61. Singer, J. David (ed.) *Quantitative International Politics: Insights and Evidence.* New York and London, The Free Press, 1968.
62. Smoker, Paul 'A Mathematical Study of the Present Arms Race'. *General Systems Yearbook*, vol. 8, 1963, pp. 61–76.
63. Snidal, Duncan 'Relative Gain and the Pattern of International Cooperation'. *American Political Science Review*, vol. 85, no. 3, 1991, pp. 701–26.
64. Snyder, Glenn H. and Diesing, Paul *Conflict Among Nations.* Princeton, Princeton University Press, 1977.
65. Sylvan, Donald A. and Chan, Steve *Foreign Policy Decision Making: Perception, Cognition and Artificial Intelligence.* New York, Praeger, 1984.
66. Taylor, M. *The Possibility of Cooperation*, revised edition, Cambridge, Cambridge University Press, 1987.
67. Thomas, Lyn *Games, Theory and Applications.* Chichester, Ellis Horwood, (paperback edition), 1986.
68. Tversky, Amos and Kahnemann, Daniel 'The Framing of Decisions and the Psychology of Choice'. *Science*, vol. 211, no. 4481, 1981, pp. 453–8.
69. Varoufakis, Janis *Rational Conflict.* Oxford and Cambridge, MA, Blackwell, 1991.
70. Von Neumann, J. and Morgenstern, O. *Theory of Games and Economic Behavior.* Princeton, Princeton University Press, 1944.
71. Wagner, Harrison R. 'The Theory of Games and the Balance of Power'. *World Politics*, vol. XXXVIII, no. 4, 1986, pp. 546–76.
72. Wilkinson, David *Deadly Quarrels: Lewis F Richardson and the Statistical Study of War.* Berkeley and London, University of California Press, 1980.
73. Weizenbaum, Joseph *Computer Power and Human Reason: From Judgment to Calculation.* London, Penguin, 1984.
74. Winograd, Terry and Flores, Fernando *Understanding Computers and Cognition: A New Foundation for Design.* Norwood, Ablex Publishing Company, 1986.
75. Wright, George *Behavioural Decision Theory.* London, Penguin, 1984.
76. Zagare, F.C. (ed.) *International Interactions 15: Special Issue on Modelling International Conflict.* 1990.
77. Zinnes, Dina A. and Gillespie, John V. *Mathematical Models in International Relations.* New York, Praeger 1976.
78. Zinnes, Dina, Gillespie, J.V. and Tahim, G.S. 'A Formal Analysis of Some Issues in Balance of Power Theories'. *International Studies Quarterly*, vol. 22, no. 3, 1978, pp. 323–56.

Part 4
Beyond the Anglo-American Tradition

16 The world beyond: the European dimension

A.J.R. Groom*

International Relations became an academic discipline in 1919, in the aftermath of the Great War, with the establishment of a Chair in the University of Wales at Aberystwyth. Other Chairs followed quickly at Oxford and LSE in Britain as well as in the United States. Research institutes flourished too, at Chatham House in London and the Council on Foreign Relations in New York. The foundations of a discipline were being laid with stones cut in an 'Anglo-Saxon' mould. To be sure influences from continental scholars writing in English were to make a great impact later, but diplomatic historians in Britain and international lawyers in the United States had already set the frame into which the contributions of others were fitted. Thus, paradoxically, a subject whose vocation was global emerged in a manner that was surprisingly parochial.

Given the limited foreign language skills of many Anglo-American scholars and the formidable linguistic skills of many continental emigrés to Britain and the USA, this tendency to parochialism was enhanced. It has bred a certain lazy arrogance that if there is anything worthwhile in the world beyond English it will eventually find its way into the discipline because English is the *lingua franca* of the field. It is important too that we consider the implications of a particular language being the principal language of discourse for a subject. By its structure, its metaphors and its vocabulary any language imposes a pattern of thought which reflects a particular culture, yet the vocation of IR is the political sociology of global society. To view IR through the prism of one language is therefore rather like observing a

* While absolving them from any imperfections of the final product, grateful thanks are due to Fulvio Attinà, Esther Barbé, Bojko Bucar, Ricardo Caldas, Gerald Chan, Jean-Luc Domenach, Philip Everts, Michel Girard, Kjell Goldmann, Gunther Hellmann, Helge Hveem, Beate Kohler-Koch, Ekkehart Krippendroff, Paul Luif, Volker Rittberger, Jean-Jacques Roche, Dieter Senghaas, Anselm Skuhra, Marie-Claude Smouts, Ben Soetendorp, Jean-Philippe Thérien, Ivan Tiouline, László Valki, Raimo Väyrynen, Thanos Veremis and Pedro Vilanova.

219

mountain only from one vantage point. What we see may be true, but it is far from being the whole truth. At a more mundane level, anyone who has given a lecture in a foreign language knows that they are not saying quite the same thing as they would in their own language. The prominence of one language, therefore, is a grave weakness for the subject.

To some extent this has been mitigated through translation or by scholars from different cultures writing in English, but a translation is either different or second best – it cannot be the real thing. Moreover, to write in a foreign language means being the prisoner of it, although we have reason to be grateful to a Morgenthau [75], or a Schwarzenberger [86], a Deutsch [31] or a Mitrany [74].

This chapter cannot aspire to open a window on the intellectual world beyond English, but merely a shaft of light, and one limited to European languages at that. Furthermore, apart from the literature in French, this survey is based entirely on the responses of a small number of correspondents chosen in an highly eclectic manner. For the most part, the literature written in or translated into English is ignored since it is readily available to the authors of foregoing chapters. Usually an English translation of titles will be referred to in the text, and the original language title will be given in the reference section. The eclecticism of the selection and the concentration on untranslated indigenous literature means that no attempt has been made to undertake a proper survey of the study of IR in any particular country.

Correspondents were asked to bring to our attention major contemporary works of theory which have been published in the last decade or so and any classics in the field that are not readily available to scholars working in English. In a number of instances the comments of correspondents have been quoted directly without acknowledgement but with permission. To have done otherwise would have been to encumber the chapter with an inappropriate scholarly apparatus for its purpose.

A number of general conclusions can be drawn from the literature in languages other than English. With the exception perhaps of the German, Dutch and Scandinavian language areas, the disciplinary base of IR is very weak. This has both advantages and disadvantages. The advantages lie in the potential for interdisciplinary cross-fertilization, but this is infrequent because all too rarely do scholars in the field constitute a critical mass for research or for the development of a school of thought. Thus, scholars tend to become clones, either of the nearest discipline to hand or of the predominant Anglo-American framework. It is particularly noticeable that textbooks in indigenous languages are often highly derivative of the Anglo-American framework and especially of North American positivism. Although British influence on the discipline was great in the inter-war period and has recently been increasing again, the overwhelming influence has been from scholars working in North America. Given that writing in North America is itself parochial [50], we are in great danger of creating a closed system.

One result of the overwhelming dominance of English and of North America in the subject overall has been that those writing in indigenous languages have tended to resort to intellectual niches which are almost

guaranteed to them by their language. Thus, they have confined themselves
to area studies, or to the study of the foreign policy of particular actors
where the native language gives an edge to local scholars. Nevertheless, in
some respects locating one's research neither in the language of power nor in
a country at the top of a global power hierarchy can be liberating; thus
alternative defence theories have come predominantly from Europe and
peace studies from the Netherlands, Germany and Scandinavia. The tendency
to parochialism is not, however, restricted to the 'Anglo-Saxons', as the
many studies on neutrality in neutral countries or of the *tiers-monde* in
France attest.

As conceived in Britain and the United States in the early 1920s, IR had a
practical task: the scientific understanding of the causes of war and of the
conditions for peace. It had, therefore, a policy vocation, which linked it
closely in conceptual thinking to the political establishment with the
movement from a consensus on liberal internationalism in the 1920s to one
on realism in the 1940s paralleling the international situation. This is also
the case in some other European countries, although in several cases this was
counterbalanced in the 1960s and 1970s by a penchant for analyses in a
Marxist-Leninist tradition. Such a tradition was largely alien to the Anglo-
American intellectual framework, and moreover, it was considered politically
disreputable, condoned only as eccentricity on the part of a few. Indeed, the
present vogue for structuralist analyses in the Anglo-American literature
owes its origin to its prevalence in writing in French, Spanish and German.
One other respect in which the literature in English owes a considerable debt
to the literature in other European languages is that concerned with the
Third World, itself a concept taken from French.

For the purposes of this chapter, the literature is grouped by language or
region, some languages themselves constituting a region: namely French,
German, and Dutch as well as the Scandinavian, East European and
Mediterranean regions. The division is as arbitrary as the selection of works
is eclectic.

The French-speaking world

For IR this world is limited to the French language communities in Belgium,
Canada and Switzerland as well as to France itself. In addition, some
scholars beyond these communities use French as an international medium.
While France may dominate in numbers of scholars and works, there is a
substantial IR community in French Canada centred upon Montreal, Ottawa
and Quebec City [58]. However, it seems to constitute more a sub-North
American grouping in its academic ties and aspirations than a French or
Euro-centric group. Similarly, in the Suisse romande, intellectual ties seem to
be strongly transatlantic rather than European. Perhaps this is because the
Graduate Institute of International Studies in Geneva is bilingual (French and
English), and, as the principal focal point for IR in Switzerland with historic
ties stretching back to 1928, its finance and its English-speaking student

body have been primarily linked with the United States. While IR is well established in the political science department at Louvain-la-Neuve which has just celebrated its centenary, the Walloon IR community is a small one.

There can be little doubt that French social science has been very influential at the international level. Indeed, it has impressive achievements which put it at the acknowledged forefront to be emulated by others. It is hard, however, to avoid the impression that IR is not at the cutting edge of French social science and therefore not in the forefront internationally. Part of this may be due to an identity problem. The subject is rarely an acknowledged part of a social science faculty, and where, as is often the case, it is linked organically with political science, it is usually as a junior partner. The subject lacks a full range of teaching and research centres on a national scale, there are few professors and students and most academic journals are not of a conceptual nature. In short, a well-established organizational framework is missing.

Although there are many respected IR scholars in France, they do not constitute a critical mass. Moreover, they are separated from each other and spread among a wide range of differing faculties. There is no professional association, and networks or invisible colleges of scholars are rare. Thus, the preconditions for growth and for IR to become one of France's leading social sciences are not yet in place. However, the necessary intellectual resources and the growing interest are sufficient for growth to occur relatively quickly. Smouts has written a brief review of IR in France [90] and, Hoffman, perhaps significantly not a Frenchman, wrote the IR chapter in Grawitz and Leca's survey of political science as a whole [44]. On the more limited subject of international organization, Thérien [94] offers a French Canadian view which is full of insights. Lyons has provided a well-known and still useful 'francophile' survey [66].

For the outsider, there are a number of obstacles to understanding the study of IR in France. The organizational and structural map of French academic life is difficult to read so that establishing ties and making contacts are no easy matters. The status of French academics is also confusing for those used to the English-speaking world. As civil servants, French academics appear to be much closer to government and to the state than would be the case in the English language world. This is not, of course, to impugn their academic freedom but simply to note that the state, and particularly state finance and state educational objectives, play a much greater part in French academic life than they do in the English language world.

The French academic structure is hierarchical and competitive to a degree which is alien to the English language world. This contributes to, and indeed facilitates, what seems to outsiders to be the closed world of French academic life, particularly in IR. It is a life that is turned in upon itself and one which, because of its particular structure, is difficult for outsiders to penetrate. Few persist. This factor of closure may also help to explain why French scholars play a surprisingly and regrettably minor role in the international discourse. For them it seems not to be the natural extension of academic life at home but rather an alien environment made more so, perhaps, through being dominated in the case of IR by an academic discourse and language that is Anglo-American. Happily, however, this state of affairs is changing rapidly.

Nevertheless, the relative isolation of the French academic world does have advantages. It gives IR world-wide an element of diversity and an independent academic discourse. To the outsider the shock of the new and of the different can be salutary. There is a separate, autonomous, intellectual agenda and academic discourse.

Given the French penchant for intellectualizing, it is quite startling to discover that the French study of IR is largely atheoretical. The failure of French scholars to take to IR theory may lie in the legal intellectual tradition and the home that IR and political science have often found in law faculties in France. A recent example of such writing is Touscoz's monograph [96]. The IR literature in France seems to be tied firmly to the conceptual notion of a state-centric world, as would befit its legal origins and strong legalistic traditions. Where IR is conceived more from a sociological, political or economic point of view, the degree of state-centricity lessens. While there have been some major contributions to IR theory by French authors, they have not usually been of startling originality.

The work of Aron, himself a sociologist, has been translated into English and widely read beyond the Hexagon. Aron puts an acceptable face on realism. However, his major work for IR, *Peace and War: A Theory of International Relations* [3], was 20 years behind Carr's *The Twenty Years' Crisis* [23] and Schwarzenberger's *Power Politics* [86]. His formulation was clear and he offered some interesting insights, but the subject was not moved forward. The same might be said of the writing of Merle. He is clearly an important figure in France, but the study of the subject outside of France would not have faltered without his contribution. Nevertheless, his rather gloomy essay on the 'problématique' of IR studies in France [71] and his works on actors [69] in, and the sociology of, IR repay reading [70]. *Forces et Enjeux* in IR is a collection of his essays [68]. The international importance of Aron and Merle is that they are shared between French scholars and the outside world and have been widely read both in France and beyond. Thus, they constitute a starting point for a discourse.

The recent conceptual work of Badie and Smouts is an exciting breath of fresh air [6, 5]. Their joint monograph [6] develops Merle's approach, taking us far beyond the state system into a world characterized by issues, processes and structures emanating from society, culture and politics at a global level. But neither they nor we are yet on firm analytical ground, although they are helping to clear the way. In a different way French scholars also make a valuable contribution. It is always stimulating to read a good conjunctural analysis by French writers whether daily in *Le Monde*, in a recent collection by Laïdi [62] or the writings of Zorgbibe [104] or Grosser [45, 46], who is one of the rare specialists in French foreign policy and an expert on Franco-German relations. Ideas flow and the arguments frequently sting the sensibilities of the 'Anglo-Saxon' mind and its *amour propre*. The contribution of Hassner to conferences and the like is a case in point. Two writers in the Suisse romande, Braillard and de Senarclens, have also made a mark in preparing excellent textbooks in IR theory [18, 20, 19, 26].

In one major sub-field of the study of IR in particular – strategic studies – the conceptual contribution of French writers has been considerable. In the hey-day of that subject in the 1960s, the contributions of Generals Beaufre [11, 10] and Gallois [41] were considerable. Indeed, both are major theorists of deterrence who formulated clearly different conceptions of that notion from the principal writers, and indeed practitioners, of strategic studies in the English-speaking world. At the same time Debray [28, 27] was introducing the English-speaking world to many of the theoretical concepts of Latin-American revolutionaries, and adding his own contribution to that particular aspect of strategic studies. The writings of Beaufre, Gallois and Debray were, for the most part, translated into English, and they exerted a considerable influence as well as gaining, for different reasons, a certain intellectual notoriety. Strategic studies continue to be a fecund field in France, as the publications of CEDSI in Grenoble and other centres attest. Among recent monographs that of Poirier [81] is noteworthy, and the tradition of polemology long associated with the name of Bouthoul lives on in Bigo and Hermant's volume [14]. Klein's work is well known among arms controls specialists beyond France [55].

It is not surprising, given the general strength of the social sciences in France, that work in other areas should impinge upon the study of IR. Mention has already been made of the strength of French legal studies and their influence beyond France, particularly in other Latin countries. However, there are at least three other major areas of conceptual influence and one which is likely to be of growing influence in the future.

The phrase 'tiers monde' or Third World was adopted by scholars in the English language world – an indication of innovation. The French contribution to development studies, and in the conceptualization of the Third World in general, has been significant. One individual whose standing is high is the economist Perroux [79]. The question of development studies leads quickly on to structural analyses. The reassertion of such analyses in the mainstream of Anglo-American IR has had not a little to do with the French-inspired conception of the tiers monde, but there is more to it than that. It was not for nothing that Wallerstein named his centre after Braudel [21]. It would not be an exaggeration to say that Braudel has had an immense indirect conceptual influence upon the contemporary study of IR from a conceptual point of view, particularly but not exclusively in North America.

Another such pervasive, indirect (if baleful) conceptual influence has been that of the postmodernists. Ironically, while Foucault and Co. [38, 37, 39, 36] are passé in Paris, they are exciting young minds in the English-speaking world. Less obtusely, the longstanding French interest in political geography [33], and its high standing in the academic world, is likely to be of seminal influence beyond the borders of France. In the English-speaking world, political geography is poised to enter once again into the mainstream of the study of IR. The leading French place in this field will have an indirect influence on the study of IR elsewhere in the decades to come, since political geography is likely to constitute one of the cutting edges of our discipline in the near future. Thus, once again, the French intellectual influence on the global study of IR from a conceptual point of view is more likely to be indirect than direct. But what of empirical work undertaken in France?

It is this aspect of French IR which strikes the outside observer as being most productive. The contribution of French Africanists and Orientalists is outstanding. In part their excellence is one of the happier legacies of Empire, but it also denotes a continued intellectual openness to the world in area studies which is curiously lacking in both the university system in general and in theoretical approaches to IR. Moreover, French scholars, being intellectuals, often present their empirical work in a contextual setting that leads to a happy fusion of conceptual musings and empirical detail. Nevertheless, there is a curious *lacuna* in the study of European integration. Given the central role of France in this enterprise, it is surprising, to say the least, that neither in conceptual nor empirical studies have French-speaking scholars led the way, although the Belgian scholar Barréa [9] is an exception to the rule.

The German-speaking world

The German-speaking IR world is dominated by the community of scholars in Germany, but in the last two decades there have been some significant developments in Austria which have yet to find a counterpart in German-speaking Switzerland. Perhaps the latter is to be explained by the concentration of research in the field in the Suisse romande with the almost solitary exception of the late and lamented Frei [40]. The German-speaking world is more outward looking than the French, particularly towards the United States. Moreover, practically every scholar is able to use English as a working language and frequently does. In part, this is because German is not a global language, and in part, it is due to the occupation of both Germany and Austria and the prior emigration of major scholars such as Morgenthau, Deutsch and Schwarzenberger and scholar–practitioners such as Kissinger to the English-language world.

The development of political science in Germany was brought to a rude halt by the Nazis. It was re-established in West Germany in the 1960s with a sizeable IR component. In East Germany, Western standards of academic freedom did not prevail. In any case, there has since been a rather unseemly wholesale dismantling of structures and the sacking of individuals, notwithstanding that some such individuals had managed to preserve a degree of integrity in difficult circumstances and had potentially much to offer.

The Nazi and Soviet past has also had an influence on the way IR has been treated in Germany. The geopolitical and Marxist traditions are both heavily imbued with historical resonances. Nevertheless, the study of IR in Germany has been noteworthy for a non-Soviet Marxist interpretation, particularly in the areas of peace research and North–South relations. One reason for this is that the study of IR in the German-speaking world came of age after the emotional and political upheavals of May 1968 in Paris and the Vietnam War. Earlier, as political science and IR found its feet, the teaching and research staff had tended to come from history, law and journalism, whereas in the late 1960s a new generation of young scholars came to the fore with a radical intellectual agenda.

In Austria there was a somewhat different agenda which reflected particular Austrian concerns such as neutrality [15, 76], the role of small states [49] and Austrian foreign policy [59]. In addition there was a concern for East–West relations and developments in the Third World. The Continental tradition of international law also trickled on in the burgeoning IR community.

Although the three German-speaking areas are physically contiguous and there is an element of centre–periphery in their relationship, they form three distinct communities. What is more, in Germany IR is closely linked with political science and is not institutionally separate in terms of a professional association. Indeed, in political science generally, there was some rivalry between professional associations, each of which has an IR section. This rivalry is now a thing of the past with the international politics section of the Germany Association of Political Science (DVPW) taking the lead and establishing its own journal. This division, the close association with the North American IR community and the subsequent activity in English, has lessened the potential impact of what is a sizeable community of scholars, although there are some indications that the IR community in Germany is developing its own specific *persona*.

Although much research in Germany has been presented in English, textbooks are important for teaching purposes. Czempiel's [25] introductory text for students not only portrays existing approaches to, and models of, IR but sets out Czempiel's own process-oriented model of international politics as a form of cascading interdependence. Another book that offers an overview of, and an introduction to, German IR research is that of Rittberger [84]. This edited volume has more than 20 contributors and gives the reader a flavour of the German IR community. Knapp and Krell [56] have edited perhaps the most up-to-date and comprehensive textbook in German with chapters on the discipline in general, the main actors and issue areas in IR. Moreover, it introduces the reader to the specialist literature.

Krippendorff published two books in the mid-1980s [61, 60] concerned with modern state formation over a long historical period, relating, in particular, to the role of the military in state formation and the simultaneous expansion of the European state on a world-wide basis through colonialism and imperialism. At the same time, Krippendorff's colleague Albrecht [1] produced an analysis of the contemporary system using the concept of dominance as the key to understanding political structures in general and the international system in particular. A related interest in structures, foundations, institutions and interests remains evident [105]. As might be expected in an intellectual community renowned for the production of philosophical giants, the study of IR in Germany frequently reflects philosophical concerns. An example of this is Meyers's [73] well-researched and documented introduction to the philosophical foundations of IR. An edited volume by Bellers and Woyke [12] provides a survey of methods for analysing IR.

German writers have developed a significant interest in international political economy, particularly in terms of North–South relationships. Elsenhans [35] seeks to demonstrate that Third World underdevelopment can be explained satisfactorily neither by structural dependency on the developed countries nor by the existence of indigenous capitalist structures. Instead, he analyses the formation of a class of bureaucrats which appropriates the surplus for investment with the aim of enhancing its own privileges and to secure its legitimacy by way of clientelism. Senghaas's [88] historical critique of developmental theory is based on comparative historical research of the varied developmental experience of European societies which he uses to enrich the discussion of development strategies for contemporary developing countries. This book has now been translated into English and was received with glowing reviews. Menzel's [67] highly topical intellectual history of Third World studies comes to the conclusion that the grand theories, strategies and policies in the field of development have failed.

It was in the area of conflict studies that German IR first made a significant impact beyond the confines of the German-speaking world. A seminal role was played by the Hessische Stiftung für Friedens und Konfliktforschung which remains a leader in the field [24]. Each year the three principal peace research institutes publish a *Friedensgutachten* or experts' report on peace. Since the 1960s the name of Senghaas [87] has been one to conjure with, and Gantzel is also in the forefront [42]. Not surprisingly, the East–West conflict has excited a good deal of German interest. Link [65] offers an original German contribution to this debate. Haftendorn's contribution on foreign policy has also been widely noted in Germany and abroad [48]. German scholars, especially the Tübingen School led by Rittberger, have been particularly innovative, both conceptually and in their empirical work, in using regime analysis in the context of the East–West conflict system. The edited volumes by the Rittberger team [34, 83] and by Kohler-Koch [57] bear witness to German strength in this field.

Finally, an overview of all these developments can be found in the third volume of the *Survey of Political Science*, which deals with foreign policy and IR [101]. Despite all its impressive achievements, German IR seems to lack self-confidence and an institutional *persona*. The training of many German IR specialists in the United States has clearly borne fruit, but it has probably also detracted from an intellectual independence which would be to the benefit of all.

The Dutch-related world

The IR community in the Netherlands has had an historical significance for, and makes a continuing contribution to, the wider IR community in the English medium. The particular historical contribution can be illustrated by the early development of peace research in the Netherlands, centred on Groningen, and the personal contribution to integration theory of Lijphart [63]. Since the International Court of Justice is in The Hague it is hardly surprising that historically there has been a strong international legal influence in Dutch writing on IR. At present the Dutch IR community writes mainly in English, and while it may not have such a high profile as in the past, it has a solid basis in a number of universities which gives rise to a stream of publications not only on Dutch-related topics but more generally.

In Belgium, the Dutch language community has easy access to two international languages but, like the French-speaking community in that country, it seems not to have made its mark. This is surprising given the large amount of international activity that takes place in Belgium, at both the governmental and non-governmental level. In South Africa, the Afrikaans-speaking community likewise has easy access to an international medium, and the bi-lingualism of the state has meant that many Afrikaner scholars of note publish in English as well as Afrikaans. The literature from South Africa is considered in Chapter 17.

There remains, nevertheless, especially in the Netherlands, a noteworthy literature which is only available in Dutch. Lijphart's inaugural lecture [64] for example is a classic on the paradigm debate of the 1960s. Soetendorp and van Staden [92] give the views of several members of the Dutch IR community on contending theories in IR. There is a similar overview in a recent issue of *Acta Politica* [91]. Monographs on particular topics include an analysis by Baehr of human rights [7] and two published doctoral theses, one on the ethical debate about nuclear deterrence [100] and the other a critical analysis of Morgenthau's theory [77]. Finally, note should be made of a popular introduction to peace research by one of its founding fathers, Röling [85]. The major contributions of Dutch scholars are, however, usually available in English.

The Scandinavian world

The English-medium IR world is much in debt to its Scandinavian colleagues who have made major contributions in such areas as peace and conflict research, development studies and foreign policy analysis. Moreover, Scandinavian journals such as the *Journal of Peace Research, Cooperation and Conflict* and *Security Dialogue* are read the world over. Since practically everything noteworthy in the field of IR in the Scandinavian countries is published in English, it is, therefore, reflected amply in other chapters.

Scandinavian scholars have developed close ties with the IR community in North America, and indeed, have become leaders of the field there, as in the case of the Holsti brothers. Furthermore, the Scandinavians have also developed links with the British IR community. Although the Scandinavian community is a very open one, there is a distinct Scandinavian network which is exemplified not only in the journals but also in the recent establishment of a Nordic International Studies Association.

Leaving aside the impressive contribution to the literature in English, some Scandinavian works have not been translated, many of them concerned with regional or national issues in Scandinavia. A more general view is offered by Goldmann [43], whose textbook makes a clear distinction between the security–political international system and the economic–political international system. National issues are represented by Apunen's study of Finland's foreign policy which integrates theoretical perspectives with historical and political analyses [2] and two works by Hveem which consider Norway's role in a new international economic order [51] and Norway in the world [52]. Finally, note should be taken of a major study by von Bonsdorff, [102] published in both Swedish and Finnish, which is an analysis of the historical evolution of international society and the impact of war and technology upon it. The book also considers various methods by which permanent peace may be achieved.

The Mediterranean countries

Four countries on the Northern shore of the Mediterranean have much in common in so far as the study of IR is concerned. In Italy, Spain, Greece and Turkey, the number of scholars is small but the subject is beginning now to take root. A small but firm base is being created in each country, and although the main media of communication are English or French at the international level, a literature in the indigenous languages exists. In most cases, scholars find themselves in departments of political science or law and have to struggle to establish the validity of their subject. They are likely, however, to win the battle.

In Italy, IR is approximately 20 years old, but in another sense it is far older. For example, the influence of Machiavelli has been great in political science and IR throughout the Western world. Moreover, in current research attention is once again being given to Gramsci, and most political scientists know of the names and work of Pareto and Mosca. Strategists, too, acknowledge Douhet as one of their founding fathers. Thus, Italian authors have been a formative part of our political and social culture.

In the more narrowly circumscribed world of recent conceptual publications, Bonanate has published an important essay on the *Concept of Order in International Politics* [17], and more recently his *Ethics and International Politics* has provided a thoughtful contribution to the growing international interest in the normative aspects of IR [16]. Attinà's *Contemporary International Politics* [4] stresses the importance of rules and institutions in the organization of the international system and explains international change by utilizing the concept of international cleavages. Papasca and Mascia [78] move away from state-centric theories and look towards pluralistic world society approaches, thus providing a different paradigmatic framework.

The situation in Spain is very similar to that in Italy in terms of academic structure and activity. A literature in Spanish has begun to circulate over the last 20 years and del Arenal's [30] *Theory of IR in Spain* deals with IR as a discipline in that country. The founder of modern Spanish IR is Truyol y Serra [98] and his *Theory of IR as Sociology*, first published in 1957, proved to be a seminal work in the Spanish context. Later he looked at the historical development of international society, paying particular attention to the development of international law and international organizations and the role of transnational actors. [97] Mesa introduced a Marxist approach to Spanish IR [72]. The most widely used textbook in Spain at the moment is by del Arenal [29]. Spanish authors are also beginning to write substantial commentaries on the works of established authors in the field such as Barbé's introductory essay to a selection of the works of Morgenthau [8].

In Greece and Turkey there has been a significant expansion in the area of IR, although the base is very small. In the Greek case this has been helped by the return to Greece of well-known scholars from overseas, as well as that of young scholars who have gone abroad for their doctoral research but who are now beginning to build careers in Greece. For the most part, these scholars publish in English or French, since this enables them to contribute directly to the international mainstream in IR.

The same may be said of Turkey, except that the university system is much larger, giving a stronger incentive to produce monographs for the Turkish-language market. As in Greece, the standard of acceptance in the university system is publication in an international language. Research, therefore, tends to be published abroad with texts or analytical articles on current policy being published at home in the indigenous language.

Eastern Europe

The academic framework in Eastern Europe has undergone as revolutionary change since 1989 as has its political and economic structure. In some ways the pecking order has changed. In the past the academies of science had large numbers of well-staffed research institutes, many of which produced work of doubtful quality, while the universities were concerned essentially with teaching and had less prestige. The scale of the research institutes in many East European countries was staggering when compared with Western Europe in terms of numbers. Bulgaria, for example, had a research infrastructure in the social sciences more appropriate to a country the size of Britain. All this has now changed. Many of the academy institutes have been abolished and their personnel sacked. Others have been privatized, and university academics in the universities are now envied, not so much for their salaries which are derisory, forcing academics to take two or three jobs, but because at least they provide steady employment.

As one researcher from Eastern Europe put it, in a subject like IR where research was highly politicized, 'we couldn't write anything worthwhile beforehand, and we are having to learn how to do it now'. But this is being attempted at a time when there is no hard currency available for the purchase of books and journals, and even the basic materials for research, such as photocopying, are in short supply. The process of academic liberalization began before the political changes of 1989, and while some countries have changed their academic structure entirely, others, such as Hungary, have had a more evolutionary process. To illustrate the literature from Eastern Europe, we shall cite examples from a country with a large academic establishment, namely Russia, and that from a small country, Slovenia.

Dolnykova's [32] book on *The Methodology and Techniques of Forecasting Foreign Policy in Non-Socialist Countries* gives an interesting review of what Soviet authors made of Western theories and approaches before the great changes. Pozdnyakov's [82] book is a pioneering attempt for that time, using a systems approach to elaborate on the theoretical and methodological aspects of foreign policy and IR. The Soviet penchant for modelling was revealed in Khroustalev's [54] study of basic frameworks for developing formal approaches to, and modelling of, IR. Two young scholars, Zagorski and Lebedeva [103], provided the first attempt in the Russian literature to develop a methodological approach to the study of the process of negotiations, while Tiuline [95] edited a unique collection which attempted to combine methodological frameworks with applied research in the context of several case studies. Thus this literature reveals an early attempt at rigour. Previous Soviet IR literature revealed an acute awareness of developments in the West. Since 1991, however, most Russian IR scholars have been consumed with problems of conceptualizing Russian foreign policy.

In the case of Slovenia it is interesting and understandable that the focus of interest has similarly shifted from global issues to the European region and especially to issues concerned with Slovenia as a new and independent state. This can be seen in the edited volumes by Simoniti [89] on *Europe 1992*, and Bucar [22] on the emergence of Slovenian statehood. However, textbooks, such as that by Benko [13], and monographs are published on a variety of subjects such as Svetlicic [93] on transnational corporations, Juznic [53] on *Colonialism and Decolonisation*, Türk [99] on non-intervention and Petric [80] on the international aspects of the right to self-determination. This literature perhaps reflects the pivotal position of the former Yugoslavia in the non-aligned movement.

The East European academic world is at present catastrophic, but there is great potential, since there is now a significant possibility of exercising academic integrity, even if the physical means to do so are sadly lacking. Moreover, there is an intellectual curiosity that now can be given full rein, and some younger and older scholars are taking advantage of this. It was especially difficult for IR scholars to maintain academic freedom as conceived in a Western sense in the past. For ordinary mortals, compromise was necessary and it ill-behoves privileged West Europeans to cast the first stone. East Europeans have to put their own house in order, but they can be helped by a sympathetic exposition of Western academic standards and perhaps by volumes such as this.

Conclusion

The IR literature in Europe in languages other than English is considerable, but its impact is not commensurate with its size or its quality. Differences of language, poor institutional backing and the absence of professional associations frequently prevent the growth of research networks which could create a critical mass. However, these impediments are slowly being removed. The exchanges of students and staff through the ERASMUS programme and the TEMPUS programme are beginning to have an effect. The first pan-European conference on IR held at Heidelberg in September 1992 proved a great success in that more than 200 papers were presented at a conference attended by over 400 scholars from all parts of Europe. The second such conference will be held in Paris in September 1995, and in the meantime a *European Journal of IR*, published by Sage, is about to be launched. At the same time, the Annual Joint Sessions of workshops of the European Consortium for Political Research usually include several workshops with an IR theme. Thus networks are being built up slowly, and transnational research groups are emerging. With luck and hard work, by the time the successor volume to this handbook is published, the study of IR in Europe will be flourishing on a pan-European basis.

Bibliography

1. Albrecht, Ulrich *Internationale Politik*. Munich, Vienna, Oldenbourg Verlag, 1986.
2. Apunen, Osmo *Paasikiven-Kekkosen linja*. Helsinki, Tammi, 1977.
3. Aron, Raymond *Peace and War: A Theory of International Relations*. Melbourne, FL, Frieger, 1981.
4. Attinà, Fulvio *La Politica Internazionale Contemporanea*. Milan, Angeli, 1989.
5. Badie, Bertrand *Culture et politique*, third edition. Paris, Economica, 1993.
6. Badie, Bertrand and Smouts, Marie-Claude *Le retournement du monde – sociologie de la scène internationale*. Paris, Dalloz, 1992.
7. Baehr, P.R. *Mensenrechten*. Meppel, Boom, 1989.
8. Barbé, Esther, 'Estudio preliminar', en *Escritos sobre política internacional de Hans J. Morgenthau*. Madrid, Tecnos, 1990.
9. Barréa, Jean *L'intégration politique externe*. Louvain, Nauwelaerts, 1969.
10. Beaufre, André *Deterrence and Strategy*. London, Faber, 1965.
11. Beaufre, André *Introduction à la Stratégie*. Paris, Economica, 1985.
12. Bellers, Jürgen and Woyke, Wichard (eds) *Analyse internationaler Beziehungen*. Opladen, Leske und Budrich, 1989.
13. Benko, Vlado *Mednarodni odnosi*. Maribor, Zalozba Obzorja, 1987.
14. Bigo, Didier and Hermant, Daniel (eds) *Approches polémologiques*. Paris, Fondation pour les études de défense nationale, 1991.
15. Birnbaum, Karl E. and Neuhold, Hanspeter (eds) *Neutrality and Non-Alignment in Europe*. Vienna, Wilhelm Braumüller, 1981.
16. Bonante, Luigi *Etica e Politica Internazionale*. Turin, Einaudi, 1992.
17. Bonanate, Luigi, 'Sistema Internazionale' in Luigi Bonanate (ed.) *Politica Internazionale*. Florence, La Nuova, 1979.
18. Braillard, Philippe *Théories des systèmes et relations internationales*. Brussels, Bruylant, 1977.
19. Braillard, Philippe *Théories des relations internationales*. Paris, PUF, 1977.
20. Braillard, Philippe 'The Social Sciences and the study of international relations'. *International Journal of Social Science*, vol. 36, no. 102, 1984, pp. 627–42.
21. Braudel, Fernand *Civilisation matérielle, économie et capitalisme XVe – XVIIIe siècle*. Paris, Colin, 1979, 3 vols.

22. Bucar, Bojko (ed.) *Nastajanje slovenske drzavnosti (Zbornik referatov): Slovenija in svet.* Ljubljana, Slovenski politolosko drustva, 1992.
23. Carr, E.H. *The Twenty Years' Crisis.* London, Macmillan, 1981.
24. Czempiel, Ernst-Otto *Friedensstrategien. Systemwandel durch Internationale Organisationen, Demokratisierung und Wirtschaft.* Paderborn, Ferdinand Schöningh, 1986.
25. Czempiel, Ernst-Otto *Internationale Politik.* Paderborn, Ferdinand Schöningh, 1981.
26. de Senarclens, Pierre *La politique internationale.* Paris, Colin, 1992.
27. Debray, Régis *A Critique of Arms.* Harmondsworth, Penguin, 1977.
28. Debray, Régis *Revolution in the Revolution.* Harmondsworth, Penguin, 1967.
29. del Arenal, Celestino *Introducción a las relaciones internacionales.* Madrid, Tecnos, 1990.
30. del Arenal, Celestino *La Teoría de las Relaciones Internacionales en España.* Madrid, International Law Association, 1979.
31. Deutsch, Karl *The Nerves of Government.* New York, Free Press, 1964.
32. Dolnykova, Ripsime N. *Metodologiya i metodika prognozirovaniya vneshney politiki nesotsialiaticheslikh gosudarstv.* Moscow, Nauka, 1986.
33. Durand, Marie-François *et al.* *Le monde – espaces et systèmes.* Paris, Dalloz, 1992.
34. Efinger, Manfred, Rittberger, Volker and Zürn, Michael *Internationale Regime in den Ost-West-Beziehungen.* Frankfurt-on-Main, Haag und Herchen, 1988.
35. Elsenhans, Hartmut *Abhängiger Kapitalismus oder bürokratische Entwicklungsgesellschaft. Versuch über den Staat in der Dritten Welt.* Frankfurt, New York, Campus, 1981.
36. Foucault, Michel *Histoire de la sexualité.* Paris, Gallimard, 1976–78, 3 vols.
37. Foucault, Michel *L'archéologie du savoir.* Paris, Gallimard, 1969.
38. Foucault, Michel *Les mots et les choses.* Paris, Gallimard, 1966.
39. Foucault, Michel *Surveiller et punir.* Paris, Gallimard, 1975.
40. Frei, Daniel *Internationale Zusammenarbeit. Theoretische Ansätze und empirische Beiträge.* Konigstein/Taunus, Athenäum, 1982.
41. Gallois, Pierre *Balance of Terror.* Boston, Houghton Mifflin, 1961.
42. Gantzel, Klaus Jürgen (ed.) *Die Kriege nach dem Zweiten Weltkrieg bis 1990. Daten und Tendenzen.* Hamburg, LIT, 1992.
43. Goldmann, Kjell *Det internationella systemet: en teori och dess begränsningar.* Stockholm, Aldus/Bonniers, 1978.
44. Grawitz, Madeleine and Leca, Jean (eds) *Traité de science politique* Vol. 1. Paris, PUF, 1985.
45. Grosser, Alfred *Affaires extérieres: la politique de la France 1944–1984.* Paris, Flammarion, 1984.
46. Grosser, Alfred *L'Allemagne en occident: La Républic fédérale 40 ans après.* Paris, Fayard, 1984.
47. Haftendorn, Helga *Sicherheit und Entspannung. Zur Außenpolitik der Bundesrepublik Deutschland 1955–1982.* Baden-Baden, Nomos, 1986.
48. Haftendorn, Helga and Schlissler, Jakob (eds) *Rekonstruktion amerikanischer Stärke. Sicherheits-und Rustungskontrollpolitik der USA während der Reagon-Administration.* Berlin, de Gruyter, 1988.
49. Höll, Otmar (ed.) *Small States in Europe and Dependence.* Vienna, Wilhelm Braumüller, 1983.
50. Holsti, Kalevi, J. *The Dividing Discipline.* Boston, Allen & Unwin, 1985.
51. Hveem, Helge *En ny ekonomik verdensordusing og Norge.* Oslo, Universitetsforlaget, 1977.

234   A.J.R GROOM

52. Hveem, Helge, Lodgaard, Sverre and Skjelsbæk, Kjell 'Norge i verdenssamfunnet' in A.M. Klanssein and H.F. Dahl (eds) *Det norske samfunn*. Oslo, Gryldendal Forlag, 1983.
53. Juznic, Stane *Kolonializem in dekolonizacija*. Maribor, Zalozba Obzorja, 1980.
54. Khroustalev, Mark M. *Systemnoye modelirovaniye mezhdunarodnykh otnosheni*. Moscow, MGIMO, 1987.
55. Klein, Jean *Sécurité et désarmement en Europe*. Paris, IFRI-Economica, 1987.
56. Knapp, Manfred and Krell, Gert (eds) *Einführung in die Internationale Politik*. Munich, Vienna, Oldenbourg Verlag, 1991.
57. Kohler-Koch, Beate (ed.) *Regime in den internationalen Beziehungen*. Baden-Baden, Nomos, 1989.
58. Korany, Bahgat (ed.) *Analyse des relations internationales: approches, concepts et données*. Montreal, Gaëtan Morin, 1987.
59. Kramer, Helmut (ed.) *Österreich im internationalen System. Zusammenfassung der Ergebnisse und Ausblick*. Vienna, Braumüller, 1983.
60. Krippendorff, Ekkehart *Internationale Politik. Geschichte und Theorie*. Frankfurt-on-Main, Campus Verlag, 1986.
61. Krippendorff, Ekkehart *Staat und Krieg. Die historische Logik politischer Unvernunft*. Frankfurt-on-Main, Suhrkamp Verlag, 1985.
62. Laïdi, Zaki (ed.) *L'ordre mondiale relâché*, second edition. Paris, Presses de la Fondation Nationale des Sciences Politiques, 1993.
63. Lijphart, Arend *Democracy in Plural Societies*. London, Yale University Press, 1980.
64. Lijphart, Arend *Paradigmata in de Leer der Internationale Betrekkingen*. Amsterdam, De Bussy, 1969.
65. Link, Werner *Der Ost–West–Konflikt. Die Organisation der internationalen Beziehungen im 20. Jahrhundert*. Stuttgart, Verlag W. Kohlhammer, 1980.
66. Lyons, Gene M. 'Expanding the Study of International Relations: The French Connection', *World Politics*, vol. 35, no. 6, 1982, pp. 135–149.
67. Menzel, Ulrich *Das Ende der Dritten Welt und das Scheitern der großen Theorie*. Frankfurt, Suhrkamp, 1992.
68. Merle, Marcel *Forces et Enjeux dans les Relations Internationales*. Paris, Economica, 1981.
69. Merle, Marcel *Les acteurs dans les relations internationales*. Paris, Economica, 1986.
70. Merle, Marcel *Sociologie des relations internationales*, fourth edition. Paris, Dalloz, 1988.
71. Merle, Marcel 'Sur le 'problématique' de l'étude des relations internationales en France'. *Revue française de science politique*, vol. 33, no. 3, 1983, pp. 403–27.
72. Mesa, Roberto *Teoría y Práctica de Relaciones Internacionales*. Madrid, Taurus, 1980.
73. Meyers, Reinhard *Weltpolitik in Grundbegriffen, Bd.1: Ein lehr – und ideengeschictlicher Grundriß*. Düsseldorf, Droste Verlag, 1979.
74. Mitrany, David *A Working Peace System*. Chicago, Quadrangle Books, 1966.
75. Morgenthau, Hans J. *Politics among Nations*. New York, McGraw-Hill, 1993.
76. Neuhold, Hanspeter and Tahlberg, Hans (eds) *The European Neutrals in International Affairs*. Vienna, Wilhelm Braumüller, 1984.
77. Nobel, J.W. *De utopie van het realisme. De machtstheorie van Hans J. Morgenthau en de dritiek op het Amerikaanse beleid in de Koude Oorlog*. Amsterdam, Jan Mets, 1986.
78. Papasca, Antonio and Mascia, Marco *Le Relazioni Internazionali nell'Era dell'Interdipendenza e dei Diritti Umani*. Padova, Cedam, 1992.

79. Perroux, François *A New Concept of Development: Basic Tenets*. New York, UNESCO, 1984.
80. Petric, Ernest *Pravica do samoodlocbe (mednarodni vidiki)*. Maribor, Zalozba Obzorja, 1984.
81. Poirier, Lucien *Des stratégies nucléaires*. Paris, Complexe, 1990.
82. Pozdnyakov, Elgiz A. *Vneshnepoliticheskaya deyatelnost gosudarstva i mezhgosudarstvennyie otnosheniya*. Moscow, Nauka, 1986.
83. Rittberger, Volker (ed.) *Regime Theory and International Relations*. Oxford, Clarendon Press, 1993.
84. Rittberger, Volker (ed.) *Theorien der Internationalen Beziehungen. Bestandsaufnahme und Forschungsperspektiven*. Opladen, Westdeutscher Verlag, 1990.
85. Röling, B.V.A. *Vredeswetenschap, Inleiding in de polemologie*. Utrecht, Spectrum, 1981.
86. Schwarzenberger, Georg *Power Politics*. London, Stevens, 1964.
87. Senghaas, Dieter *Konfliktformationen im internationalen System*. Frankfurt, Suhrkamp Verlag, 1988.
88. Senghaas, Dieter *Von Europa lernen. Entwicklungsgeschichtliche Betrachtungen*. Frankfurt, Suhrkamp, 1982.
89. Simoniti, Iztok (ed.) *Evropa 1992 (Razprave, eseji, dokumenti)*. Ljubljana, Gospodarski vestnik, 1989.
90. Smouts, Marie-Claude 'The Study of International Relations in France' in Hugh C. Dyer and Leon Mangasarian (eds) *The Study of International Relations*. London, Macmillan, 1989, pp. 221–8.
91. Soetendorp, R.B. 'De Vergelijkende Analyse van Buitenlands Beleid: Vooruitgang of Stilstand?' *Acta Politica*, vol. XXVIII, no. 1, 1993.
92. Soetendorp, R.B. and van Staden, A. (eds) *Internationale Betrekkingen in Perspectief*. Utrecht, Aula, 1987.
93. Svetlicic, Marjan *Zlate mreze transnacionalk*. Ljubljana, Delvaska enotnost, 1985.
94. Thérien, J-P. 'L'apport de la littérature francophone à l'étude des organisations internationales' in Robert Cox (ed.) *Multilateralism and the United Nations System*. United Nations University, in press, and *International Social Science Journal*, no. 138, 1993.
95. Tiuline, Ivan (ed.) *Systemnyi podkhod: Analiz i prognozirovaniye mezhdunarodnykh otnosheniy. Opyt prikladnykh issledovaniy*. Moscow, MGIMO, 1991.
96. Touscoz, Jean *Droit international*. Paris, Presses Universitaires de France, 1993.
97. Truyol y Serra, Antonio *La sociedad internacional*. Madrid, Alianza, 1991.
98. Truyol y Serra, Antonio *La teoría de las Relaciones Internacionales como Sociología (Introducción al estudio de las Relaciones Internacionales*. Madrid, Instituto de Estudios Políticos, 1973.
99. Türk, Danilo *Nacelo neintervencije (v mednarodnih odnosih in v mednarodnem pravu)*. Ljubljana, Mladinska knjiga, 1984.
100. van der Bruggen, K. *Verzekerde vrede of verzekerde vernietiging: ontwikkeling van een theorie van gerechtvaardigde afschrikking*. Kampen, Kok, 1986.
101. von Beyme, Klaus, Czempiel, Ernst-Otto, Kielmansegg, Peter Graf and Schmoock, Peter (eds) *Politik-Wissenschaft, Eine Grundlegung*. Stuttgart, Kohlhammer, 1987.
102. von Bonsdorff, Göran *Världspolitik i teknikens tidsålder*. Ekenäs tryckeri, Ekenäs, 1961.
103. Zagorski, Andrei V. and Lebedeva, Marina M. *Teoriya i metodologiya analiza mezhdunarodnykh peregovorov*. Moscow, MGIMO, 1989.

104. Zorgbibe, Charles *Dictionnaire de politique internationale.* Paris, Presses Universitaires de France, 1988.
105. Zürn, Michael *Interessen und Institutionen in der internationalen Politik. Grundlegung und Anwendungen des situationsstrukturellen Ansatzes.* Opladen, Leske und Budrich, 1992.

17 Beyond the north-west: Africa and the east

Stephen Chan*

Introduction

In a crude positivism that accompanied early realism, Third World states were seen as having no independent foreign policies but took or received their places only within the competing foreign policies of the superpowers. Any independent instances or systems of thought were disregarded both by policy-makers and academics. Even into the 1960s, with new states proliferating, and driven partly towards independence by forms of nationalist and, by extension, some internationalist thought, IR theory lacked nuance when viewing the Third World or even non-Western members of the developed world.

As theory began to centre itself around the concept of an international system, this system was seen to have both organizing and socializing aspects. No nationalism, no matter how radical in the opposed views it expressed about the international system, could avoid being socialized, eventually, by that system. The international system was the point of theoretical focus. For some, it is the culmination of a broadening and deepening process of human organization and communitarianism that has arrived at internationally common values and obligations. For others, it is a system which provides international benefits that, under national conditions, would warrant allegiance and contracturalism. In both cases, a globalism takes precedence over any state particularism. Yet, paradoxically, normative theory has avoided Third World texts and critical bodies of knowledge.

* Stephen Chan alone is responsible for the conclusions of this chapter. He is grateful for the assistance of Gerald Chan, Victoria University of Wellington; Takashi Inoguchi, University of Tokyo; Hiroshi Momose, Tsudajuku University, Tokyo; Haider Nizamani, Institute of Strategic Studies, Islamabad; Mahmood Sariolghalam, National University of Iran, Teheran; Brigadier Mustafa Kamal Uddin, Bangladesh Institute of International and Strategic Studies, Dhaka; Wang Yi, Chinese People's Institute of Foreign Affairs, Beijing.

When IR became a separate discipline, its emphasis on the international system separated it from area studies. One of the few IR scholars to have straddled disciplinary boundaries is James Piscatori, whose work on Islamic international relations has not only identified Islam as an international actor [100] but has defined, with their national foundations [101], the various sorts of Islam that act internationally. The idea of the national and cultural foundations of international action has prompted this author to complain about theoretical IR schools which tend to ignore it [27, 28, 29, 30]. Although scholars such as Rengger have recently acknowledged that culture plays a role in international action [115], there has been little thought as to where such claims might lead. Survey volumes, such as Dyer and Mangasarian's [36], outline unevenly some non-Western IR without articulating the theoretical problems that would accompany the erosion of IR's universalism.

A note on other disciplines

Increasingly, in other disciplines, the dissident particulars are being treated seriously, indeed centrally, as, for example, the nature of the state in comparative politics which is seen as determined by its functions. At its base, comparative politics undertakes a typologizing project: different groups of functions identify different types of state. This raises an acute question for IR. If, as Luciani et al. [84] argue, there are several types of Arab state and, according to Ergas et al. [38], some six types of African state, unrelated to the Arab types, at what reified level of international action is there an inter-state system, since it has no homogeneous base?

In Third World studies and related development studies, Manor et al. argue for the importance of cultural studies and cultural pluralism [87]. The particulars of the past affect, if not undermine, the universalism suggested by a Western image of the modern world. It is history that has had most to say about how these particulars of the past work – or, rather, how they are brought into play and manipulated. Hobsbawm, looking at European [54], and Ranger looking at African history [113], together producing an historical overview [55], suggest the invention of traditions. In the African context, Vail et al. [130], Kaarsholm et al. [72], and Lan [82] have produced similar suggestions. Traditions, using motifs from the past, are abstracted or invented to mobilize peoples in the face of external threats, whether of formal colonialism or of conquest by an external other. The point here is that there is an external counterpoint to the basis of internal nationalism and the traditions invented for nation-building. A view of internationalism accompanies nationalism; and if there are many national cultures, then there is also a heterogeneity of international values. The contribution of history has been paralleled and amplified by anthropology. The work of Gellner is powerful here [44] and that of Davis suggests an explanation anchored in national traditions as to why Libya's internationalism can seem bizarre [33]. The point is that Third World studies, history, and anthropology have central concepts of a nation-state, while IR has tended to deal with states and to give less attention to the 'nation'.

Structuralism and exception

It might be argued that IR does indeed accommodate Third World thought through its Latin American-derived structuralist paradigm, since the work, *inter alia*, of Frank and Furtado, has a salient place in IR. As Kay points out, however, Latin-American structuralism may be subdivided into different schools [75], and, although extensive fieldwork has been done in different parts of Latin America, no comparable fieldwork exists in African structuralism. The paradigm has nevertheless been widely adopted in Africa for two non-academic reasons. First, it provides an explanation of the African condition that is founded on systemic immiseration. Second, it provides an intellectual foundation for the notion of united African resistance to the declared Western progenitors of this immiseration. Since 1975 African political conferences have mirrored academic conferences in their condemnation of imperialism and neo-colonialism. Because immiseration is held to originate on a systemic basis, because it is part of the structural dynamics of the international system, a great deal of African IR, such as Amin's [14], without ever having been remotely pro-Soviet, has been anti-Western.

The borrowing from Latin America ignores, however, basic differences between the two continents. In one, races and cultures were destroyed or marginalized and, although what emerged as the periphery was rebellious, that same periphery was ascertainable of the culture and language of the metropole. Latin America was an object in the international politics of the Latin metropole but shared in many respects its subjectivity – elements of its identity. The African experience was both more successful in that races were not necessarily destroyed but also much more fragmented. The same sort of bond, in terms of identity and in terms of collaboration between homogenizible classes in both metropole and periphery, did not exist. This has led to a tension in contemporary African IR. One school of thought, more prominent in Francophone than Anglophone Africa, has sought to present Africa not as an object but as a culturally secure, autonomous subject in its own right. Recently Amin has published works against Eurocentrism [16] and in favour of delinking from the West [17], so that Africa might provide its own foundation in international relations. The most prominent Anglophonic representative of this school is Mazrui, but he insists upon the West's appreciation of Third World culture rather than preaching culture as part of the Third World's autonomy [89]. In addition, African IR reveals various structuralist approaches.

The production of knowledge differs markedly even within the same geographical regions of Africa. Zambia, for instance, has not produced a single book on any aspect of IR, not least because of a paucity of paper and printing materials, so that the lack of produced knowledge might itself be taken as a consequence of immiseration. The reductionist association of lack and want on the one hand, with immiseration on the other, has led to some of the cruder works in African IR. Few works are IR-specific; they take in several disciplines and help to service a political critique of the society in which their production is situated – as well as of the global system. The individual characteristics of local society and government can lead to an individualized application of structuralism. In Zimbabwe, the work of Raftopoulos very elegantly accomplishes this [102]. Zimbabwe has, in general, avoided the cruder reductionisms of structuralism, and insightful works on domestic issues, set in their international structural context, have appeared: Shivji [127] and Shivji *et al.* [126] on the democratization debate in Africa; Mandaza and Sachikonye *et al.* on democratization in Zimbabwe [86]; and Mandaza *et al.* on the political economy of Zimbabwian independence [85]. The close links between Western capital and immiseration, and the risk of reductionism, are not always avoided; Nabudere [93], however, does this sort of analysis with elegance and local fit. Zimbabwe has its own tradition of atheoretical but nevertheless scholarly analysis of regional relations, [71] and [39], for example, and Patel has described Zimbabwean foreign policy development [98, 99].

In Nigeria there is a firm structuralist school, centred on the University of Ife, and some local textbook production which, in the field of IR, mirrors many US textbooks. But there is also concern for Nigeria's place in the world on the often undeclared realist assumption that Nigeria has more 'power' than other African states and has therefore a relationship with the great powers that is not fully dependent. Garba [41] and Adebo [1] paint broad international canvasses, while Ogunbadejo analyses Nigerian–Soviet relations [96], and Nwankwo has written about *perestroika* and *glasnost* [95]. Full-length treatments have appeared on how major powers formulate foreign policy towards Nigeria, among them that of Fafowora [40] and shorter texts on chemical warfare and world peace [97].

All this means a tripartite depiction of at least sub-Saharan IR. In some Francophone countries there is a degree of cultural assertion, and IR theory is represented by forms of structuralism. In addition, realism can be said to underlie some of the atheoretical analyses that have emerged from Nigeria. In South Africa, however, both cultural considerations and some aspects of all three mainstream paradigms coexist. The cultural component underlies much Afrikaner IR, and, as Vale suggests, until recently it dominated the South African discipline [131]. In Geldenhuys's work one sees, first, how cultural underlays helped to produce a diplomacy of isolation [43], and second, how it opened out into a fierce realism: power with a military edge [42], on behalf of a highly idiosyncratic state and its interests. Power relationships, particularly within the immediate region, have sparked a considerable literature, as has the perception that such relationships have an in-built structure where state interests merely mask those of capital [83]. Under such conditions, the inherent liberalism of the pluralist paradigm has seemed markedly lacking. This has led Du Pisani and Van Wyk to complain of a lack of theoretical IR in South Africa [35], although Du Pisani himself has represented, from the point of conflict resolution, the possibilities of plural levels of action and actor in IR [34]. Recently, there have been additions to the principal school of conflict resolution and peace research in South Africa, that surrounding Van Der Merwe in Cape Town [132]. The ground is changing in South Africa, in IR as in so much else, and IR in all its forms is thriving.

A typology of five

There are five themes in non-northwestern IR. The first is a drive towards the modernization of knowledge, to be acknowledged as part of a global discipline. The second concerns the question of culture and tradition, on which other disciplines have an effect. The third contributes to a politics of, perhaps even an ideology of, resistance to the West. The fourth relates to the tensions within a realist system and, particularly, those that exist between non-northwestern countries and the superpowers. The fifth also falls within realism, but it is established in terms of power relationships within a set region.

In the second part of this chapter, these themes will be found in six 'eastern' examples. All are non-Western; some are developing, though none share the full characteristics of underdevelopment found in most of Africa; some are on the verge of development; and one is seen, in technological terms, as the quintessence of development. Each has sought to modernize, and this is reflected in IR. Within this survey, a hypothesis may be tested: those closest to modernization are also those who have sought most to 'modernize' their IR knowledge. This applies even to unorthodox or 'revolutionary' states such as Iran and China. However, the undercurrents of tradition, culture, assertion of identity and resistance to the international system are never far below the surface.

Iran

The present religious rhetoric of Iran has been accepted by the West without nuance. Amin has remarked upon the dualism of Iranian society [15], and Gilsenan maintains that the West was surprised by the Ayatollah's revolution because it had equated institutional modernization with cultural–ideological modernization [47]. In fact, 20th-century Iranian history might be written in terms of the tension between institutional superstructure and cultural infrastructure. In any case, there is, as Ayubi has pointed out, a sophisticated juristic base to the Islamic state [18], and the notion of a crudely theological state is here a contradiction in terms. There are four aspects to bear in mind about Iranian IR. First, it is written mostly in Farsi and is prolific. Second, it reflects the tension between modernization and culture but, in so far as universities and research institutes share some aspirations towards modernity, there remains much institutional modernism in IR theory. Third, Iranian IR theory is sophisticated. Fourth, there is a wealth of atheoretical analytical material. Here, however, the concern is with theory, as it is with the English-language *Iranian Journal of International Affairs* [66], where the 'Notes for Authors' pointedly warn that 'descriptive materials are unlikely to be accepted'.

In Iranian IR theory there is enquiry into the nature of the international system [19], into the relationship between the dominant system and the Third World [118] and into the relationship between international power and international society [77]. In other words, all of the 'classical' IR enquiries are present. Moreover, Iranian IR is cognisant of Western IR. Ghazan made an early critique of IR theories [46], but other works in this mould appeared after the revolution [94, 123] and Sariolghalam published works on methodology [120].

In the field of the theory of strategy and security, Moghtader has written on collective security [90] and Roshandel on the evolution of the concept of strategy [116]. In foreign policy analysis Behzadi [24] and Ghavam [45], a decade apart, produced survey works on foreign policy; Kazemi investigated diplomacy in a changing world [76]; and Seifzadeh placed foreign policy within a systematic conceptual framework [124].

Seifzadeh has also considered the question of modernization [122]. Sariolghalam has written on rationality within Iranian development [121], what is entailed by developmental culture [117] and on cultural denomi-nators within a developmental culture [119]. There is an awareness in much of this literature that, below the level of institutions that may be modernized, there is something that is non-Western, even if not necessarily anti-Western. This is perhaps most noticeable in a curious not-quite-peripheral literature, published under academic imprints with academic apparatus, such as footnotes, but which are really polemical works or works of complaint. Sheikholeslami, for example, asserts that Israel has 'effectively played on the old prejudices of the West against the Middle Eastern peoples, portraying them as violent, unreliable and undemocratic. In Israeli propaganda, the West sees confirmation of its own attitudes' [125]. The tension within Iranian IR is, in fact, a tension between modernization and culture.

Pakistan

Because separate independence from an India which was seen in oppositional terms both culminated and authenticated the nationalist cause in Pakistan, Pakistani IR has been concerned with security: first as a defence of the nation; and, second, no matter how the nation was constituted, security from India is of paramount importance. Thus Pakistani IR has been concerned primarily with historical narratives of security policy. There has, however, been a second string to the Pakistani bow. Beginning with the 1956 Suez crisis, 'fraternal feelings' to other Muslim countries, and to Islam in general, have featured in Pakistani IR [37].

Irfani writes about Islam and its place in the search for identity [67]. He has also written a most interesting riposte to Fukuyama's thesis on the end of history, pointing out that it lacked Third World sources and argumen-tation. In the process he portrayed the vast literatures on methodology written, first, in Arabic, and then as they have appeared in non-Arab Islamic countries [68]. An Islamic approach can provide an intellectual structure for enquiry. Manzoorudin has compared Western theories of integration with those derived from Islam [88]. This was the only consciously comparative and theoretical text of its kind to be found in the late 1950s. In more recent times, there have been enquiries into the imperialized base of theory. Waseem, for example, argues that European culture, introduced through colonialism, has in fact benefited the building of institutions [134], although he comments less on whether there is any parallel in its effect on local culture and ideology.

In less atheoretical studies, for example of strategy [74], a realist foundation can be detected, but it is hardly articulated as theory. Similarly, Rauf's work [114] on conflict management and confidence-building measures has realist assumptions. Where theory does raise its head explicitly, it is in discussions of the nature of the state in post-colonial societies [12].

Bangladesh

The conditionality of the successful struggle for independence remains a major factor in Bangladeshi IR. Strategic Studies, therefore, has become the primary work of IR, and it is largely atheoretical, although it does consider in conceptual terms the problems of small states. Relations with India, primarily strategic relations, form a large part of the literature. Bangladeshi strategists also pay attention to China, and from there, the focus widens to south Asian security and cooperation in general to neighbouring regional groups such as ASEAN and, finally, to other Third World groupings such as the Non-Aligned Movement. In this sense, Bangladeshi IR is parochial, but the Bangladesh Institute of International and Strategic Studies does publish an excellent journal [22]. While its concern is largely strategic, articles can be of high quality and Rob Khan's survey of Strategic Studies in the Third World seeks to provide a preliminary conceptual base, not only beyond Bangladesh, but beyond IR, to such subjects as development studies [78].

While there is no theoretical wing in Bangladeshi IR, there are isolated instances of theory. Afroze [4] and Talukder [128] have considered various theoretical platforms from which the question of small states might be addressed, while Afroze has studied small states from empirical and comparative perspectives, looking at Bhutan and Maldives [2] and at Nepal by itself [3]. Ahmed has published an interesting theoretical enquiry into the relationship between a state and foreign policy [8]. Structuralism finds a brief platform in Ahmed and Khan's study of Indian foreign policy, when dealing with the class structure of underlying values [9].

There is an undeclared sense of pluralism in Bangladeshi works on south Asian co-operation. With one exception, however, integration or adjustment theory are absent, and the possibilities of co-operation are dealt with analytically and in policy terms [5, 6, 11, 50, 103, 58]. In the work on co-operation with ASEAN, however, theoretical work intrudes explicitly [21]. Similarly, relations with the Non-Alignment Movement have been considered by Hassan [51] and with the Middle East by Mostafa [92].

India

The object of so much Pakistani and Bangladeshi IR, India itself has a vast IR output which is simultaneously, in its affiliation to Western paradigmatic models, very small indeed. Here, a magisterial survey by Rana and Misra already exists, and it has been published in several forms [111, 112]. Rana laments the atheoretical nature of Indian IR, even when it comes to the study of an international movement dear to the Indian political heart such as the Non-Aligned Movement [110]. He himself, a much respected if lone figure in Indian IR, has written on realist theory [109], on the systemic capabilities of non-alignment [108], on conceptual approaches to regionalism [105], a conceptual study of Indian foreign policy under Nehru [106] and on international political modernization [104]. He has also contributed a study of Western and non-Western IR theories [107]. In general, however, Indian IR is both atheoretical and non-comparative.

According to Rana, there are two reasons for this. The first is that area studies, considered more important, have marginalized IR as a discipline both methodologically and in terms of funding. The second is because of the primary importance attached to security and strategic studies [107]. As in Pakistani and Bangladeshi IR, a realist context may be assumed a priori in many works on strategy and security, although it is not fully articulated. Moreover, Indian IR writing about non-alignment is, in one sense, theoretical, although the basis of this theory is not pluralism but normative. Non-alignment is seen as a moral path in a realist world, related not to an ethical system but linked to the historical Indian experience of non-violent resistance. The result is that this is not so much a normative internationalism as a chauvinism. It must also be noted that although institutional IR is narrow, interesting work is done outside the discipline and in intellectual life outside the universities. In development studies, for example, the wholly original work of Rajni Kothari is an exciting contribution to knowledge.

Kothari has made his life's work the lateral growth of freedom. He maintains that only when sufficient lateral growth has occurred can there be the critical mass for a breakthrough upwards. Kothari, like John Burton, locates the basis of international action at the level of the individual and identifies the power of culture at its grassroots' origins. But he works in structures and categories that are different from those used in the West. The spread of freedom, power and action takes place laterally among individuals, then at village level and among villages [81]. Any further spread demands the identification of a class structure, but, in view of immense Third World poverty, these cannot be the classes of Western structuralism [79]. New social norms from alternative social groupings lead to new cultural values, and, eventually, there is a new normative international order [80]. Kothari seems to be pointing to a series of exponential self-determinations that overcome the structures of the state and international system.

Kothari has already had some effect on Western IR, through the journal *Alternatives* which has served as a vehicle for the World Order Models Project with a further penchant for both development studies and IR expressionism. Kothari's influence has been immense and if Rana is the grandmaster of Indian theory on the international system, Kothari is the pioneer of new thought on what might be called the international condition.

China

China maintained a comprehensive autonomy from the external world until very recently. It was only in the late 1970s and early 1980s that China accepted the international system on the system's terms, rather than seeking to impose its own. Up to the European Renaissance, and some would even say until the European Industrial Revolution, there was a parallel but separate Chinese history to that of the West. The historical antecedents to contemporary thought in China are thus located outside the European experience. If Western IR theorists view (or perhaps construct from) Thucydides an antique conceptual precursor of realism, the same is true in China with regard to Sunzi Bingfa's work (usually called Sun Tsu or Sun Tzu in English), *The Art of War*. Chinese theorists also use Zhan Guo Ce's *Annals of the Warring States* and San Guo Zhi's *History of the Three Kingdoms* which date from the eighth century BC and were acknowledged by Mao and his commanders as strategic exemplars. Chan maintains that Mao also used them, and other classical writings, for diplomatic strategy and that for a quarter-century after the revolution they helped form a proto-theory of the international system. In 1974 it was articulated as the Three World Theory. The author has described its cultural roots [25] and has also noted a Clausewitzian sense of policy limits in its application [26]. According to Yee, Chinese foreign policy commenced its contemporary pragmatism in 1979 [139], and it is from this date, 30 years after the revolution, that forms of modern IR can be traced.

The Three World Theory, its proto-theoretical predecessor, and the first stirrings of theory in the freer period of pragmatism that followed 1979, were all concerned with poles of power. This has been noted by Yahuda [138], although his survey does not really reflect the richness of Chinese enquiry over the last ten years. It should be noted, however, that China is still officially a Marxist/Leninist/Maoist state, and the published works of official institutions, such as universities and research academies, must acknowledge, if not seek to reflect, this. It should also be said that the term 'theory' has a different connotation in China from that in the West. There is no pure knowledge, only theory which may be applied. In China, moreover, methodology has a literary nature, and a poetic phrase or a metaphor can assume immense weight in argument. But theorizing is only a little over a decade old, and the project can seem tentative and naïve at times.

Most scholars engaged in theoretical work are young, and have had some international university education. Wang Jisi, for example, used this background to outline Chinese reactions to Western IR; he also discusses the problems in formulating a coherent Chinese conceptual framework [133]. This is the only work in this part of the survey to be written in English.

Zhang Jiliang *et al.* have published a lengthy review of major IR themes and theories from a Chinese perspective [142]. Underlying this study are a set of realist assumptions with a faint echo of Chinese structuralism. Bai Xi, on the other hand, is more innovative in his realist connotations, and he has a refined sense of an international system and its dynamics and interactions [20]. From the Shanghai 'school', more liberal than Beijing IR writing, has come an edited collection entitled *Initial Attempts at International Relations Theory* [48], in which each contributor discusses a separate aspect of IR theory and its development.

These works form a significant counterpoint to established schools, which are still working from the Chinese Marxist/Leninist/Maoist structuralism. Here again, it is the Shanghai effort that is most daring. Yu Kaixiang *et al.* accept socialism as a starting point but seek ways of developing and reforming it to meet the challenges of world politics [140]. Other work is more anchored in past methodologies. In the departmental chairman's preface to the edited collection by the Beijing University Department of International Politics, for example, he argues that 'the study of international politics must not depart from the guidance of Marxism' [23]. Xu Guofu's *et al.* [137] book is used as a military textbook and includes reviews of the international strategic situation.

Even in the works of the 'old' school of Chinese IR, therefore, there is an underlying urge to confront a changing world. Meanwhile, there is a growing number of largely atheoretical works analysing aspects of the global situation, including the most authoritative Chinese journal on international politics, *World Economics and Politics* (in Chinese) [136].

Japan

Japan is the most unambiguously 'modern' and developed country represented in this chapter. It also has the most extensive scholarly provision for the study of world politics, with links to similar scholarly bodies all over the world. The possibility of a genuinely theoretical IR would seem greatest under such conditions. Entry to the world of Japanese IR is also facilitated by the English-language surveys and commentaries of Takashi Inoguchi, who has been prolific. A survey of Japanese political science, with bibliography, appeared a decade ago in the *International Handbook of Political Science*, dealing among other things with IR and methodology [60]. More recently, Inoguchi has contributed a chapter to Dyer and Mangasarian [61] setting out with great clarity the sub-divisions and methodological approaches in Japanese IR. He has also co-authored a powerful set-piece in Der Derian and Shapiro [13], arguing a contextuality for theory. Although he does not advocate a culture-based IR as such, he utilizes in part a Japanese methodology which the Japanese call, 'let the facts speak out'. Two 'facts' of world history are presented: global conflict and its related balance of power, and people's wars of liberation. From the former has come the realist paradigm in IR. Inoguchi sees no theoretical articulation of the latter, and he argues that there cannot be one unless historical and local contexts are examined, as well as the cross-fertilizations of other contexts [13]. Inoguchi has also produced an in-depth study of Japanese foreign policy [62].

Another extremely useful guide to Japanese IR available in English is the Japan Foundation *Bibliography for Japanese Studies*. The 1991 edition has a full chapter on IR (by Inoguchi [63]). The *Japan Association of International Relations International Newsletter* [70] is also in English, and there is a short English-language intellectual history of Japanese IR by Momose, concentrating mostly on international history [91]. Theory features in the Japan Association of International Relations' Japanese-language scholarly journal, *International Relations*, each issue of which has an appendix of English-language summaries. Issues in 1992 dealt with the question of sovereignty in both theory and practice [64], post-cold war perspectives, including articles on security regimes and confidence building measures [65] and included a riposte to Fukuyama's end of history thesis which pointed out the cultural heterogeneity of the world [129].

Drawing from the work of Inoguchi, a summary picture of Japanese IR would look like this: eight areas of sub-disciplinary concentration include (1) theoretical research, (2) behavioural studies, (3) international political economy, (4) international organization, (5) strategic studies, (6) peace research, (7) diplomatic history and (8) area and country studies. Japanese theoretical research in political science generally can be divided into eight methodological groupings, three 'traditional' and five 'modern'. 'Traditional' schools are (1) based on Japanese intellectual history, enquiring particularly into the endogenous nature of development and self-transformation; (2) concerned with indigenous political theories that better explain the Japanese political system than Western ones (here, cultural referents are widely but not exclusively used) and (3) forms of Marxist, structuralist and dialectical thought. Inoguchi includes critical theory into the traditional schools but without explanation.

The 'modern' schools cover (1) survey-based research, (2) content analysis, (3) simulation and gaming studies, (4) aggregate data analysis, and (5) mathematical modelling. Inoguchi points out that IR, as a separate discipline, is only a recent development in Japan. Moreover, he maintains that Marxist and structuralist works are based less on a belief in theory than on the need for what he calls 'opposition science' though the term 'oppositional knowledge' might give a more nuanced suggestion of the link between thought, through praxis, to political activity in this case.

Inoguchi does not reveal whether there is also a tension between the other traditional schools and modernity as it is politically practised in Japan. His own contribution to the Der Derian and Shapiro book, however, launches a subtle but clear objection to the assumed universalism of modern experience found in Western IR.

Conclusion

In his memorial tribute to Hedley Bull, Adam Watson spoke of Bull's recognition of a global society, 'in place of the imperial world society dominated by the Europeans' [135]. Bull located the correct starting point of a post-imperial world. If China and Japan are anything to go by, the western

Pacific rim will be a fertile area, not only economically, but in the study of IR.

In this chapter, theoretical IR accompanies other modernizations. It cannot precede it. It can stand alongside culturally based rejections of the West, as in Iran and, to a tentative extent, China, provided certain levels of modernization have been reached in other sectors. In more underdeveloped societies, particularly those located in areas of regional tension, IR theory will, inevitably, be overshadowed by strategic studies. The question of culture as an academic object is raised differently from country to country. Inoguchi has raised it in a most subtle non-static context of cross-fertilizations. This might be a point of departure for a future enquiry: the world may be, to arguable extents, socialized in its in-system behaviour. To this extent, universal IR may be possible. However, its varied foundation belief systems and intellectual methodologies may mean that there is a less universal acculturation. Here, IR must take into account the dissident particulars.

Bibliography

1. Adebo, S.O. *Our International Years*. Ibadan, Spectrum, 1988.
2. Afroze, S. 'Foreign Policy of Small States: A Comparative Study of Bhutan and Maldives'. *BIISS Journal*, vol. 8, no. 2, 1987.
3. Afroze, S. 'Dilemmas in Nepalese Foreign Policy'. *BIISS Journal*, vol. 8, no. 4, 1987.
4. Afroze, S. 'Do Small States Behave Differently from Big States? A Critique of Maurice East's Alternative Model'. *BIISS Journal*, vol. 14, no. 1, 1993.
5. Ahamed, E. *SARC: Seeds of Harmony*. Dhaka, University Press, 1985.
6. Ahamed, E. and Kalam, A. (eds) *Bangladesh, South Asia and the World*. Dhaka, Academic Publishers, 1992.
7. Ahmed, A.T.S. 'Bangladesh–China Relations: An Assessment'. *BIISS Journal*, vol. 13, no. 2, 1992.
8. Ahmed, I. 'State and Foreign Policy: A Theoretical Abstraction'. *BIISS Journal*, vol. 13, no. 3, 1992.
9. Ahmed, I. and Khan, A.R. *India's Policy Fundamentals, Neighbours and Post-Indira Developments*. Dhaka, BIISS Papers no. 3, 1985.
10. Ahmed, K.U. 'Bangladesh–Burma Relations: The Politico–Economic Dimensions'. *BIISS Journal*, vol. 7, no. 4, 1986.
11. Alam, S. 'SAARC in the Foreign Policy Objectives of Bangladesh'. Paper presented at the First Annual Conference of the Bangladesh Society of International Studies, Dhaka (BIISS), 1989.
12. Alavi, H. and Shanin, T. (eds) *Introduction to Sociology of Developing Countries*. London, Macmillan, 1982.
13. Alker Jr., H.R., Biersteker, T.J. and Inoguchi, T. 'From Imperial Power Balancing to People's Wars: Searching for Order in the Twentieth Century' in J. Der Derian and M.J. Shapiro (eds) *International/Intertextual Relations*. Lexington, Lexington Books, 1989.
14. Amin, S. *Imperialism and Unequal Development*. Hassocks, Harvester, 1977.
15. Amin, S. *The Crisis of Arab Society* (in Arabic). Cairo, Dar al-Mustaqbal al-'Arabi, 1985.

16. Amin, S. *Eurocentrism*. London, Zed, 1989.
17. Amin, S. *Delinking*. London, Zed. 1990.
18. Ayubi, N. *Political Islam: Religion and Politics in the Arab World*. London, Routledge, 1991.
19. Azghandi, A. *The International System* (in Farsi). Teheran, Ghomes, 1991.
20. Bai Xi. *An Introduction to Contemporary International Relations* (in Chinese). Beijing, Beijing University of Politics and Law Press, 1991.
21. Bangladesh Institute of International and Strategic Studies. *ASEAN Experiences of Regional and Inter-regional Cooperation: Relevance for SAARC*. Dhaka, BIISS, 1988.
22. *Bangladesh Institute of International and Strategic Studies Journal (BIISSJ)*, 1/46 Elephant Road, Dhaka 1000, Bangladesh.
23. Beijing University Department of International Politics (ed.) *Perspectives on International Relations* (in Chinese). Beijing, Beijing University Department of International Politics, 1990.
24. Behzadi, H. *Principles of Foreign Policy* (in Farsi). Teheran, Badr, 1981.
25. Chan, S. 'China's Foreign Policy and Africa: The Rise and Fall of China's Three World Theory'. *Round Table*, no. 296, 1985.
26. Chan, S. *Issues in International Relations: A View From Africa*. London, Macmillan, 1987, chapter 5.
27. Chan, S. 'Small Revolutions and the Study of International Relations: The Problematique of Affiliation'. *Political Science*, vol. 43, no. 2, 1991.
28. Chan, S. 'Revolution, Rebellion and Romance. Some Notes Towards the Resacralisation of I.R.' *Paradigms*, vol. 7, no. 1, 1993.
29. Chan, S. 'Cultural and Linguistic Reductionisms and a New Historical Sociology for International Relations'. *Millennium*, vol. 22, no. 3, 1993
30. Chan, S. 'Culture and Absent Epistemologies in International Relations'. *Theoria*, 81/2, 1993.
31. Choudhury, N. 'Burma's Foreign Policy: Continuity and Change'. *BIISS Journal*, vol. 7, no. 2, 1986.
32. Chowdhury, I.A. *Bangladesh's External Relations: The Strategy of a Small Power in a Subsystem*. Canberra, Australian National University unpublished PhD thesis, 1980.
33. Davis, J. *Libyan Politics: Tribe and Revolution*. London, I.B. Tauris, 1987.
34. Du Pisani, A. *Critical Evaluation of Conflict Resolution Techniques: From Workshop to Theory*. Cape Town, University of Cape Town unpublished PhD thesis, 1988.
35. Du Pisani, A. and Van Wyk, K. 'A Restricted Palette: Reflections on the State of International Relations in South Africa'. *International Affairs Bulletin*, vol. 15, no. 1, 1991.
36. Dyer, H.C. and Mangasarian, L. (eds) *The Study of International Relations: The State of the Art*. London, Macmillan, 1989.
37. Eayrs, J. (ed.) *The Commonwealth and Suez – a documentary survey*. London, Oxford University Press, 1964, p. 261.
38. Ergas, Z. (ed.) *The African State in Transition*. London, Macmillan, 1987.
39. Evans, M. *The Front-line States, South Africa and Southern African Security*. Harare, University of Zimbabwe, 1986.
40. Fafowora, O.O. *Pressure Groups and Foreign Policy: A Comparative Study of British Attitudes and Policy towards Secessionist Moves in the Congo and in Nigeria*. Ibadan, Heinemann Educational, 1990.
41. Garba, J. *Diplomatic Soldiering: The Conduct of Nigerian Foreign Policy 1975–1979*. Ibadan, Spectrum, 1991.

42. Geldenhuys, D. 'The Destabilization Controversy: an analysis of high risk foreign policy options for South Africa'. *Politikon*, vol. 9, no. 2, 1982.

43. Geldenhuys, D. *The Diplomacy of Isolation – South African Foreign Policy Making*. Johannesburg, Macmillan, 1984.

44. Gellner, E. *Spectacles and Predicaments*. Cambridge, Cambridge University Press, 1979.

45. Ghavam, A. *Principles of Foreign Policy and International Relations* (in Farsi). Teheran, Samt, 1991.

46. Ghazan Chegal, A. *A Critique of International Relations Theories* (in Farsi). Teheran, Institute for Advanced International Studies, 1974.

47. Gilsenan, M. 'Approaching the Islamic Revolution'. *MERIP Reports*, no. 102, 1982.

48. Guoji Guanxi Lilun Chutan (ed.) *Initial Attempts at International Relations theory* (in Chinese). Shanghai, Foreign Languages Education Press, 1991.

49. Hafiz, M.A. 'Bangladesh–Pakistan Relations: Still Developing'. *BIISS Journal*, vol. 6, no. 3, 1985.

50. Hafiz, M.A. and Iftekharuzzaman (eds) *South Asian Regional Cooperation: A Socio-Economic Approach to Peace and Stability*. Dhaka, Hakkani, 1985.

51. Hassan, S. 'Bangladesh, Zia and the Non Aligned Movement'. *BIISS Journal*, Special Issue no. 1, 1981.

52. Hassan, S. *India–Bangladesh Political Relations During the Awami League Government 1972–1975*. Canberra, Australian National University unpublished PhD thesis, 1987.

53. Higgott, R. and Richardson, J.L. (eds) *International Relations: Global and Australian Perspectives on an Evolving Discipline*. Canberra, Australian National University, 1991.

54. Hobsbawm, E.J. *Nations and Nationalism since 1780*. Cambridge, Cambridge University Press, 1990.

55. Hobsbawm, E.J. and Ranger, T. (eds) *The Invention of Tradition*. Cambridge, Cambridge University Press, 1983.

56. Hussain, S.A. *China and Pakistan: Diplomacy of an Entente Cordiale*. Oxford, Oxford University Press, 1974.

57. Iftekharuzzaman. 'The India Doctrine: Relevance for Bangladesh' in M.G. Kabir and S. Hassan (eds) *Issues and Challenges Facing Bangladesh Foreign Policy*. Dhaka, Bangladesh Society of International Studies, 1989.

58. Iftekharuzzaman and Ahmed, I. (eds) *Bangladesh and SAARC: Issues, Perspectives and Outlook*. Dhaka, BIISS and Academic Publishers, 1992.

59. *India Quarterly*, Sapru House, Barakhambra Road, New Delhi 110001, India.

60. Inoguchi, T. 'Japan' in W.G. Andrews (ed.) *International Handbook of Political Science*. Westport, Greenwood, 1982.

61. Inoguchi, T. 'The Study of International Relations in Japan' in H.C. Dyer and L. Mangasarian (eds) *The Study of International Relations: The State of the Art*. London, Macmillan, 1989.

62. Inoguchi, T. *Japan's International Relations*. London, Pinter, 1991.

63. Inoguchi, T. 'International Relations' in *An Introductory Bibliography for Japanese Studies, vol. vii, part 1, Social Sciences 1986–87*. Compiled by the Toho Gakkai. Tokyo, Japan Foundation, 1991.

64. *International Relations*, vol. 101, 1992 (in Japanese).

65. *International Relations*, vol. 100, 1992 (in Japanese).

66. *Iranian Journal of International Affairs*. Institute for Political and International Studies, P.O. Box 19395/1793, Teheran, Iran.

67. Irfani, S. 'Islamic Revival: Quest of Identity and Legitimacy – Implications for Pakistan'. *Strategic Studies*, vol. xiii, no. 1, 1989.
68. Irfani, S. 'The Return of History'. *Strategic Studies*, vol. xiv, no. 3, 1991.
69. Islam, M.R. *Ganges Water Dispute: Its International Legal Aspects*. Dhaka, University Press, 1987.
70. *Japan Association of International Relations International Newsletter*, Hitotsubashi University, Naka 2-1, Kunitachi, Tokyo 186, Japan.
71. Johnson, P. and Martin, D. (eds) *Destructive Engagement: Southern Africa at War*. Harare, Zimbabwe Publishing House, 1986.
72. Kaarsholm, P. (ed.) *Cultural Struggle & Development in Southern Africa*. London, James Currey, 1991.
73. Kabir, M.G. and Hassan, S. (eds) *Issues and Challenges Facing Bangladesh Foreign Policy*. Dhaka, Bangladesh Society of International Studies, 1989.
74. Kamal, N. 'Change and Development in Strategic Studies'. *Strategic Studies*, vol. 1, no. 4, 1978.
75. Kay, C. *Latin American Theories of Development and Underdevelopment*. London, Routledge, 1989.
76. Kazemi, A.A. *Diplomacy and Changing International Relations* (in Farsi). Teheran, Institute for Political and International Studies, 1986.
77. Kazemi, A.A. *Power, Society and International Relations* (in Farsi). Teheran, Ghomes, 1990.
78. Khan, A.R. 'Strategic Studies in the Third World: A Suggested Approach'. *BIISS Journal*, vol. 5, no. 2, 1984.
79. Kothari, R. 'Communications for Alternative Development: Towards a Paradigm'. *Development Dialogue*, 1–2, 1984.
80. Kothari, R. *Transformation and Survival: In Search of a Humane World Order*. New Delhi, Ajanta, 1988.
81. Kothari, R. 'Peace as a Technological Fix'. *Paradigms*, vol. 7, no. 1, 1993.
82. Lan, D. *Guns & Rain: Guerillas and Spirit Mediums in Zimbabwe*. London, James Currey, 1985.
83. Legassick, M. and Innes, D. 'Capital Restructuring and Apartheid: A Critique of Constructive Engagement'. *African Affairs*, vol. 76, no. 305, 1977.
84. Luciani, G. (ed.) *The Arab State*. London, Routledge, 1990.
85. Mandaza, I. (ed.) *Zimbabwe: The Political Economy of Transition 1980–1986*. Harare, CODESRIA, 1987.
86. Mandaza, I. and Sachikonye, L. (eds) *The One Party State and Democracy*. Harare, SAPES Books, 1991.
87. Manor, J. (ed.) *Rethinking Third World Politics*. London, Longman, 1991.
88. Manzoorudin, A. 'Integration of the Muslim World: Problems and Prospects'. *Pakistan Horizon*, vol. xi, no. 4, 1958.
89. Mazrui, A.A. *Cultural Forces in World Politics*. London, James Currey, 1990.
90. Moghtader, H. Collective Security in Theory and Practice (in Farsi) in A. Ghaderi (ed.) *The Evolution of Concepts*. Teheran, Institute for Political and International Studies, 1991.
91. Momose, H. 'International Relations and History'. *Commission of History of International Relations Newsletter*, no. 5, 1991.
92. Mostafa, M.G. 'Bangladesh Foreign Policy: The Middle East Factor'. *BIISS Journal*, vol. 7, no. 1, 1986.
93. Nabudere, D.W. *The Crash of International Finance Capital*. Harare, SAPES Books, 1989.

94. Naghibzadeh, A. 'New Interpretations of International Relations' (in Farsi) in A. Ghaderi (ed.) *The Evolution of Concepts*. Teheran, Institute for Political and International Studies, 1991.

95. Nwankwo, A. *Perestroika and Glasnost: their Implications for Africa*. Enugu, Fourth Dimension, 1990.

96. Ogunbadejo, O. 'Soviet Policies in Africa' in S. Chan (ed.) *Exporting Apartheid: Foreign Policies in Southern Africa 1978–1988*. London, Macmillan, 1990.

97. Okecha, S.A. *War, Chemicals and World Peace*. Lagos, Nigerian Institute of International Affairs Lecture Series 72, 1991.

98. Patel, H.H. *No Master, No Mortgage, No Sale: The Foreign Policy of Zimbabwe*. Nairobi, Centre for Research, Documentation and University Exchanges Working Paper 2, 1987.

99. Patel, H.H. 'Zimbabwe's Mediation in Mozambique and Angola 1989–1991' in S. Chan and V. Jabri (eds) *Mediation in Southern Africa*. London, Macmillan, 1993.

100. Piscatori, J.P. *Islam in a World of Nation States*. Cambridge, Cambridge University Press, 1986.

101. Piscatori, J. (ed.) *Islamic Fundamentalisms and the Gulf Crisis*. Chicago, American Academy of Arts and Sciences, 1991.

102. Raftopoulos, B. *Beyond the House of Hunger: The Struggle for Democratic Development in Zimbabwe*. Harare, Zimbabwe Institute of Development Studies Working Paper 17, 1991.

103. Rahman, A. *Political Economy of SARC*. Dhaka, University Press, 1985.

104. Rana, A.P. 'Nehru and International Political Modernization: A View from the Seventies'. *India Quarterly*. January–March, 1979.

105. Rana, A.P. 'Regionalism as an Approach to International Order: A Conceptual Overview'. *International Studies*. October–December, 1979.

106. Rana, A.P. *The Imperatives of Nonalignment: A Conceptual Study of India's Foreign Policy Strategy in the Nehru Period*. New Delhi, Macmillan, 1979.

107. Rana, A.P. 'The Development of International Studies in India: A Profile of Some Critical Constraints' in K.P. Misra and R.C. Beal (eds) *International Relations Theory: Western and Non-Western Perspectives*. New Delhi, Vikas, 1980.

108. Rana, A.P. 'Nonalignment as a Developmental Foreign Policy Strategy: A Conceptual Enquiry into its Systemic Capabilities'. *Indian Journal of Political Science*. December, 1980.

109. Rana, A.P. 'Strategic Considerations in India's Foreign Policy: A Preliminary Framework of Enquiry'. *Political Science Review*. January–March, 1982.

110. Rana, A.P. 'The Legitimacy Crisis of Contemporary Nonalignment: A Paradigmatic Enquiry and Research Proposal'. *Paradigms*, vol. 1, no. 2, 1987.

111. Rana, A.P. *The Study of International Relations in India*. New Delhi, Allied Publishers, nd.

112. Rana, A.P. and Misra, K.P. *The India Report on Research on Continuity and Change in Global Affairs: Towards a Transnational Community of Scholars*. Washington DC, International Studies Association Third World Assembly of International Studies, 1988.

113. Ranger, T. *Peasant Consciousness and Guerilla War in Zimbabwe*. London, James Currey, 1985.

114. Rauf, T. 'Conflict Management and Confidence Building Measures in Regional Conflicts in the Third World'. *Strategic Studies*, vol. iv, no. 1, 1980.

115. Rengger, N.J. 'Culture, Society and Order in World Politics' in J. Baylis and N.J. Rengger (eds) *Dilemmas of World Politics*. Oxford, Clarendon Press, 1992.

116. Roshandel, J. 'The Evolution of the Concept of Strategy' in A. Ghaderi (ed.) *The Evolution of Concepts*. Teheran, Institute for Political and International Studies, 1991.

117. Sariolghalam, M. 'Development Culture and the Third World' (in Farsi). *Political-Economic Monthly*, May, 1989.

118. Sariolghalam, M. *Development, the Third World and the International System* (in Farsi). Teheran, Safeer, 1989.

119. Sariolghalam, M. 'Non-Economic Prerequisites, Cultural Denominators and Development' (in Farsi). *Political-Economic Monthly*, April, 1990.

120. Sariolghalam, M. *The Evolution of Method and Research in International Relations* (in Farsi). Teheran, National University Press, 1992.

121. Sariolghalam, M. *Rationality and Development* (in Farsi). Teheran, Safeer, 1993.

122. Seifzadeh, H. *Modernization and Development* (in Farsi). Teheran, Safeer, 1988.

123. Seifzadeh, H. *Theories of International Relations* (in Farsi). Teheran, Safeer, 1988.

124. Seifzadeh, H. 'Developing a Conceptual Framework in Systematic Foreign Policy Analysis' (in Farsi). *Journal of the School of Law and Political Science*, no. 1, 1991.

125. Sheikholeslami, A.R. 'Zionism, Fascism and the Formation of the State of Israel'. *The Iranian Journal of International Affairs*, vol. 1, no. 1, 1989.

126. Shivji, I.G. (ed.) *State and Constitutionalism: An African Debate on Democracy*. Harare, SAPES Books, 1991.

127. Shivji, I.G. *Fight My Beloved Continent: New Democracy in Africa*. Harare, SAPES Books, 1992.

128. Talukder, M. *The Security of Small States in The Third World*. Canberra, Canberra Papers on Strategy and Defence no. 25, 1982.

129. Usuki, E. 'An End to the "End of History" Debates' (in Japanese). *International Relations*, vol. 99, 1992.

130. Vail, L. (ed.) *The Creation of Tribalism in Southern Africa*. London, James Currey, 1989.

131. Vale, P. '"Whose World is it Anyway?" International Relations in South Africa' in H.C. Dyer and L. Mangasarian (eds) *The Study of International Relations: The State of the Art*. London, Macmillan, 1989.

132. Van Der Merwe, H.W. *Pursuing Justice and Peace in South Africa*. London, Routledge, 1989.

133. Wang Jisi 'International Relations Theory and the Study of Chinese Foreign Policy' in T. Robinson and D. Shambaugh (eds) *Ideas and Interpretation of Chinese Foreign Policy*. Oxford, Oxford University Press, 1993.

134. Waseem, M. 'Europe and the Institutionalization of the Third World' in A.A. Kadeer (ed.) *Europe and the Third World*. Karachi, Area Study Centre for Europe, 1985.

135. Watson, A. 'Hedley Bull – In Memoriam' in R. O'Neill and D.N. Schwartz (eds) *Hedley Bull on Arms Control*. London, Macmillan, 1987.

136. *World Economics and Politics* (in Chinese). Institute of World Economy and Political Studies, Chinese Academy of Social Sciences, Beijing 100732, P.R. China.

137. Xu Guofu (ed.) *Contemporary World Politics, Economics and International Relations* (in Chinese). Beijing, People's Liberation Army Press, 1988.

138. Yahuda, M.B. 'International Relations Scholarship in the People's Republic of China' in H.C. Dyer and L. Mangasarian (eds) *The Study of International Relations: The State of the Art*. London, Macmillan, 1989.
139. Yee, H.S. 'The Three World Theory and post-Mao China's global strategy'. *International Affairs*, vol. 59, no. 2, 1983.
140. Yu Kaixiang (ed.) *World Politics, World Economics and International Relations* (in Chinese). Shanghai, Shanghai People's Press, 1988.
141. Zafar, M.A. *India and the Superpowers*. Dhaka, University Press, 1983.
142. Zhang Jiliang (ed.) *A General Introduction to International Relations Theory* (in Chinese). Beijing, World Affairs Press, 1989.

Index of names

Index of concepts